D0022962

LEGAL ASPECTS
OF SPECIAL EDUCATION
AND PUPIL SERVICES

LEGAL ASPECTS
OF SPECIAL EDUCATION
AND PUPIL SERVICES

JULIE K. UNDERWOOD

University of Wisconsin–Madison

JULIE F. MEAD

University of Wisconsin–Madison

ALLYN AND BACON

Boston   London   Toronto   Sydney   Tokyo   Singapore

Series Editor: *Ray Short*
Editorial Assistant: *Christine M. Shaw*
Marketing Manager: *Ellen Mann*
Production Administrator: *Annette Joseph*
Production Coordinator: *Susan Freese*
Editorial-Production Service: *TKM Productions*
Manufacturing Buyer: *Megan Cochran*
Cover Administrator: *Linda Knowles*
Cover Designer: *Suzanne Harbison*

Copyright © 1995 by Allyn & Bacon
A Simon & Schuster Company
Needham Heights, Mass. 02194

All rights reserved. No part of the material protected by this copyright notice may be
reproduced or utilized in any form or by any means, electronic or mechanical,
including photocopying, recording, or by any information storage and retrieval system,
without the written permission of the copyright owner.

 This textbook is printed on
recycled, acid-free paper.

Library of Congress Cataloging-in-Publication Data

Underwood, Julie.
    Legal aspects of special education and pupil services / Julie K.
Underwood, Julie F. Mead.
        p.   cm.
    Includes bibliographical references and index.
    ISBN 0-205-13777-6
    1. Special education—Law and legislation—United States.
I. Title.
KF4209.3.U53   1995
344.73'0791--dc20
[347.304791]   94-39877
                                                         CIP

Printed in the United States of America
10 9 8 7 6 5 4 3 2 1   00 99 98 97 96 95

CONTENTS

PREFACE

Few educators would dispute the fact that the role of the school changed significantly in the 1970s and 1980s. Both the population served and the services provided have changed dramatically. A number of factors have contributed to this. First, federal legislation prohibiting discrimination (e.g., Title VI, Title VII, Title IX, Section 504) forced schools to reflect on and, in many situations, alter traditionally accepted practices. Schools have been litigating the interpretation and application of these federal statutes and regulations regularly since their passage.

In addition, Congress passed the Education for All Handicapped Children Act (EAHCA) of 1975 (now called the Individuals with Disabilities Education Act [IDEA]), thought by many to be the single most significant piece of federal legislation to affect the public schools in the 1970s and 1980s. IDEA and the resulting state legislation altered the population of some school districts to include children with disabilities who had never previously been served by schools. In addition, the act altered the model of delivering services to children in most school districts. Finally, it had the effect of significantly "legalizing" (i.e., making schools directly accountable through statutes, court decisions, and hearing officer decisions) a portion of the schools' curriculum and delivery model.

The special needs population has become an area of increasing concern for school administrators. A significantly expanding number of students fall into the category of special needs students. The number of special education students (IDEA eligible) as a percentage of the school population has risen steadily from 1974 to the present. The nationwide average percentage of special education students is about 10 percent. In addition, schools serve students who have other special needs or who are otherwise at risk. Children at risk are generally defined as those who are not likely to complete high school successfully. Currently, there are legal protections for those children to help them deal with their problems, protect them from discrimination, or enhance their chances of success. Many students who are not IDEA eligible receive other pupil services provided in the public schools such as counseling and guidance services. Others may be served by special programs because of their economic status (Chapter 1), family status (teen-parent programs), housing situation (McKinney programs), or heritage (bilingual programs). Currently, administering these special education and pupil service programs requires more than half the time of a typical school principal.

The costs of administering these programs have also increased dramatically through the passing decades. For example, when the Education of the Handicapped Act (EHA) was first enacted, local educators were assured that a sizable percentage of the necessary funding would be paid by the federal government. However, that expectation was not met. Although the dollar expenditure has increased, the percentage of cost this represents has fallen. As early as 1985, a survey conducted by *Education Daily* found that nearly three-quarters of the respondents indicated that special programs were placing a financial burden on their districts.

Special education and pupil services are also an increasing concern for school attorneys. In addition to increased cost and numbers of students, the legislation has brought increased litigation to schools. For example, although EHA cases comprised only 6 percent of cases actually filed against school districts in 1988, they ranked second in terms of claims against school districts' errors and omissions policies. Litigation in the area of special education and the delivery of pupil services was the only area of school law litigation to increase during the 1980s. This is compared with a decline in the number of reported cases in every other category of school law litigation during the same time period.

In sum, special education and pupil services is an important area of concern in the nation's public schools and courts. IDEA and related legislation have modified the school population, the type of services provided in the schools, and the service delivery mode. It is a confusing area for program administrators as well as program recipients and their advocates because of the complicated network of federal and state legislation, regulations, and court decisions. The ambiguity, coupled with the stakes involved, has caused a litigation explosion in the area.

This book is intended to address the need for synthesized information on special education and pupil services for administrators, attorneys, and students. It covers more than just the legal ins and outs of IDEA; today, the needs and concerns are much more comprehensive. Servicing the needs of special populations includes additional programming and regulations. One must be aware not only of the law of special education but also nondiscrimination, discipline, privacy, and negligence as well. *Legal Aspects of Special Education and Pupil Services* is targeted at a broad audience. It is written with the student, attorney, and practitioner in mind. All of these individuals may sit in a class or workshop together, and all are equally in need of current reference materials. Hopefully, writing for these differing audiences within one text will provide a bridge of information as they work together on the issues of individual students' needs.

It has become apparent to us that the genesis of this book lies in 1984, when Julie Underwood taught a workshop on special education law while teaching at the University of North Dakota. In preparing for the workshop, a search for materials found little in terms of published pieces. There were, of course, cases, statutes, regulations, and journal articles on subjects within the topic, but nothing was compiled and edited for specific use. Scissors and tape transformed the pieces and bits into a workshop handout. Over the next years, Underwood taught many of these workshops. She now is called on to do workshops on very specific issues within this topic, has a regular graduate and law school course in special education law, has served as a state-level reviewing officer, and represents clients in special education and pupil service litigation. That first handout has spawned 11 years of additional bits, pieces, articles, and papers filling two semi-organized file cabinets. It is clear to both of us that the original workshop handout evolved into this manuscript.

Chapter 1 begins with a brief overview of the U.S. legal system. The next two chapters deal with various forms of discrimination and the constitutional and statutory issues related to its prohibition. Chapter 4 provides an in-depth examination of the Individuals with Disabilities Education Act and all its components. Subsequent chapters examine student discipline, child abuse and neglect, juvenile justice, negligence, student records and privacy, student health concerns, and preschool and early childhood education.

Each chapter is further divided into subtopics. Each subtopic is discussed and the current legal reasoning on the topic is explored. Case law is used to illustrate that reasoning by means of edited judicial opinions. Sections entitled Additional Commentary provide additional information on the subtopic from other cases or legislative action. A glossary follows the content chapters, and indexes of subjects and cases may be found at the end of the book.

As with any legal textbook, this book is not intended to replace the advice and counsel of an independent attorney. It is intended to advise students and practitioners so they can undertake preventive law (doing things right the first time) and defensive law in the sense that they may become empowered in their practice through understanding the parameters of the law. It is not intended to turn educators into lawyers or to replace the local school attorney. Since state practices differ in many areas, if there is a specific question or if you are involved in litigation, it is best to seek individual legal advice.

ACKNOWLEDGMENTS

We now come to the time of acknowledging all of those who have helped us with this manuscript. Since, as mentioned, it has evolved over a number of years, this is a difficult task. First, I, Julie Underwood, would like to acknowledge my mother and my sister, both of whom have been special education teachers. They are now public school administrators and still deal daily with the concerns of special students. I would also like to acknowledge my father, who was a public school administrator. Through his leadership, he changed many districts to be truly inclusive environments in an era when that was neither legally mandated nor socially expected. Both of my parents gave me an early basis of respecting and including any individual, no matter how different from me that person seemed to be. I grew up in a household where people who were deaf, paraplegic, non-English speakers, non-White, or cognitively disabled were common visitors. I thought that every child went to Easter Seal Camp or knew someone with no hands. It is from this background that I entered the true world and discovered how much work was left to be done before all people are accepted and all children have an equal chance, even in public education.

I would also like to acknowledge the patience of the other half of my family. I thank my husband, Bill Young, for his time and understanding, and my children for giving up some of their time with their mother. I am not certain that they all understand how much this project meant to me, but they were all supportive in my efforts.

Similarly, I, Julie Mead, would like to acknowledge the influence of my late grandmother, Ellen McCabe Byrne. Her tales of teaching in a one-room schoolhouse and the pride and joy she related in learning with her students first ignited my interest in education as a profession. She also taught me that it is not the package but the present inside that should be the educator's focus. I wish also to thank my parents who made it clear to me and each of my seven siblings that education was of paramount importance in their lives as individuals and as parents.

I, too, would like to acknowledge my immediate family. First, I thank David Mead, my husband, who provides the encouragement and support I need to juggle my many roles. Second, I would like to acknowledge my daughter, Caitlin, whose giggles and smiles are a constant delight and a source of inspiration.

Finally, we express our gratitude to those who worked with us on this project. First, we are indebted to the students at the University of Wisconsin–Madison who piloted each draft of this book in the class entitled Legal Aspects of Special Education and Pupil Services. Their comments and criticisms were all very helpful. Many of their insights and retold experiences are reflected in this book. Also, special thanks must be given to Kathleen Doherty and Lorraine Scurti for their technical assistance in putting this manuscript together, typing, retrieving cases, creating tables, and, most importantly, not letting us lose the originals. Our thanks are also extended to the reviewers of this book: Craig R. Fiedler (University of Wisconsin–Oshkosh) and the late Philip R. Jones (Virginia Polytechnic Institute and State University). Phil will be greatly missed by this community.

LEGAL ASPECTS
OF SPECIAL EDUCATION
AND PUPIL SERVICES

Chapter 1

THE LEGAL SYSTEM

INTRODUCTION

By their very nature, i.e., state operated, everything within a public school is, in one way or another, subject to the dictates of legal institutions, be they the United States Congress or just state actors, such as the principal of a local school. Every public school is an arm of the state. Legal institutions permeate public education.

The U.S. legal structure is complex because of the concept of federalism. There are three levels of government—federal, state, and local—and four types of law—constitutional, statutory, judicial, and administrative—within each level. Thus, each school district must operate within the federal precedents, in addition to its state and local precedents (see Table 1.1).

FEDERAL SOURCES OF LEGAL AUTHORITY

Constitutions

A constitution is that original agreement under which the participants enter into a society. It establishes the rules by which the government will operate, by setting forth governmental re-

sponsibilities and limitations. The United States Constitution is the preeminent law of the land, and all other forms of legal authority must be in compliance with it. The U.S. Constitution sets forth the three branches of government and defines the parameters under which each must operate. The Bill of Rights, the first ten amendments, describes additional limitations on governmental authority held in common to all of the branches. Because the Bill of Rights has been made applicable to the state governments as well, these are now limitations on state and local governments. The amendments made applicable to the states and of concern to schools are:

First Amendment:	Establishment of religion clause
	Free exercise of religion clause
	Freedom of speech
	Freedom of the press
	Freedom of association
	Right of assembly
Fourth Amendment:	Freedom from unreasonable search and seizures

TABLE 1.1 Sources of Legal Authority

FEDERAL	STATE	LOCAL DISTRICT
Constitution	Constitution	Not applicable
Statutes	Statutes	Policies
Administration (Dept. of Education)	Administration (State Dept. of Education)	Administrative decisions
Judicial—Federal Courts	Judicial—State Courts	Judicial—Board as hearing body

Fifth Amendment: Freedom from self-
incrimination

Eighth Amendment: Ban on cruel and
unusual
punishments

Tenth Amendment: Reserved powers

Eleventh Amendment: State immunity

Thirteenth Amendment: Ban on involuntary
servitude

Fourteenth Amendment: Due process clause
Equal protection
clause

Statutes

Statutory law is made of those statutes or laws enacted by the legislative body; it represents the current will of the people. The authority of the U.S. Congress is prescribed by the U.S. Constitution, through its body and amendments. The Tenth Amendment states: "The powers not delegated to the United States by the Constitution, nor prohibited by it to the States, are reserved to the States respectively, or to the people." This provision simply means that if the authority has not been given specifically to the federal government, the federal government has no direct authority over those concerns. Regulation of education, since it is not specifically granted as a federal power, has been deemed to be a power reserved to the states. Thus, the federal government has no authority to directly regulate education. The influence the federal government has had on education cannot be denied. This power, however, has come through a more indirect route.

Article I sets forth the powers of the Congress. Article I, Section VII, sets forth the congressional power to spend for the general welfare. Through this power, Congress has had a significant impact on education by directing state and local policy by spending money for particular causes. For example, the statutes outlined in Table 1.2 provide funds for specific uses.

Congress has used another form of legislation to achieve indirect regulation—the creation of incentive monies. In this situation, Congress has provided funds for states upon the enactment of particular legislation. In essence, it is a

TABLE 1.2   General Funding Statutes

FEDERAL STATUTE	PURPOSE	CITATION
Title IV of the Civil Rights Act	Provides funds for technical assistance and training re: race, national origin, and sex equity issues	42 U.S.C. 2000c
Women's Education Equity Act	Provides funds for educational equity for females	20 U.S.C. 3041
Carl Perkins Vocational Education Act	Provides funds for quality vocational education programs with attention to special needs populations	20 U.S.C. 2301
Chapter I of Education Consolidation and Improvement Act (ECIA)	Provides funds for remedial programs for disadvantaged students	20 U.S.C. 3801
Emergency School Aid Act	Provides monies for desegregation efforts	20 U.S.C. 1601
Bilingual Education	Ensures equal educational opportunity for students with limited English	20 U.S.C. 3281

TABLE 1.3 Incentive Funding Statutes

FEDERAL STATUTE	PURPOSE	CITATION
Individuals with Disabilities Education Act (IDEA)	Ensures appropriate special education and related services	20 U.S.C. 1400
McKinney Homeless Assistance Act	Ensures appropriate education for homeless children	42 U.S.C. 11301
Child Abuse Reporting and Prevention Act	Ensures mandatory reporting of child abuse and neglect	42 U.S.C. 5101

bribe. For example, all the statutes in Table 1.3 grant federal funds for states that have enacted the particular legislation set forth in the federal statute.

A final form of indirect federal regulation through spending powers is conditional funding. During the 1970s, Congress enacted a number of regulatory statutes, generally civil rights statutes. These statutes contain limitations on the actions of institutions that receive federal funds. In the Supreme Court case *Grove City College v. Bell*,[1] the application of these statutes was narrowed, requiring that a program receive federal funds directly before it is obligated to abide by these statutes. However, Congress amended these statutes in the Civil Rights Restoration Act so that a program need only indirectly receive funds to be bound. In essence, the definition of *program* or *activity* was broadened so that receipt of federal funds in any part of an enterprise imbues the entire organization. Even though there is technically no direct regulation, these congressional actions have significantly impacted most of U.S. society (see Table 1.4).

Congress also has the power to regulate commerce, as indicated in Article I, Section VIII.

TABLE 1.4 Conditional Funding Statutes

FEDERAL STATUTE	PURPOSE	CITATION
Title IX of the Education Amendments	Prohibits sex discrimination in educational institutions	20 U.S.C. 1681
Section 504 of the Rehabilitation Act	Prohibits disability discrimination	29 U.S.C. 794
Title VII of the Civil Rights Act Civil Rights Act	Prohibits discrimination in employment on the basis of sex, race, or national origin	42 U.S.C. 2000e
Age Discrimination Act	Prohibits age discrimination	42 U.S.C. 6101
Family Educational Rights and Privacy Act	Protects student privacy in school records	20 U.S.C. 1232g
Equal Access Act	Prohibits content-based discrimination for access to high school forums	20 U.S.C. 4071

Under this power, Congress has enacted legislation that has regulated the work force. The work force is actually considered interstate commerce because people move back and forth between state lines and because larger businesses have an effect on interstate commerce. For example, the Fair Labor Standards Act[2] regulates the working conditions of many Americans, including those who work for state and local government. The Americans with Disabilities Act[3] has significantly broadened protections for people who have disabilities.

Finally, Congress has the obligation to eradicate discrimination, i.e., implement the Civil War amendments (the Thirteenth, Fourteenth, and Fifteenth Amendments). Implementation of this would be contained in statutes such as Title VI of the Civil Rights Act of 1964,[4] designed to eliminate racial discrimination.

Administrative Rules and Regulations

The next source of federal legal authority is administrative rules and regulations impacting education. Although many different federal agencies are involved in some type of educational program, the U.S. Department of Education is the major agency through which the federal government demonstrates its commitment or authorizes services in education. The Office of Education was created in 1867 and established as a separate department in 1979. During the Reagan years, there was a push to close it, and there has been a decline in staff and funding since 1980. However, in some ways it grew in stature and security during the Reagan/Bush administrations with the appointment of various secretaries and the development of President Bush's education agenda.

As an administrative agency it is the role of the Department of Education to issue regulations implementing federal statutes and to monitor for compliance. Here, its ultimate power is the withholding of federal funds to institutions found to be in noncompliance of federal regulations. Courts grant a good deal of discretion to the administrative agencies charged with implementing and monitoring federal statutes. As such, the Department of Education has a significant amount of control over public education across the nation.

STATE SOURCES OF LEGAL AUTHORITY

Each of the 50 states has some requisites in its own constitution about the provision of education within the state. These vary in terms. Some say that the legislature must provide for a "uniform" system of education; others stipulate a "free" system of education or a "thorough and efficient" form of education. The distinctions have significant meaning in terms of finance equity litigation and the rights of children to an education in each state. Generally, a state constitution directs the state legislature to provide and fund a system of public education. Legislatures certainly would have the discretion to implement a system of education without a constitutional mandate, since, unlike the federal government, state legislatures have broad plenary powers. But the state constitutions require action. The state constitutions have each mandated that the state legislatures implement educational systems. Here rests the power to directly control public education. How each state legislature has dealt with that authority differs from state to state and from time to time, since the legislature can make changes at any time. Each state has set up some kind of system of schools, but the authority used to regulate those schools varies.

One option is that the legislature can keep all of the authority to regulate education itself. In this situation, the legislature directs such items as curriculum, graduation standards, and teacher certification through statutes. As an alternative, the legislature can delegate its authority to regulate to an administrative agency: the state department of education or state department of public instruction. Some states have given broad authority to the state departments of education to develop regulations for certifi-

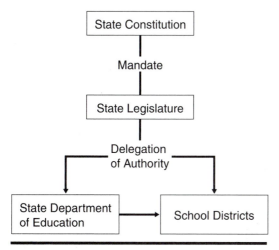

FIGURE 1.1 Delegation of State Authority

cation, curriculum, and so on. In this structure, the state department could then delegate some of this authority to school districts. Finally, the legislature may delegate its authority to the local school districts upon their creation. There are some states in which the legislature has created the system of schools, created their funding mechanism, and then transferred all other power directly to the local school boards. This would be the true example of local control (see Figure 1.1).

FEDERAL AND STATE JUDICIAL STRUCTURES

Courts basically have three functions: (1) settle controversies between parties, (2) construe or interpret legislation, and (3) determine the constitutionality of governmental actions. In order to carry out these functions, the courts work within some requirements. Courts must decide the dispute in front of them; however, they cannot legislate. Additionally, they must make their decisions based on the general rules covering similar disputes, and those sources of rules are constitutions, statutes, administrative regulations, or judicial decisions.

This latter category, judicial decisions, makes up the body of case law in the United States. Case law is either the interpretation or application of constitutions, statutes, or administrative regulations or the development of common law. A good example of this is the issue of negligence. States do not generally have any statutes or administrative rules regarding negligence, nor does the issue rise to constitutional proportions. However, there is a system of common law rules that determine who will be liable for an injury. Judges apply common law rules to the situation in front of them to determine the outcome in the new situation.

Probably the most important rule in the development of case law is that, in applying legal authority to the facts in front of them, courts are bound by the interpretations of courts that are their superior. Figure 1.2 illustrates the federal and state court structure. In the federal system and in most state systems, there are three levels of courts. The bottom level is composed of trial courts. Lawsuits typically begin in trial courts. There, the true facts are verified and the law is applied to those facts to determine the result. If a party is not satisfied with the result, it has the opportunity of appeal. Appellate courts do not make independent determinations of fact. The only way an appellate court would overturn a decision of fact is if it is not supported by the evidence on the record. Appellate courts primarily determine if the law was correctly developed and applied to the facts. In most states and at the federal level, there is a second level of appeal: the supreme court. Most supreme courts have control of their docket, so that an appealing party does not have a right to be heard. A supreme court can refuse to review a case, in which instance the decision of the lower court stands.

The pattern of appeal, the appellate structure, sets forth the superior/subordinate relationship and determines which interpretations a lower court is bound by. In essence, a court must apply those interpretations set forth by courts above it in the appellate chain. Thus, state appeals courts

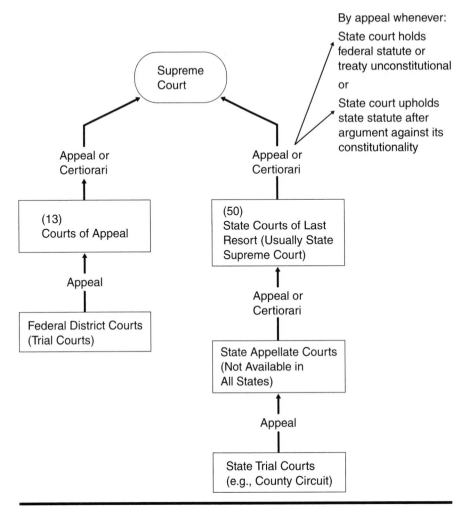

By appeal whenever:

State court holds federal statute or treaty unconstitutional

or

State court upholds state statute after argument against its constitutionality

Supreme Court

Appeal or Certiorari

Appeal or Certiorari

(13)
Courts of Appeal

(50)
State Courts of Last Resort (Usually State Supreme Court)

Appeal

Appeal or Certiorari

Federal District Courts (Trial Courts)

State Appellate Courts (Not Available in All States)

Appeal

State Trial Courts (e.g., County Circuit)

FIGURE 1.2 Federal and State Court Structure

and state trial courts must abide by the decisions of that state's supreme court but not by decisions of supreme courts in other states. The federal and state courts are linked only at the level of the United States Supreme Court, so that all courts in the nation are bound by their interpretations. State courts are not bound by other federal court decisions, either federal district courts or federal circuit courts of appeal. Equally true, federal district courts are not bound by the opinions of courts outside of their circuit. See Figure 1.3 for a map of the federal judicial circuits. This pattern of binding precedent explains the inconsistent rulings and interpretations over the same or similar issues across the nation and indicates the authority that must be attended to in any given locale.

Summing up the concept of judicial review and case law, one thing that must be remembered is that courts do not make law; they settle controversy and construe and interpret legislation and constitutions for the cases that are brought in front of them. In order to do that, they must use rules of precedent, be they consti-

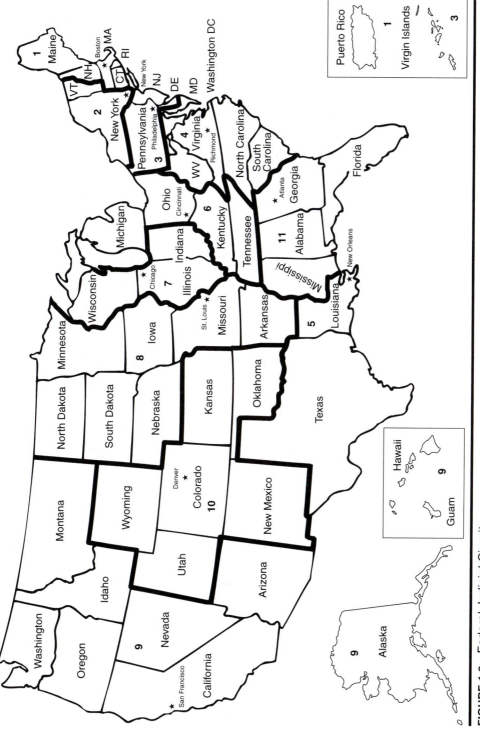

FIGURE 1.3 Federal Judicial Circuits

7

tutional precedent, legislative precedent, administrative precedent, or binding judicial precedent. That said, it is equally important to recognize that the judicial system is a highly political institution that both considers and reflects the political ideology and values of society.

ENDNOTES

1. 465 U.S. 555, 104 S. Ct. 1211 (1984).
2. 29 U.S.C. 206.
3. 42 U.S.C. 12101.
4. 42 U.S.C. 2000d.

CHAPTER 2

DISCRIMINATION AND CHILDREN AT RISK

INTRODUCTION

American society places a high value on education. Education is seen as the best way to improve oneself in society—a way to climb the social and economic ladder to success. The U.S. legal system, however, has not incorporated this value into law, in that the right to an education has not been found to be a federal constitutional right.[1] However, the right to access to the American public school system has been guaranteed on an equal basis regardless of race, sex, religion, national origin, or disabling condition. Although access to education has been opened considerably over the last 30 years, children who are female, disabled, minority, and of lower socioeconomic status still run the highest risk of school failure. The education a child receives once within the system may not be equal in quality to that received by others nor meet his or her needs. Many experts attribute this to a lack of commitment on the part of the public school system to provide services and make these students successful.

Over the last 30 years, the courts and the U.S. Congress have interpreted and implemented legislation to ensure equal treatment of students by outlawing discrimination on the basis of race, sex, national origin,[2] and disability.[3] In addition, federal and state legislatures have enacted programs that are intended to meet the needs of special student populations, those children "at risk," by providing additional protections or services.

Children at risk are generally defined as those who are not likely to complete high school

successfully. Currently, there are legal protections for those children to help them deal with their problems, protect them from discrimination, and enhance their chances of success. The contemporary emphasis on providing educational resources to meet the unique educational needs of various groups of students began in the mid-1960s with the Elementary and Secondary Education Act (ESEA). Much of the money made available under that program was to be spent to supplement the needs of children who, although not necessarily poor themselves, lived in areas with concentrations of low-income families. These children were labelled "educationally deprived" and were provided with a variety of compensatory educational programs.

In the late 1960s, attention was focused on the needs of children whose home language was not English. In 1974, a major judicial controversy was settled that mandated the protection of the rights of students with limited English-speaking ability.[4] In 1978, the Bilingual Education Act was reauthorized, providing federal financial assistance for programs to aid limited English-speaking children.

In the 1970s, congressional action primarily focused on antidiscrimination legislation. In addition, judicial and legislative action began to coalesce around the notion that more than 3 million children with disabilities living in the United States should no longer be excluded from public education. In 1975, the Education for All Handicapped Children Act was passed to provide additional federal funding for those states agreeing to provide a free and appropriate education to children with disabilities.

In the 1980s, the nation's focus shifted to school reform and improving educational outcomes. The major educational legislation from Congress involved only amending previously existing legislation. The exception is the McKinney Homeless Assistance Act, involving services for those who are homeless.

The following section will present legislation and litigation that prohibits discrimination and provides additional protections for at-risk children. First, the theoretical bases for nondiscrimination will be presented, then various types of discrimination and entitlement programs will be discussed. Although not within the theoretical purview of discrimination, a section on homelessness is included in this chapter, since these children are also severely at risk.

LEGAL FRAMEWORK

Discrimination litigants may rely on constitutional or statutory bases, or both. The appendix at the end of this chapter presents the major federal antidiscrimination provisions and the standards used by the courts to implement them.

Constitutional Standards

The primary constitutional vehicle is the federal equal protection clause,[5] although state constitutions contain similar provisions. The constitutional provisions apply only to governmental action; they prohibit unequal treatment only at the hands of the government or state actors, not private individuals. In interpreting the federal provision, a series of tests has been developed. The tests are basically a pattern of standards to determine when a classification of people is appropriate to serve the ends specified by the government. The more heinous the classification, the greater the justification required to uphold it.

Governmental action that facially discriminates against an individual on the basis of a suspect classification can only be justified if it is necessary to a compelling state interest. A *suspect classification* is a politically powerless group, which is an insular minority and has immutable characteristics. Groups that the court has been willing to recognize as suspect include classifications based on race and national origin. Thus, to uphold a governmental classification on the basis of race, the state must show that its actions are necessary to a compelling state interest and narrowly tailored to achieve those interests. Under this standard, frequently called *strict scrutiny,* a classification is rarely upheld.[6]

Most governmental classifications are held to a test of rationality, i.e., the court only looks to see if the classification is rationally related to a legitimate state interest. Classifications on the basis of age, economic circumstances, and sexual orientation are examples of classifications that have not received a suspect classification. Therefore, under this more lenient rationality standard, most classifications are upheld.

The gap between these two standards, one in which it is nearly impossible for the state to succeed and the other in which it is nearly impossible for the state to lose, caused courts to become dissatisfied with this rigid standard. As a result, a middle tier was created. Here, the classification must be substantially related to achieve an important governmental interest.[7] Courts have applied this heightened scrutiny to gender-based classifications, and some have applied it to disability and sexual orientation.

Equal protection challenges are powerful vehicles for those who believe they have been subject to overt governmental classifications based on race or gender. However, most discrimination issues do not involve facial discriminatory treatment, but rather involve facially neutral policies that have a discriminatory impact on a particular group. For example, a school district would not write a policy that required all non-White students to attend a particular school, but a facially neutral policy drafting attendance zones may have the same effect. In these instances under the federal equal protection clause, in order to prevail the individuals must show that the discriminatory result was intended or that the discrimination was purposeful.[8]

Statutory Standards

Because the constitutional provisions do not apply to all forms of discrimination and because of the difficulty in providing discriminatory intent in many situations involving governmental discrimination, plaintiffs have more often turned to statutory provisions to challenge possible discrimination. Title VI, Title VII,[9] and Title IX[10] are the primary statutory vehicles for litigating discrimination in educational institutions. Title VI protects any person in any federally funded program or activity from discrimination on the basis of race, color, or national origin. Title VII is in some ways broader, since it prohibits discrimination on the basis of race, color, national origin, and religion and gender. Its scope, however, is narrower in that it applies only to employers with 15 or more employees, employment agencies, and labor organizations covering employment issues such as hiring, promotion, compensation, fringe benefits, and other terms and conditions of employment. Title IX prohibits gender discrimination in any educational program or activity that receives federal funding. Individuals can bring a private action against an institution that is bound by these statutes,[11] and under Title VI and Title IX, federal funds can be withdrawn from institutions that are not in compliance.[12] Under all three, if successful, an individual can receive damages for discrimination.[13]

The legal theories and standards used by the court in interpreting these statutes are all very similar. They have devised two standards: discriminatory treatment and disparate impact. Discriminatory treatment covers that category of discriminatory activity that classifies people facially, e.g., policies that exclude women or minorities for certain benefits. Once a facially

discriminatory practice or policy is brought to the court, there is an inference of discrimination. This inference can be rebutted in slightly different ways for each statute. Under Title VI, like the constitutional provision, the institution must show the action is necessary to a compelling state interest. Under Title VII, the institution may show a nondiscriminatory reason for the actions, such as a bona fide occupational qualification. However, the plaintiff still has an opportunity to prove that this reason is merely a pretext for discrimination. Under Title IX, the institution must show that the action is justified by a substantial disruption to the environment or to prevent physical or mental health dangers. Like the constitutional theories, the plaintiff must prove intentional discrimination.

The second standard, disparate impact, covers that category of discriminatory activity in which an institution's actions are facially neutral but have a disparate impact on a protected group. In these cases, discriminatory intent need not be proven.[14] Once it is shown that the action has a disparate impact on the protected group, the institution may still prevail if there is proof that the action is required for a nondiscriminatory reason or serves legitimate goals.[15] The plaintiff may still prevail by showing that the institution's interest could still be served by nondiscriminatory means.

RACE

Segregation

More than 40 years have elapsed since the United States Supreme Court issued its landmark decision that outlawed apartheid practices in U.S. public schools.[16] Before this decision, the courts had allowed the doctrine of "separate but equal" to stand. This doctrine was established in an 1896 Supreme Court decision also involving public school segregation.[17] *Brown v. Board of Education* was the culmination of five cases from Kansas, South Carolina, Virginia, Delaware, and Washington, DC. The individual cases brought a broad spectrum of types of segregation in many regions of the United States. In all but the Delaware case, the lower courts had denied relief to African-American children, finding that there were equivalent facilities or ordering equivalent facilities to be established, but not ordering integration. The major point argued to the Court was whether the doctrine of "separate but equal" was constitutional. In a unanimous decision, the Court found: "We conclude that in the field of public education the doctrine of 'separate but equal' has no place. Separate educational facilities are inherently unequal."[18] Clearly, this has been one of the most important decisions in U.S. history. It has changed the educational lives of children, regardless of race. It has also been used as a springboard and theoretical basis for the integration of U.S. society for other groups and into other arenas.

Nonetheless, racial discrimination still remains a serious problem in most public schools. Even in the 1980s, over 60 percent of the African-American students in America attended predominantly African-American schools. In addition, minority students are more often suspended from schools, tracked into low-ability groups, and have been found more likely to not finish school with a high school diploma.

De jure segregation, segregation enforced by law, is prohibited constitutionally and under state and federal statutes. In 1969, the Supreme Court ordered all school districts operating in states that had de jure segregation to become unitary immediately. The districts could accomplish this through rezoning, busing, or other devices, but unitary status was mandated. However, schools remain racially unbalanced due to other factors, such as housing patterns and attendance area boundaries. In these situations, referred to as *de facto segregation,* the districts have no affirmative duty to cure the racial imbalance that they neither caused nor created.

Racial balance is not to be achieved for its own sake. It is to be pursued when racial imbalance has been caused by a constitutional violation. Once the racial imbalance due to the de jure violation has been remedied, the school district is under no duty to remedy imbalance that is caused by demographic factors.[19]

In either situation, the courts do not require statistical balance in the public schools, but imbalances must be justified by nondiscriminatory bases.

The constitutional command to desegregate schools does not mean that every school in every community must always reflect the racial composition of the school system as a whole. . . . [I]t should be clear that the existence of some small number of one-race schools . . . is not in and of itself the mark of a system which still practices segregation by law. [But] . . . the burden upon school authorities will be to satisfy the court that their racial composition is not the result of present or past discriminatory action on their part.[20]

Judicial and Office for Civil Rights orders requiring pairing of schools, redrawing of attendance districts, assignment of students across district lines, and busing students to non-neighborhood schools have all been upheld as measures to remedy racial segregation. School district policies allowing for open enrollment within the district alone have been found not to be a sufficient remedy for segregation. The issue of whether a district is in fact segregated and which remedy is sufficient is heavily dependent on the facts of the individual case. Once a district has been held to be segregated, the court retains jurisdiction throughout the remedy implementation. The most famous desegregation case, *Brown v. Board of Education,* is still under judicial control. This case was first decided by the district court in 1951. As recently as February 1993, this case involved eight Supreme Court decisions, one reported Circuit Court of Appeals decision, and three reported district court decisions.

Districts are released from supervision once they have achieved unitary status. Unitary status has been determined to be achieved when a previously segregated school district has not been segregated for a number of years, considering factors such as faculty and staff assignments, extracurricular activities, facilities, and student attendance. In essence, the district must show that it has eradicated the vestiges of past discrimination.[21] This requirement was recently altered by the Supreme Court in *Freeman v. Pitts,*[22] when the Supreme Court ruled that a district's judicial supervision could be withdrawn in stages at the district court's discretion even before the district has achieved balance in all aspects of its functioning. In this case, the school district had been declared unitary with respect to student assignments, transportation, physical facilities, and extracurricular activities. The district court retained supervisory authority in the areas of faculty assignments, resource allocation, and quality of education. The Supreme Court found that in making this determination to release from judicial supervision, the primary consideration should be whether the district has made a good-faith commitment to implement the judicial decree and the redresses underlying constitutional violations upon which the suit was predicated. The district court's control over a school district ends after the time necessary for the district to remedy the effect of past discrimination.[23]

BROWN v. BOARD OF EDUCATION OF TOPEKA
Supreme Court of the United States, 1954.
347 U.S. 483, 74 S. Ct. 686.

Mr. Chief Justice WARREN delivered the opinion of the Court.

These cases came to us from the States of Kansas, South Carolina, Virginia, and Delaware. They are premised on different facts and different local conditions, but a common legal question justifies their consideration together in this consolidated opinion.

In each of the cases, minors of the Negro race, through their legal representatives, seek the aid of the courts in obtaining admission to the public schools of their community on a nonsegregated basis. In each instance, they have been denied admission to schools attended by white children under laws requiring or permitting segregation according to race. This segregation was alleged to deprive the plaintiffs of the equal protection of the laws under the Fourteenth Amendment. In each of the cases other than the Delaware case, a three-judge federal district court denied relief to the plaintiffs on the so-called "separate but equal" doctrine announced by this Court in *Plessy v. Ferguson*, 163 U.S. 537, 16 S. Ct. 1138, 41 L. Ed. 256. Under that doctrine, equality of treatment is accorded when the races are provided substantially equal facilities, even though these facilities be separate. In the Delaware case, the Supreme Court of Delaware adhered to that doctrine, but ordered that the plaintiffs be admitted to the white school because of their superiority to the Negro schools.

The plaintiffs contend that segregated public schools are not "equal" and cannot be made "equal," and that hence they are deprived of the equal protection of the laws. Because of the obvious importance of the question presented, the Court took jurisdiction. Argument was heard in the 1952 Term, and reargument was heard this Term on certain questions propounded by the Court. . . .

In the first cases in this Court construing the Fourteenth Amendment, decided shortly after its adoption, the Court interpreted it as proscribing all state-imposed discriminations against the Negro race. The doctrine of "separate but equal" did not make its appearance in this Court until 1896 in the case of *Plessy v. Ferguson, supra,* involving not education but transportation. American courts have since labored with the doctrine for over half a century. In this Court, there have been six cases involving the "separate but equal" doctrine in the field of public education. In *Cumming v. Board of Education of Richmond County*, 175 U.S. 528, 20 S. Ct. 197, 44 L. Ed. 262, and *Gong Lum v. Rice*, 275 U.S. 78, 48 S.

Ct. 91, 72 L. Ed. 172, the validity of the doctrine itself was not challenged. In more recent cases, all on the graduate school level, inequality was found in that specific benefits enjoyed by white students were denied to Negro students of the same educational qualifications. . . . In none of these cases was it necessary to re-examine the doctrine to grant relief to the Negro plaintiff. And in *Sweatt v. Painter*, the Court expressly reserved decision on the question whether *Plessy v. Ferguson* should be held inapplicable to public education.

In the instant cases, that question is directly presented. Here, unlike *Sweatt v. Painter*, there are findings below that the Negro and white schools involved have been equalized, or are being equalized, with respect to buildings, curricula, qualifications and salaries of teachers, and other "tangible" factors. Our decision, therefore, cannot turn on merely a comparison of these tangible factors in the Negro and white schools involved in each of the cases. We must look instead to the effect of segregation itself on public education.

In approaching this problem, we cannot turn the clock back to 1868 when the Amendment was adopted, or even to 1896 when *Plessy v. Ferguson* was written. We must consider public education in the light of its full development and its present place in American life throughout the Nation. Only in this way can it be determined if segregation in public schools deprives these plaintiffs of the equal protection of the laws.

Today, education is perhaps the most important function of state and local governments. Compulsory school attendance laws and the great expenditures for education both demonstrate our recognition of the importance of education to our democratic society. It is required in the performance of our most basic public responsibilities, even service in the armed forces. It is the very foundation of good citizenship. Today it is a principal instrument in awakening the child to cultural values, in preparing him for later professional training, and in helping him to adjust normally to his environment. In these days, it is doubtful that any child may reasonably be expected to succeed in life if he is denied the opportunity of an education. Such an opportunity, where the state has undertaken to provide it, is a right which must be made available to all on equal terms.

We come then to the question presented: Does segregation of children in public schools solely on the basis of race, even though the physical facilities and other "tangible" factors may be equal, deprive the children of the minority group of equal educational opportunities? We believe that it does.

In *Sweatt v. Painter*, in finding that a segregated law school for Negroes could not provide them equal educational opportunities, this Court relied in large part on "those qualities which are incapable of objective measurement but which make for greatness in a law school." In *McLaurin v. Oklahoma State Regents*, the Court, in requiring that a Negro admitted to a white graduate school be treated like all other students, again resorted to intangible considerations: "his ability to study, to engage in discussions and exchange views with other students, and, in general, to learn his profession." Such considerations apply with added force to children in grade and high schools. To separate them from others of similar age and qualifications solely because of their race generates a feeling of inferiority as to their status in the community that may affect their hearts and minds in a way unlikely ever to be undone. The effect of this separation on their educational opportunities was well stated by a finding in the Kansas case by a court which nevertheless felt compelled to rule against the Negro plaintiffs:

> *Segregation of white and colored children in public schools has a detrimental effect upon the colored children. The impact is greater when it has the sanction of the law; for the policy of separating the races is usually interpreted as denoting the inferiority of the Negro group. A sense of inferiority affects the motivation of a child to learn. Segregation with the sanction of law, therefore, has a tendency to [retard] the educational and mental development of Negro children and to deprive them of some of the benefits they would receive in a racial[ly] integrated school system.*

Whatever may have been the extent of psychological knowledge at the time of *Plessy v. Ferguson*, this finding is amply supported by modern authority. Any language in *Plessy v. Ferguson* contrary to this finding is rejected.

We conclude that in the field of public education the doctrine of "separate but equal" has no place. Separate educational facilities are inherently unequal. Therefore, we hold that the plaintiffs and others similarly situated for whom the actions have been brought are, by reason of the segregation complained of, deprived of the equal protection of the laws guaranteed by the Fourteenth Amendment. This disposition makes unnecessary any discussion whether such segregation also violates the Due Process Clause of the Fourteenth Amendment.

Because these are class actions, because of the wide applicability of this decision, and because of the great variety of local conditions, the formulation of decrees in these cases presents problems of considerable complexity. On reargument, the consideration of appropriate relief was necessarily subordinated to the primary question—the constitutionality of segregation in public education. We have now announced that such segregation is a denial of the equal protection of the laws. In order that we may have the full assistance of the parties in formulating decrees, the cases will be restored to the docket, and the parties are requested to present further argument on Questions 4 and 5 previously propounded by the Court for the reargument this Term. The Attorney General of the United States is again invited to participate. The Attorneys General of the states requiring or permitting segregation of public education will also be permitted to appear as *amici curiae* upon request to do so by September 15, 1954, and submission of briefs by October 1, 1954.

It is so ordered.

ADDITIONAL COMMENTARY

1. Severe conflict surrounded the implementation of the *Brown* decisions. The best known is probably the attempts of the state of Arkansas to block the integration of the schools in Little Rock. The Arkansas National Guard was used to prevent African-American students from entering the formerly White school. Federal troops were called in to protect these students and gain access to the schools for them. *Cooper v. Aaron*, 358 U.S. 1 (1958).

2. In 1968, the Supreme Court held that "freedom of choice" plans were only an acceptable method of redressing de jure segregation if it did in fact move the district toward unitary status. *Green v. County School Board of New Kent County*, 391 U.S. 430 (1968).

3. In *Griffin v. County School Board of Prince Edward County*, 377 U.S. 218 (1964), the Supreme Court held that a state could not avoid integration by closing its public schools and providing education through county assistance to private schools.

4. Explaining color-conscious remedies, the Fifth Circuit Court of Appeals stated:

   The Constitution is both color blind and color conscious. To avoid a conflict with the equal protection clause, a classification that denies a benefit, causes harm, or imposes a burden must not be based on race. . . . But the Constitution is color conscious to prevent discrimination being perpetuated and to undo the effects of past discrimination. The criterion is the relevancy of color to a legitimate governmental purpose.
   U.S. v. Jefferson County Board of Education, 372 F.2d 836 at 876 (5th Cir. 1966).

5. Once a district achieves unitary status, but resegregation occurs, plaintiffs must prove the discriminatory intent of the state caused the resegregation. Resegregation caused by other forces does not require mandatory integration methods. *Riddick by Riddick v. School Board of Norfolk*, 784 F.2d 521 (4th Cir. 1986).

6. The decisions have allowed additional options to be provided to students as a part of integration efforts, including enrichment courses, early childhood programs, and reductions in student-teacher ratios. *Milliken v. Bradley*, 433 U.S. 267 (1977).

7. In *Missouri v. Jenkins*, U.S., 110 S .Ct. 1651 (1990), the Supreme Court upheld a lower court's order to levy excess taxes to fund desegregation remedies.

8. Recently, there have been proposals to implement single-race, single-sex institutions in an effort to provide good role models and environments particularly for African-American males. The districts of both Milwaukee and Detroit have experimented with this option, developing the programs so as to not exclude others but to clearly focus on the needs of this population.

OTHER DISCRIMINATORY PRACTICES

Even after a district is declared to be unitary, discriminatory practices can continue to adversely effect the education of students. Practices such as ability grouping and discriminatory disciplinary measures may have the effect of isolating groups from one another. Nationally, at the high school level, Black students are suspended three times as often as Whites. Minority students comprise 25 percent of the school population, and yet they comprise 40 percent of all students suspended or expelled. It is often alleged that this is caused not by minority students presenting an actual disruption more often than White students, but by racism in the public schools.

Although discipline policies are written in a race-neutral manner, they are too often applied discriminatorily. Policies generally contain vague terms and leave the teachers and administrators with a good deal of discretion in their application. Unfortunately, this can lead to discriminatory applications and interpretations. Such discriminatory application of disciplinary rules would be grounds for judicial relief.[24] If the rules are racially neutral on their face, to be successful, the plaintiff has to present evidence of discriminatory motives. Since actual proof of animus is extremely rare, the courts have held that, absent a legitimate educational reason if the practice would foreseeably result in discrimination, discriminatory intent can be inferred.

There has been much litigation in the area of discriminatory testing and ability grouping.[25] Many classification and testing practices have been challenged as biased on the bases of race, culture, and gender. Academic classification of students has tended to concentrate minority students in less advanced school programs. The percentage of minority students assigned to special education programs for the educable mentally retarded and less advanced academic programs is two to three times that of the general school population in over half the school districts nationally.[26] This would be of less concern if it were believed that this result was brought about truly by ability or disability rather than biased testing and classification practices.

This argument is also applied when schools and states conduct competency tests. Recently, more states and districts have moved to the use of a competency test for promotion and graduation. Even by the late 1980s, a majority of states had some form of mandated competency testing, and one-third of the states conditioned graduation on a competency test.[27] The discriminatory effect of these tests was litigated in *Debra P. v. Turlington*.[28] In this case, the plaintiffs challenged the implementation of a minimum competency test for graduation on the grounds that (1) there was insufficient notice of the change in requirements (13 months), (2) the test was not a valid reflection of the material being taught in the school curriculum, and (3) it had a disparate impact on minority students who embarked on their educational career in segregated schools. Initially, the test was enjoined from use as a graduation requirement until students had time to prepare and students who had been enrolled in a segregated system had graduated. The injunction was finally lifted after the court was convinced of the instructional validity of the examination.

TERESA P. v. BERKELEY UNIFIED SCHOOL DISTRICT
724 F. Supp. 698
(U.S. District Court, Northern District of California 1989)

JENSEN, District Judge.

I. INTRODUCTION

. . . .

II. FINDINGS OF FACT

2. Plaintiff class, . . . consists of all students currently enrolled in the Berkeley Unified School District (the BUSD or District), who are of limited English proficiency [LEP] by reason of having a first or home language other than English and who consequently have a barrier to equal participation in the BUSD programs.

. . . .

[As of June 15, 1988, 571 LEP students were enrolled in the District.]

III. CONCLUSIONS OF LAW

Plaintiffs challenge the Language Remediation Program of the Berkeley Unified School District (BUSD) on two grounds. First, plaintiffs argue that the BUSD violated section 1703(f) of the Equal Educational Opportunities Act (EEOA), 20 U.S.C. § 1701 et seq., which requires appropriate action by school districts to overcome special educational barriers. Second, plaintiffs allege that the BUSD violated Title VI of the Civil Rights Act of 1964, 42 U.S.C. § 2000d, which prohibits racial discrimination in programs receiving federal aid. As relief, plaintiffs request that the Court issue an injunction ordering the BUSD to design and implement a comprehensive plan to ensure plaintiffs equal educational opportunity and effective participation in the learning process.

Based on the findings of fact and a review of the applicable law, this Court concludes that plaintiffs have failed to establish a violation of either section 1703(f) or Title VI.

A. Plaintiffs' EEOA Section 1703(f) Claim

1. Legal Framework

Plaintiffs' first cause of action is based on section 1703(f) of the EEOA, which provides that:

> No state shall deny equal educational opportunity to an individual on account of his or her race, color, sex, or national origin, by—
>
> (f) the failure by an educational agency to take appropriate action to overcome language barriers that impede equal participation by its students in its instructional programs.
>
> 20 U.S.C. § 1703(f).

The EEOA does not define appropriate action nor does it provide criteria for a court to evaluate whether or not a school district has taken "appropriate action.". . .

The clearest statement of this requirement is set forth by the Fifth Circuit in *Castaneda v. Pickard*, 648 F.2d 989 (5th Cir. 1981). *Castaneda* held that in evaluating a school system's language remediation program, a court must conduct the following three-prong analysis.

First, the court must determine whether the school district is pursuing a program "informed by an educational theory recognized as sound by some experts in the field, or, at least, deemed a legitimate experimental strategy." Id. at 1009. Second, the court must establish whether "the programs and practices actually used by the school system are reasonably calculated to implement effectively the educational theory adopted by the school." Id. at 1010. Third, the court must determine whether the school's program, although premised on sound educational theory and effectively implemented, "produces results indicating that the language barriers confronting students are actually being overcome." Id.

. . . .

[1] This Court agrees with, and will heed, the warnings stated by the *Castaneda* Court itself that

courts should not substitute their educational values and theories for the educational and political decisions properly reserved to local school authorities and the expert knowledge of educators, since they are ill-equipped to do so. Id. at 1009.

. . . .

a. Sound Educational Theory

The EEOA does not require school districts to adopt a specific educational theory or implement an ideal academic program. That Congress utilized the term "appropriate action," rather than "bilingual education," indicates that Congress intended to leave educational authorities substantial latitude in formulating programs to meet their EEOA obligations. *Castaneda,* 648 F.2d at 1009.

. . . .

Although plaintiffs advocate a program that emphasizes native tongue instruction, they introduced no objective evidence demonstrating that the efficacy of this approach, whatever it may be, for teaching LEP students English, or helping them succeed in a mainstream environment, renders the alternative programs preferred by BUSD pedagogically unsound.

b. Implementation of the Educational Program

(1) Effective Teachers

Plaintiffs maintain that the training of the bilingual teacher and tutor is crucial to the proper implementation of a language remediation program. Plaintiffs argue that by failing to hire teachers and tutors qualified to provide the highly technical and specialized instruction required by the ESL approach, the BUSD has failed to implement a sound educational program.

Plaintiffs contend that in order to implement its language remediation program, BUSDs teachers must have skills based on academic course work in ESL methodology, the developmental needs of LEP students, language proficiency assessment procedures, applied linguistics, general language acquisition, and second language acquisition. Plaintiffs contend that the BUSD should assure this competence by hiring teachers with a language development specialist credential, a bilingual-crosscultural certificate of proficiency or a bilingual-crosscultural specialist credential.

. . . .

By including in the EEOA the obligation to remove language barriers through appropriate action, Congress intended to ensure that school districts make "genuine and good faith efforts, consistent with local circumstances and resources," to remedy the language deficiencies of their LEP students. *Castaneda,* 648 F.2d at 1009. To this end, a school district that chooses to fulfill its EEOA obligations by means of a bilingual program must make good faith efforts to provide teachers competent to teach such a program. Id. at 1012. . . .

The threshold question is, of course, whether or not the credentialed teachers contemplated by plaintiffs are in fact available to a school district who seeks them out. The evidence at trial did not fully resolve this issue but did suggest that it is highly unlikely that the BUSD could fill all necessary positions with fully credentialed teachers in the basic language groups and that it is impossible to cover all languages represented in the BUSD school population. The record in this case established that the mix of teachers newly hired or reassigned to language remediation responsibilities by the BUSD, included both credentialed and non-credentialed teachers. Those without credentials were assessed as to relevant bilingual skills, required to participate in district level training sessions, and to make substantial progress toward completion of requirements for credentials as a condition of employment. The situation with tutors was much the same. The BUSD looks to college graduates or students with two years college at a minimum, finds some with native language ability, and provides relevant district level training to all.

The other major assumption of plaintiffs in this area is that it is necessary to hold language-specific credentials in order to deliver remediation programs which do not violate the EEOA. The evidence in the record does not support this assumption. Rather, it tends to show an alternative assumption: that good teachers are good teachers no matter what the educational challenge may be. There is in fact evidence in the record showing that there is no difference in achievement success of LEP students in the BUSD between students with credentialed teachers and students who do not have credentialed teachers.

. . . .

The third prong of the *Castaneda* test involves consideration of the program's results. Neither the EEOA nor the *Castaneda* court explains how it is that a federal court is to judge the results of a school district's language remediation program. *Castaneda* simply indicated that the program should "produce results indicating that the language barriers confronting students are actually being overcome." 648 F.2d at 1010.

Measuring the success or failure of educational programs is one of the great challenges that faces our educators and is a challenge that this Court approaches with, at least, great trepidation. Other courts have also expressed a similar reluctance. . . . It is surely beyond the competence of this Court to fashion its own measure of academic achievement, and the Court will necessarily defer to the measuring devices already used by the school system.

In this case, the CAP [California Assessment Program] and CTBS [California Test of Basic Skills] standardized achievement scores, used by California schools, relative to English and to academic subject matter, as well as the classroom grades of the BUSDs LEP students, all point to the effectiveness of the program in teaching English to LEP students and in contributing to their academic achievement. These scores show that the BUSDs LEP students are learning at rates equal to or higher than their counterparts in California. LEP students in the BUSD have a record of achievement which is the same or better than the record of LEP students in schools identified by plaintiffs' experts as having effective language remediation programs. Extremely strong attendance patterns provide further proof, through non-academic criteria, that LEP students are fully participating in the BUSDs educational program.

. . . .

Plaintiffs' claim that the BUSD has failed to implement a sound educational program, has not been sustained. Accordingly, this Court concludes that plaintiffs have failed to establish a violation of section 1703(f) of the EEOA.

B. Plaintiffs' Title VI Claim

. . . .

Plaintiffs' second claim for relief is based on Title VI of the Civil Rights Act of 1964, 42 U.S.C. § 2000d, and its implementing administrative regulations. Section 601 of the Act provides that:

No person in the United States shall, on the ground of race, color, or national origin, be excluded from participation in, be denied the benefits of, or be subjected

to discrimination under any program or activity receiving federal financial assistance.
42 U.S.C. § 2000d.

Regulations issued under this statutory mandate require that recipients of federal funding may not:

[U]tilize criteria or methods of administration which have the effect of subjecting individuals to discrimination because of their race, color, or national origin, or have the effect of defeating or substantially impairing accomplishment of the objectives of the program as respect individuals of a particular race, color, or national origin.
34 C.F.R. § 100.3(b)(2), originally adopted as 45 C.F.R. § 80.3(b)(2).

. . . .

The case law makes clear that in order to establish a prima facia case of discrimination, plaintiffs must show a discriminatory intent on the part of the BUSD or show that the BUSDs language remediation program, although neutral on its face, has a discriminatory effect on the BUSDs LEP students. Plaintiffs have not offered evidence and in fact do not argue that the BUSD harbors any racially discriminatory intent whatsoever in the delivery of any of its educational programs. Proof that the BUSDs program has a disparate impact on LEP students is, therefore, the only avenue that remains open to them to establish that the BUSD violates Title VI.

. . . . Although there are relatively few Title VI disparate impact cases, the cases that do exist all hold that plaintiff can only establish a prima facie case by offering proof of discriminatory intent or proof that the challenged action has a discriminatory impact.

. . . .

Since plaintiffs in the case have not offered any evidence, statistical or otherwise, of racially discriminatory effect, this Court concludes that plaintiffs have utterly failed to sustain their burden of proof under Title VI.

IV. CONCLUSION

Based on these findings of fact and conclusions of law, this Court holds that plaintiffs have failed to establish a violation of section 1703(f) of the EEOA or section 601 of Title VI. Accordingly, this Court enters judgment in favor of defendants.

IT IS SO ORDERED.

ADDITIONAL COMMENTARY

1. In *Morales v. Shannon*, 516 F.2d 411 (5th Cir. 1975), *cert. denied*, 423 U.S. 1034 (1975), the court found that the high concentration of Mexican-American students in low-track academic programs was the result of nonbiased measures.

   Given that ability groupings are not unconstitutional per se, the statistical results of the groupings here are not so abnormal or unusual in any instance as to justify an inference of discrimination. The record shows no more than the use of a non-discriminatory teaching practice or technique, a matter which is reserved to educators under our system of government.

   516 F.2d at 414.

2. In *Lemon v. Bossier Parish School Board*, 444 F.2d 1400 (5th Cir. 1971), the court struck student classification practices because they were found to be contrary to a prior desegregation order. However, in *Georgia State Conference of Branches of NAACP v. State of Georgia*, 775 F.2d 1403 (11th Cir. 1985), the court upheld the use of ability groups even though the districts had not achieved unitary status.

3. In two separate cases, plaintiffs alleged that standardized intelligence tests used for placing students were biased. In *Larry P. v. Riles*, 495 F.Supp. 926 (N.D. Cal. 1979) *aff'd*, 793 F.2d 969 (9th Cir. 1984), the court enjoined the district from using the results of intelligence tests to place minority students in classes for the mentally retarded. The court was not convinced that the tests were valid for the placement of minority students since they were normed for White middle-class students. However, the court in *Parents in Action on Special Education v. Hannon*, 506 F.Supp. 831 (N.D. Ill. 1980), reached the opposite result, and allowed intelligence tests to be used as one factor in placement.

LANGUAGE AND ETHNICITY

Title VI and the equal protection clause can also be used to prohibit discrimination on the basis of national origin or ethnicity. When ethnicity or national origin are used as a classification on its face, discrimination under Title VI is readily proven. The Supreme Court in *Plyler v. Doe*[29] applied a heightened, but not strict, level of scrutiny when ruling on the Texas statute, which excluded children of illegal aliens from public schools.

However, when the alleged discrimination is not clear on its face, that is when a policy or practice results in differential results, relief under either theory is more difficult to achieve. In *Castaneda v. Pickard*,[30] the court found no constitutional or Title VI violations in the district's enrollment and student classification practices, even though the end result was essentially a district segregated between Hispanics and Whites.[31]

Generally, grievances raised by minority students, other than segregation, often involve linguistic barriers. State or school board rules can require that the basic language of instruction in all schools be English. The state, however, cannot instruct in the English language exclusively, by denying interpretation and bilingual instruction to students who do not use the English language. The principal sources of federal legislation that cover linguistic barriers to educational opportunities are found in Title VI of the Civil Rights Act of 1964,[32] the Equal Educational Opportunities Act of 1974,[33] and the Bilingual Education Act of 1978.[34]

The most noted case in the field is the United States Supreme Court case, *Lau v. Nichols*.[35] There, non-English-speaking Chinese students maintained that failure to provide methods for bridging the language gap violated Title VI of the Civil Rights Act of 1964. The statute bans discrimination "on the grounds of race, color, or national origin" in "any program or activity receiving federal financial assistance." The Department of Health, Education, and Welfare had issued guidelines that state:

> Where inability to speak and understand the English language excludes national origin-minority groups children from effective participation in the educational program offered by a school district, the district must take affirmative steps to rectify the language deficiency.[36]

The Supreme Court held in favor of the children, and in so doing observed that there is not equality of treatment where the students do not understand English but are instructed solely in English. The Court concluded that:

> Basic English skills are at the very core of what these public schools teach. Imposition of a requirement that, before a child can effectively participate in the educational program, he must already have acquired those basic skills is to make a mockery of public education. We know that those who do not understand English are certain to find their classroom experiences wholly incomprehensible and in no way meaningful.[37]

The Court did not define the relief required for the children but instead noted that the lower judge had the discretion to fashion appropriate relief by way of an injunction.

The Equal Educational Opportunities Act's (EEOA) provisions relating to linguistic minorities states:

> No state shall deny equal educational opportunity to an individual on account of his or her race, color, sex, or national origin, by . . . (f) the failure by an educational agency to take appropriate action to overcome language barriers that impede equal participation by its students in its instructional programs.[38]

This statute is broader than Title VI of the Civil Rights Act because it applies to all public educational agencies and programs, to any individual, and regardless of evidence of intentional discrimination. Most importantly, it has been held that the EEOA imposes an affirmative duty on schools "to take appropriate action to overcome language barriers."[39] To be successful in an EEOA case, the students must be able to identify their language barriers and show how their language barrier impedes their participation in the instructional program. Plaintiffs must next show how the defendants have failed to take appropriate steps to rectify the problem and finally identify the connection between the defendant's failure and the students' learning problems.[40] The courts have given the educational experts a great deal of discretion in determining what remedies would be appropriate in each particular case. The EEOA does not necessarily require any particular form of program or even formal bilingual or bicultural education.[41]

Although the EEOA is most commonly used to redress the grievances of non-English-speaking minorities, it has been used by children who speak "Black English." In one case, 11 African-American children were experiencing educational difficulties due to their use of "Black English." The court found that they were being denied equal opportunities under the EEOA by the school district's failure to train teachers in that vernacular and help the students bridge the gap from their language to standard American English.[42]

The most specific statute in the area is the Bilingual Education Act (BEA). In part, it states:

> [T]here are large and growing numbers of children of limited English proficiency . . . the Congress declares it to be the policy of the United States, in order to establish equal educational opportunity for all children . . . (A) to encourage the establishment and operation, where appropriate, of educational programs using bilingual education practices, techniques and methods, (B) to encourage the establishment of special alternative instructional programs for students of limited English proficiency in school districts where the establishment of bilingual educational programs is not practicable . . . , and (C) for those purposes

to provide financial assistance to local educational agencies and, ... to State educational agencies. ... The programs assisted ... are designed to meet the educational needs of individuals of limited English proficiency with particular attention to children having the greatest need for such programs.[43]

Fiscal incentives are intended to induce school districts with high concentrations of linguistic minorities to undertake bilingual and bicultural programs. Like the EEOA, the BEA does not impose any particular philosophy of bilingual education. The statute and implementing regulations use the concepts of *limited English proficiency,* meaning children with sufficient difficulty in understanding, speaking, reading, or writing the English language to deny them the opportunity to learn successfully in English;[44] *transitional bilingual education,* meaning "structured English language instruction, and to the extent necessary to allow a child to achieve competence in the English language, instruction in the child's native language";[45] *developmental bilingual education,* meaning "a full-time program of instruction ... in structured English language instruction and instruction in a second language";[46] and *special alternative instructional programs,* meaning "programs of instruction ... [that] have specially designed curricula and are appropriate for the particular linguistic and instructional needs of the children enrolled."[47] The BEA stresses appreciation of students' cultural heritage in all courses to the extent the same are necessary to allow a child to progress through the educational system.[48]

PLYLER v. DOE
457 U.S. 202, 102 S. Ct. 2382, 72 L. Ed. 786 (1982)

Justice BRENNAN delivered the opinion of the Court.

The question presented by these cases is whether, consistent with the Equal Protection Clause of the Fourteenth Amendment, Texas may deny to undocumented school-age children the free public education that it provides to children who are citizens of the United States or legally admitted aliens.

I.

****

In May 1975, the Texas Legislature revised its education laws to withhold from local school districts any state funds for the education of children who were not "legally admitted" into the United States. The 1975 revision also authorized local school districts to deny enrollment in their public schools to children not "legally admitted" to the country. Tex. Educ. Code Ann. § 21.031 (Vernon Supp. 1981).

****

II.

The Fourteenth Amendment provides that "[n]o State shall ... deprive any person of life, liberty, or property, without due process of law; nor deny to any person within its jurisdiction the equal protection of the laws.". . .

****

"The Fourteenth Amendment to the Constitution is not confined to the protection of citizens. It says: 'Nor shall any state deprive any person of life, liberty, or property without due process of law; nor deny to any person within its jurisdiction the equal protection of the laws.' These provisions are universal in their application, to all persons within the territorial jurisdiction, without regard to any differences of race, of color, or of nationality; and the protection of the laws is a pledge of the protection of equal laws." *Yick Wo, supra,* at 369, 6 S. Ct. at 1070.

****

Our conclusion that the illegal aliens who are plaintiffs in these cases may claim the benefit of the Fourteenth Amendment's guarantee of equal protection only begins the inquiry. The more difficult question is whether the Equal Protection Clause has been violated by the refusal of the State of Texas to reimburse local school boards for the education of children who cannot demonstrate that their presence within the United States is lawful, or by the imposition by those school boards of the burden of tuition on those children. . . .

III.

****

A.

Sheer incapability or lax enforcement of the laws barring entry into this country, coupled with the failure to establish an effective bar to the employment of undocumented aliens, has resulted in the creation of a substantial "shadow population" of illegal migrants—numbering in the millions—within our borders. This situation raises the specter of a permanent caste of undocumented resident aliens, encouraged by some to remain here as a source of cheap labor, but nevertheless denied the benefits that our society makes available to citizens and lawful residents. The existence of such an underclass presents most difficult problems for a Nation that prides itself on adherence to principles of equality under law.

The children who are plaintiffs in these cases are special members of this underclass. Persuasive arguments support the view that a State may withhold its beneficence from those whose very presence within the United States is the product of their own unlawful conduct. These arguments do not apply with the same force to classifications imposing disabilities on the minor children of such illegal entrants. . . . Even if the State found it expedient to control the conduct of adults by acting against their children, legislation directing the onus of a parent's misconduct against his children does not comport with fundamental conceptions of justice.

****

Public education is not a "right" granted to individuals by the Constitution. *San Antonio Independent School Dist. v. Rodriguez*, 411 U.S. 1, 35, 93 S. Ct. 1278, 1298, 36 L. Ed. 2d 16 (1973). But neither is it merely some governmental "benefit" indistinguishable from other forms of social welfare legislation. Both the importance of education in maintaining our basic institutions, and the lasting impact of its deprivation on the life of the child, mark the distinction. The "American people have always regarded education and [the] acquisition of knowledge as matters of supreme importance." *Meyer v. Nebraska*, 262 U.S. 390, 400, 43 S. Ct. 625, 627, 67, L. Ed. 1042 (1923). We have recognized "the public schools as a most vital civic institution for the preservation of a democratic system of government," *Abington School District v. Schempp*, 374 U.S. 203, 230, 83 S. Ct. 1560, 1575, 10 L. Ed. 2d 844 (1963) (BRENNAN, J., concurring). . . . "[A]s . . . pointed out early in our history, . . . some degree of education is necessary to prepare citizens to participate effectively and intelligently in our open political system if we are to preserve freedom and independence." *Wisconsin v. Yoder*, 406 U.S. 205, 221, 92 S. Ct. 1526, 1536, 32 L. Ed. 2d 15 (1972). And these historic "perceptions of the public schools as inculcating fundamental values necessary to the maintenance of a democratic political system have been conformed by the observations of social scientists." *Ambach v. Norwick, supra*, 411 U.S., at 77, 99 S. Ct., at 1594. . . . In sum, education has a fundamental role in maintaining the fabric of our society. We cannot ignore the significant social costs borne by our Nation when select groups are denied the means to absorb the values and skills upon which our social order rests.

****

. . . . But more directly, "education prepares individuals to be self-reliant and self-sufficient participants in society." *Wisconsin v. Yoder, supra*, 406 U.S., at 221, 92 S. Ct., at 1536. Illiteracy is an enduring disability. The inability to read and write will handicap the individual deprived of a basic education each and every day of his life. The inestimable toll of that deprivation on the social economic, intellectual, and psychological well-being of the individual, and the obstacle it poses to individual achievement, make it most difficult to reconcile the cost or the principle of a status-based denial of basic education with the framework of equality embodied in the Equal Protection Clause.

****

These well-settled principles allow us to determine the proper level of deference to be afforded § 21.031. Undocumented aliens cannot be treated as a suspect class because their presence in this country in violation of federal law is not a "constitutional irrelevancy." Nor is education a fundamental right; a State need not justify by compelling necessity every variation in the manner in which education is provided to its population. *See San Antonio Independent School Dist. v. Rodriguez, supra*, at 28-39, 93 S. Ct., at 1293-1300. But more is involved in these cases than the abstract question whether § 21.031 discriminates against a suspect class, or whether education is fundamental right. Section 21.031 imposes a lifetime hardship on a discrete class of children not accountable for their disabling status. The stigma of illiteracy will mark them for the rest of their lives. By denying these children a basic education, we deny them the ability to live within the structure of our civic institutions, and foreclose any realistic possibility that they will contribute in even the smallest way to the progress of our Nation. In determining the rationality of § 21.031, we may appropriately take into account its costs to the Nation and to the innocent children who are its victims. In light of these countervailing costs, the discrimination contained in § 21.031 can hardly be considered rational unless it furthers some substantial goal of the State.

IV.

****

V.

****

[W]e discern three colorable state interests that might support § 21.031.

First, appellants appear to suggest that the State may seek to protect itself from an influx of illegal immigrants. While a State might have an interest in mitigating the potentially harsh economic effects of sudden shifts in population, § 21.031 hardly offers an effective method of dealing with an urgent demographic or economic problem. There is no evidence in the record suggesting that illegal entrants impose any significant burden on the State's economy. To the contrary, the available evidence suggests that illegal aliens underutilize public services, while contributing their labor to the local economy and tax money to the state fisc. . . .

Second, while it is apparent that a State may "not . . . reduce expenditures for education by barring [some arbitrarily chosen class of] children from its schools," *Shapiro v. Thompson*, 394 U.S. 618, 633, 89 S. Ct. 1322, 1330, 22 L. Ed. 2d 600 (1969), appellants suggest that undocumented children are appropriately singled out for exclusion because of the special burdens they impose on the State's ability to provide high-quality public education. But the record in no way supports the claim that exclusion of undocumented children is likely to improve the overall quality of education in the State. . . . Of course, even if improvement in the quality of education were a likely result of barring some number of children from the schools of the State, the State must support its selection of this group as the appropriate target for exclusion. In terms of educational cost and need, however, undocumented children are "basically indistinguishable" from legally resident alien children.

Finally, appellants suggest that undocumented children are appropriately singled out because their unlawful presence within the United States renders them less likely than other children to remain within the boundaries of the State, and to put their education to productive social or political use within the State. Even assuming that such an interest is legitimate, it is an interest that is most difficult to quantify. . . . It is difficult to understand precisely what the State hopes to achieve by promoting the creation and perpetuation of a subclass of illiterates within our boundaries, surely adding to the problems and costs of unemployment, welfare, and crime. It is thus clear that whatever savings might be achieved by denying these children an education, they are wholly insubstantial in light of the costs involved to these children, the State, and the Nation.

VI.

If the State is to deny a discrete group of innocent children the free public education that it offers to other children residing within its borders, that denial must be justified by a showing that it furthers some substantial state interest. No such showing was made here. Accordingly, the judgment of the Court of Appeals in each of these cases is

Affirmed.

(Footnotes omitted.)

– – – –

LAU v. NICHOLS
414 U.S. 563, 94 S. Ct. 786 (1974)

Mr. Justice DOUGLAS delivered the opinion of the Court.

. . . . The District Court found that there are 2,856 students of Chinese ancestry in the school system who do not speak English. Of those who have that language deficiency, about 1,000 are given supplemental courses in the English language. About 1,800, however, do not receive that instruction.

This class suit brought by non-English-speaking Chinese students against officials responsible for the operation of the San Francisco Unified School District seeks relief against the unequal educational opportunities, which are alleged to violate, inter alia, the Fourteenth Amendment. No specific remedy is urged upon us. Teaching English to the students of Chinese ancestry who do not speak the language is one choice. Giving instructions to this group in Chinese is another. There may be others. Petitioners ask only that the Board of Education be directed to apply its expertise to the problem and rectify the situation.

****

. . . [Section] 8573 of the Education Code provides that no pupil shall receive a diploma of graduation from grade 12 who has not met the standards of proficiency in 'English,' as well as other prescribed subjects. Moreover, by § 12101 of the Education Code (Supp. 1973) children between the ages of six and 16 years are (with exceptions not material here) 'subject to compulsory full-time education.'

Under these state-imposed standards there is no equality of treatment merely by providing students with the same facilities, textbooks, teachers, and curriculum; for students who do not understand English are effectively foreclosed from any meaningful education.

Basic English skills are at the very core of what these public schools teach. Imposition of a requirement that, before a child can effectively participate in the education program, he must already have acquired those basic skills is to make a mockery of public education. We know that those who do not understand English are certain to find their classroom experiences wholly incomprehensible and in no way meaningful.

We do not reach the Equal Protection Clause argument which has been advanced but rely solely on § 601 of the Civil Rights Act of 1964, 42 U.S.C. § 2000d, to reverse the Court of Appeals.

That section bans discrimination based 'on the ground of race, color, or national origin,' in 'any program or activity receiving Federal financial assistance.' The school district involved in this litigation receives large amounts of federal financial assistance. The Department of Health, Education, and Welfare (HEW), which has authority to promulgate regulations prohibiting discrimination in federally assisted school systems, 42 U.S.C. § 2000d–1, in 1968 issued one guideline that '(s)chool systems are responsible for assuring that students of a particular race, color, or national origin are not denied the opportunity to obtain the education generally obtained by other students in the system.' 33 Fed Reg. 4955. In 1970 HEW made the guidelines more specific, requiring school districts that were federally funded 'to rectify the language deficiency in order to open' the instruction to students who had 'linguistic deficiencies,' 35 Fed. Reg. 11595.

. . . . HEW's regulations, 45 CFR 80.3(b)(1), specify that the recipients may not

'(ii) Provide any service, financial aid, or other benefit to an individual which is different, or is provided in a different manner, from that provided to others under the program;

'(iv) Restrict an individual in any way in the enjoyment of any advantage or privilege enjoyed by others receiving any service, financial aid, or other benefit under the program.'

Discrimination among students on account of race or national origin that is prohibited includes 'discrimination . . . in the availability or use of any academic . . . or other facilities of the grantee or other recipient.' *Id.*, § 80.5(b).

Discrimination is barred which has that effect even though no purposeful design is present: a recipient 'may not . . . utilize criteria or methods of administration which have the effect of subjecting individuals to discrimination' or have 'the effect of defeating or substantially impairing accomplishment of the objectives of the program as respect individuals of a particular race, color, or national origin.' *id.*, § 80.3(b)(2).

It seems obvious that the Chinese-speaking minority receive fewer benefits than the English-speaking majority from respondents' school system which denies them a meaningful opportunity to participate in the educational program—all earmarks of the discrimination banned by the regulations. In 1970 HEW issued clarifying guidelines, 35 Fed. Reg. 11595, which include the following:

'Where inability to speak and understand the English language excludes national origin-minority group children from effective participation in the educational program offered by a school district, the district must take affirmative steps to rectify the language deficiency in order to open its instructional program to these students.'

'Any ability grouping or tracking system employed by the school system to deal with the special language skill needs of national origin-minority group children must be designed to meet such language skill needs as soon as possible and must not operate as an educational deadend or permanent track.'

Respondent school district contractually agreed to 'comply with title VI of the Civil Rights Act of 1964 . . . and all requirements imposed by or pursuant to the Regulation' of HEW (45 CFR pt. 80) which are 'issued pursuant to that title . . .' and also immediately to 'take any measures necessary to effectuate this agreement.' The Federal Government has power to fix the terms on which its money allotments to the States shall be disbursed. *Oklahoma v. United States Civil Service Commission*, 330 U.S. 127, 142–143, 67 S. Ct. 544, 552–554, 91 L. Ed. 794. Whatever may be the limits of that power, *Steward Machine Co v. Davis*, 301 U.S. 548, 590, 57 S. Ct. 883, 892, 81 L. Ed. 1279 *et seq.*, they have not been reached here. Senator Humphrey, during the floor debates on the Civil Rights Act of 1964, said: 'Simple justice requires that public funds, to which all taxpayers of all races contribute, not be spent in any fashion which encourages, entrenches, subsidizes, or results in racial discrimination.'

We accordingly reverse the judgment of the Court of Appeals and remand the case for the fashioning of appropriate relief.

Reversed and remanded.

(Footnotes omitted.)

ADDITIONAL COMMENTARY

1. In *Morales v. Shannon*, the court accepted the district's defense that segregation on the basis of language and ethnicity came about as part of ability grouping rather than segregation. 516 F.2d 411 (5th Cir. 1975). Also *Castaneda v. Pickard*, 781 F.2d 456 (5th Cir. 1986). But see *Gomez v. Illinois State Board of Education*, 811 F.2d 1030 (7th Cir. 1987) when the court was willing to examine evidence to determine if the programs used by the school were academically sound. Also *Rios v. Read*, 480 F.Supp. 14 (E.D.N.Y. 1978).

2. It is clear that use of bilingual programs cannot become an excuse to funnel non-native-English speakers into a totally separate dual system with no possibility of reintegration once English skills are improved. *Cintron v. Brentwood Union Free School District*, 455 F.Supp. 57 (E.D.N.Y. 1978).

3. In *Idaho Migrant Council v. Board of Education*, the court found that the obligation to ensure that needs of students with limited English proficiency were addressed fell on the State Department of Education as well as the local school district. 647 F.2d 69 (9th Cir. 1981).

4. With California's November 1994 passage of Proposition 187 foreclosing a variety of social services (including education) to illegal aliens, another chapter in discrimination on the basis of natural origin will open. As this book goes to press, an injunction barring the law's implementation in schools is in place. Lengthy litigation is expected to follow.

GENDER

It may be surprising to have to deal with issues of sex discrimination in public schools, since they are coeducational. However, differences in the treatment and opportunities afforded male and female students are commonplace. Some are obvious, such as exclusion of females from athletics and traditionally male pursuits. Others are more subtle, such as course materials that maintain sexual stereotypes, test bias, and sexual harassment.

Sex equity litigation in the 1970s focused on constitutional equal protection challenges. The challenges and forms of discrimination are analogous to race discrimination:

> There can be no doubt that our nation has had a long and unfortunate history of sex discrimination. Traditionally, such discrimination was rationalized by an attitude of "romantic paternalism" which, in practical effect, put women not on a pedestal, but in a cage.
> . . . .
> As a result of notions such as these, our statute books gradually became laden with gross, stereotyped distinctions between the sexes and, indeed, throughout much of the nineteenth century the position of women in our society was, in many respects, comparable to that of blacks under the pre-Civil War slave codes.
> . . . .
> It is true, of course, that the position of women in America has improved markedly in recent decades. Nevertheless, it can hardly be doubted that, in part because of the high visibility of the sex characteristic, women still face pervasive, although at times more subtle, discrimination in our educational institutions, in the job market and, perhaps most conspicuously, in the political arena.[49]

The standard of review currently used in gender discrimination cases was set forth by the U.S. Supreme Court in 1976.[50] It is not one that requires strict scrutiny, as in race discrimination cases, but does require some heightened scrutiny. "[C]lassifications by gender must serve important governmental objectives and must be substantially related to achievement of those objectives."[51]

The Civil Rights Act of 1964 prohibits discrimination on the basis of sex, but its provisions do not apply to students. In 1972, Congress enacted Title IX, which states:

> No person in the United States shall, on the basis of sex, be excluded from participation in, be denied the benefits of, or be subjected to discrimination under any education program or activity receiving federal financial assistance.[52]

The implementing regulations of this statute specifically prohibit sex discrimination in admissions, counseling, courses, financial aids and scholarships, and extracurricular activities. A student may not be precluded from any right, privilege, advantage, or opportunity because of sex. Under Title IX, a school that receives federal financial assistance may not require or refuse participation in any course by any of its students on the basis of sex. This includes courses in physical education, industrial arts, business, vocational education, technical education, home economics, and so on. Some segregation may occur within the course, such as separating sexes when playing contact sports or separating vocal groups for vocal range. In addition, whenever a school finds that a course has a disparate distribution of enrollment on the basis of sex, it must take action to determine that sex bias on the part of the school—through scheduling, counseling, and the like—is not responsible for the result.[53] The regulations exclude textbooks and curricular content from its scope[54] to avoid possible first amendment speech issues.[55]

Title IX has had a significant impact in increasing the opportunities for females in the area of sports. Its provisions require equal opportunities for both sexes. Title IX does not require that the programs for each gender be identical, but that the amount and extent of participation available must be equivalent, i.e., "male and female athletes should receive equivalent treatment, benefits, and opportunities."[56] In some instances, this will require integration of previously single-sex sports. The regulations state:

> [A] recipient may operate or sponsor separate teams for members of each sex where selection for such teams is based upon competitive skill or the activity involved is a contact sport. However, where a recipient operates or sponsors a team in a particular sport for members of one sex but operates or sponsors no such team for members of the other sex, and athletic opportunities for members of that sex have previously been limited, members of the excluded sex must be allowed to try-out for the team offered unless the sport involved is a contact sport. For the purposes of this part, contact sports include boxing, wrestling, rugby, ice hockey, football, basketball and other sports the purpose or major activity of which involves bodily contact.[57]

Discrimination on the grounds of pregnancy[58] or marriage[59] is also covered by Title IX.

> A recipient shall not discriminate against any student, or exclude a student from its education program or activity, including any class or extracurricular activity, on the basis of such student's pregnancy, . . . or recovery therefrom, unless the student requests voluntarily to participate in a separate portion of the program or activity of the recipient.[60]

Even when litigated under constitutional grounds, classification of students due to pregnancy or marriage has been regularly found to be invalid.[61]

Many schools, however, still offer a separate program (sometimes separate also in terms of time and location) to students who are pregnant or parents. These programs may be made available to students, but participation must be voluntary and the program must be equivalent to the mainstream program.[62]

Sexual harassment has been determined to be a form of sex discrimination.[63] Federal regulations define *sexual harassment* as:

> Unwelcome sexual advances, requests for sexual favors, and other verbal or physical conduct of a sexual nature constitutes sexual harassment when (1) submission to such conduct is made either explicitly or implicitly a term or condition of an individual's employment, (2) submission to or rejection of such conduct by an individual is used as the basis for employment decisions affecting such individual, or (3) such conduct has the purpose or effect of unreasonably interfering with an individual's work performance or creating an intimidating, hostile, or offensive working environment.[64]

A school may be responsible for sexual harassment that has occurred at the hands of its administrators. Further, it may be responsible for the harassing behaviors of others if the district knew or should have known of the conduct and failed to take "immediate and appropriate corrective action."[65] This would include sexual harassment perpetrated by teachers, students, and others entering the school.[66]

Recently, the Supreme Court has determined that a student can recover monetary damages in a Title IX action. *Franklin v. Gwinnett* allowed a high school student to recover monetary damages in a Title IX action in which she alleged sexual harassment at the hands of a teacher. This remedy is an addition to the previous court decisions that merely granted injunctive or declaratory relief.

MISSISSIPPI UNIVERSITY FOR WOMEN v. HOGAN
458 U.S. 718, 102 S. Ct. 3331, 73 L. Ed. 2d 1090 (1982)

Justice O'CONNOR delivered the opinion of the Court.

This case presents the narrow issue of whether a state statute that excludes males from enrolling in a state-supported professional nursing school violates the Equal Protection Clause of the Fourteenth Amendment.

I.

The facts are not in dispute. In 1884, the Mississippi Legislature created the Mississippi Industrial Institute and College for the Education of White Girls of the State of Mississippi, now the oldest state-supported all-female college in the United States. 1884 Miss. Gen. Laws, Ch. 30, § 6. The school, known today as Mississippi University for Women (MUW), has from its inception limited its enrollment to women.

****

Respondent, Joe Hogan, is a registered nurse but does not hold a baccalaureate degree in nursing. Since 1974, he has worked as a nursing supervisor in a medical center in Columbus, the city in which MUW is located. In 1979, Hogan applied for admission to the MUW School of Nursing's baccalaureate program. Although he was otherwise qualified, he was denied admission to the School of Nursing solely because of his sex. School officials informed him that he could audit the courses in which he was interested, but could not enroll for credit.

****

II.

We begin our analysis aided by several firmly established principles. Because the challenged policy expressly discriminates among applicants on the basis of gender, it is subject to scrutiny under the Equal Protection Clause of the Fourteenth Amendment. *Reed v. Reed*, 404 U.S. 71, 75, 92 S. Ct. 251, 253, 30 L. Ed. 2d 225 (1971). That this statutory policy discriminates against males rather than against females does not exempt it from scrutiny or reduce the standard of review. . . . Our decisions also establish that

the party seeking to uphold a statute that classifies individuals on the basis of their gender must carry the burden of showing an "exceedingly persuasive justification" for the classification. . . . The burden is met only by showing at least that the classification serves "important governmental objectives and that the discriminatory means employed" are "substantially related to the achievement of those objectives." *Wengler v. Druggists Mutual Ins. Co.*, 446 U.S. 142, 150, 100 S. Ct. 1540, 1545, 64 L. Ed. 2d 107 (1980).

Although the test for determining the validity of a gender-based classification is straightforward, it must be applied free of fixed notions concerning the roles and abilities of males and females. Care must be taken in ascertaining whether the statutory objective itself reflects archaic and stereotypic notions. Thus, if the statutory objective is to exclude or "protect" members of one gender because they are presumed to suffer from an inherent handicap or to be innately inferior, the objective itself is illegitimate. . . .

****

III. A.

The State's primary justification for maintaining the single-sex admissions policy of MUW's School of Nursing is that it compensates for discrimination against women and, therefore, constitutes educational affirmative action. . . .

In limited circumstances, a gender-based classification favoring one sex can be justified if it intentionally and directly assists members of the sex that is disproportionately burdened. . . .

It is readily apparent that a State can evoke a compensatory purpose to justify an otherwise discriminatory classification only if members of the gender benefited by the classification actually suffer a disadvantage related to the classification. . . .

****

. . . Mississippi has made no showing that women lacked opportunities to obtain training in the field of nursing or to attain positions of leadership in that field when the MUW School of Nursing opened its door or that women currently are deprived of such opportunities. In fact, in 1970, the year before the School of Nursing's first class enrolled, women earned 94 percent of the nursing baccalaureate degrees conferred in Mississippi and 98.6 percent of the degrees earned nationwide. . . .

Rather than compensate for discriminatory barriers faced by women, MUW's policy of excluding males from admission to the School of Nursing tends to perpetuate the stereotyped view of nursing as an exclusively woman's job.

****

The policy is invalid also because it fails the second part of the equal protection test, for the State has made no showing that the gender-based classification is substantially and directly related to its proposed compensatory objective. To the contrary, MUW's policy of permitting men to attend classes as auditors fatally undermines its claim that women, at least those in the School of Nursing, are adversely affected by the presence of men.

MUW permits men who audit to participate fully in classes. Additionally, both men and women take part in continuing education courses offered by the School of Nursing, in which regular nursing students also can enroll. . . .

Thus, considering both the asserted interest and the relationship between the interest and the methods used by the State, we conclude that the State has fallen far short of establishing the "exceedingly persuasive justification" needed to sustain the gender-based classification. Accordingly, we hold that MUW's policy of denying males the right to enroll for credit in its School of Nursing violates the Equal Protection Clause of the Fourteenth Amendment.

B.

In an additional attempt to justify its exclusion of men from MUW's School of Nursing, the State contends that MUW is the direct beneficiary "of specific congressional legislation which, on its face, permits the institution to exist as it has in the past." The argument is based upon the language of § 901(a) in Title IX of the Education Amendments of 1972, 20 U.S.C. § 1681(a). Although § 901(a) prohibits gender discrimination in education programs that receive federal financial assistance, subsection 5 exempts the admissions policies of undergraduate institutions "that traditionally and continually from [their] establishment [have] had a policy of admitting only students of one sex" from the general prohibition. . . .

Section 5 of the Fourteenth Amendment gives Congress broad power indeed to enforce the command of the Amendment and "to secure to all persons the enjoyment of perfect equality of civil rights and the equal protection of the laws against State denial or invasion. . . ." *Ex parte Virginia,* 100 U.S. (10 Otto) 339, 346, 25 L. Ed. 676 (1880). Congress' power under § 5, however, "is limited to adopting measures to enforce the guarantees of the Amendment; § 5 grants Congress no power to restrict, abrogate, or dilute these guarantees." *Katzenbach v. Morgan,* 384 U.S. 641, 651, n.10, 86 S. Ct. 1717, 1724, n.10, 16 L. Ed. 2d 828 (1966). Although we give deference to congressional decisions and classifications, neither Congress nor a State can validate a law that denies the rights guaranteed by the Fourteenth Amendment. . . .

****

IV.

Because we conclude that the State's policy of excluding males from MUW's School of Nursing violates the Equal Protection Clause of the Fourteenth Amendment, we affirm. . . .

(Footnotes omitted.)

— — — —

FRANKLIN v. GWINNETT
—U.S.—, 112 S. Ct. 1028, 117 L. Ed. 2d 208 (1992)

Justice WHITE delivered the opinion of the Court.

****

I.

Petitioner Christine Franklin was a student at North Gwinnett High School in Gwinnett County, Georgia, between September 1985 and August 1989. Respondent Gwinnett County School District operates the high school and receives federal funds. According to the complaint filed on December 29, 1988, in the United States District Court for the Northern District of Georgia, Franklin was subjected to continual sexual harassment beginning in the autumn of her tenth grade year (1986) from Andrew Hill, a sports coach and teacher employed by the district. Among other allegations, Franklin avers that Hill engaged her in sexually-oriented conversations in which he asked about her sexual experiences with her boyfriend and whether she would consider having sexual intercourse with an older man, . . . that Hill forcibly kissed her on the mouth in the school parking lot, . . . that he telephoned her at her home and asked if she would meet him socially, . . . and that, on three occasions in her junior year, Hill interrupted a class, requested that the teacher excuse Franklin, and took her to a private office where he subjected her to coercive intercourse. . . . The complaint further alleges that though they became aware of and investigated Hill's sexual harassment of Franklin and other female students, teachers and administrators took no action to halt it and discouraged Franklin from pressing charges against Hill. . . . On April 14, 1988, Hill resigned on the condition that all matters pending against him be dropped. . . . The school thereupon closed its investigation.

II.

In *Cannon v. University of Chicago*, 441 U.S. 677, 99 S. Ct. 1946, 60 L. Ed. 2d 560 (1979), the Court held that Title IX is enforceable through an implied right of action. We have no occasion here to reconsider that decision. Rather, in this case we must decide what remedies are available in a suit brought pursuant to this implied right. . . .

****

. . . . Unquestionably, Title IX placed on the Gwinnett County Schools the duty not to discriminate on the basis of sex, and "when a supervisor sexually harasses a subordinate because of the subordinate's sex, that supervisor 'discriminate[s]' on the basis of sex." *Meritor Savings Bank, FSB v. Vinson*, 477 U.S. 57, 64, 106 S. Ct. 2399, 2404, 91 L. Ed. 2d 49 (1986). We believe the same rule should apply when a teacher sexually harasses and abuses a student. Congress surely did not intend for federal monies to be expended to support the intentional actions it sought by statute to proscribe. . . .

C.

Finally, the United States asserts that the remedies permissible under Title IX should nevertheless be limited to backpay and prospective relief. In addition to diverging from our traditional approach to deciding what remedies are available for violation of a federal right, this position conflicts with sound logic. . . . [I]n this case the equitable remedies suggested nothing for petitioner, because she was a student when the alleged discrimination occurred. Similarly, because Hill—the person she claims subjected her to sexual harassment—no longer teaches at the school and she herself no longer attends a school in the Gwinnett system, prospective relief accords her no remedy at all. The government's answer that administrative action helps other similarly-situated students in effect acknowledges that its approach would leave petitioner remediless.

V.

In sum, we conclude that a damages remedy is available for an action brought to enforce Title IX. The judgment of the Court of Appeals, therefore, is reversed and the case is remanded for further proceedings consistent with this opinion.

So ordered.

(Footnotes omitted.)

ADDITIONAL COMMENTARY

1. Title IX does not prohibit school boards from converting all-girl high schools to coeducational institutions. Such a school closure in New York City was challenged based on the theory that the single-sex school provided an environment in which girls were more likely to succeed academically, in accordance with the intent of the statute. The plaintiffs further challenged the closure by arguing that coeducational systems would be an unwise practice in light of their argument that girls achieved less when educated with boys. The court upheld the school closure and found that Congress did not intend the statute to require districts to provide special programs for one sex, absent a showing of past imbalances. Further, the court ruled that even if it was an unwise practice,

it was not the sort of school action the statute was designed to redress. *Jones on Behalf of Michele v. Board of Education of City School District of City of New York,* 632 F. Supp. 1319 (E.D. N.Y. 1986).

2. Title IX does not authorize establishment of new single-sex schools. *Garrett v. Board of Education of School District of City of Detroit,* 775 F. Supp. 1004 (E.D. Mich. 1991).

3. In a Title IX case, an educational institution is liable upon finding hostile environment/sexual harassment perpetrated by its supervisors upon employees if the official representing the institution knew, or in exercise of reasonable care should have known, of the harassment's occurrence, unless the official can show that appropriate steps were taken to halt the harassment.

Lipsett v. University of Puerto Rico, 864 F.2d 881, (1st Cir. (Puerto Rico) 1988).

4. The fact that high school grooming codes prohibited only male students from wearing hair below the ear lobe or over the collar did not constitute sex-based discrimination within the meaning of Title IX. *Trent v. Perritt,* 391 F. Supp. 171, (S.D. Miss. 1975).

5. The difference in girls' and boys' junior and senior high basketball rules, as laid down by an association, consisting of voluntary group of schools, did not violate Title IX where there was no evidence that any "educational program or activity" involved in the present case received "federal financial assistance." *Dodson v. Arkansas Activities Association,* 468 F. Supp. 394, (E.D. Ark. 1979).

POVERTY

Since classification on the basis of wealth has not received heightened scrutiny under constitutional analysis and is not a protected class under federal statutes, litigation does not focus on issues of discrimination. Children's educational issues relating to poverty focus on entitlement or compensatory programs. The first major federal entitlement program for at-risk students was the Elementary and Secondary Education Act (ESEA) of 1965. It provided funds to state and local schools through Title I, which is now Chapter 1 of the Education Consolidation and Improvement Act (ECIA) for economically and educationally disadvantaged students. The money must be used to supplement students' educational needs in "core academic subjects," defined as at least, but not limited to, mathematics and reading/language arts. Services comparable to those provided in the public schools are to be provided to children who attend private schools in areas with high concentrations of low-income families.

Since 1965, most of the nation's public school districts and many private schools have used Chapter 1 programs to help millions of economically disadvantaged children. Students who receive Chapter 1 services are at high risk for academic failure. Half of these students score below the fifteenth percentile on national achievement tests. Many have moved and changed schools often during the school term. Half of the Chapter 1 students qualify economically for free or reduced lunch programs; slightly more than one-third are minorities. Eligible students receive supplementary small-group instruction in reading, writing, and communication skills. According to repeated national studies, children who participate in Chapter 1 programs do better in school than similar children who do not participate in Chapter 1 programs. And some children, such as the children of migrant workers or children in states where there are no kindergartens, attend school in Chapter 1 programs when they otherwise might not attend school at all.[68]

Most Chapter 1 money is used to provide extra help in reading and math for elementary school children whose test scores show that they are not working at or near the level of other children their age. These educational programs are possible because Chapter 1 funds pay the salaries of teachers and classroom aides to work with economically disadvantaged children in small groups in their own classrooms or in special workrooms, and because Chapter 1 funds purchase extra materials and equipment designed to help children who are having trouble learning to read and do math. In addition, Chapter 1 funds are used to train Chapter 1 and regular teachers so they are better prepared to help children in need of special assistance. Finally, Chapter 1 funds are used for programs to train and encourage parents to become more involved with their children's education.

In *Bell v. New Jersey and Pennsylvania*,[69] the United States Supreme Court held that the federal government may recover from the states funds that had been misused. In the wake of the opinion, there were a number of cases involving the Secretary of Education's decision seeking repayment of misused Chapter 1 funds. What is to be learned from these cases[70] is that the administrative interpretations of the statute will be granted discretion by courts when attempting to interpret the program. States and districts must comply with the nonsupplant requirement and the comparability requirement, and spend funds only on programs within the stated Chapter 1 purposes.

HOMELESS

The McKinney Homeless Assistance Act,[71] enacted by Congress in 1987, is a package of several programs dealing with homeless people. The act has as its stated educational intent that homeless children have access to a free, appropriate public education on an equal basis with nonhomeless children. The act provides funds for states that adopt consistent statutes. One part of the model statute to be adopted by states prohibits states from using state residency laws to bar homeless children from attending public schools. The stated policy of the sections regarding education is:

> *(1) each state educational agency shall assure that each child of a homeless individual and each homeless youth have access to a free, appropriate public education which would be provided to the children of a resident of a State and is consistent with the State school attendance laws; and*
>
> *(2) in any State that has a residency requirement as a component of its compulsory school attendance laws, the State will review and undertake steps to revise such laws to assure that the children of homeless individuals and homeless youth are afforded a free and appropriate public education.*[72]

The McKinney Act provides federal funds to states that develop a state plan to provide education to the homeless. The state plans must be designed so that local educational agencies will comply with the federal act's provision for access. School districts in participating states must enroll homeless children in either the district in which the child was originally enrolled or in the district in which the child is actually living, whichever is determined to be in the child's best interest.[73] The placement of the child must be made without regard to whether the child is living with the parents.[74] School districts must provide other educational services in a nondiscriminatory manner to homeless children such as special education, compensatory education, and transportation.[75] Since the act creates no mechanism for the administrative enforcement of the benefits to which homeless children are entitled, appeals must be made to federal district court to gain relief.[76]

APPENDIX: DISCRIMINATION IN EDUCATION—A LEGAL FRAMEWORK

BASIS IN LAW	CONSTITUTIONAL/STATUTORY LANGUAGE	OBJECTIVE	SCOPE OF PROTECTION	COURT APPLIED STANDARDS	IDENTIFIED/POSSIBLE CLASSES	ILLUSTRATIVE CASES
14th Amendment of the U.S. Constitution U.S. Const. Amend. XIV, Sec. 1	". . . No State shall make or enforce any law which shall abridge the privileges or immunities of citizens of the United States; nor shall any State deprive any person of life, liberty or property, without due process of law; nor deny to any person within its jurisdiction the equal protection of the laws."	Give rights, services, etc., to a group or class.	Anyone subject to a governmental action.	*Strict scrutiny is applied to a Suspect Class (an insular minority; politically powerless with immutable characteristics).* *Action must be necessary to a compelling state interest.*	Race (identified)	*Brown v. Board of Education of Topeka,* 347 U.S. 483, 74 S. Ct. 686 (1954).
				Heightened scrutiny is applied to a Quasi-Suspect Class. *Action must be substantially related to an important state interest.*	Gender (identified) Ethnicity, alienage (disability—possible)	*Mississippi University for Women v. Hogan,* 458 U.S. 718, 102 S. Ct. 3331 (1982). *Plyler v. Doe,* 457 U.S. 202, 102 S. Ct. 2382 (1982).
				Minimal scrutiny is applied to all remaining classes. *Action must be rationally related to a legitimate state interest.*	All others: economic status, sexual orientation, marital status (disability—possible)	

BASIS IN LAW	CONSTITUTIONAL/STATUTORY LANGUAGE	OBJECTIVE	SCOPE OF PROTECTION	COURT APPLIED STANDARDS	IDENTIFIED/ POSSIBLE CLASSES	ILLUSTRATIVE CASES
Title VI 42 U.S.C. Sec. 2000d Civil Rights Act of 1964, Pub. Law 88-352	"No person in the United States shall, on the ground of race, color, or national origin, be excluded from participation in, be denied the benefits of, or be subjected to discrimination under any program or activity receiving Federal financial assistance."	Give rights, services, etc., to a group or class.	Anyone subject to any federally funded program or activity.	*Discriminatory Treatment* requires that action pass *strict scrutiny test* (necessary to a compelling state interest). *Disparate Impact* requires that *there must be a nondiscriminatory reason* to support the classification.	Race National Origin	*Lau v. Nichols*, 414 U.S. 563, 94 S. Ct. 786 (1974).
Title VII 42 U.S.C. Sec. 2000e	"It shall be unlawful employment practice for any employer . . . to fail or refuse to hire or discharge any individual, or otherwise to discriminate against any individual with respect to his compensation, terms, conditions, or privileges of employment because of such individual's race, color, religion, sex or national origin . . . ."	Give employment opportunities to a group or class.	Anyone employed or seeking employment.	*Discriminatory Treatment* requires that employer prove there is a bonafide occupational qualification. *Disparate Impact* requires that there be a nondiscriminatory reason or business necessity for the action.	Race (has been applied to reverse discrimination) Religion Gender National Origin	*Griggs v. Duke Power Co.*, 401 U.S. 424, 91 S. Ct. 849 (1971).
Title IX 20 U.S.C. Sec. 1681	"No person in the United States shall, on the basis of sex, be denied the benefits of, or be subjected to discrimination under any education program or activity receiving Federal financial assistance . . . ."	Gives rights, services, etc., to all, regardless of gender.	Anyone subject to any federally funded educational program or activity.	*Discriminatory Treatment* requires proof of substantial disruption to environment or result in physical or mental health dangers. *Disparate Impact* requires proof that gender bias was not responsible for result.	Gender, marital status, pregnancy Students as well as employees.	*North Haven Board of Education v. Bell*, 456 U.S. 512, 102 S. Ct. 1912 (1982).

continued

BASIS IN LAW	CONSTITUTIONAL/STATUTORY LANGUAGE	OBJECTIVE	SCOPE OF PROTECTION	COURT APPLIED STANDARDS	IDENTIFIED/ POSSIBLE CLASSES	ILLUSTRATIVE CASES
Section 504 29 U.S.C. Sec. 794 Rehabilitation Act of 1975 Pub. Law 93-112	". . . no otherwise qualified individual with handicaps in the United States . . . shall, solely by reason of her or his handicap, be excluded from the participation in, or denied the benefits of, or be subjected to discrimination under any program or activity receiving federal financial assistance . . . ."	Give rights, services, etc., to individuals who are handicapped.	Anyone subject to any federally funded program or activity.	Must prove otherwise qualified and denied benefits solely on the basis of handicap. Reasonable accommodations to allow access and participation must be made.	Any handicapped individual.	Southeastern Community College v. Davis, 442 U.S. 397, 99 S. Ct. 2361 (1979). Sullivan by Sullivan v. Vallejo City Unified School District, 731 F. Supp. 947, 59 Ed. Law Rptr. 73 (E.D. Cal. 1990).
20 U.S.C. 1681 Civil Rights Restoration Act of 1987 Pub. Law 100-259	". . . certain aspects of recent decisions and opinions of the Supreme Court have unduly narrowed and cast doubt upon the broad application of title IX . . . . section 540 . . . and title VI . . . ." ". . . legislative action is necessary to restore the prior consistency . . . (of) broad institution-wide application of those laws as previously administered."	To restore the broad scope of coverage and application of prior law by clarification of definition of "program or activity."	Any person protected under Sec. 504, Title IX or Title VI.	Apply standards as established for applicable law.	As covered by applicable cases.	In response to: Grove City College v. Bell, 465 U.S. 555, 104 S. Ct. 1211 (1984).

BASIS IN LAW	CONSTITUTIONAL/STATUTORY LANGUAGE	OBJECTIVE	SCOPE OF PROTECTION	COURT APPLIED STANDARDS	IDENTIFIED/ POSSIBLE CLASSES	ILLUSTRATIVE CASES
Americans with Disabilities Act of 1990 42 U.S.C. Secs. 12101-12213	Forbids employment "discrimination" against any "qualified individual with a disability." Forbids employer, before making a job offer, to "conduct a medical examination . . . or make inquiries . . . as to whether such applicant is an individual with a disability. . . . " Forbids employer from "not making reasonable accommodations . . . (for) an otherwise qualified individual . . . unless (it) would impose an undue hardship."	Prevents discrimination in employment of persons with disabilities who are qualified to perform the duties with reasonable accommodations.	Qualified individual with disability as defined by this act. Covers employment, governmental programs and services, public accommodations and services, and telecommunications.	Court-applied standards are not yet established.	To be identified.	No appeals decisions identified at this time.
Equal Educational Opportunities Act 20 U.S.C. 1703(f)	"No state shall deny equal educational opportunity to an individual on account of his or her race, color, sex, or national origin by . . . failure by an educational agency to take appropriate action to overcome language barriers that impede equal participation by its students in its instructional program."	Give rights, services, etc.	Any individual in any public educational agency or program regardless of intent to discriminate.	Student must show: 1. Language barrier impedes participation in educational program. 2. Defendants failed to take steps to rectify the problem. 3. Connection between failure and learning problems.	Race Gender National Origin	Martin Luther King School Children v. Michigan Board of Education, 451 F. Supp. 1324 (E.D. Mich. 1978). Morales v. Shannon, 516 F.2d 411 (5th Cir. 1975), cert. den'd, 423 U.S. 1034.

ENDNOTES

1. San Antonio Independent School Dist. v. Rodriguez, 411 U.S. 1 (1973).

2. No state shall deny equal educational opportunity to an individual on account of his or her race, color, sex, or national origin, by:

(a) the deliberate segregation by an educational agency of students on the basis of race, color, or national origin among or within schools . . .

(c) the assignment by an educational agency of a student to a school, other than the one closest to his or her place of residence within the school district in which he or she resides, if the assignment results in a greater degree of segregation of students on the basis of race, color, sex, or national origin . . .

(d) discrimination by an educational agency on the basis of race, color, or national origin in the employment, employment conditions, or assignment to schools of its faculty or staff, except to fulfill the purposes of subsection (f) below . . .

(e) the transfer by an educational agency, whether voluntary or otherwise of a student from one school to another if the purpose and effect of such transfer is to increase segregation of students on the basis of race, color, or national origin among the schools of such agency; or

(f) the failure by an educational agency to take appropriate action to overcome language barriers that impede equal participation by its students in its instructional programs. 20 U.S.C. 1703.

3. Section 504, 29 U.S.C. 794 and IDEA, 20 U.S.C. 1401 will be treated fully and in separate subsequent chapters.

4. Lau v. Nichols, 414 U.S. 563, 94 S. Ct. 786 (1974).

5. U.S. Const. amend XIV, Sec. 1.

6. However, note that the elimination of racial discrimination may be considered a compelling state interest. Therefore, race-based governmental actions that are necessary to this end may be upheld.

7. *E.g.*, Craig v. Boren, 429 U.S. 190, 197 (1976).

8. *See* Dayton Bd. of Educ. v. Brinkman, 443 U.S. 526, 536 (1979).

9. Originally, Title VII did not apply to educational institutions. This exemption has been repealed. However, there exists an exemption for educational institutions for "individuals of a particular religion" 42 U.S.C. 2000e-1 (1988).

10. Title IX has been determined to apply to both students and employees. North Haven Bd. of Educ. v. Bell, 456 U.S. 512 (1982).

11. Cannon v. University of Chicago, 441 U.S. 677 (1979).

12. 42 U.S.C. 2000d and 20 U.S.C. 1681.

13. Franklin v. Gwinnett County Public Schools, 112 S. Ct. 1028 (1992).

14. Griggs v. Duke Power Company, 401 U.S. 424 (1971).

15. Wards Cove Packing Company v. Antonio, 490 U.S. 642 (1989).

16. Brown v. Bd. of Educ., 347 U.S. 483 (1954).

17. Plessy v. Ferguson, 163 U.S. 537 (1896).

18. *Brown*, 347 U.S. 483, at 494 (1954).

19. Freeman v. Pitts, 112 S.Ct. 1430, 1447 (1992).

20. Swann v. Charlotte-Mecklenburg Bd. of Educ., 402 U.S. 1, at 24-26 (1971).

21. Bd. of Educ. of Oklahoma City v. Dowell, 111 S. Ct. 630 (1991); Green v. County School Bd., 391 U.S. 430, 88 S. Ct. 1689 (1968).

22. 112 S. Ct. 1430 (1992).

23. Bd. of Educ. of Oklahoma City v. Dowell, 111 S. Ct. 630 (1991).

24. Sherpell v. Humnoke School Dist., 619 F. Supp. 670 (E.D. Ark. 1985).

25. Discriminatory testing and classification practices are dealt with in more detail in Chapter 4.

26. "GAO Critics OCR Efforts to Limit Biased School Tracking," *School Law News,* May 9, 1991, p. 3.

27. John Marshall, *State Initiatives in Minimum Competency Testing for Students* (Policy Issue Series, No. 3). Bloomington, IN: Consortium on Educational Policy Studies, 1987.

28. 474 F. Supp. 244 (M.D. Fla. 1979), aff'd in part, 644 F.2d 397 (5th Cir. 1981).

29. 457 U.S. 202 (1982).

30. 648 F.2d 989 (5th Cir. 1989).

31. *See also* Morales v. Shannon, 516 F.2d 411 (5th Cir. 1975), *cert. denied*, 423 U.S. 1034 (1975).

32. 42 U.S.C. 2000d *et seq.*

33. 20 U.S.C. 1701, *et seq.*

34. 20 U.S.C. 3281, *et seq.*

35. 414 U.S. 563, 94 S. Ct. 786 (1974).

36. 35 C.F.R. 11595.

37. Lau v. Nichols, 414 U.S. 563, at 566.

38. 20 U.S.C. 1703(f).

39. Morales v. Shannon, 516 F.2d 411, 415 (5th Cir. 1975), *cert. denied.*, 423 U.S. 1034 (1975).

40. *See* Martin Luther King School v. Michigan Bd. of Educ., 451 F. Supp. 1324, 1330 (E.D. Mich. 1978).

41. *See e.g.,* Guadalupe Org., Inc., v. Tempe Elementary School, 587 F.2d 1022 (9th Cir. 1978).

42. Martin Luther King School v. Michigan Bd. of Educ., 451 F. Supp. 1324 (E.D. Mich. 1978).

43. 20 U.S.C. 3282.

44. 20 U.S.C. 3283(1).

45. 20 U.S.C. 3283(4)(A).

46. 20 U.S.C. 3283(5)(A).

47. 20 U.S.C. 3283(6).

48. 34 C.F.R. 500.4.

49. Frontiero v. Richardson, 411 U.S. 677, 684-87 (1973).

50. Craig v. Boren, 429 U.S. 190, 97 S. Ct. 451 (1976).

51. 429 U.S. at 197, 97 S. Ct. at 457.

52. 20 U.S.C. 1681(a).

53. 34 C.F.R. 106.36.

54. 34 C.F.R. 106.42.

55. 40 Fed. Reg. 24135.

56. 44 Fed. Reg. 71414 (1979).

57. 34 C.F.R. 106.41(b). Title IX's regulations allow school districts to choose whether coeducational participation in a contact sport will be permitted. *See* Yellow Springs Exempted Village School Dist. Bd. v. Ohio High School Athletic Ass'n, 647 F.2d 651 (6th Cir. 1981). However, a number of courts have required districts to allow a female to at least try out for all-male contact sports on constitutional equal protection grounds. Force v. Pierce City R.VI School Dist., 570 F. Supp. 1020 (W.D. Mo. 1983) (football); Clinton v. Nagy (football), 411 F. Supp. 1396 (N.D. Ohio 1974); Att'y General v. Massachusetts Interscholastic Athletic Ass'n, 393 N.E. 2d 284 (Mass. 1979) (all sports); Darrin v. Gould, 540 P.2d 882 (1975) (football); Commonwealth v. Pennsylvania Interscholastic Ass'n, 334 A.2d 839 (1975) (all sports); Leffel v. Wisconsin Interscholastic Athletic Ass'n, 444 F. Supp. 1117 (E.D. Wis. 1978) (all sports). Mularadelis v. Haldane Central School Bd., 427 N.Y.S.2d 458 (1980).

58. 34 C.F.R. 106.40(b)(1).

59. 34 C.F.R. 106.40(a).

60. 34 C.F.R. 106.40(b)(1).

61. *E.g.,* Indiana High School Athletic Ass'n v. Raike, 329 N.E. 2d 66 (Ind. Ct. App. 1975); Bell v. Lone Oak Indep. School Dist., 507 S.W.2d 636 (Tex. Civ. App. 1974); Davis v. Meek, 344 F. Supp. 298 (N.D. Ohio 1972); Beeson v. Kiowa County School Dist., 567 P.2d 801 (Colo. Ct. App. 1977).

62. Rather than excluding students who are parents, as has been the historical norm, Wisconsin's experiment with AFDC (Aid to Families with Dependent Children) (Learn Fare) requires school attendance as a prerequisite to eligible school-age recipients and their children.

63. Meritor Savings Bank v. Vinson, 106 S. Ct. 2399 (1986). *See also* Alexander v. Yale University, 631 F.2d 178 (2nd Cir. 1980), where the court determined that sexual harassment was actionable under Title IX but dismissed the case as moot since the student had graduated.

64. 29 C.F.R. 1604.11(a) (1985).

65. 29 C.F.R. 1604.11(d).

66. Schools may also be held responsible under Section 1983 for sexual molestation of student at the hands of school employees. *E.g.,* Caplinger v. Doe, 975 F.2d 137 (5th Cir. 1992) *cert. denied,* 113 S. Ct. 1066 (1993).

67. 20 U.S.C. 3801.

68. Underwood, J. (1988). Legal protections for at risk children. In J. Lakebrink (Ed.), *Children at risk* pp. 90–118). Springfield, IL: Charles C. Thomas.

69. 103 S. Ct. 2187 (1983).

70. *E.g.,* Bennett v. Kentucky Dep't of Educ., 105 S. Ct. 1544 (1985); Bennet v. New Jersey, 105 S. Ct. 1555 (1985); Virginia Dep't of Educ. v. Sec'y of Educ., 806 F.2d 78 (4th Cir. 1986); Florida Dep't of Educ. v. Bennett, 769 F.2d 1501 (11th Cir. 1985).

71. 42 U.S.C. 11432.

72. 42 U.S.C. 11432(e)(1).

73. 42 U.S.C. 11432(e)(3).

74. 42 U.S.C. 11432(e)(4).

75. 42 U.S.C. 11432(e)(5).

76. A recent court ruling held that homeless children may seek enforcement of the various provisions of the McKinney Act by filing complaints under 42 U.S.C. § 1983 (Lampkin v. District of Columbia, 27 F.3d 605 (D.C. Cir. 1994)).

CHAPTER 3

SECTION 504 IN EDUCATION

INTRODUCTION

Section 504 of the Rehabilitation Act of 1973 states:

> [N]o otherwise qualified individual with a disability . . . shall solely by reason of her or his disability, be excluded from the participation in, be denied the benefits of, or be subjected to discrimination under any program or activity receiving Federal financial assistance.[1]

This broad statute grants the right to be free from discrimination to a diverse array of people. Section 504 applies to all individuals, not just the school-age population. In schools, not only students but also parents, teachers, administrators, custodians, and all staff are protected by the guarantees of Section 504. This coverage was increased with the 1990 passage of the Americans with Disabilities Act (ADA).[2] However, it is important to remember that Section 504 is a discrimination statute, not an entitlement statute. Although its eligibility is broader, the benefits to the individual are narrower.

INTERRELATIONSHIP BETWEEN SECTION 504 AND THE INDIVIDUALS WITH DISABILITIES EDUCATION ACT

As is a common pattern for the U.S. Congress, this discrimination statute was shortly followed by a companion piece of legislation that offered financial incentives for states that agreed to meet exacting standards in order to guarantee equal access to their elementary and secondary education programs. Passed in 1975, the Education for All Handicapped Children Act (EAHCA) compliments Section 504. In 1990,

EAHCA was amended and renamed the Individuals with Disabilities Education Act (IDEA). Together, these two acts, Section 504 and IDEA, form the anchor that secures educational rights for children with disabilities. In essence, IDEA presents the "carrot" of financial assistance that school districts must accept to avoid the "stick" of Section 504. It is important to recognize that Section 504 provides the foundation from which IDEA develops. The specifics of IDEA will be discussed in detail in subsequent chapters.

The relationship between Section 504 and IDEA has largely been determined by the courts. In *Smith v. Robinson*,[3] the Supreme Court drew the parallels and distinctions for the purposes of litigation between 504 and IDEA.

> *Section 504 and the EHA [now IDEA] are different substantive statutes. While the EHA guarantees a right to a free appropriate public education, . . . Sec. 504 protects handicapped persons of all ages from discrimination in a variety of programs and activities receiving federal financial assistance. . . . The significant difference between the two, as applied to special education claims, is that the substantive and procedural rights assumed to be guaranteed by both statutes are specifically required only by the EHA. . . . There is no suggestion that Sec. 504 adds anything to petitioners' [students'] substantive right to a free appropriate public education. . . . Where Sec. 504 adds nothing to the substantive rights of a handicapped child, we cannot believe that Congress intended to have the careful balance struck in the EHA upset by reliance on Sec. 504 for otherwise unavailable damages or for an award of attorney's fees.[4]*

The Court found that since IDEA was the more specific of the two statutes, complainants involving IDEA had to exhaust the remedies available in IDEA before seeking redress under Section 504. However, IDEA and Section 504 are truly companion statutes and Section 504 has ramifications that not only undergird IDEA, but exceed IDEA's requirement.

ELIGIBILITY

The interrelationship between the two statutes is very apparent in the area of eligibility. Section 504 eligibility is much broader than IDEA. A visual depiction of this interrelationship is shown in Figure 3.1.

To qualify for protection under Section 504, an individual must be one who "(i) has a physical or mental impairment which substantially limits one or more of such person's major life activities, (ii) has a record of such an impairment, or (iii) is regarded as having such an impairment."[5] A major life activity is defined in the regulations as including: "caring for one's self, performing manual tasks, walking, seeing, hearing, speaking, breathing, learning and working."[6] A physical or mental impairment includes any disabling condition or disorder, and does not have to be severe or permanent.[7]

All People

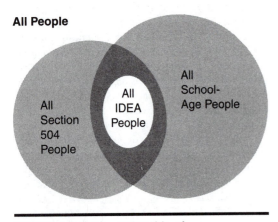

FIGURE 3.1   Interrelationship of Eligibility Standards

The definition of *handicapped* under this statute is significantly broader than in IDEA.

The definition is not just limited to someone who currently has a disability; it also includes those who "have a record" or are "regarded" as having an impairment. Persons with a record of an impairment are those who no longer have an impairment as well as those who may have been misclassified as having an impairment, such as "persons with histories of mental or emotional illness, heart disease, or cancer, persons who have been misclassified as mentally retarded."[8]

Persons who may be regarded as having an impairment may be those who have a disorder or impairment that does not currently affect or substantially limit a major life activity.[9] The purpose is to protect those people who have minor impairments that do not actually impact their abilities to perform or who have no real impairments at all but are hampered within society by unrealistic or stereotypical attitudes of others. Thus, for example, the Supreme Court determined that a person who had tuberculosis, then in remission, was "handicapped" under the statutory definition. In the same case, the Eleventh Circuit Court of Appeals had stated that "[e]ven when not directly affected by tuberculosis, Arline falls within the coverage of Section 504 because she 'has a record of such an impairment, . . .' and is 'regarded as having such an impairment.'"[10]

Further, the condition does not have to be permanent or severe—only substantially limiting one or more major life activities. Thus, diabetes,[11] epilepsy,[12] and back injuries[13] have been found to be conditions that fell under Section 504 protection. However, unusual physical attributes generally do not, e.g., left-handedness[14] and crossed eyes.[15] Obesity is one condition that has gone both ways.[16]

DISCRIMINATION

Section 504 prohibits discrimination against an otherwise qualified person with disabilities[17];

however, one must show that he or she is "qualified." With respect to employment, a person who is disabled is one who, with reasonable accommodation, can perform the essential functions of the job in question. With respect to public preschool, elementary, secondary, or adult educational services, a person who is disabled is "(i) of an age during which nonhandicapped persons are provided such services, (ii) of any age during which it is mandatory under state law to provide such services to handicapped persons, or (iii) to whom a state is required to provide a free appropriate public education" under IDEA.[18]

Although most substantive parts of a child's education are dealt with under IDEA, there are situations where 504 coverage is important for K–12 public school students, such as when the alleged discrimination does not effect the child's educational program but rather another school-operated program. For example, there are a number of cases in which students are denied the benefits of an extracurricular program due to a physical disability.[19] The regulations state that recipients "afford handicapped students an equal opportunity for participation in . . . nonacademic and extracurricular services and activities."[20] For example, a student sought permission to allow a service dog into a building,[21] another wanted to participate in a European field trip,[22] and yet another wanted to play football.[23] In all cases, the students prevailed, given the protection of Section 504.

Programs must be offered in the same basis to students with and without disabilities. In *Riley v. Jefferson County Board of Education*,[24] the court found that the school district could not charge the parents of students with disabilities higher rates for an after-school program, even if the student's care incurred higher costs for the program. In short, people may not be excluded from, or treated differently within a program, because of a disabling condition.

Another form of discrimination prohibited under Section 504 is denial of physical access to a program or activity.[25] This concept is an important and often misunderstood component of Section 504. Although each program run by a recipient must be made readily accessible to people with disabilities, not every part of every facility need be usable by every person with disabilities.[26] The key is allowing equal opportunity for participation in classes, libraries, theaters, or other aspects of the school. The Office for Civil Rights (OCR) has even upheld the designation of a particular school as accessible to the disabled, rather than requiring a district to make every building accessible. Common sense can be of use in these situations, so that schedules may be altered to provide access to a program that would regularly meet in a non-accessible location. However, it should be noted that people with disabilities should have ready access to these programs and not have to rely on others to carry them or be the only person using a particular door as an access to a building.[27]

A letter from the OCR[28] set forth some concerns about students with disabilities receiving services comparable to nondisabled student and issued a list of problems that districts should consider in assessing their compliance with Section 504.

— Classes for students with disabilities were held in storage rooms, home economics rooms, partitioned offices, and other areas that were not conducive to an appropriate learning environment.

— Classroom sizes were not adequate to accommodate some of the specific educational, physical, and/or medical needs of students with disabilities.

— Teachers were not provided adequate support or supplies to enable them to give their students an equal education. In some instances, it was found that teachers had to go to unusual lengths to obtain supplies. In one school district, no clerical or secretarial staff was available for teachers of students with disabilities and thus teachers had to leave their classes to answer the telephone, whereas teachers of nondisabled students had appropriate clerical assistance.

— Students with disabilities who use bus transportation received an instructional schoolday substantially shorter than that of nondisabled students. In one school district, bus transportation was not provided to a student with a disability on days when the weather was inclement.

— Some mobility-impaired students did not receive transportation until five months into the school term because the school district did not own an accessible bus.

— Some students with disabilities had school bus rides in excess of 4 hours and 45 minutes each day because of bus scheduling. These rides were much longer than the bus rides of other students. As a result, many of these students with disabilities arrived in wet underclothes. Others became hyperactive and required additional medication.

REASONABLE ACCOMMODATION

In addition to prohibiting discrimination, Section 504 requires recipients to provide reasonable accommodations to persons with disabilities. Often, the reasonable accommodation being sought is program accommodation. In *Southeastern Community College v. Davis,*[29] the Supreme Court attempted a definition of *reasonable accommodations* within an academic setting.

> *Section 504 by its terms does not compel educational institutions to disregard the disabilities of handicapped individuals or to make substantial modifications in their programs to allow disabled persons to participate. . . . An otherwise qualified person is one who is able to meet all of the program's requirements in spite of his handicap.*[30]

Consistent with this ruling, the court in *Brookhart v. Illinois State Board of Education*[31] held that the state was not required to lower its graduation requirements to accommodate students with disabilities. However, nonsubstantive accommodations—particularly in program delivery, e.g., testing alterations, scheduling modifications, and additional time for tasks—are required when necessary to provide an education for students with disabilities that reflects the students' skills rather than their disabling condition.

Questions arise as to what constitutes a reasonable accommodation under Section 504; in other words, What must a school provide to a student who is defined as disabled under Section 504 but not under IDEA? Here, it is important to note that Section 504 and IDEA both entitle eligible students to a free appropriate public education (FAPE).[32] Section 504 regulations define FAPE as "the provision of regular or special education and related aids and services that are designed to meet the individual educational needs of handicapped persons as adequately as the needs of nonhandicapped persons are met."[33] Stated another way, FAPE, under Section 504, requires only those measures necessary to avoid or eradicate discrimination on the basis of disability. As Chapter 4 will describe in detail, this standard differs somewhat from the requirements of FAPE under IDEA.

The student with an orthopedic impairment that does not require him or her to receive special education under IDEA provides an instructive example. In such a situation, the student may seek protection and services under Section 504. What is important to remember is that although coverage for Section 504 is broader, the rights and services are not as extensive. Therefore, such a student may need accommodations such as accessible classrooms, modified assignments to allow for differing physical abilities or alternate modes of expression, extended time on tests—whatever is needed to allow the student to demonstrate his or her abilities rather than the manifestations of the impairments with which he or she lives.

When affirmative accommodations or services are necessary to provide nondiscriminatory educational services to a child with disabilities, the accommodation should be noted in a service plan.[34] These accommodations may require receipt of special education services.[35] For example, a child who was asthmatic and had an allergic reaction to cigarette smoke was covered by Section 504 and the district was required to make reasonable accommodations to allow him to attend school.[36] Despite the observations in *Davis,* indicating that Section 504 does not impose an affirmative obligation on schools to provide related services to students, other courts have upheld such an obligation. In *Elizabeth S. v. Gilhool,*[37] a class action suit was filed to seek the provision of related services to children qualified under Section 504 but not under IDEA. Among the named individuals in that action was an insulin-dependent child seeking blood sugar tests and insulin injections and a hydrocephalic child seeking catheterization. The action ended without a court opinion when the state issued regulations providing related services to Section 504 eligible children.

A letter from OCR[38] sets forth current expectations for school districts under Section 504:

Section 504 applies to all qualified handicapped persons in federally funded programs and activities. The IDEA applies only to children having impairments specified in that statute and regulation who require special education to benefit from an education. Students who are handicapped under Section 504 are entitled to appropriate educational services even if they do not meet the definition of "handicapped" under the IDEA. As a result, school districts may not categorically limit services to students who are eligible under the IDEA. Some examples of students who may be handicapped under Section 504 but may not be eligible for services under the IDEA are those who have diabetes, AIDS, or Attention Deficit Disorder (ADD).

To determine if a student is handicapped under Section 504, school districts must establish standards and procedures for the evaluation and placement of the student in question. The placement decision must be made based upon information from a variety of sources and considered by a group of persons, including those knowledgeable about the child, the meaning of the evaluation data, and the placement options available. If it is determined that the student is handicapped, the student is then entitled to regular or special education and related aids and services that are designed to meet the individual educational needs of the student as adequately as the needs of nonhandicapped persons are met. Procedural safeguards, including notice, an opportunity to examine relevant records, an impartial hearing with opportunity for participation by the person's parents or guardian and representation by counsel, and a review procedure, apply to the identification, evaluation and placement process.

Section 504 also has implications for schools when dealing with the general public and parents. It is important to remember that these groups also must receive reasonable accommodations, if necessary, to make general services available to them on the same basis as nondisabled persons. For example, *Rothschild v. Grottenthaler*[39] established the principle that parent-oriented activities, such as parent-teacher conferences, that are "incident to their children's education" must be made accessible to people with disabilities by reasonable accommodations. Therefore, accommodations such as moving a meeting or program to a room accessible by wheelchair or providing a sign language interpreter may be necessary.

DUE PROCESS PROCEDURES

Complaints under Section 504 can be filed with the Department of Education within 180 days of the violation.[40] The complaint should be sent to the Office for Civil Rights of the Department of Education in the region where the school district is located. The complaint need not be on any particular form in order for investigation to proceed, but it must contain the following:

1. The name, address, and telephone number of the complaining party
2. The basis for the complaint, such as disability discrimination

3. The name(s) of who has been affected by the discrimination (individuals or groups of individuals)
4. The name and address of the discriminating agency, if known
5. The approximate date of the discriminatory conduct
6. A brief description of what happened
7. The signature of the complaining party

An administrative investigation follows. Because administrative action in such cases is generally futile to resolution of the individual situation, the majority of courts permit individuals to bring actions directly in court. Although Section 504 complaints are not a viable avenue for remedying many types of practices that may affect only one individual—because the IDEA often preempts Section 504—it is important to recognize Section 504 as a tool for remedying systemic practices and policies. For example, a practice of always conducting special education classes in separate, segregated facilities could be attacked through a complaint to the Office for Civil Rights. An investigation could lead to an order for the school to stop the practice, and this would then affect all special education students in the school.

An individual complaint may be filed and would result in a due process hearing. School districts must have available an impartial hearing process (similar to that required under IDEA) for resolving disputes. The regulations do not contain specific procedural guidelines, therefore OCR applies a standard of reasonableness in assessing a hearing process. It is possible even for IDEA hearing officers to resolve Section 504 issues, in conjunction with or apart from IDEA claims. If this is not possible due to specific state statutes or regulations, the school districts in the state must offer alternative hearing procedures.[41]

SOUTHEASTERN COMMUNITY COLLEGE v. DAVIS
442 U.S. 397, 99 S. Ct. 2361, 60 L. Ed. 2d 980 (1979)

Mr. Justice POWELL delivered the opinion of the Court.

****

Respondent, who suffers from a serious hearing disability, seeks to be trained as a registered nurse. During the 1973–1974 academic year she was enrolled in the College Parallel program of Southeastern Community College, a state institution that receives federal funds. Respondent hoped to progress to Southeastern's Associate Degree Nursing program, completion of which would make her eligible for state certification as a registered nurse. . . .

On the basis of an examination at Duke University Medical Center, respondent was diagnosed as having a "bilateral, sensori-neural hearing loss." A change in her hearing aid was recommended, as a result of which it was expected that she would be able to detect sounds "almost as well as a person would who has normal hearing." But this improvement would not mean that she could discriminate among sounds sufficiently to understand normal spoken speech. Her lipreading skills would remain necessary for effective communication: "While wearing the hearing aid, she is well aware of gross sounds occurring in the listening environment. However, she can only be responsible for speech spoken to her, when the talker gets her attention and allows her to look directly at the talker."

Southeastern next consulted Mary McRee, Executive Director of the North Carolina Board of Nursing. On the basis of the audiologist's report, McRee recommended that respondent not be admitted to the nursing program. In McRee's view, respondent's hearing disability made it unsafe for her to practice as a nurse. In addition, it would be impossible for respondent to participate safely in the normal clinical training program, and those modifications that would be necessary to enable safe participation would prevent her from realizing the benefits of the program. . . .

****

II.

[T]his is the first case in which this Court has been called upon to interpret § 504. . . . Section 504 by its terms does not compel educational institutions to disregard the disabilities of handicapped individuals or to make substantial modifications in their programs to allow disabled persons to participate. Instead, it requires only that an "otherwise qualified handicapped individual" not be excluded from participation in a federally funded program "solely by reason of his handicap," indicating only that mere possession of a handicap is not a permissible ground for assuming an inability to function in a particular context.

. . . . An otherwise qualified person is one who is able to meet all of a program's requirements in spite of his handicap.

The regulations . . . reinforce, rather than contradict, this conclusion. According to these regulations, a "[q]ualified handicapped person" is, "[w]ith respect to postsecondary and vocational education services, a handicapped person who meets the academic and technical standards requisite to admission or participation in the [school's] education program or activity. . . ." 45 CFR § 84.3(k)(3) (1978). An explanatory note states: "The term 'technical standards' refers to all nonacademic admissions criteria that are essential to participation in the program in question." 45 CFR pt. 84, App. A, p. 405 (1978).

A further note emphasizes that legitimate physical qualifications may be essential to participation in particular programs. We think it clear, therefore, that HEW interprets the "other" qualifications which a handicapped person may be required to meet as including necessary physical qualifications.

III.

The remaining question is whether the physical qualifications Southeastern demanded of respondent might not be necessary for participation in its nursing program. It is not open to dispute that, as Southeastern's Associate Degree Nursing program currently is constituted, the ability to understand speech without reliance on lipreading is necessary for patient safety during the clinical phase of the program. As the District Court found, this ability also is indispensable for many of the functions that a registered nurse performs.

Respondent contends nevertheless that § 504, properly interpreted, compels Southeastern to undertake affirmative action that would dispense with the need for effective oral communication. First, it is suggested that respondent can be given individual supervision by faculty members whenever she attends patients directly. Moreover, certain required courses might be dispensed with altogether for respondent. It is not necessary, she argues, that Southeastern train her to undertake all the tasks a registered nurse is licensed to perform. Rather, it is sufficient to make § 504 applicable if respondent might be able to perform satisfactorily some of the duties of a registered nurse or to hold some of the positions available to a registered nurse.

Respondent finds support for this argument in portions of the HEW regulations discussed above. In particular, a provision applicable to postsecondary educational programs requires covered institutions to make "modifications" in their programs to accommodate handicapped persons, and to provide "auxiliary aids" such as sign-language interpreters.

. . . . Yet the only evidence in the record indicates that nothing less than close, individual attention by a nursing instructor would be sufficient to ensure patient safety if respondent took part in the clinical phase of the nursing program. . . . [I]t also is reasonably clear that § 84.44(a) does not encompass the kind of curricular changes that would be necessary to accommodate respondent in the nursing program. In light of respondent's inability to function in clinical courses without close supervision, Southeastern, with prudence, could allow her to take only academic classes. Whatever benefits respondent might realize from such a course of study, she would not receive even a rough equivalent of the training a nursing program normally gives. Such a fundamental alteration in the nature of a program is far more than the "modification" the regulation requires.

****

. . . . It is undisputed that respondent could not participate in Southeastern's nursing program unless the standards were substantially lowered. Section 504 imposes no requirement upon an educational institution to lower or to effect substantial modifications of standards to accommodate a handicapped person.

****

V.

Accordingly, we reverse the judgment of the court below, and remand for proceedings consistent with this opinion.

So ordered.
(Footnotes omitted.)

— — — —

GRUBE v. BETHLEHEM AREA SCHOOL DISTRICT
United States District Court, E.D. Pennsylvania, 1982.
550 F. Supp. 418

HUYETT, District Judge

****

The student is enrolled in his senior year at Freedom High School in the Bethlehem Area School District (School District). . . .

Richard is a vigorous, athletically inclined high school student whose only physical problem is the absence of his right kidney which was removed when he was 2 years of age as a result of a congenital malformation. . . . Richard was selected to be a member of his school's varsity football team for this year. He was awarded first string positions with the offensive and defensive squads. Richard prepared this summer to participate in the team. He attended team work-outs. He joined in pre-season team exercises which included physical contact. A few days before the first scrimmage, Richard was informed that he had been declared ineligible for the team by the Superintendent of Schools because he lacks one kidney. Richard is qualified by virtue of athletic ability to play on his school's varsity football team. Richard was barred from the football team solely as a result of his lack of one kidney.

****

The plaintiffs' complaint presents two legal theories. First, they assert that Richard has been discriminated against in violation of the Rehabilitation Act of 1973 (Act) § 504. 29 U.S.C.A. § 706(7) (Supp. 1981). Secondly, they assert that he has been deprived of his fourteenth amendment right to equal protection giving rise to an action under 42 U.S.C. § 1983. . . .

Section 504 of the Act as amended provides: "No otherwise qualified handicapped individual in the United States . . . shall, solely by reason of his handicap, be excluded from the participation in, be denied the benefits of, or be subjected to discrimination under any program or activity receiving Federal fi-

nancial assistance. . . ." 29 U.S.C.A. § 794 (Supp. 1981). In interpreting this section, the Supreme Court has held that an "otherwise qualified" person "is one who is able to meet all of a program's requirements in spite of his handicap." *Southeastern Community College v. Davis*, 442 U.S. 397, 406, 99 S. Ct. 2361, 2367, 60 L. Ed. 2d 980 (1979). The Court interpreted § 504 as follows:

> *Section 504 by its terms does not compel educational institutions to disregard the disabilities of handicapped individuals or to make substantial modifications in their programs to allow disabled persons to participate. Instead, it requires only that an "otherwise qualified handicapped individual" not be excluded from participation in a federally funded program "solely by reason of his handicap," indicating only that mere possession of a handicap is not a permissible ground for assuming an inability to function in a particular context.*
> *Id., 442 U.S. at 405, 99 S. Ct. at 2366.*

Three lower courts have addressed the import of § 504 in contexts similar to the present case. In *Kampmeier v. Nyquist*, 553 F.2d 296 (2d Cir. 1977), the Court of Appeals for the Second Circuit considered an appeal from the denial of a preliminary injunction sought on behalf of children with one eye who were barred from participation in their school's contact sports programs. The school's decision to bar the children was based upon the opinion of the school physician. The medical evidence the children introduced to refute the school physician's opinion was equivocal. Referring to the school's reliance on the opinion of the school physician, the court stated: "The plaintiffs have presented little evidence—medical, statistical or otherwise—which would cast doubt on the substantiality of this rationale." Noting that the equities in the case were very close, the court concluded that this absence of evidence was fatal to plaintiffs' claim. On the evidence presented, it could not be said that the school district lacked "substantial justification" for its action.

In *Poole v. South Plainfield Board of Education*, 490 F. Supp. 948 (D.N.J. 1980), the plaintiff was a high school student with one kidney who was barred from his school's wrestling team. Before the court were the defendant's motions to dismiss for lack of subject matter jurisdiction and in the alternative, for judgment on the pleadings. The court denied both motions because on the facts as assumed in the opinion, the plaintiff had demonstrated a right to recovery. The school system's medical director advised the system that it was inadvisable to permit a student with one kidney to participate in contact sports. The student refuted this opinion with medical opinions by his own experts. It was apparent to the court that both the school system physician and the board itself were making a philosophical and not a medical judgment. . . .

****

The final case dealing with similar facts is *Wright v. Columbia University*, 520 F. Supp. 789 (E.D. Pa. 1981). In *Wright*, the court heard plaintiff's request for a temporary restraining order in an adversial hearing. The plaintiff who had only one eye had been barred by the defendant from playing collegiate football. The plaintiff presented evidence from a highly qualified ophthalmologist that no substantial risk of serious eye injury related to football exists. The *Wright* court concluded that this testimony distinguished the case before it from *Kampmeier* where the plaintiffs offered "little evidence." Like the *Poole* court, the court in *Wright* concluded that the defendant was motivated by good intentioned, but impermissible "paternalistic" thinking.

Turning to the present case, I begin with reluctance an analysis which compels me to disturb a well-intended decision of local school authorities. The administration of our public schools is a matter almost always better left in the hands of members of the community which the schools serve. . . .

The school district has advanced two reasons as "substantial justification" for its action. First, according to Dr. LaFrankin, was his concern for the liability that might be imposed upon the school district if Richard loses the use of his kidney. This concern may be answered by the releases which the parents and son have offered to execute. . . . The

district's second justification for precluding Richard from participating in football is concern for his health, safety, and welfare. This concern is based on a risk perceived by the district that Richard could lose his one functioning kidney.

This case began when Dr. Delp decided that it would be helpful to get an opinion from Richard's kidney physician with regard to his ability to play. . . . The letters that were produced from Dr. Lennart were equivocal. . . . The evidence is clear that neither Dr. Lennart, Dr. Delp, nor Dr. Hemmerlie had any facts which would permit them to make a rational medical evaluation of the existence of a risk. In an understandable abundance of caution, all three eventually concluded that the safest course was to say that Richard could not play. I conclude that the opinion of these three doctors cannot serve as substantial justification for the district's actions where their decision lacks a medical basis.

Dr. Moyer's conclusion was that the risk of injury to the kidney is so slim that there is no medical reason why Richard cannot play football. Essentially, his testimony is consistent with that portion of Dr. Lennart's correspondence which concluded that whether Richard should engage in contact sports is not a medical issue.

Richard's selection for the team established that he is otherwise qualified to play football. For the reasons stated above, the defendant's decision to preclude him from playing lacks substantial justification. Accordingly, I conclude that the plaintiffs have made a strong showing of likelihood of success on the merits.

****

1. The motion is GRANTED.
2. THE DEFENDANT IS PRELIMINARILY ENJOINED FROM PRECLUDING THE PLAINTIFF RICHARD WILLIAM GRUBE FROM PARTICIPATING AS A MEMBER OF THE FREEDOM HIGH SCHOOL FOOTBALL TEAM ON THE SAME TERMS AND CONDITIONS AS APPLY TO ALL OTHER MEMBERS OF THE TEAM.
3. THE PLAINTIFFS SHALL GIVE SECURITY IN THE SUM OF $1,000.00.

(Footnotes omitted.)

— — — —

ROTHSCHILD v. GROTTENTHALER
907 F. 2d 286 (Second Circuit 1990)

ALTIMARI, Circuit Judge:

The central questions presented on this appeal is whether a public school district which receives federal financial assistance must provide sign-language interpreter services, at school district expense, to deaf parents of non-hearing impaired children at certain school-initiated activities.

****

BACKGROUND

The parties stipulate that plaintiffs-appellees Kenneth and Karen Rothschild are deaf parents of two non-hearing impaired children who attend schools operated by defendant-appellant Ramapo Central School District. It is also stipulated that the Rothschilds use American Sign Language as their primary method of communication. . . .

****

The Rothschilds commenced this action in May 1989, seeking declaratory and injunctive relief, as well as damages, under section 504 of the Rehabilitation Act and 42 U.S.C. § 1983. The Rothschilds contended that, although they are invited to attend School District meetings, conferences, and other events concerning their children's education, they cannot effectively communicate with teachers and other School District personnel at these activities without the services of a sign-language interpreter. They claimed that, without a sign-language interpreter, the opportunity afforded them to participate in School District activities concerning their children's education is not equal to the opportunity afforded non-hearing impaired parents.

****

Our inquiry begins, as it must, with the language of section 504. That section, in pertinent part, provides:

> *No otherwise qualified individual with handicaps in the United States, as defined in section 706(8) of this title, shall, solely by reason of her or his handicap, be excluded from the participation in, be denied the benefits of, or be subjected to discrimination under any program or activity receiving Federal financial assistance. . . .*

. . . . To establish a prima facie violation of section 504, a plaintiff must prove that 1) he or she is a "handicapped person" as defined in the Rehabilitation Act; 2) he or she is "otherwise qualified" to participate in the offered activity or to enjoy its benefits; 3) he or she is being excluded from such participation or enjoyment solely by reason of his or her handicap; and 4) the program denying the plaintiff participation receives federal financial assistance. . . .

In the present case, the School District concedes that the Rothschilds are handicapped persons within the meaning of the Rehabilitation Act, . . . and that the School District receives federal financial assistance. . . . The School District does not seriously contest that the Rothschilds are denied the opportunity to participate in school-initiated activities concerning their children's education by reason of their handicaps. Rather, the heart of the School District's argument is that the Rothschilds are not "otherwise qualified" for the offered activities. . . .

****

An "otherwise qualified" handicapped individual is one "who is able to meet all of a program's requirements in spite of his handicap." *Southeastern Community College v. Davis*, 442 U.S. 397, 406, 99 S. Ct. 2361, 2367, 60 L. Ed. 2d 980 (1979); . . . A recipient of federal financial assistance may consider an individual's handicap if it "could reasonably be viewed as posing a substantial risk that the applicant would be unable to meet [the recipient's] reasonable standards." *Doe v. New York Univ.*, 666 F.2d at 775 (citing *Southeastern Community College*, 442 U.S. at 413 n. 12, 99 S. Ct. at 2371 n. 12). However, where an individual's handicap is unrelated to reasonable requirements for participation in the activity, section 504 prohibits denying that individual's participation on the sole basis of his or her handicap. . . . If the Rothschilds are "otherwise qualified" for the parent-oriented activities offered by the School District, the Rothschilds must be afforded an equal opportunity to participate in those activities.

The Rothschilds are "otherwise qualified" for the parent-oriented activities incident to their children's education that are offered by the School District. The Rothschilds are parents of school children enrolled in the School District. They are concerned with their children's educational development. They are interested in meeting with teachers and other School District personnel and are able to meet them at the scheduled times and locations. The Rothschilds' inability to effectively communicate without the services of a sign-language interpreter simply has no bearing on the reasonable requirements for participating in school-initiated activities incident to their children's education. . . .

****

. . . . The School District and Superintendent Grottenthaler contend that the Rothschilds are not "otherwise qualified" because they are not eligible to receive educational service. . . . While the School District is subject to section 504 in providing educational services, that is not the only area in which it must refrain from discrimination on the basis of handicap. In hiring employees, for example, the School District is obviously subject to the definition of qualified handicapped person in Regulation 104.3(k)(1). So too, the School District is subject to the definition of qualified handicapped person in Regulation 104.3(k)(4) with respect to "other services" which, in this case, include parent-teacher conferences, meetings with School District personnel, and other parent-oriented services related to the education of its students. The Rothschilds are not excluded from the protection of section 504 merely because they are parents and not school children.

****

Mindful of the need to strike a balance between the rights of the Rothschilds and the legitimate financial and administrative concerns of the School District, the district court limited the scope of activities for which the School District would be required to provide a sign-language interpreter. It stated:

We take pains, however, to emphasize that the [school] district's obligation, and correspondingly, the plaintiffs' entitlement, is limited to "school-initiated conferences incident to the academic and/or disciplinary aspects of their child's education." To the extent that the plaintiffs wish to voluntarily participate in any of the plethora of extra-curricular activities that their children may be involved in, we think they, like other parents, must do so at their own expense.

. . . . This seems a "reasonable accommodation," . . . which permits the Rothschilds to be involved in their children's education while preserving the responsible administration of the School District. . . . The School District's refusal to modify its program to accommodate the Rothschilds' handicap is "unreasonable and discriminatory.". . .

. . . . In light of the foregoing, the district court's judgment is affirmed in part, and vacated and remanded in part for modification not inconsistent with this opinion.
(Footnotes omitted.)

— — — —

HAWAII STATE DEPARTMENT OF EDUCATION
17 EHLR 360 (O.C.R. 1990)

****

FINDINGS OF FACT

[ ] is 18 years old, an age at which educational services are provided to nonhandicapped persons by HDOE. He was diagnosed by HDOE [Hawaii State Department of Education] as Learning Disabled and was determined to need special education. As such, he has a condition which substantially limits the major life activity of "learning."

****

. . . . Students who do not pass the HSTEC [Hawaii State Test of Essential Competency] do not receive a high school diploma. Special education students who complete high school but fail to pass the HSTEC may receive an alternate diploma.

****

The complainant asserted that [ ] needed a reader to help him take the HSTEC because his handicap substantially impairs his ability to read. . . . HDOE records show that a request for such a reader originated in the principal's office, on [ ]s behalf, in February 1990. The request was denied by HDOE administrators.

The official HDOE policy regarding accommodation for handicapped students taking the HSTEC is set forth in an October 19, 1988 memorandum from the Superintendent. This policy specifies that a reader may be furnished for "certified blind" students. The memorandum also states that no student may receive the assistance of a reader in completing the reading portion of the test, EC #1. Blind students are required to take this portion of the exam in braille. . . .

****

ANALYSIS

It is established that the student resides in the area served by HDOE. Because he is a school aged student with an acknowledged disability which significantly limits his ability to learn, he is a qualified handicapped person within the meaning of Section 504. In its diagnosis of his handicap, HDOE implicitly recognizes that he has difficulty processing information by means of reading.

Section 104.4(b)(1)(iii) and (b)(2) of the Section 504 regulation require recipients to provide services in such a manner as to afford handicapped students an equal opportunity to obtain the same result or reach the same level of achievement as is afforded nonhandicapped students. Several sections of the regulation make it clear that "equal opportunity to obtain the same result" on tests requires that the tests be administered in such a way that they measure the student's proficiency in the subject tested, rather than his or her unrelated handicap. For example, § 104.35(b)(3) requires that tests administered during the evaluation process be selected and administered so as to ensure that instruments designed to measure specific skills do so, rather than reflecting the student's impaired sensory, manual or speaking skills. Section 104.44(c), relating to *post*secondary education, requires that, in administering course examinations to students with impaired sensory, manual or speaking skills, a recipient must use methods which ensure that examination results reflect the students' achievement in the course, rather than their impairments.

****

OCR recognizes that section EC #1 of the HSTEC is intended specifically to measure reading competency. It follows that to read this portion of the test to a student would defeat the purpose of the test. OCR finds that requiring students to complete this section without a reader's assistance is not discriminatory. The other sections of the current test are not intended to measure reading competency. To the extent that the form in which these tests are administered requires reading competency, their administration without adjustments discriminates against students who have handicaps that make it difficult to assimilate or process information by reading. Since these sections are not specifically intended to measure reading competency, it may be necessary to furnish handicapped students with an accommodation which ensures that their handicap does not interfere with their ability to process the information necessary to take the test, so that the test can accurately measure the specifically designated competency. Such an accommodation may include oral administration of those portions of the test.

Because the needs and abilities of handicapped students vary, Section 504 requires that educational decisions be made for them on an individual basis. School districts must therefore make individual determinations of the adjustments needed to afford handicapped students an equal opportunity to pass an examination. By deciding that readers could *only* be provided for the HSTEC to visually impaired students, the HDOE failed to consider the individual needs of students with other handicaps. It thereby denied those students who needed adjustments an equal opportunity to pass the examination and receive a high school diploma.

****

ADDITIONAL COMMENTARY

1. Students who have disabilities have the right to comparable programs and may not be excluded from programs solely due to their disabling condition. Thus, when such students were denied enrollment in a school's summer recreational program because of the disability, the OCR found a Section 504 violation. Students, if otherwise qualified, must be allowed to enroll and be provided with reasonable accommodations. *Clayton*
School District, 16 E.H.L.R. 766 (OCR 1990). Because a school district offers some summer school programming does not require the district to offer summer school for all students. E.g., *Charlotte-Mecklinburg School District*, 18 I.D.E.L.R. 929 (OCR 1991).

2. In undertaking new construction and remodeling, school districts must adhere to the Uniform Federal Accessibility Standards and the American

National Standard Specification for Making Buildings and Facilities Accessible to and Usable by the Physically Handicapped. 34 C.F.R. 104.23. Copies of these may be obtained through the American National Standards Institute, Inc., 1430 Broadway, New York, NY 10018.

3. A joint memorandum from the Office for Civil Rights (OCR) and Office for Special Education and Rehabilitative Services (OSERS, 18 I.D.E.L.R. 116 (1991), regarding children with attention-deficit disorder (ADD) who have been determined to not be eligible under IDEA but are protected by Section 504, offered some guidelines and suggestions.

Should it be determined that the child with ADD is disabled for purposes of Section 504 and needs only adjustments in the regular classroom, rather than special education, those adjustments are required by Section 504. A range of strategies is available to meet the educational needs of children with ADD. Regular classroom teachers are important in identifying the appropriate educational adaptations and interventions for many of these children.

State education agencies (SEAs) and local education agencies (LEAs) should take the necessary steps to promote coordination between special and regular education programs. Steps also should be taken to train regular education teachers and other personnel to develop their awareness about ADD and its manifestations, as well as the adaptations that can be implemented in regular education programs to address the instructional needs of these children. Examples of adaptations in regular education programs could include the following:

Providing a structured learning environment; repeating and simplifying instructions about in-class and homework assignments; supplementing verbal instructions with visual instructions; using behavioral management techniques; adjusting class schedules; modifying test delivery; using tape recorders, computer-aided instruction, and other audio-visual equipment; selecting modified textbooks or workbooks; and tailoring homework assignments.

Other provisions range from consultation to special resources and may include reducing class size; use of one-on-one tutorials; classroom aids and note takers; involvement of a "services coordinator" to oversee implementation of special

programs and services, and possible modification of nonacademic times such as lunchroom, recess, and physical education.

4. To determine if someone is disabled within the employment area, the focus should be on the individual, not solely on the impairment. The person does not have to unemployable, in general, to be disabled, but the disability must substantially limit the major life activity—working—within the individual's prospective field. *Black Ltd. v. Marshall*, 497 F. Supp. 1088 (D. Haw. 1980).

5. Cases involving students who are alcoholics or drug addicts also raise issues. These students are likely to be classified as disabled under Section 504 but not IDEA. However, Section 504 does not prevent the discipline of those students for possession or use of illegal substance. The regulations state,

Of great concern to many commentators was the question of what effect the inclusion of drug addicts and alcoholics as handicapped persons would have on school disciplinary rules prohibiting the use or possession of drugs or alcohol by students. Neither such rules nor their application to drug addicts or alcoholics is prohibited by this regulation, provided that the rules are enforced evenly with respect to all students. 34 C.F.R. Part 104 App. A. 366 (1987).

For greater detail, see Chapter 5, Discipline, in this text.

6. Recently, a formal letter of inquiry was submitted to the Office for Civil Rights concerning whether the requirement under Section 504 for a free appropriate public education is limited by the "reasonable accommodation" standard (*Zirkel*, 20 I.D.E.L.R. 134 (OCR 1993). The response reads in part:

The key question to your letter is whether OCR reads into that Section 504 regulatory requirement for a free appropriate public education (FAPE) a "reasonable accommodation" standard or similar limitation. The clear and unequivocal answer to that is no. Section 104.33(a) guarantees all qualified individuals with disabilities FAPE which consists of regular and special education and related aids and services that are designed to meet the individual needs of qualified persons with disabilities as adequately as the individual education needs of other persons are met and that are designed and delivered in accordance with the Department's regulation, 34 C.F.R. § 104.22(b)(1).

. . .

The regulation establishes different compliance standards for different educational contexts. A reasonable accommodation limitation on the responsibilities of recipients is contained in Subpart B of the regulation which covers employment. See 34 C.F.R. 104.12. Subpart E, which covers postsecondary and vocational education, contains a similar limitation on the recipient's obligation to modify its academic requirements to ensure that they do not discriminate or have the effect of discriminating on the basis of disability. If a recipient can demonstrate that an academic requirement is essential to the program of instruction being pursued by the student with a disability or to directly related licensing requirement, failure to modify the requirement will not be regarded as discriminatory. See 34 C.F.R. § 104.44. Such limitations are not contained in Subpart D, covering elementary and secondary education. We conclude therefore that the regulation writers intended to create a different standard for elementary and secondary students than for employees and postsecondary/vocational students.

This response suggests that when considering the educational programming for students with disabilities, FAPE under Section 504 sets a baseline beneath which a school district may not fall regardless of the costs of achieving FAPE for that child. However, the response has prompted some to question whether there is disagreement between the executive and judicial branches of government concerning how the terms "reasonable accommodation" and FAPE should be reconciled under the law. *See* Dagley, D., & Evans, C. (1994). *The Reasonable Accommodation Standard for Section 504 Eligible Students.* Paper presented at the Annual Meeting of the National Council of Professors of Educational Administration, Palm Desert, CA.

7. A school district's federal funding my be terminated for violating Section 504. Additionally, the Eleventh Circuit Court of Appeals upheld the suspension of a district's funding for failure to cooperate with an OCR investigation. *Freeman v. Cavazos,* 939 F.2d 1527 (11th Cir. 1991).

8. An example of a service plan for students under Section 504 is shown in Figure 3.2.

SECTION 504 EVALUATION SUMMARY AND EDUCATION PLAN

Student Name _____ ID _____ Birthdate _____

Address _____ Telephone _____

Date of Meeting _____ School _____ Grade _____

PARTICIPANTS (Group of persons knowledgeable about the child, including parent, and the results of the evaluation data.)

SUMMARY OF EVALUATION DATA (Information from a variety of sources, including, as relevant, aptitude and achievement test, teacher recommendations, physical condition, social or cultural background, and adaptive behavior. Information varies based upon the evaluative information required on a case-by-case basis.)

DETERMINATION OF WHETHER THE CHILD HAS A DISABILITY UNDER SECTION 504

_____ Child does not have a physical or mental impairment which substantially limits one or more major life activities, such as caring for one's self, performing manual tasks, walking, seeing, hearing, speaking, breathing, learning, and working.

_____ Child has a physical or mental impairment which substantially limits one or more major life activities, such as caring for one's self, performing manual tasks, walking, seeing, hearing, speaking, breathing, learning, and working, but:

_____ Child does not have a disability under the Individuals with Disabilities Act (IDEA); or

_____ Child does not need special education.
(Note: If the child has a disability under the IDEA and needs special education, the MDC Summary Report must be used; not this form.)

EDUCATIONAL PLAN

DESCRIPTION OF ACCOMMODATIONS (Specific accommodations, related services, or supplementary aids needed for the child to benefit from his or her education. For each area identified, include as appropriate the amount of services needed, goals/objectives, educational setting in which services will be provided, staff responsible for providing the service, special equipment or adaptive devices required, and duration of services (which must be reviewed at least annually).

PLACEMENT (If the school in which the services being provided to the child must be changed as a result of this Educational Plan, identify the new school and educational program below. The educational program must be in the least restrictive environment in which the services may be provided.)

Parents have been informed of their rights under Section 504 including information about the evaluation, the education planning meeting, and the provision of procedural safeguards, including the right to request an impartial hearing and review procedure.

_____ YES

FIGURE 3.2 Example of Service Plan

ENDNOTES

1. 29 U.S.C. 794.

2. 42 U.S.C. 12101. This statute increased the coverage of 504 to employers of 15 or more employees effective in 1994 and of 25 or more employees effective in 1992. Since public schools were previously subject to 504, due to receipt of federal financial assistance, this would not effect them. The only major impact the ADA will have on schools is the provision relating to the exclusion of drug addiction as a disabling condition.

3. 468 U.S. 992 (1984).

4. Smith v. Robinson, 468 U.S. 992 at 1016-1021 (1984).

5. 29 U.S.C. 706(8)(B).

6. 34 C.F.R. 104.3(j)(2)(ii).

7. The regulations provide a nonexhaustive list:

> *(A) any physiological disorder or condition, cosmetic disfigurement, or anatomical loss affecting one or more of the following body systems: neurological; musculoskeletal; special sense organs; respiratory, including speech organs; cardiovascular; reproductive, digestive, genito-urinary; hemic and lymphatic; skin; and endocrine; or (B) any mental or psychological disorder, such as mental retardation, organic brain syndrome, emotional or mental illness, and specific learning disabilities 45 C.F.R. 84.3 (j)(2)(i).*

8. 34 C.F.R. Part 104 App. A. 366; 45 C.F.R. Part 84 Appt. 345.

9. 45 C.F.R. 84.3(j)(2)(iv); 34 C.F.R. 104.3 (j)(2)(iv).

10. *Arline v. School Bd. of Nassau County,* 772 F.2d 759, 764 (11th Cir. 1985), *aff'd* 480 U.S. 273 (1987).

11. *E.g.,* Atascadero State Hospital v. Scanlon, 473 U.S. 234 (1985).

12. *E.g.,* Costner v. U.S., 720 F.2d 539 (8th Cir. 1983).

13. *E.g.,* Perez v. Philadelphia Housing Authority, 677 F.Supp. 357 (E.D. Pa. 1987), *aff'd,* 841 F.2d 1120 (3rd Cir. 1988).

14. *E.g.,* Torres v. Bolger, 781 F.2d 1134 (5th Cir. 1986).

15. Jasany v. U.S. Postal Service, 755 F.2d 1244 (6th Cir. 1985).

16. OCR Memorandum, 307 E.H.L.R. 17 (OCR 1989).

17. The regulations state:

> *No qualified handicapped person shall, on the basis of handicap, be excluded from participation in, be denied benefits of or otherwise be subjected to discrimination under any program or activity which receives or benefits from Federal financial assistance.*
> *34 C.F.R. 104.4(a).*

18. 34 C.F.R. 104.3(k).

19. For athletics, *see, e.g.,* Kampmeier v. Nyquist, 553 F.2d 296 (2nd Cir. 1977); Cavallaro v. Ambach, 575 F. Supp. 171 (W.D. N.Y. 1983); Poole v. South Plainfield Bd. of Educ., 490 F. Supp. 948 (D. N.J. 1980).

20. 34 C.F.R. 104.37.

21. Sullivan v. Vallejo City Unified School Dist., 731 F. Supp. 947 (E.D. Cal. 1990).

22. Wolff v. South Colonie Central School Dist., 534 F. Supp. 758 (N.D. N.Y. 1982).

23. Grube v. Bethlehem, 550 F. Supp. 418 (E.D. Pa. 1982).

24. 15 EHLR 441: 632 (N.D. Ala. 1989).

25. The regulation states:

> *No qualified handicapped person shall, because a recipient's facilities are inaccessible to or unusable by handicapped persons, be denied the benefits of, be excluded from participation in, or otherwise be subjected to discrimination.*
> *34 C.F.R. 104.21.*

26. The regulations require school districts to "operate each program or activity . . . so that the program or activity, when reviewed in its entirety is readily accessible to handicapped persons. 34 C.F.R. 104.22 (1989).

27. 34 C.F.R. 104.4 (6)(1)(iii). *E.g.,* Garaway Local School District, 17 E.H.L.R. 237 (OCR 1990).

28. OCR Letter 1992.

29. 442 U.S. 397, 99 S. Ct. 2361 (1979).

30. 442 U.S. at 405.

31. 697 F.2d 179 (7th Cir. 1983).

32. 34 C.F.R. 104.22(a).

33. 34 C.F.R. 104.33(b)(1).

34. *See* 34 C.F.R. 104.33, 104.35, 104.36.

35. Williams, 18 I.D.E.L.R. 229 (OCR 1991).

36. Middlebury Community Schools, 257 E.H.L.R. 593 (OCR 1984).

37. No. C.A. 86-0218 (M.D. Pa. Nov. 27, 1989).

38. OCR, 1992.

39. 907 F.2d 286 (2nd Cir. 1990).

40. *See* Hall v. Knott County Bd. of Educ., 941 F.2d 402 (6th Cir. 1991); I.D. v. Westmoreland School Dist. 788 F. Supp. 634 (D. N.H. 1992).

41. Komer, 18 I.D.E.L.R. 230 (OCR 1991).

CHAPTER 4

THE INDIVIDUALS WITH DISABILITIES EDUCATION ACT

INTRODUCTION

Educational philosophy toward children in the United States who have disabilities has passed through many phases. In the 1700s and 1800s, most children with disabilities were not sent to school. In the latter 1800s and early 1900s, children who were disabled and who went to school were segregated in special classes under the guise of the philosophy of relieving stress on the teacher and other children. These sentiments, represented in *State ex rel Beattie v. Board of Education*,[1] were persuasive. Frequently, academic instruction suffered in these classes. By the mid-1900s, society had shifted its thinking to recognize the worth of individuals with disabilities. Teaching self-reliance and life skills was seen as a worthwhile goal. Again, those who received an education did so in segregated facilities.[2] However, many social and educational leaders began to suggest that segregation in the educational process was inherently wrong.

The United States Supreme Court adopted the notion that racial segregation was inherently unequal in *Brown v. Board of Education of Topeka*.[3] Here the Court found that forcing African-American children to be educated in segregated facilities was inherently unequal because of the stigma attached to being educated separately and because of the deprivation of interaction with children of other backgrounds. This idea of the inequities produced in segregated facilities carried from segregation on the basis of race to segregation on the basis of disability.

The concept of integrating children who have disabilities has paralleled the movement of integrating children of different races. Congress made initial efforts to provide for special education by enacting specific funding programs. In 1966,[4] a provision in Title VI established the Bureau of Education for the Handicapped to provide leadership in special education. In 1970,[5] the Education of the Handicapped Act was passed, which provided for grants to states to encourage special education programming.

During the 1970s, many advocacy groups were pushing to improve the rather haphazard approach to educating students with disabilities in the United States. In addition to lobbying at the local, state, and federal levels, they helped develop impact litigation. Two of these cases culminated in landmark decisions in 1971 and 1972.[6] In *Pennsylvania Association for Retarded Children v. Pennsylvania*,[7] the district court approved a consent decree that enjoined the state from denying education to mentally retarded children. The case was based on the constitutional theories of equal protection and due process and echoes its desegregation roots. The court ordered:

> *[A] free, public program of education and training appropriate to the child's capacity, within the context of the general educational policy that, among the alternative programs of education and training required by statute to be available, placement in a regular public school class is preferable to placement in a special public school class [i.e., a class for "disabled" children] and*

placement in a special public school class is preferable to placement in any other type of program of education and training.[8]

In *Mills v. Board of Education*,[9] the court similarly approved a consent decree. There, the judgment went so far as to set out an elaborate framework for due process requirements relating to labeling, placement, and exclusion of students. These cases served as the impetus for cases in other states and the outline for federal and state legislation.

In 1970, only 10 states mandated education for students with disabilities. This number changed rapidly in the early 1970s; nonetheless, by 1975, about three million children with disabilities were not receiving an education. Congress passed federal grant legislation to encourage states to adopt appropriate procedures for providing education to children with disabilities. The civil rights movement and related activities provided a favorable political atmosphere for the enactment of strong legislation. In response to many concerns, as an initial measure, Congress passed an interim funding bill that required states, as a condition of receiving federal funds, to adopt "goals of providing full educational opportunities to all handicapped children."[10] The interim bill was adopted to give Congress a year to study the issues. The following year, Congress enacted the Education for All Handicapped Children Act of 1975 (EAHCA),[11] which became effective in 1977.

Technically, the EAHCA is an amendment to the 1970 Education of the Handicapped Act (EHA), which had provided for grants to states to provide special education. The EAHCA amends Part B of the EHA. Although it is a funding statute, it creates individual rights in that, in order for states to receive the funding, they must comply with statutory framework for the provision of special education. All 50 states[12] now accept this federal funding and comply with its requirements. This is significant because the law provides the important elements of due process, integration, parental involvement, and nondiscriminatory testing and evaluation. The details of these requirements were set out in regulations finalized in 1977.[13]

To say that EAHCA revolutionized the education of children with disabilities is no understatement. The major principles of the act established an entirely new method and philosophy about how schools treat and educate children with disabilities. In addition, for the first time, some measure of continuity and consistency characterized special education from state to state. Turnbull and Turnbull[14] set forth the major principles of EAHCA as follows:

1. Zero reject—the right to be included in a free, appropriate, publicly supported educational system
2. Nondiscriminatory classification—the right to be fairly evaluated and diagnosed so that correct educational placement and program can be achieved
3. Individualized and appropriate education—the right to a meaningful educational experience
4. Least restrictive educational placement—the right to normalization
5. Procedural due process—the right to protest and remain where you are until that protest is heard and decided upon
6. Participatory democracy—the right to participate in the educational process

Through regulations detailing precise procedural guidelines, EAHCA attempted to define the major components of a free appropriate public education for children with disabilities. Briefly, the law requires procedures for referring children suspected of needing special education, a multiple-disciplinary team to consider eligibility, a team to develop an individualized education program (IEP) for any child who qualifies, placement in an educational setting appropriate to the child's needs, and procedures for parental notification and participation in the process. In addition, strict time limitations, periodic reassessment, and procedures for dispute resolution are prescribed.

There have been a number of amendments to this statute. The substantive changes are incorporated within the text and noted as appropriate. There is, however, one marked change that needs to be noted separately. In 1990, Congress reauthorized EAHCA and changed its title to the "Individuals with Disabilities Education Act of 1990" (IDEA). The language of the statute was changed throughout, replacing the phrase "handicapped child" to "child with disabilities" to reflect a more individual-oriented language and to make the language consistent with the Americans with Disabilities Act.

Not surprisingly, courts have been asked to construe all the major components of IDEA (EAHCA). Parents, school districts, and state educational authorities have petitioned the court for clarification of the purpose and breadth of IDEA. Litigation has defined the application of the act with respect to:

1. Eligibility
2. Appropriateness
3. Assessment
4. The individualized education program (IEP)
5. Least restrictive environment
6. Related services
7. Residential placements
8. Changes in placement
9. Private schools
10. Due process procedures
11. Remedies for violations

Sections examining each of these issues in depth follow.

STATE EX REL. BEATTIE v. BOARD OF EDUCATION
169 Wis. 231
April 3–April 29, 1919

Appeal from a judgment of the municipal court of Langlade County: T. W. Hogan, Judge. *Reversed.*

This is an action of mandamus brought in the municipal court of Langlade County to compel the *Board of Education of the City of Antigo* to reinstate and admit petitioner's son to the public schools of said city. . . .

Merritt Beattie, thirteen years of age . . . , has been a crippled and defective child since his birth, being afflicted with a form of paralysis which affects his whole physical and nervous make-up. He has not the normal use and control of his voice, hands, feet, and body. By reason of said paralysis his vocal cords are afflicted. He is slow and hesitating in speech and has a peculiarly high, rasping, and disturbing tone of voice, accompanied with uncontrollable facial contortions, making it difficult for him to make himself understood. He also has an uncontrollable flow of saliva which drools from his mouth on to [sic] his clothing and books, causing him to present an unclean appearance. He has a nervous and excitable nature. It is claimed on the part of the school board that his physical condition and ailment produces a depressing and nauseating effect upon the teachers and school children; that by reason of his physical condition he takes up an undue portion of the teacher's time and attention, distracts the attention of other pupils, and interferes generally with the discipline and progress of the school. . . . It appears that he is normal mentally and that he kept pace with the other pupils in the respective grades, although the teachers had difficulty in understanding him, . . . At the beginning of the school year in 1917 Merritt presented himself to the Second Ward public school, but on the second day those in charge refused to accept him as a pupil. . . . On September 13, 1917, the Board of Education had a regular meeting to consider the demand of the petitioner that his son be reinstated and admitted to the public schools. The matter was considered for an hour, during which time one member of the board moved that the boy be reinstated in the schools. This motion did not receive a second, . . . [T]he petitioner brought this action to compel his reinstatement. . . .

. . . .

... The duty confronting the school board was a delicate one. It was charged with the responsibility of saying whether this boy should be denied a constitutional right because the exercise of that right would be harmful to the school and to the pupils attending the same. He should not be excluded from the schools except for considerations affecting the general welfare. But if his presence in school was detrimental to the best interests of the school, then the board could not, with due regard to their official oaths, refrain from excluding him, even though such action be displeasing and painful to them. . . . The action of the board in refusing to reinstate the boy seems to have been the result of its best judgment exercised in good faith and the record discloses no grounds for the interference of courts with its action.

. . . .

By the Court.—Judgment reversed, and cause remanded with instructions to dismiss the petition.

— ▬ ▬ ▬

MILLS v. BOARD OF EDUCATION OF THE DISTRICT OF COLUMBIA
348 F. Supp. 866
(U.S. District Court, District of Columbia 1972)

WADDY, District Judge.

****

THE PROBLEM

The genesis of this case is found (1) in the failure of the District of Columbia to provide publicly supported education and training to plaintiffs and other "exceptional" children, members of their class, and (2) the excluding, suspending, expelling, reassigning and transferring of "exceptional" children from regular public school classes without affording them due process of law.

The problem of providing special education for "exceptional" children (mentally retarded, emotionally disturbed, physically handicapped, hyperactive and other children with behavioral problems) is one of major proportions in the District of Columbia. . . .

****

PLAINTIFFS ARE ENTITLED TO RELIEF

Plaintiffs' entitlement to relief in this case is clear. The applicable statutes and regulations and the Constitution of the United States require it.

Statutes and Regulations

Section 31-201 of the District of Columbia Code requires the following:

Every parent, guardian, or other person residing [permanently or temporarily] in the District of Columbia who has custody or control of a child between the ages of seven and sixteen years shall cause said child to be regularly instructed in a public school or in a private or parochial school or instructed privately during the period of each year in which the public schools of the District of Columbia are in session . . . ."

****

. . . . The Court need not belabor the fact that requiring parents to see that their children attend school under pain of criminal penalties presupposes that an educational opportunity will be made available to the children. The Board of Education is required to make such opportunity available. . . .

****

Thus the Board of Education has an obligation to provide whatever specialized instruction that will benefit the child. By failing to provide plaintiffs and their class the publicly supported specialized education to which they are entitled, the Board of Education violates the above statutes and its own regulations.

The Constitution-Equal Protection and Due Process

The Supreme Court in *Brown v. Board of Education,* 347 U.S. 483, 493, 74 S.Ct. 686, 691, 98 L.Ed. 873 (1954) stated:

Today, education is perhaps the most important function of state and local governments. Compulsory school attendance laws and the great expenditures for education both demonstrate our recognition of the importance of education to our democratic society. It is required in the performance of our most basic public responsibilities, even service in the armed forces. It is the very foundation of good citizenship. Today it is a principal instrument in awakening the child to cultural values, in preparing him for later professional training, and in helping him to adjust normally to his environment. In these days, it is doubtful that any child may reasonably be expected to succeed in life if he is denied the opportunity of an education. Such an opportunity, where the state has undertaken to provide it, is a right which must be made available to all on equal terms.

****

In *Hobson v. Hansen, supra,* Judge Wright found that denying poor public school children educational opportunities equal to that available to more affluent public school children was violative of the Due Process Clause of the Fifth Amendment. A fortiori, the defendants' conduct here, denying plaintiffs and their class not just an equal publicly supported education but all publicly supported education while providing such education to other children, is violative of the Due Process Clause.

Not only are plaintiffs and their class denied the publicly supported education to which they are entitled many are suspended or expelled from regular schooling or specialized instruction or reassigned without any prior hearing and are given no periodic review thereafter. Due process of law requires a hearing prior to exclusion, termination of classification into a special program.

****

[The] Court having reviewed the record of this cause including plaintiffs' Motion, . . . it is hereby ordered, adjudged and decreed that summary judgment in favor of plaintiffs and against defendants be, and hereby is, granted.

****

(Footnotes omitted.)

— — — —

Legislative History
SENATE REPORT REGARDING P.L. 94-142
EDUCATION FOR ALL HANDICAPPED CHILDREN ACT OF 1975
S. REP. NO. 168, 94th Cong., 1st Sess. 1975
(reprinted in 1975 U.S.C.C.A.N. 1425 at 1431)

NEED FOR LEGISLATION

****

In recent years decisions in more than 36 court cases in the States have recognized the rights of handicapped children to an appropriate education. States have made an effort to comply; however, lack of financial resources have prevented the implementation of the various decisions which have been rendered.

The Education Amendments of 1974 incorporated the major principles of the right to education cases. That Act added important new provisions to the Education of the Handicapped Act which require the States to: establish a goal of providing full educational opportunities to all handicapped children; provide procedures for insuring that handicapped children and their parents or guardians are guaranteed procedural safeguards in decisions regarding identification, evaluation, and educational placement of handicapped children; establish procedures to in-

sure that, to the maximum extent appropriate, handicapped children, including children in public or private institutions or other care facilities, are educated with children who are not handicapped; and that special classes, separate schooling, or other removal of handicapped children from the regular education environment occurs only when the nature or severity of the handicapped is such that education in regular classes with the use of supplementary aids and services cannot be achieved satisfactorily; and, establish procedures to insure that testing and evaluation materials and procedures utilized for the purposes of classification and placement of handicapped children will be selected and administered so as not to be racially or culturally discriminatory.

Whereas the actions taken at the State and national levels over the past few years have brought substantial progress, the parents of a handicapped child or a handicapped child himself must still too often be told that adequate funds do not exist to assure that child the availability of a free appropriate public education. The courts have stated that the lack of funding may not be used as an excuse for failing to provide educational services. Yet, the most recent statistics provided by the Bureau of Education for the Handicapped estimate that of the more than 8 million children (between birth and twenty-one years of age) with handicapping conditions requiring special education and related services, only 3.9 million such children are receiving an appropriate education. 1.75 million handicapped children are receiving no educational services at all and 2.5 million handicapped children are receiving an inappropriate education. (Table 1 contains the estimated number of handicapped children served and unserved, by type of handicap.)

TABLE 1 Estimated Number of Children with Disabilities Served and Unserved by Type of Disability 1974–75

	1974–75 SERVED (PROJECTED)	1974–75 UNSERVED	TOTAL HANDICAPPED CHILDREN, SERVED AND UNSERVED	PERCENT SERVED	PERCENT UNSERVED
Total age 0–19	3,947,000	3,939,000	7,886,000	50	50
Total age 6 to 19	3,687,000	3,062,000	6,699,000	55	45
Total age 0–5	260,000	927,000	1,187,000	22	78
Speech impaired	1,850,000	443,000	2,293,000	81	19
Mentally retarded	1,250,000	257,000	1,507,000	83	17
Learning disabilities	235,000	1,731,000	1,966,000	12	88
Emotionally disturbed	230,000	1,080,000	1,310,000	18	82
Orthopedically and other health impaired	235,000	93,000	328,000	72	28
Deaf	35,000	14,000	49,000	71	29
Hard of hearing	60,000	268,000	328,000	18	82
Visually handicapped	39,000	27,000	66,000	59	41
Deaf-blind and other multi-handicapped	13,000	27,000	40,000	33	67

Source: Bureau of Education for the Handicapped, U.S. Office of Education. (Note that the term *orthopedically impaired* is used in place of *crippled* to conform with legislative change made by S.6.)

The long range implications of these statistics are that public agencies and taxpayers will spend billions of dollars over the lifetimes of these individuals to maintain such persons as dependents and in a minimally acceptable lifestyle. With proper education services, many would be able to become productive citizens, contributing to society instead of being forced to remain burdens. Others, through such services, would increase their independence, thus reducing their dependence on society.

There is no pride in being forced to receive economic assistance. Not only does this have negative effects upon the handicapped person, but it has far-reaching effects for such person's family.

Providing educational services will ensure against persons needlessly being forced into institutional settings. One need only look at public residential institutions to find thousands of persons whose families are no longer able to care for them and who themselves have received no educational services.

Billions of dollars are expended each year to maintain persons in these subhuman conditions. This Nation has long embraced a philosophy that the right to a free appropriate public education is basic to equal opportunity and is vital to secure the future and the prosperity of our people. It is contradictory to that philosophy when that right is not assured equally to all groups of people within the Nation. Certainly the failure to provide a right to education to handicapped children cannot be allowed to continue.

Parents of handicapped children all too frequently are not able to advocate the right of their children because they have been erroneously led to believe that their children will not be able to lead meaningful lives. However, over the past few years, parents of handicapped children have begun to recognize that their children are being denied services which are guaranteed under the Constitution. It should not, however, be necessary for parents throughout the country to continue utilizing the courts to assure themselves a remedy. It is this Committee's belief that the Congress must take a more active role under its responsibility for equal protection of the laws to guarantee that handicapped children are provided equal educational opportunity. It can no longer be the policy of the Government to merely establish an unenforceable goal requiring all children to be in school. S.6 takes positive necessary steps to ensure that the rights of children and their families are protected.

****

ELIGIBILITY

The Individuals with Disabilities Education Act requires states to ensure that special education and related services will be provided for all children with disabilities. The law mandates that children with disabilities aged 3 to 21 (inclusive) be provided with programs appropriate to individual needs.[15] IDEA also permits and will provide funding assistance for any district that extends that age category to include children from birth to age 3.

However, determining who receives service under IDEA is not as simple as it might seem. The statute defines a *child with disabilities* as one with "mental retardation, hearing impairments including deafness, speech or language impairments, visual impairments, autism, traumatic brain injury, other health impairments, or specific learning disabilities; and who by reason thereof need[s] special education and related services."[16] Somewhere around 10 percent of the school-age population meet the criteria for service.[17]

IDEA assigns considerations of eligibility to a "multiple-disciplinary team" (M-team). In other words, the school must assemble a team of teachers and evaluators to consider the child's current functioning, identify strengths and weaknesses, identify any unmet educational needs, and make recommendations for meeting those needs. The team must be comprised of individuals with expertise in the disability area or area that the school suspects the child to exhibit. In order to ensure that decisions are founded on valid data, the M-team must evaluate the child and consider that child's skills in relation to the law. In essence, the M-team serves as a gatekeeping body. Its members determine whether a child meets or fails criteria for eligibility for service. One of the M-team's primary responsibilities is to identify under which specified disability or disabilities a child demonstrates the need for special education and related services. However, it should be noted that children do not qualify simply by reason of exhibiting a disability. Rather, that disability must translate into the need for educational services not provided as a matter of course in the conventional classroom. In other words, in order to qualify for special education and related services under IDEA, a child must demonstrate that his or her disability hinders educational progress. Therefore, although many children may require accommodations to be successful in regular education, not all of them will receive services under IDEA because they do not exhibit needs exceptional enough to meet the eligibility requirements of the act.

This process of categorization and labelling causes a number of problems. First, in order to qualify for services, a child must be classified according to one of the listed disabilities. The school district must affix a label to the child. Labeling children often stigmatizes them. The focus shifts to the label and obscures the child as a unique individual with unique needs. The school begins to deal with a "learning disabled child" rather than educating "Judy." In addition, schools are forced to fit children into one of these categories and are then asked to disregard those same categories when determining the child's programming and placement. Further, many children clearly exhibit multiple characteristics that implicate a number of categories, thus making it difficult to place them in one position or an another or even to identify a primary disability. For some of these children, the possibility exists that because they do not fit neatly into one category or another, they receive no services under IDEA.

Another problem related to this initial labelling process is the referral procedure that initiates the M-team evaluation. Most referral procedures require the referring person to identify the suspected disability area from a list of those specified in IDEA. This initial suspicion is used to assign professionals to the M-team. However, if the referring person indicates the wrong category, the child may be improperly evaluated. This error may lead to prolonging the evaluation time in order to allow for more and more experts to be added to the M-team for additional assessments. In the alternative, the child may be declared ineligible for services based on the disability suspected and then be re-referred later for another evaluation for a different disability. This process may occur several times if the child continues to have difficulty in school. The opposite problem may also arise. If the referring person checks numerous categories in the hopes of catching the right one, the child will have to submit to numerous assessments, some of them unnecessary, conducted by each assigned M-team member. Such evaluations are time consuming and may make meeting the required 90-day limit difficult.

After being categorized, the child must jump an additional hurdle in order to receive services. It must be demonstrated that a child's particular disability has so impaired the traditional learning processes that special education is required. For example, a child who has diabetes and needs only insulin injections to cope with his or her condition may be considered "disabled." However, that child would not be qualified or eligible under IDEA because that "disability" presents no need for special education.[18] Another example is a child who has a hearing impairment that is not substantial enough to significantly impact learning. Such a child would not qualify for services or be categorized as disabled under IDEA.[19]

Litigation relating to eligibility has posed the logical question of whether it must be proven that the child will benefit from special education before he or she is eligible to receive services under IDEA. This issue was presented to the First Circuit Court of Appeals in the case of *Timothy W. v. Rochester School District*.[20] In this case, a child who was severely disabled was denied services by the school district under a claim that he was allegedly unable to benefit from services provided in special education, i.e., the child was severely disabled and thus probably would not benefit from traditional educational services. The district court found that the school district was not obligated to provide services to the child because the legislature could not have mandated it to do a futile act. The First Circuit Court of Appeals reversed that decision and determined that traditional educability was not an eligibility requirement under IDEA. In essence, IDEA followed the zero-reject principle—that is, Congress intended every child to be served under the act and, in fact, those children with severe and profound disabilities were given first priority by Congress.

Although the holding in *Timothy W.* seems to indicate that no child with a disability can be excluded from the benefits of IDEA, there still remains the nagging question of whether some child may be found too severe to be covered by the act. Timothy W. was very severely disabled and profoundly mentally retarded. However, the court noted that there was considerable evidence that he "is aware of his surrounding environment, makes or attempts to make purposeful movements, responds to tactile stimulation, responds to his mother's voice and touch, recognizes familiar voices, responds to noises, and parts his lips when spoon fed."[21] He had educational needs, defining education broadly in terms of self-sufficiency skills.

There lingers a question, however, of what a court would do if a child is nonresponsive or unaware of his or her surroundings. The First Circuit referred to the case of *Parks v. Pavkovic*[22] in which the Seventh Circuit Court of Appeals speculated about a hypothetical case of a child who was in a coma and might be uneducable. Although the First Circuit found these judicial opinions irrelevant since Timothy W. was not in a coma, there remains a question of whether some child might be so unresponsive as to be deemed to have no educational needs, even using a broad definition of education.

Such a situation was presented to the Second Level Appeal Panel in the State of Illinois before *Timothy W.* The panel determined the eligibility of a child who was 6 years old, had remained under water for five minutes, and was in a comatose or semicomatose state. Five years after the accident, the child, who had only reflexive responses, was seeking special education services. The state-level review panel found the child was not eligible for special education because he did not have adequate cognitive power to benefit from the education—in essence, the child was so nonresponsive that he had no educational needs. The district's decision to discontinue evaluative procedures because of the lack of demonstrable cognitive functioning was found to be justified in light of the continued prolonged static condition. The panel found that the services required were not educational in nature since the child was nonresponsive and not able to be educated. Thus, here the court found educability was an eligibility requirement.[23] However, in 1990, OSERS reached a different result when it ruled that a school district must provide services to a comatose child.[24] Therefore, it remains uncertain whether the zero-reject principle is truly absolute.

TIMOTHY W. v. ROCHESTER SCHOOL DISTRICT
875 F.2d 954 (1st Cir. 1989)

BROWNES, Circuit Judge

I. BACKGROUND

Timothy W. was born two months prematurely on December 8, 1975, with severe respiratory problems, and shortly thereafter experienced an intracranial hemorrhage, subdural effusions, seizures, hydrocephalus, and meningitis. As a result, Timothy is multiply handicapped and profoundly mentally retarded. He suffers from complex developmental disabilities, spastic quadriplegia, cerebral palsy, seizure disorder and cortical blindness. His mother attempted to obtain appropriate services for him, and while he did receive some services from the Rochester Child Development Center, he did not receive any educational program from the Rochester School District when he became of school age.

. . . .

. . . . In a meeting on March 7, 1980, the school district decided that Timothy was not educationally handicapped—that since his handicap was so severe he was not "capable of benefitting" from an education, and therefore was not entitled to one. During 1981 and 1982, the school district did not provide Timothy with any educational program.

. . . .

In response to a letter from Timothy's attorney, on January 17, 1984, the school district's placement team met. . . . The placement team recommended that Timothy be placed at the Child Development Center so that he could be provided with a special education program. The Rochester School Board, however, refused to authorize the placement team's recommendation to provide educational services for Timothy. . . .

On November 17, 1984, Timothy filed a complaint in the United States District Court. . . .

. . . .

On July 15, 1988, the district court rendered its opinion. . . . The court made rulings of law and findings of fact. It first ruled that "under EAHCA [the Education for All Handicapped Children Act], an initial determination as to the child's ability to benefit from special education, must be made in order for a handicapped child to qualify for education under the Act." After noting that the New Hampshire statute (RSA 186-C) was intended to implement the EAHCA, the court held: "Under New Hampshire law, an initial decision must be made concerning the ability of a handicapped child to benefit from special education before an entitlement to the education can exist." The court then reviewed the materials, reports and testimony and found that "Timothy W. is not capable of benefitting from special education. . . . As a result, the defendant [school district] is not obligated to provide special education under either EAHCA [the federal statute] or RSA 186-C [the New Hampshire statute]." Timothy W. has appealed this order. . . .

****

II. THE LANGUAGE OF THE ACT

A. The Plain Meaning of the Act Mandates a Public Education for All Handicapped Children

The Education for All Handicapped Children Act, [hereinafter the Act], 20 U.S.C. §§ 1400 et seq., was enacted in 1975 to ensure that handicapped children receive an education which is appropriate to their unique needs. In assessing the plain meaning of the Act, we first look to its title: The Education for *All* Handicapped Children Act (emphasis added). The Congressional Findings section of the Act states that there were eight million handicapped children, that more than half of them did not receive appropriate educational services, and that one million were ex-

cluded entirely from the public school system. 20 U.S.C. § 1400(b)(1), (3), and (4). Given these grim statistics, Congress concluded that "State and local educational agencies have a responsibility to provide education for *all* handicapped children . . . ." 20 U.S.C. § 1400 (b)(8) (emphasis added). . . .

The Act's mandatory provisions require that for a state to qualify for financial assistance, it must have "in effect a policy which assures *all* handicapped children the right to a free appropriate education" 20 U.S.C. § 1412(1) (emphasis added). The state must "set forth in detail policies and procedures which the State will undertake . . . to assure that—there is established a goal of providing full educational opportunity to *all* handicapped children . . . [and that] a free appropriate public education will be available for *all* handicapped children between the ages of three and eighteen . . . not later than September 1, 1978, and for *all* handicapped children between the ages of three and twenty-one . . . not later than September 1, 1980 . . . ." 20 U.S.C. § 1412 (2)(A) and (B) (emphasis added). The state must also assure that "*all* children residing in the State who are handicapped, *regardless of the severity of their handicap*, and who are in need of special education and related services are identified, located, and evaluated . . . ." 20 U.S.C. § 1412(2)(C) (emphasis added). *See also* 20 U.S.C. § 1414(a)(1)(A). The Act further requires a state to:

> establish[ ] priorities *for providing a free appropriate public education to all handicapped children, . . . first with respect to handicapped children who are not receiving an education, and second* with respect to handicapped children within each disability, with the most severe handicaps *who are receiving an inadequate education . . .*
> 20 U.S.C. §1412(3) (emphasis added). See also 20 U.S.C. § 1414 (a)(1)(C).

Thus not only are severely handicapped children not excluded from the Act, but the most severely handicapped are actually given *priority* under the Act.

****

The language of the Act could not be more unequivocal. The statute is permeated with the words "*all* handicapped children" whenever it refers to the target population. It never speaks of any exceptions for severely handicapped children. . . . Nor is there any language whatsoever which requires as a prerequisite to being covered by the Act, that a handicapped child must demonstrate that he or she will "benefit" from the educational program. Rather, the Act speaks of the *state's* responsibility to design a special education and related services program that will meet the unique "needs" of all handicapped children. The language of the Act in its entirety makes clear that a "zero-reject" policy is at the core of the Act, and that no child, regardless of the severity of his or her handicap, is to ever again be subjected to the deplorable state of affairs which existed at the time of the Act's passage, in which millions of handicapped children received inadequate education or none at all. In summary, the Act mandates an appropriate public education for all handicapped children, regardless of the level of achievement that such children might attain.

B. Timothy W.: A Handicapped Child Entitled to an Appropriate Education

Given that the Act's language mandates that all handicapped children are entitled to a free appropriate education, we must next inquire if Timothy W. is a handicapped child, and if he is, what constitutes an appropriate education to meet his unique needs.

(1) *handicapped children:*

****

There is no question that Timothy W. fits within the Act's definition of a handicapped child: he is multiply handicapped and profoundly mentally retarded. He has been described as suffering from severe spasticity, cerebral palsy, brain damage, joint contractures, cortical blindness, is not ambulatory, and is quadriplegic.

(2) *appropriate public education:*

The Act and the implementing regulations define a "free appropriate publiceducation" to mean "special education and related services which are provided at public expense . . . [and] are provided in conformity with an individualized education program." 34 C.F.R. §300.4; 20 U.S.C. § 1401(a)(18).

****

The record shows that Timothy W. is a severely handicapped and profoundly retarded child in need of special education and related services. Much of the expert testimony was to the effect that he is aware of his surrounding environment, makes or attempts to make purposeful movements, responds to tactile stimulation, responds to his mother's voice and touch, recognizes familiar voices, responds to

noises, and parts his lips when spoon fed. The record contains testimony that Timothy W.'s needs include sensory stimulation, physical therapy, improved head control, socialization, consistency in responding to sound sources, and partial participation in eating. The educational consultants who drafted Timothy's individualized education program recommended that Timothy's special education program should include goals and objectives in the areas of motor control, communication, socialization, daily living skills, and recreation. The special education and related services that have been recommended to meet Timothy W.'s needs fit well within the statutory and regulatory definitions of the Act.

****

III. LEGISLATIVE HISTORY

An examination of the legislative history reveals that Congress intended the Act to provide a public education for all handicapped children, without exception . . . .

****

IV. CASE LAW

****

C. Education Is Broadly Defined

The courts have also made clear that education for the severely handicapped under the Act is to be broadly defined. In *Battle*, 629 F.2d at 275, the court stated that under the Act, the concept of education is necessarily broad with respect to severely and profoundly handicapped children, and "[w]here basic self help and social skills such as toilet training, dressing, feeding and communication are lacking, formal education begins at that point.". . .

****

D. Proof of Benefit Is Not Required

The district court relied heavily on *Board of Education of Hendrick Hudson Central School District v. Rowley*, 458 U.S. 176, 102 S. Ct. 3034, 73 L.Ed. 2d 690 (1982), in concluding that as a matter of law a child is not entitled to a public education unless he or she can benefit from it. The district court, however, has misconstrued Rowley. In that case, the Supreme Court held that a deaf child, who was an above average student and was advancing from grade to grade in a regular public school classroom, and who was already receiving substantial specialized instruction and related services, was not entitled, in addition, to a full time sign-language interpreter, because she was already benefitting from the special education and services she was receiving. The Court held that the school district was not required to *maximize* her educational achievement. It stated, "if personalized instruction is being provided with sufficient supportive services to permit the child to benefit from the instruction, . . . the child is receiving a 'free appropriate public education' as defined by the Act," *id.* at 189, 102 S. Ct. at 3042, and that "certainly the language of the statute contains no requirement . . . that States maximize the potential of handicapped children." *Id.* at 189, 102 S. Ct. at 3042.

Rowley focused on the *level* of services and the quality of programs that a *state* must provide, not the criteria for *access* to those programs. *Id.* at 207, 102 S. Ct. at 2051. The Court's use of "benefit" in *Rowley* was a substantive limitation placed on the state's choice of an educational program; it was not a license for the state to exclude certain handicapped children. In ruling that a state was not required to provide the maximum benefit possible, the Court was *not* saying that there must be proof that a child will benefit before the state is obliged to provide any education at all. Indeed, the Court in *Rowley* explicitly acknowledged Congress' intent to ensure public education to all handicapped children without regard to the level of achievement they might attain.

****

Rowley simply does not lend support to the district court's finding of a benefit/eligibility standard in the Act. As the Court explained, while the Act does not require a school to maximize a child's potential for learning, it does provide a "basic floor of opportunity" for the handicapped, consisting of "*access* to specialized instruction and related services." *Id.* at 201, 102 S. Ct. at 3048 (emphasis added). Nowhere does the Court imply that such a "floor" contains a trap door for the severely handicapped. . . .

****

V. CONCLUSION

The statutory language of the Act, its legislative history, and the case law construing it, mandate that all handicapped children, regardless of the severity of their handicap, are entitled to a public education. The district court erred in requiring a benefit/eligibility test as a prerequisite to implicating the Act. School districts cannot avoid the provisions of the Act by returning to the practices that were widespread prior to the Act's passage, and which indeed were the impetus for the Act's passage, of unilaterally excluding certain handicapped children from a public education on the ground that they are uneducable.

****

The judgment of the district court is reversed, judgment shall issue for Timothy W. . . .

(Footnotes omitted; all "emphasis added" notations were cited from the original opinion.)

— — — —

DOE v. THE BOARD OF EDUCATION OF
THE STATE OF CONNECTICUT
753 F. Supp. 65
(U.S. District Court, District of Connecticut 1990)

ELLEN B. BURNS, Chief Judge

****

BACKGROUND

The plaintiff attended regular classes and participated in the gifted program in Darien public schools from kindergarten through fifth grade. He did well academically in school during this time, . . . [I]n January, 1987 in his sixth grade, John had emotionally deteriorated to the extent that his parents found it necessary to hospitalize him at the New York Hospital-Cornell Medical Center ("NYH-CMC") on January 9, 1987. At the hearing, John's parents described his condition at this time as depressed and violent. . . .

As the time came for John to be released from the hospital, his educational placement became a concern to his parents and the Darien School Board. A Central Planning and Placement Team ("CPPT") meeting was held on May 6, 1987 to discuss the plaintiff's educational placement. . . . Mr. Laffer stated that the hospital recommended a residential treatment facility for John. His parents had already selected the Grove School in Madison, Connecticut and requested that this placement be fully funded by the school board as an educational, and not a medical, placement. The school board offered to pay for educational costs if the placement was for medical reasons. The board also informed John's parents that a determination had to be reached as to his need for special education and for an educational placement in a residential facility before the board could assume the cost of the placement. . . .

****

The first issue to be addressed in this review is whether the plaintiff is a handicapped child in need of special education. Under 20 U.S.C. § 1401(a)(1), the term "handicapped children" is defined as "mentally retarded, hard of hearing, deaf, speech or language impaired, visually handicapped, seriously emotionally disturbed, orthopedically impaired, or other health impaired children, or children with specific learning disabilities, who by reason thereof require special education and related services." Federal regulations define the term "seriously emotionally disturbed" as

> *a condition exhibiting one or more of the following characteristics over a long period of time and to a marked degree, which adversely affects educational performance:*
>
> *(A) An inability to learn which cannot be explained by intellectual, sensory, or health factors;*
>
> *(B) An inability to build or maintain satisfactory interpersonal relationships with peers and teachers;*
>
> *(C) A general pervasive mood of unhappiness or depression; or*
>
> *(E) A tendency to develop physical symptoms or fears associated with personal or school problems.*
>
> *(ii) The term includes children who are schizophrenic. The term does not include children who are socially maladjusted, unless it is determined that they are seriously emotionally disturbed.*
>
> *34 C.F.R. § 300.5(b)(8).*

****

The plaintiff claims that he was a "socially and emotionally maladjusted child," and an "exceptional child," in need of special education at a residential facility. . . .

****

Despite the evidence of the plaintiff's behavioral difficulties, this court concludes for the following reasons that he was not a handicapped child entitled to special education. The plaintiff had some emotional difficulties, but these difficulties did not adversely affect his educational performance as required by federal and state law. The plaintiff's academic performance (both his grades and his achievement test results) before, during, and after his hospitalization were satisfactory or above. In addition, two of the plaintiff's sixth grade teachers from Darien testified that they did not notice the plaintiff had any behavior problems, other than some problems with organization. 4/5/88 Hearing Transcript at 126-42, 158-65. In fact, Dr. Picker's psychological evaluation states "it does not appear that [John's] behavioral difficulties in school have contributed to academic underachievement, the very preoccupation which consumes his conscious ideation." Board Exhibit 23 at 5. On cross-examination at the hearing, Dr. Tessler agreed with this conclusion. Hearing Transcript 3/10/88 at 44. Dr. Tessler further stated on cross-examination that "[u]p to now, he has been able to do remarkably well [in school] despite his depression." *Id.* at 59. Mr. Chorney similarly testified on cross-examination that John liked school, liked succeeding, and that his emotional problems had not significantly interfered with his academics. Hearing Transcript 3/18/88 at 34-35. Dr. Seen, the Darien school psychologist, evaluated the plaintiff in August, 1987. Board Exhibit 32. Dr. Seen found John's behavior initially somewhat anxious, but generally appropriate. Dr. Seen stated that he did not believe John's behavior was interfering with his learning. Board Exhibit 37. In sum, there was sufficient evidence presented to the state hearing officer from which she reasonably concluded that the plaintiff's education was not significantly impeded or adversely affected by his behavior problems and that he was therefore not entitled to special education. Hence, the hearing officer did not misapply Connecticut law, nor did the hearing officer's decision deny the plaintiff his right to a "free and appropriate education."

****

CONCLUSION

This court agrees with the hearing officer's decision that the plaintiff was not an "exceptional child" in need of special education. For the foregoing reasons, the decision of the state hearing officer is affirmed.

SO ORDERED.

(Footnotes omitted.)

— — — —

DOE v. BELLEVILLE PUBLIC SCHOOL DISTRICT NO. 118
672 F. Supp. 342
(U.S. District Court, Southern District of Illinois 1987)

FOREMAN, Chief Judge:

****

Plaintiff Johnny Doe is a six-year-old male child who was diagnosed as having Hemophilia B as an infant. Subsequent to that diagnosis, made in August of 1986, he was diagnosed as having Acquired Immune Deficiency Syndrome (AIDS). During the 1986-87 school year, Johnny attended kindergarten at a public school in Harmony School District No. 175. Sometime before the end of that school year, Johnny and his mother moved to a new school district where, by virtue of the timing of the move, he was required to enroll in the first grade in Belleville District No. 118.

****

. . . . EAHCA [now IDEA] defines "handicapped children" as children who are:

mentally retarded, hard of hearing, deaf, speech or language impaired, visually handicapped, seriously emotionally disturbed, orthopedically impaired, or other health impaired children, or children with specific learning disabilities, who by reason thereof require special education and related services.
20 U.S.C. § 1401(a)(1).

In this case the parties agree that the only category into which Johnny fits is that of "other health impaired children." That phrase is defined as children who have:

[1] limited strength, vitality or alertness due to chronic or acute health problems such as a heart condition,

tuberculosis, rheumatic fever, nephritis, asthma, sickle-cell anemia, hemophilia, epilepsy, lead poisoning, leukemia, or diabetes, which adversely affects a child's educational performance.
34 C.F.R. § 300.5(b)(7).

. . . . Here, the record reveals virtually no evidence that plaintiff suffers from limited strength, vitality, or alertness. Furthermore, given such evidence as is in the record of Johnny's limited strength, there is virtually no evidence that this limitation has adversely affected his educational performance.

****

Based on the Department of Education's opinions and the tenor of the statutory language, the Court concludes that EAHCA would apply to AIDS victims only if their physical condition is such that it adversely affects their educational performance; i.e., their ability to learn and to do the required classroom work. There is no such showing at the present time, and it seems clear that the only reason for the Board's determination that Johnny needs "special education" is the fact that he has a contagious disease—AIDS. In the Court's opinion, given the facts of this case as they now exist, the provisions of EAHCA would not apply to the plaintiff at this time.

****

For the above-stated reasons, the Court is of the opinion that defendants' Motion to Dismiss should be, and hereby is, DENIED.

IT IS SO ORDERED.

(Footnotes omitted.)

— — — —

KELBY v. MORGAN HILL UNIFIED SCHOOL DISTRICT
959 F.2d 240 (Ninth Circuit 1992)

Before WISDOM, . . . BREEZER and TROTT, Circuit Judges.

****

The Kelbys appeal the district court's judgment affirming the school district's determination that Richard Kelby was ineligible to receive special educa-

tion benefits pursuant to the Individuals with Disabilities Education Act (IDEA), 20 U.S.C. §§ 1400–1485 (1988). We have jurisdiction and we affirm.

I.

In 1988, Richard enrolled in a regular fifth grade class within the Morgan Hill Unified School District.

His record there, as in his previous school district, reflects poor grades, behavior problems and inconsistent work habits. The Kelbys found Richard's poor performance particularly troubling because tests have shown he has above-average intelligence. At the beginning of Richard's sixth-grade year, the Kelbys requested an assessment of and special education placement for Richard.

A school district IEP team evaluated Richard, as did an independent psychologist employed by the Kelbys. The two assessments disagreed as to the basic cause of Richard's problems. The independent psychologist, Dr. Mark Steinberg, concluded that Richard had a specific learning disability and deficits in visual memory and visual motor domain areas. The school district concluded that Richard had a behavior problem not caused by a learning disability. The school district determined that Richard was not eligible for special education assistance.

The Kelbys disagreed and requested a due process hearing. . . .

****

The IDEA's coverage includes children with "specific learning disabilities . . . who, by reason thereof require special education and related services." 20 U.S.C. § 1401(a)(1) (Supp. II 1990). State regulations define the covered disabilities, and these regulations may go beyond the federal minimum. *Town of Burlington v. Dept. of Educ.*, 736 F.2d 733. . . .

****

The Kelbys argue that given Richard's above-average I.Q. score, his below-average grades indicate that he is not receiving the "appropriate education" the IDEA guarantees to each child with a disability. The point that this argument misses is that having an unsuccessful educational experience does not, in itself, qualify a student for special education. Not every student with a learning difficulty has a "specific learning disability." As set forth in the IDEA and implementing law, a student has a specific learning disability if three factors exist: a relevant "severe discrepancy" between ability and achievement, the discrepancy must result from a disorder in a psychological process, and the discrepancy must not be correctable through regular education. *See* Cal. Educ. Code § 56337 (West 1989).

IV.

The school district's argument focuses on its experts' evaluations and on teachers' comments about Richard's behavior problems and missing homework. The IEP team determined that there was not a statutorily defined "severe" discrepancy between Richard's achievement test scores and his ability test scores. A speech and language pathologist from the school district assessed Richard and found that he did not have auditory processing problems that hindered his ability to learn in a regular classroom. . . .

The California and federal regulations provide that "no single score" shall be used to determine eligibility for special education. Cal. Code Regs. tit.5 § 3030(j)(4); 34 C.F.R. 300.532(3)(d). Therefore, the district court appropriately considered CHC's assessment with the school district's assessments and other evidence. . . . The preponderance of the evidence supports the finding that Richard's learning difficulties are not so severe that he cannot benefit adequately from the regular educational program. The district court's judgment is not clearly erroneous.

****

The judgment of the district court is AFFIRMED. (Footnotes omitted.)

ADDITIONAL COMMENTARY

1. A 1987 Office of Special Education Programs (OSEP) memo stated that the district's practice of labeling children with disabilities must be limited to eligibility requirements and could not be carried forth for determination of services and programs for children with similar disabilities. *Richards*, 211 E.H.L.R. 440 (OSEP 1987). Many states have resolved the problem of having to categorize special education students who have more than one disability by classifying the student according to the most disabling condition. For example, a student whose disruptive behavior rather than learning disabilities were responsible for his failure to succeed academically was classified as having emotional disorders rather than as having learning disabilities. However, for pur-

poses of placement and programming, the child's needs must be considered paramount rather than the label. *Maine-Endwell Central School District*, 502 E.L.H.R. 228 (S.E.A. 1981). *See also Garrick B. v. Curwensville Area School District*, 669 F. Supp. 705 (M.D. Pa. 1987).

2. In *Sequoia Union High School District*, 559 E.H.L.R. 133 (N.D. Cal. 1987), a student was determined not to be seriously emotionally disturbed but instead only socially maladjusted, and thus not eligible for services under IDEA. The student was a "punker" who demonstrated a problem with authority and social norms, had a low toleration for frustration, and was impulsive and manipulative. It was determined that his academic problems were due to truancy and substance abuse and not a disabling emotional disturbance.

3. A New Jersey hearing officer ruled that a child was severely emotionally disturbed based on an incident of alleged assault and previous behavioral history. It was noted, however, that an assault in isolation would not have been sufficient to warrant the label. *Hackensack Board of Education,* 16 E.H.L.R. 1299 (S.E.A. N.J. 1990).

4. A 1991 Office for Special Education and Rehabilitative Services (OSERS) statement explains that children with attention-deficit disorder (ADD) who are therefore in need of special education are eligible under IDEA under the categories of other health impairments, specific learning disability, or serious emotional disturbance. Therefore, a separate category for ADD is not necessary. Joint Policy Administration, 18 I.D.E.L.R. 116 (OSERS 1991); Parker, 18 I.D.E.L.R. 963 (OSEP 1992); *Loudoun County Public Schools,* 18 I.D.E.L.R. 1137 (S.E.A. Va. 1991).

5. The state of Massachusetts determined that it should err on the side of providing a child services when in doubt of whether the child was benefitting from the education provided. The state level review found that since the testimony concerning residual brain activity and purposeful behavior was inconclusive, the doubt must be resolved in favor of the student. The district was ordered to provide special education for one year with comprehensive monitoring, reporting, and assessment procedures. *Christopher C. v. Weston Public Schools*, Case No. 86-0531, 509 E.H.L.R. 154 (Mass. 1987).

6. Eligibility is clearly a decision that requires considerable educational expertise. Although courts will review a decision for procedural errors and to determine if there is evidence to support a determination, they will not make an initial determination of eligibility. See *Edwards v. Cleveland Heights-University Heights Board of Education,* 18 I.D.E.L.R. 507 (6th Cir. 1991); *Matter of Ruffel P.,* 582 N.Y.S.2d 631 (NY Fam. Ct. 1992).

APPROPRIATENESS

IDEA requires that a free appropriate education be provided to every student with disabilities eligible to receive services. Superficially, this mandate appears relatively straightforward. The simplicity of the mandate, however, has caused confusion among educators, and often conflict between educators and parents. In fact, the vast majority of due process procedures initiated involve a determination of what is an "appropriate education." What is "appropriate," of course, will differ with respect to each child, since appropriateness requires attention to the unique needs of each individual.

Statutory Definitions

The statute defines an appropriate education in very general terms. IDEA requires specially designed instruction to meet the particular needs of a child with disabilities, provided in conformity with an individual education program.[25]

The term "free appropriate public education" means special education and related services which (1) have been provided at public expense, under public supervision and direction, and without charge, (2) meet the standards of the State educational agency, (3) include an appropriate preschool, elementary, or secondary school education in the state involved, and (4) are provided in conformity with the individualized education program required under section 1414(a)(5) of this title.[26]

Section 504 and its regulations are often consulted in judicial attempts to interpret vague or ambiguous terminology in IDEA. In attempts to define "appropriate," however, Section 504 provides little additional clarity: "The provision of regular or special education and related aids and services that are designed to meet individual educational needs of handicapped persons as adequately as the needs of nonhandicapped persons are met, and are based upon adherence to procedures."[27] Thus, there are several vital aspects of the definition of "appropriate" provided in the statutes and regulations:

— Specially designed in conformity with an individual education plan
— Education as equally suitable as that offered to those without disabilities
— Based on proper evaluation
— Attention to the educational setting
— Devised with proper procedural safeguards

These phrases have not eliminated confusion in the schools and the courts. Before 1982, many interpretations of the appropriate requirement were offered; the extent of services provided to students with disabilities varied widely. On one end of the spectrum, some saw the requirement as necessitating only that the schools open enrollment to the public schools for students with disabilities. On the other end, some believed the requirement was to maximize the potential of students with disabilities. In the middle were those who believed the mandate was to spend an equal dollar amount on students with disabilities as students without disabilities. The Supreme Court ended this uncertainty when it decided *Board of Hendrick Hudson v. Rowley.*[28]

Rowley Definition

In *Rowley,* the Supreme Court adopted a definition of an "appropriate education." The Court found that "if personalized instruction [was] being provided with sufficient supportive services to permit the child to benefit from the instruction,"[29] the child was receiving the level of services required to be appropriate under the act. In addition, it provided a checklist for adequacy under the act. According to the Court, the school must provide services and instruction at public expense and under public supervision, meet the state's educational standards, approximate the grade levels used in the state's regular education, and comport with the child's IEP.

The Court described the proper judicial review process as a simple two-step process. "First, has the state complied with the procedures set forth in the Act? And second, is the individualized educational program developed through the Act's procedures reasonably calculated to enable the child to receive educational benefits?"[30] This review is more procedural than substantive. It may seem that the Court set forth no substantive standard prescribing the level of education in the Act: "[W]e do not attempt today to establish any one test for determining the adequacy of educational benefits conferred upon all children covered by the Act."[31] The Court, however, did set a general substantive standard—the child must be receiving those services necessary for him or her to receive educational benefits.

When the opinion was released, it was strongly criticized by the special education community:

> *Since the Supreme Court handed down its decision in Rowley, approximately 100 Education for All Handicapped Children Act cases have been decided by the lower courts. . . . Those critics who found Rowley's implications harsh will be relieved to find that courts have not sacrificed services for the handicapped through strict application of Rowley's minimum standard.*[32]

Congress has not amended the federal statute to increase the required level of educational services or the level of scrutiny a court can undertake in reviewing the educational services provided. With the lapse of more than 10 years since *Rowley* was decided, it appears that no amendment is eminent.

State Standards

The definition of an appropriate education includes the requirement that the special education and related services provided must "meet the standards of the State educational agency."[33] In *Rowley,* the Court emphasized that this standard constitutes a federal floor of opportunity, not a ceiling on the right to educational services.[34] As long as a state meets the minimal requirements of the act, it is free to impose higher standards on itself. However, a state standard that is weaker, or provides fewer rights to the student with disabilities, must be set aside in favor of the basic floor of opportunity guaranteed by the act.

In a number of states[35] statutes have been interpreted to impose state substantive standards that are higher than the federal requirements. For example, the Third Circuit Court of Appeals upheld a parent's preference for a residential placement by applying New Jersey's higher substantive standard as the one to "best achieve educational success." The court noted that the placement proposed by the district would have satisfied the lower *Rowley* standard, but not the higher state standard. This practice of providing students with a higher operative standard of "appropriate" provides students with the greatest access to services. However, states may, as New Jersey did, alter their statutes or regulations to conform to the lower standard set forth in *Rowley.*

A second controversy involving the requirement of state standards involves state payment of tuition for educational facilities that do not meet state certification standards. In *School Committee of the Town of Burlington v. Department of Education of Massachusetts,*[36] the Supreme Court held that parents are entitled to reimbursement for expenses incurred for a uni-

lateral placement that, after review, is determined to have been necessary to provide an appropriate education for their child. Until recently, the courts have not been in agreement regarding whether parents may be granted reimbursement for expenses of a placement at an unapproved school. Most courts have held that reimbursement is not available in these situations.[37] However, the Supreme Court recently resolved this issue in *Florence County School District v. Carter.*[38] In *Carter,* the Supreme Court approved reimbursement for parents at an unapproved school, distinguishing a 1987 precedent that had been read to preclude such reimbursement.[39] There, the Court relied on a different section of the statute and found that the state could not place a child in an unapproved facility but parents could. As stated by the Fourth Circuit Court of Appeals and affirmed by the Supreme Court:

> *Congress clearly envisioned that § 1413(a)(4)(B), and its requirement that private schools receiving funds under the Act meet state educational standards, would apply only when the child is placed in the private school by the state or local school system. The Act itself simply imposes no requirement that the private school be approved by the state in parent-placement reimbursement cases.*[40]

Practical Applications of Appropriateness

Since *Rowley,* the courts have been reviewing appropriateness of placements to determine only if instruction would be provided with enough support services to permit a child to receive educational benefits. In undertaking this review, the Supreme Court's standard, however, provides minimal information and does little to help an individualized education program team devise an IEP and agree on the appropriate level of services to be provided to a particular student.

In considering program and placement options for a particular student, it is important to keep in mind that in nearly every situation, more than one program or placement may be appropriate.

The key consideration when selecting from the array of appropriate program or placement options is that the determination of appropriateness be made on an individualized basis. This requirement forms the cornerstone of IDEA. Individualized determination of services is inherent in the term *IEP*. It is implicit in the procedural safeguards, the evaluation requirements, the determination of the least restrictive environment, and the review cycles contained in the act. In addition, IDEA even states that instruction must be "specially designed . . . to meet the unique needs of a child with a disability."[41] This language implies that individual determinations of appropriateness need to be made to ascertain and meet the particular needs of each student. The possible options for a child generally range from some programs that are minimally appropriate to clearly superb placement/program options. The courts have stated clearly that the IEP team does not have to select the best option or select only from options that maximize the student's potential.[42] The problem, then, becomes one of selecting from this array.

At this point in the process, other considerations enter into the analysis—including least restrictive environment, services available, and cost to the district. However, each of these determinations is predicated on an initial determination of appropriateness for the individual child. The array of choices *must first* be narrowed by the baseline of appropriateness.

The emphasis on individual determinations of appropriateness can never be overstated. As was discussed in the section on eligibility, since *all* children with disabilities must be served by school districts, the extent and type of services required will vary significantly. For some children, an appropriate education will be comprised entirely of rudimentary self-sufficiency skills.[42] Other children's needs may be related to behavioral and social issues, whereas others

may only need adaptations or assistance to achieve through a standard curriculum. IDEA mandates appropriate services to *all* children with disabilities; the IEP team must determine what each child's educational needs are and devise a program calculated for the child to make progress toward achieving his or her goals.

A program that is "reasonably calculated to provide educational benefits" was fairly easy for the Court to consider in *Rowley*. The similar decision for many IEP teams is not so simple. The courts have not offered much guidance as to how to determine whether a program is reasonably calculated to provide educational benefits. Some general considerations can be gleaned from the cases.

The IEP must address each of the student's disabling conditions.[44] A student should be making progress in these areas. Assessing when sufficient progress is being made is difficult and should be made on an individual basis. Courts have been willing to look at a child's progress over time to make this determination. It cannot be made in a vacuum; it requires the court to take a careful look at the child's past progress or lack thereof. Where there has been no experience with a proposed program, teacher qualifications, quality of IEP, and progress of other similar students can be used to assess appropriateness.[45] This substantive review seeks to predict whether the anticipated progress is likely to be meaningful as opposed to trivial. Such determination is the most detailed substantive review a court will undertake. Stated negatively, programs that have led to regression or stagnation have been determined to be inappropriate.[46] Stated in a positive manner, in evaluating an IEP to determine if it has been appropriate, the student should have made meaningful progress under the program.[47]

In essence, the IEP team has a threefold task. First, it must structure a program to address the unmet needs identified by the multidisciplinary team. Once the components of an appropriate program have been outlined, the team must then consider in which setting or settings the IEP can be implemented. Third, after identifying in which settings an appropriate program can be delivered, the team must consider which option represents the least restrictive environment for the child. The least restrictive environment (LRE) is that setting that "to the maximum extent appropriate" allows the student to interact with nondisabled peers.[48] In making a placement selection, the IEP team must pay strict attention to this requirement. However, note that the term *least restrictive environment* has no generic meaning. It only comes into focus when considering an individual child and what constitutes an appropriate education for that child. Observe that the regulations specifically modify the LRE requirement by the word *appropriate*. Therefore, even though a regular class placement may be appropriate and least restrictive for most students, some students will actually be restricted educationally by that setting. (Least restrictive environment is discussed in detail in a subsequent section.) Suffice it to say for now that from the array of least restrictive appropriate placement options, the one that maximizes interaction with nondisabled peers must be selected.

Cost to the District

After the IEP team has outlined the components of an appropriate program, identified those placement options in which the plan may be implemented, and determined which placement(s) meet the LRE requirement, then and only then may the district consider service availability and program cost. In other words, if the IEP team concludes that two options are equally appropriate as well as equally provide for interaction with nondisabled peers, the district may choose the less costly placement.

Courts have recognized that "cost can be a legitimate consideration when devising an appropriate program for individual students. Nevertheless, cost considerations are only relevant when choosing between several options, all of which offer an 'appropriate' education."[49] IDEA does not require that a district provide an unlimited commitment of resources to meet the needs of a student who is disabled. It must be emphasized, however, that cost can be a determinant only when more than one possible least restrictive appropriate placement option exists. Neither low nor high cost can make an inappropriate placement appropriate.

THE HENDRICK HUDSON CENTRAL SCHOOL DISTRICT
v. ROWLEY
Supreme Court of the United States, 1982

Justice REHNQUIST delivered the opinion of the Court.

****

II.

This case arose in connection with the education of Amy Rowley, a deaf student ... in the Hendrick Hudson Central School District. ... Amy has minimal residual hearing and is an excellent lipreader. During the year before she began attending Furnace Woods, a meeting between her parents and school administrators resulted in a decision to place her in a regular kindergarten class in order to determine what supplemental services would be necessary to her education. ... At the end of the trial period it was determined that Amy should remain in the kindergarten class, but that she should be provided with an FM hearing aid which would amplify words spoken into a wireless receiver by the teacher or fellow students during certain classroom activities. Amy successfully completed her kindergarten year.

As required by the Act, an IEP was prepared for Amy during the fall of her first-grade year. The IEP provided that Amy should be educated in a regular classroom at Furnace Woods, should continue to use the FM hearing aid, and should receive instruction from a tutor for the deaf for one hour each day and from a speech therapist for three hours each week. The Rowleys agreed with the IEP but insisted that Amy also be provided with a qualified sign-language interpreter in all of her academic classes. Such an interpreter had been placed in Amy's kindergarten class for a two-week experimental period, but the interpreter had reported that Amy did not need his services at that time. . . .

When their request for an interpreter was denied, the Rowleys demanded and received a hearing before an independent examiner. . . . The examiner agreed with the administrators' determination that an interpreter was not necessary because "Amy was achieving educationally, academically, and socially" without such assistance. . . . Pursuant to the Act's provision for judicial review, the Rowleys then brought an action in the United States District Court for the Southern District of New York. . . .

The District Court found that . . . "[S]he performs better than the average child in her class and is advancing easily from grade to grade." *Id.* at 532. The disparity between Amy's achievement and her potential led the court to decide that she was not receiving a "free appropriate public education," which the court defined as "an opportunity to achieve [her] full potential commensurate with the opportunity provided to other children. *Id.* at 534. . . .

. . . .

We granted certiorari. . . . Such review requires us to consider two questions: What is meant by the Act's requirement of a "free appropriate public education"? And what is the role of state and federal courts in exercising the review granted by § 1415 of the Act? . . .

III.

A.

****

According to the definitions contained in the Act, a "free appropriate public education" consists of educational instruction specially designed to meet the unique needs of the handicapped child, supported by such services as are necessary to permit the child "to benefit" from the instruction. Almost as a checklist for adequacy under the Act, the definition also re-

quires that such instruction and services be provided at public expense and under public supervision, meet the State's educational standards, approximate the grade levels used in the State's regular education, and comport with the Child's IEP. Thus, if personalized instruction is being provided with sufficient supportive services to permit the child to benefit from the instruction, and the other items on the definitional checklist are satisfied, the child is receiving a "free appropriate public education" as defined by the Act.

****

Noticeably absent from the language of the statute is any substantive standard prescribing the level of education to be accorded handicapped children. Certainly the language of the statute contains no requirement like the one imposed by the lower courts—that States maximize the potential of handicapped children "commensurate with the opportunity provided to other children." 483 F. Supp. at 534. That standard was expounded by the District Court without reference to the statutory definitions or even to the legislative history of the Act. Although we find the statutory definition of "free appropriate education" to be helpful in our interpretation of the Act, there remains the question of whether the legislative history indicates a congressional intent that such education meet some additional substantive standard. For an answer, we turn to that history.

B.

****

. . . . By passing the Act, Congress sought primarily to make public education available to handicapped children. But in seeking to provide such access to public education, Congress did not impose upon the States any greater substantive educational standard than would be necessary to make such access meaningful. Indeed, Congress expressly "recognize[d] that in many instances the process of providing special education and related services to handicapped children is not guaranteed to produce any particular outcome." S. Rep. No. 94-168, *supra*, at 11, U.S. Code Cong. & Admin. News 1975, p. 1435. Thus, the intent of the Act was more to open the door of public education to handicapped children on appropriate terms than to guarantee any particular level of education once inside.

****

(ii)

Respondents contend that "the goal of the Act is to provide each handicapped child with an equal educational opportunity." Brief for Respondents 35. We think, however, that the requirement that a State provide specialized educational services to handicapped children generates no additional requirement that the services so provided be sufficient to maximize each child's potential "commensurate with the opportunity provided to other children." . . .

The educational opportunities provided by our public school systems undoubtedly differ from student to student, depending upon a myriad of factors that might affect a particular student's ability to assimilate information presented in the classroom. The requirement that States provide "equal" educational opportunities would thus seem to present an entirely unworkable standard requiring impossible measurements and comparisons. Similarly, furnishing handicapped children with only such services as are available to nonhandicapped children would in all probability fall short of the statutory requirement of "free appropriate public education"; to require, on the other hand, the furnishing of every special service necessary to maximize each handicapped child's potential is, we think, further than Congress intended to go. Thus to speak in terms of "equal" services in one instance given less than what is required by the Act and in another instance more. The theme of the Act is "free appropriate public education," a phrase which is too complex to be captured by the word "equal" whether one is speaking of opportunities or services.

****

C.

When the language of the Act and its legislative history are considered together, the requirements imposed by Congress become tolerably clear. Insofar as a State is required to provide a handicapped child with a "free appropriate public education," we hold that it satisfies this requirement by providing personalized instruction with sufficient support services to permit the child to benefit educationally from that instruction. Such instruction and services must be provided at public expense, must meet the State's educational standards, must approximate the grade levels used in the State's regular education, and must comport with the child's IEP. In addition, the IEP, and therefore the personalized instruction, should be formulated in accordance with the requirements of the Act and, if the child is being educated in the regular classrooms of the public education system, should be reasonably calculated to enable the child to achieve passing marks and advance from grade to grade.

IV.

A.

****

. . . [A] court's inquiry in suits brought under § 1415(e)(2) is twofold. First, has the State complied with the procedures set forth in the Act. And second, is the individualized educational program developed through the Act's procedures reasonably calculated to enable the child to receive educational benefits. If these requirements are met, the State has complied with the obligations imposed by Congress and the court can require no more.

B.

[4] In assuring that the requirements of the Act have been met, courts must be careful to avoid imposing their view of preferable educational methods upon the States. The primary responsibility for formulating the education to be accorded a handicapped child, and for choosing the educational method most suitable to the child's needs, was left by the Act to state and local educational agencies in cooperation with the parents or guardian of the child. . . .

We previously have cautioned that courts lack the "specialized knowledge and experience" necessary to resolve "persistent and difficult questions of educational policy." *San Antonio School District v. Rodriguez*, 411 U.S. 1, 42, 93 S. Ct. 1278, 1301, 26 L. Ed. 2d 16 (1973). . . .

VI.

[5] Applying these principles to the facts of this case, we conclude that the Court of Appeals erred in affirming the decision of the District Court. . . .

****

(Footnotes omitted.)

—　　—　　—　　—

POLK v. CENTRAL SUSQUEHANNA INTERMEDIATE UNIT 16
853 F.2d 171 (Third Circuit 1988)

BECKER, Circuit Judge.

****

II. FACTS & PROCEDURAL HISTORY

Christopher Polk is severely developmentally disabled. . . . Although Christopher is fourteen years old, he has the functional and mental capacity of a toddler. All parties agree that he required "related services" in order to learn. He receives special education from defendants, the Central Susquehanna Intermediate Unit #16 (the IU) and Central Columbia Area School District (the school district). . . . His education consists of learning basic life skills such as feeding himself, dressing himself, and using the toilet. . . .

Although the record is not clear on this point, until 1980, the defendants apparently provided Christopher with direct physical therapy from a licensed physical therapist. . . . Christopher no longer receives direct physical therapy from a physical therapist. Instead, a physical therapist comes once a month to train Christopher's teacher in how to integrate physical therapy with Christopher's education. . . .

****

[P]laintiffs have maintained that to comply with the EHA [Education of Handicapped Act] the defendants must provide, as part of Christopher's "free appropriate public education," one session a week with a licensed physical therapist.

****

V. PLAINTIFF'S SUBSTANTIVE CLAIM (THAT THE COURT MISAPPLIED THE LEGAL STANDARD FOR EVALUATING APPROPRIATE EDUCATION)

A. The Supreme Court's Opinion in *Rowley*

We begin our discussion of the substantive protections of the EHA with the Supreme Court's opinion in *Board of Education v. Rowley*, 458 U.S. 176, 102 S.Ct. 3034, 73 L.Ed.2d 690 (1982). . . .

****

. . . . The Court thus explained that the purpose of the Act was to provide a basic level of educational opportunity, not to provide the best education money can buy. *See id.* ("certainly the language of the statute contains no requirement . . . that states maximize the potential of handicapped children"); *id.* at 197 n. 21, 102 S.Ct. at 3046 n. 21 ("Whatever Congress meant by an 'appropriate' education, it is clear that it did not mean a potential-maximizing education."); *Muth v. Central Bucks School District*, 839 F.2d 113, 119 (3d Cir. 1988) (citing *Rowley*). . . .

. . . [T]he Supreme Court in *Rowley* did not abdicate responsibility for monitoring the substantive quality of education under the EHA. Instead, it held that the education must "provide educational benefit." The Court thus recognized that the substantive, independent judicial review envisioned by the EHA was not a hollow gesture. Instead, courts must ensure "a basic floor of opportunity" that is defined by an individualized program that confers benefit.

****

. . . [T]he facts of the case (including Amy Rowley's quite substantial benefit from her education) did not force the Court to confront squarely the fact that Congress cared about the quality of special education. In the case sub judice, however, the question of how much benefit is sufficient to be "meaningful" is inescapable. Therefore we must examine the Act's notion of "benefit" and apply a standard that is faithful to congressional intent and consistent with *Rowley*.

****

. . . . Our interpretation of "educational benefit" is informed by the text of the EHA and by the legislative history concerning the passage of the 1975 amendments. The self-defined purpose of the EHA is to provide "full educational opportunity to all handicapped children." 20 U.S.C. § 1412(2)(A). Similarly, the Senate Report on the 1975 amendments defined related services as "transportation, developmental, corrective, and supportive services . . . necessary for a handicapped child to fully benefit from special education." Sen.R.No. 168, 94th Cong., 1st Sess. at

42. . . . Although the Supreme Court has instructed that Congress did not intend to provide optimal benefit, the Act's use of the phrase "full educational opportunity" and the EHA's legislative history indicate an intent to afford more than a trivial amount of educational benefit.

****

Implicit in the legislative history's emphasis on self-sufficiency is the notion that states must provide some sort of meaningful education—more than mere access to the schoolhouse door. We acknowledge that self-sufficiency cannot serve as a substantive standard by which to measure the appropriateness of a child's education under the Act. *See Rowley*, 458 U.S. at 201 n. 23, 102 S.Ct. at 3048 n. 23. Indeed, Christopher Polk is not likely ever to attain this coveted status, no matter how excellent his educational program. Instead, we infer that the emphasis on self-sufficiency indicates in some respect the quantum of benefits the legislators anticipated: They must have envisioned that significant learning would transpire in the special education classroom— enough so that citizens who would otherwise become burdens on the state would be transformed into productive members of society. Therefore, the heavy emphasis in the legislative history on self-sufficiency as one goal of education, where possible,

suggests that the "benefit" conferred by the EHA and interpreted by *Rowley* must be more than de minimis.

****

4.

To summarize, in our view, the danger of the district court's formulation is that under its reading of *Rowley* the conferral of any benefit, no matter how small, could qualify as "appropriate education" under the EHA. Under the district court's approach, carried to its logical extreme, Christopher Polk would be entitled to no physical therapy because his occupational therapy offers him "some benefit." We do not believe that such a formulation reflects congressional intent in light of the importance of related services (particularly physical therapy) in the statutory and regulatory scheme. Just as Congress did not write a blank check, neither did it anticipate that states would engage in the idle gesture of providing special education designed to confer only trivial benefit. Put differently, and using *Rowley*'s own terminology, we hold that Congress intended to afford children with special needs an education that would confer meaningful benefit.

****

. . . . The judgment of the district court will therefore be reversed and the case remanded for further proceedings consistent with this opinion.

— — — —

ASHWAUBENON SCHOOL DISTRICT
18 IDELR 377 (1991)

****

I. SUMMARY OF THE CASE
On March 29, 1991, Mary Jo, on behalf of Todd, requested a due process hearing to resolve several issues concerning Todd's special education identification and placement at Pioneer School in the Ashwaubenon School District. The hearing was held . . . before Hearing Officer Dr. Craig Fiedler. . . .

****

II. STATEMENT OF ISSUES
A. Does the law require the School District to place Todd in the "most appropriate" integrated EMR program?

****

C. Does the law require the School District to integrate Todd with non-handicapped children according to "best educational practices?"

****

III. STATEMENT OF FACTS
A. Todd is an 11 year old boy, born on June 19, 1980, who resides in the Ashwaubenon School District with his mother, Mary Jo.

B. The most recent M-Team report for Todd indicates that he meets the eligibility criteria in Wis. Admin. Code P.I. § 11.35 for the handicapping conditions of mental retardation ("cognitive disability"), emotional disturbance, and speech/language handicap. The report also states that Todd consistently performs three to four years below his age and peer group in educational performance.

****

D. Todd's most recent M-Team report notes that Todd displays disruptive behavior problems at school and apparently suffers from Attention Deficit Disorder (ADD).

****

IV. CONCLUSIONS OF LAW

A. Does the Law Require the School District to Place Todd in the "Most Appropriate" Integrated EMR Program?

In determining whether a State has met the requirements of the Education of the Handicapped Act (recently retitled the "Individuals with Disabilities Education Act"), the United States Supreme Court has stated that:

> Insofar as a State is required to provide a handicapped child with a "free appropriate public education," we hold that it satisfies this requirement by providing personalized instruction with sufficient support services to permit the child to benefit educationally from that instruction.
> Board of Education v. Rowley, 458 U.S. 176, 203 (1982)

. . . . After a thorough review of all the evidence and testimony, Dr. Fiedler concluded that Todd will benefit educationally only if his IEP is implemented in an integrated EMR program, rather than an ED program.

Educating Todd in an integrated EMR program requires placement outside of the Ashwaubenon School District. Both federal and state law require that a handicapped child be placed as close as possible to the child's home. 34 C.F.R. § 300.552(a)(3), Wis. Admin. Code P.I. § 11.06(2). Dr. Fiedler properly considered the least restrictive environment requirements of the law, and noted that the individual educational needs of the child govern placement determination. *Independent School District No. 77.* 3 EHLR 503:144 (Minn. 1981).

In paragraph no. 2 of his Order, Dr. Fiedler stated that:

> The appropriate educational placement for Todd is in an integrated EMR program. The Ashwaubenon School District must make provisions to transfer Todd to the nearest, most appropriate integrated EMR program.

I conclude that the first sentence of the above Order is properly supported by law, the testimony and the evidence. The second sentence of the Order, however, by including the word "most," holds the School District to a higher standard than that required by law.

In *Rowley*, the Supreme Court interpreted the Education of the Handicapped Act (the "Act") to determine what is required of States in providing handicapped children with a "free and appropriate education." The Court concluded that:

> . . . .
> . . . Whatever Congress meant by an "appropriate" education, it is clear that it did not mean a potential-maximizing education. Id. at p. 197, n. 21

A similar decision was reached by the Ninth Circuit Court of Appeals in *Department of Education v. Katherine D.*, 727 F.2d 809 (9th Cir. 1983). In determining whether homebound education for a child with cystic fibrosis constituted an appropriate education, the court held that the child "was entitled only to an appropriate, not the best, education at public expense." *Id.* at 814, n. 4.

I conclude, therefore, that the Ashwaubenon School District cannot be required to transfer Todd to the "most" appropriate integrated EMR program. . . .

****

C. Does the Law Require the School District to Integrate Todd with Non-Handicapped Children According to "Best Educational Practices?"

Federal and state statutes and regulations require that handicapped children are educated in the least restrictive environment. 20 U.S.C. § 1415(5)(B), 34 C.F.R. § 300.550, Wis. Stats. § 115.85(1), Wis. Admin. Code P.I. § 11.06(1)(b)(1). These laws require that handicapped children are educated with non-handicapped children "to the maximum extent appropriate." Handicapped children may only be educated outside the regular education environment when the nature or severity of the child's handicap is such that education in regular classes with the use of supplementary aids and services cannot be achieved satisfactorily.

In paragraph 3 of his Order, Dr. Fiedler states that:

> The Ashwaubenon School District must make a reasonable effort to educate Todd for a greater percentage of

his school day in regular education classes. The decision to integrate Todd in nonacademic and academic regular education classes must be based on best educational practices, adequate instructional support for Todd and the regular education teacher, and input and participation of Ms. [ ].

In its appeal, the School District objects to the language "best educational practices" on the grounds that it imposes a substantive legal standard on the School District without basis in existing law.

I believe Dr. Fiedler's decision regarding greater integration of Todd in regular education class is well-supported by the law, the evidence and the testimony. I agree with the School District, however, that the correct legal standard for mainstreaming is "to the maximum extent appropriate," not according to "best educational practices." Therefore, the School District must integrate Todd in nonacademic and academic regular education classes to the maximum extent appropriate.

****

ORDER

For the reasons stated above,

IT IS ORDERED that:

1. The Ashwaubenon School District must make provisions to transfer Todd to the nearest, appropriate integrated EMR program. . . . [;]

2. must consider existing integrated EMR program placement options in reaching a decision on the appropriate educational placement for Todd for the 1991–92 school year. . . . [and]

3. must integrate Todd in nonacademic and academic regular education classes to the maximum extent appropriate.

****

— ▬ ▬ ▬

SHERRI A.D. v. KIRBY
975 F. 2d 193 (Fifth Circuit 1992)

GOLDBERG, Circuit Judge.

I. BACKGROUND

Twenty year-old Sherri A.D. is profoundly mentally retarded, deaf and blind. . . . All parties to this action agree that an appropriate educational program for Sherri should include motor development, communication, socialization and recreational components. Emphasis must be placed on assisting Sherri to develop independence in the activities of daily living, such as toileting, washing, and eating.

It is unclear from the record where Sherri lived from birth to age six. It appears, however, that she was not institutionalized, although she functioned then, as now, at the cognitive level of a one to two year-old child. In 1978, an "admission, review and dismissal committee" ["ARD"] of Sherri's local public school district ["School District"] decided to place Sherri at the Texas School for the Blind and Visually Impaired ["School for the Blind"], the only residential institution in Texas established for the specific purpose of educating blind and visually impaired people at public expense until they attain age twenty-two.

In 1985, the School for the Blind and the Texas Education Agency ["TEA"] developed new eligibility criteria for students at the School for the Blind. The School for the Blind then notified Sherri's School District that Sherri might no longer be eligible for continuing admission to the School. On March 14, 1986, an ARD convened at the School for the Blind determined that Sherri did not meet the new eligibility criteria and should be returned to a community placement and educated by her local School District. Representatives of the School District initially agreed, but soon changed their position for reasons not revealed in the record.

On March 27, 1986, Sherri's grandmother, Nell D., acting as Sherri's guardian and next friend, requested a due process hearing under the Education for All Handicapped Children Act ["EAHCA"]. Following the hearing, the School District convened two ARDs to decide whether the March 14, 1986 ARD had reached the correct decision. The ARDs convened by the School District found that the School for the Blind was the least restrictive placement available to accommodate Sherri's needs.

****

Because the School District's ARDs reached a different decision than did the ARD convened at the School for the Blind, and because Nell D. did not believe she could care for Sherri at home, Nell D. appealed to a special education hearing officer, alleging that the School for the Blind's eligibility criteria were discriminatory or otherwise unlawful, and that the School for the Blind was the least restrictive environment in which Sherri could receive free, appropriate special education services to which she is entitled until age twenty-two. [A hearing officer and then a district court (magistrate judge) both found that Sherri should be moved to a community residence and receive educational services from the local school district.]

****

B. Review of Applicable Law

Under EAHCA, the principle of "mainstreaming" disabled individuals with able-bodied individuals is well established. . . . Even in cases in which mainstreaming is not a feasible alternative, there is a statutory preference for serving disabled individuals in the setting which is least restrictive of their liberty and which is near the community in which their families live. . . . The decisions of both the special education hearing officer and the magistrate judge appear to have been based upon this understanding of EAHCA and relevant Texas regulations.

While the School for the Blind might be capable of providing services from which Sherri may obtain "educational benefit" (the standard for "appropriateness" of free public education under *Rowley*), the School for the Blind is not the least restrictive environment in which Sherri may receive appropriate educational services. The capacity of the School for the Blind to provide educational services to Sherri may in some respects far exceed what EAHCA requires. However, EAHCA does not mandate that every child with a disability receive optimal services. *Lunceford*, 475 F.2d at 1583 ("The EAHCA does not secure the best education money can buy; it calls upon government, more modestly, to provide an ap-

propriate education for each child"); . . . Instead, EAHCA requires that "appropriate" educational services be delivered in the least restrictive environment available, with a preference for mainstreaming when possible. The concern for enhancing the disabled child's ability to obtain educational benefit must be balanced with concerns about limited public resources, the need to provide basic educational opportunities to disabled and able-bodied children alike, and the concern to serve the disabled child in the environment which is least restrictive of the child's liberty.

****

There is evidence that Sherri can be appropriately served in the community. A special education hearing officer and an expert from Sherri's School District agree that Sherri can obtain educational services in the School District from which she will be able to obtain educational benefit. The fact that her ability to obtain benefit from community-based services cannot be known for certain until Sherri has been given the opportunity is no argument against giving her that opportunity.

Sherri is twenty now. When she turns twenty-two, her eligibility for education and residence at the School for the Blind will terminate. The parties do not contemplate that she would require institutionalization at some other facility thereafter. All parties concede, and the special education hearing officer specifically found, that if Sherri were to remain at the School for the Blind, her progress over the course of the next two years would not be significant. As plaintiff herself points out, Sherri has only made a few months' worth of progress in cognitive age since she entered the School for the Blind fourteen years ago. If she would be able to work in a sheltered workshop and live in a community residence after receiving two more years of free, appropriate education under her IEP at the School for the Blind, as plaintiff claims, surely she will be able to do the same with the education she will receive under the same IEP implemented in her local school district. Plaintiff agrees that Sherri can and should eventually live in the community. It would seem that the time is now.

****

ADDITIONAL COMMENTARY

1. A placement that allows little or no interaction with nondisabled peers is allowed if it is necessary to provide an appropriate placement. In *Johnston v. Ann Arbor Public Schools*, 569 F. Supp. 1502 (E.D. Mich. 1983), the court upheld the placement of a child with cerebral palsy in a special school, since it had been determined that a class in a conventional school could not be made appropriate even with the addition of supplemental aids and services. *Also e.g., Liscio v. Woodland Hills School District*, 734 F. Supp. 689 (W.D. Pa. 1989); *David D. v. Dartmouth School Commission*, 775 F.2d 411 (1st Cir. 1985).

2. The concept that an appropriate education is not necessarily the best possible education, but is one that provides the child with disabilities with needed functional skills, was well stated in *Rettig v. Kent City School District*, 788 F.2d 328 (6th Cir. 1986). The student was an autistic and mentally delayed 16-year-old. His parents were initially satisfied with his progress, but conflicts developed over his program and the instructional techniques used. In ruling, the court determined that an appropriate education for a child with severe disabilities was one that would give him a reasonable chance to acquire the skills he needed to function independently, or at least outside of residential care. The court indicated that this did not mean that the student was entitled to the best or perfect education, nor was the school required to provide all available services, nor experiment with every new technique that might be suggested, nor provide a state-of-the-art program.

3. A student's promotion from grade to grade does not automatically mean that a program is appropriate. *Hall v. Vance County Board of Education*, 774 F.2d 629 (4th Cir. 1985); *In re Van Overeem*, 555 E.H.L.R. 182 (1983). Both of these cases involved children with specific learning disabilities. Both children were able to progress from grade to grade but were achieving far below their learning potentials and far below the grade level expected for their ages. Therefore, the rulings indicate that mere promotion from grade to grade is not sufficient to demonstrate that current programming is conferring educational benefit when individual evaluations show little age-appropriate skill acquisition.

4. Several cases have addressed the issue of whether the regular schoolday or calendar must be extended for particular students with disabilities. The courts have unanimously held that when an extended program is necessary for the child to benefit, one must be provided. These cases have typically hinged on whether the child has a regression-recoupment problem. A regression-recoupment problem occurs when a child suffers a disproportionate degree of regression during that time when he or she is not receiving services and it takes an unacceptable length of time for the child to recoup those skills that have been lost. This analysis has been applied to academic as well as nonacademic skills. *E.g., Alamo Heights Independent School District v. State Board of Education*, 790 F.2d 1153 (5th Cir. 1986); *see also Yaris v. Special School District of St. Louis County*, 728 F.2d 1055 (8th Cir. 1984).

5. The term *education* is broadly defined under IDEA. For students with severe physical or emotional disabilities, education is often largely nonacademic. In these situations, "educational benefit" is a very broad concept, which could include, for example, only basic life skills or gross motor skills. *See Jefferson County Board of Education v. Breen*, 853 F.2d 853 (11th Cir. 1988); *Timothy W. v. Rochester*, 875 F.2d 954 (1st Cir. 1989).

6. The courts have generally limited their review of a state's choice of instructional methods. Where a student is making progress with the selected method, the court will not question whether another method might work better. *E.g., Evans v. District No. 17*, 841 F.2d 824 (8th Cir. 1988). *Bertolucci v. San Carlos Elementary School District*, 721 F. Supp. 1150 (N.D. Cal. 1989).

7. The Seventh Circuit in *Board of Education of Community Consolidated School District No. 21 v. Illinois State Board of Education*, 938 F.2d 712 (7th Cir. 1991), held that "it is permissible to consider parental hostility to an IEP as part of the prospective evaluation required by the [IDEA] of the placement's expected educational benefits." A similar result was reached in a Utah hearing examiner's decision in a related services issue. *Davis School District*, 18 I.D.E.L.R. 696 (S.E.A. Utah 1992). These cases may be limited to ex-

treme situations since both decisions focus on the point that the parents had been so adverse to the proposed placement that they had "poisoned" the child's mind, i.e., the child had been convinced by the parents that the proposed placement was unworkable.

8. In *Union School District v. Smith,* 15 F.3d 1519 (9th Cir. 1994), the court found that a local school district had denied a child with autism an appropriate education by offering placement in a class for communicatively handicapped. The class included no other autistic children and the teacher had not been trained to work with autistic children. Therefore, the court held that the placement did not adequately address the child's unique needs. The court also found appropriate the parents' unilateral placement of the child in a private facility that was certified by the state to provide counseling but not special education itself.

ASSESSMENT

Identification

As part of the school district's obligations under IDEA, it must actively engage in a process to identify children who may have a disabling condition.[50] This affirmative responsibility is frequently referred to as the requirement for "child find." In other words, a local district may not wait for children with disabilities to arrive on its doorstep, but rather must attempt to find those children residing within its boundaries who may qualify for service under IDEA. This responsibility includes seeking children who may qualify who attend private schools or who are home schooled within its jurisdiction.

One of the common procedures in the identification and referral process is screening of all children. This schoolwide screening is not an "evaluation" under IDEA.[51] Schools regularly screen all children for hearing and vision problems. Any deviation from the expected norm for a child is reported to the parent with a recommendation that the child be evaluated by the family's physician or a referral for a special education evaluation. Group testing or screening also occurs regularly in other ways in the school—classroom teachers daily administer substantive educational examinations on various topics, the school administers standardized achievement tests, and so on. The results of these tests are used in many ways, and, due to a discrepancy in performance, may be used for some as a basis for a referral for a special educa-

tion evaluation. The distinction between an evaluation and a screening as set out in the regulations is that evaluations are "procedures used selectively with an individual child."[52]

Referrals

Districts may receive referrals regarding children with suspected special needs from a variety of sources. Naturally, classroom teachers may refer those students they believe are exhibiting academic problems for assessment to determine whether they qualify for special education and related services. In addition, parents may directly request that a district evaluate their child to determine eligibility for special education. If the school refuses, the parent may initiate due process proceedings.

Individualized Evaluation

Before a school can plan a program and provide services to a child suspected of having a disabling condition, an evaluation must be conducted. This evaluation process is an extremely important component of IDEA, for it represents the first mechanism employed by the act to define appropriateness for an individual child. The evaluation serves three main purposes. First, it must describe the child's functioning, documenting that child's strengths and weaknesses. Second, the evaluation must identify and define any outstanding needs the child exhibits. Those unmet needs form the basis for considerations of eligibility and, if the child qualifies, will be targeted by the individualized education program. As described in the section regarding eligibility, a child must not only have a disability but must also demonstrate needs that require special educational services to qualify for service under IDEA. Therefore, the evaluation results form the foundation of appropriateness and will directly impact the provision of a free appropriate public education for eligible students.

The evaluation process also marks the onset of the act's procedural guarantees regarding parents. Not only must parents be provided with written notice that the school proposes to evaluate the student, but they must consent to the preplacement evaluation before it is conducted.[53] This may be the parents' first encounter with special education services, so the notification and consent procedures are important. The notice must be understandable and, presented in the parents' language, explain all of the procedural safeguards, the evaluations that are proposed, the specific tests, and a description of the general types of tests to be performed. The notice must also explain why these evaluations are being proposed.[54] The parents' consent must be voluntary and can be revoked at any time.[55] If the parents refuse to consent to the evaluation, the school may initiate due process proceedings to compel the evaluation.

Once consent to evaluate has been given, the school district must complete its evaluation in a timely manner. Delays in evaluation may be grounds for complaints to the Office for Civil Rights (OCR). OCR has ruled that significant delays have the effect of denying a free appropriate public education for those students who eventually qualify.[56]

In addition, regulations require that evaluations be designed to describe the child's current functioning. Those regulations require the following:

(a) Tests and other evaluation materials:

(1) Are provided and administered in the child's native language or other mode of communication, unless it is clearly not feasible to do so;

(2) Have been validated for the specific purpose for which they are used; and

(3) Are administered by trained personnel in conformance with the instructions provided by their producer.

(b) Tests and other evaluation materials include those tailored to assess specific areas of educational need and not merely those that are designed to provide a single general intelligence quotient.

(c) Tests are selected and administered so as best to ensure that when a test is administered to a child with impaired sensory, manual, or speaking skills, the test results accurately reflect the child's aptitude or achievement level or whatever factors the test purports to measure, rather than reflecting the child's impaired sensory, manual, or speaking skills (except where those skills are the factors which the test purports to measure).

(d) No single procedure is used as the sole criterion for determining an appropriate educational program for a child.

(e) The evaluation is made by a multi-disciplinary team or group of persons, including at least one teacher or other specialist with knowledge of the suspected disability.

(f) The child is assessed in all areas related to the suspected disability, including, if appropriate, health, vision, hearing, social and emotional status, general intelligence, academic performance, communicative status, and motor abilities.[57]

In short, evaluations must consist of multiple procedures, be designed to accurately and thoroughly describe a student's abilities, and be conducted by a team of individuals knowledgeable about and qualified for the tasks they perform. Failure to comply with any of these requirements places a district in violation of both IDEA and Section 504. For example, the Office for Civil Rights ruled that a Massachusetts school district violated these rules when it had guidance counselors and special education teachers administer psychological and intelligence tests for which they were not properly trained to perform. Likewise, the same district was cited for failure to consistently test for proficiency in either English or a child's native language when the primary home language was other than English.[58] In another action, following a due process hearing, a New Hampshire district was found to be out of compliance with IDEA (then EAHCA) because the tests administered to a particular student were chosen to justify a predisposed conclusion that the student no longer qualified for special education. Therefore, the evaluation was not an assessment of the student's true strengths and weaknesses.[59]

Response to Inquiry from Robert S. Black, Director, South Carolina Office of Programs for Handicapped, State Department of Education
16 EHLR 1400 (OSEP 1990)
Digest of Inquiry
(August 9, 1990)

****

If a state's guidelines require attempts at intervention before evaluating a child for special education eligibility, must a school district obtain parental consent prior to conducting an achievement screening measure during the intervention process?

****

In your letter you asked:

If, as part of this intervention process, the assistance team decides that it is necessary to have someone other than the regular classroom teacher administer an achievement screening measure to an individual child, would written parental permission for such be required?

The EHA-B [now IDEA] requires written parental consent prior to two actions: (1) before conducting a preplacement evaluation and (2) before the initial placement of a child with a handicapping condition into a program that provides special education and related services. *See* 34 CFR § 300.504. According to the definition of the term "evaluation" at 34 CFR § 300.500, "'[e]valuation' means procedures used selectively with an individual child and does not include basic tests administered to or procedures used with all children in a school, grade, or class." Therefore, a school's general screening activities would not be subject to the EHA-B requirement for parental consent because all of the children in a school, grade, or class are tested as part of the screening activity.

The EHA-B requirement to obtain parental consent does apply with respect to an initial evaluation if a public agency uses selective procedures that single out a particular child in order to determine whether that child has a handicapping condition. Selective procedures include the use of a test or procedure that is not used for all children in a school, grade, or class.

The question you asked in your letter indicated that the test you described would be considered part of a screening process. However, during a telephone conversation between members of our staffs, it was determined that the testing would be done selectively only for children suspected of having a handicapping condition. This testing situation is considered an evaluation according to the EHA-B definition at 34 CFR § 300.500. Therefore, in response to your question, written parental consent is required in the situation you described in your letter. . . .

****

Independent Evaluations

If parents disagree with the results of the evaluation, they have the right to seek an independent educational evaluation.[60] Upon request, the school must inform the parents of where they can get an independent evaluation. Once obtained, the independent evaluation must be considered by the school in any decision making and in any hearing. Cost of an independent evaluation often becomes a significant issue. Parents have the right to a publicly funded independent evaluation *after* the parents disagree with an evaluation conducted by the school. Thus, the school is not obligated to pay for independent evaluations conducted prior to its own, even if later used in the process.[61] If the school believes its evaluation was appropriate, and the independent evaluation was duplicative or erroneous, the case may go to hearing. At that point, if the hearing officer agrees, the school will not be responsible for the cost of the independent evaluation.[62] Thus, practically speaking, unless the school is willing to go to hearing on the issue, it will pay the cost of the independent evaluation. Additionally, evaluations that are requested by a hearing officer are the school's financial responsibility.

The results of evaluations initiated by the parents and at private expense must be considered by the multidisciplinary team.[63] However, the district is under no obligation to accept those results if the results of the school's evaluation differ and the school is confident in the results it obtained.

Discrimination

In addition to the preceding guidelines, districts must ensure that the tests employed are accurate and fair. To qualify for financial assistance under the statute each state must establish:

> *[P]rocedures to assure that testing and evaluation materials and procedures utilized for the purposes of evaluation and placement of children with disabilities will be selected and administered so as not to be racially or culturally discriminatory.*[64]

The largest group of evaluation cases has focused on alleged racial discrimination in special education placements. The most noted case on this issue is *Larry P. v. Riles,* which questioned the overrepresentation of African-American children in special education. There, the court enjoined the use of nonvalidated intelligence tests and ordered the reevaluation of all African-American children whose placements were based on the use of the invalid IQ test.

Reevaluation

Each student must be reevaluated at least every three years.[65] This evaluation must conform with the evaluation procedures with just a few differences. Although notification is necessary, parental consent for the reevaluation is not required.[66] Further, the notice need not list the specific tests to be administered.[67]

The three-year reevaluation rule establishes a minimum for reassessment. Students should be reevaluated more frequently if conditions warrant or if a new evaluation is requested by either the parent or the teacher.

LARRY P. v. RILES
793 F.2d 969 (Ninth Circuit 1981)

POOLE, Circuit Judge:

The State Superintendent of Public Instruction appeals a decision holding that IQ tests used by the California school system to place children into special classes for the educable mentally retarded (E.M.R.) violated federal statutes and the equal protection clauses of the United States and California Constitutions. The district court enjoined the use of non-validated IQ tests, and ordered the state to develop plans to eliminate the disproportionate enrollment of black children in E.M.R. classes. We affirm on the statutory grounds and reverse on the federal and state constitutional issues.

I. PROCEDURE BELOW

The initial complaint for declaratory and injunctive relief was filed in 1971, with six black elementary schoolchildren in the San Francisco Unified School District as named plaintiffs. Appellees challenged as unconstitutional the use of standardized intelligence tests for placement of black children in E.M.R. classes in San Francisco. The defendants were the city and state superintendents, the members of the State Board of Public Instruction and the members of the City Board of Education. . . .

****

From 1968 until trial in 1977, black children have been significantly overrepresented in E.M.R. classes. For example, in 1968–69, black children were about 9% of the state population, yet accounted for 27% of the E.M.R. population.

"These apparent overenrollments could not be the result of chance. For example, there is less than one in a million chance that the overenrollment of black children and the underenrollment of non-black children in the E.M.R. classes in 1976–77 would have resulted under a color-blind system." To explain this overenrollment, the defendants proffered a theory that there is a higher incidence of mental retardation among the black population. The district court found that this theory fails to account for the problem, because even "if it is assumed that black children have a 50 percent greater incidence of this type of mental retardation, there is still less than a one in

100,000 chance that the enrollment could be so skewed towards black children. . . . [Further,] the disproportionate E.M.R. enrollment of black children is not duplicated in the classes for the so-called 'trainable mentally retarded' children."

****

ISSUES

(3) Whether the district court erred in holding that appellant's use of the IQ tests violated the Rehabilitation Act of 1973 and the Education For All Handicapped Children Act of 1975, because the court clearly erred in finding that appellant had failed to show the tests were validated for black children and that appellant had failed to use a variety of statutorily mandated evaluation tools.

(4) Whether the district court erred in holding that appellant's action violated Title VI, because the court clearly erred in finding that the tests were not validated, that placement in E.M.R. classes for non-E.M.R. students was not a benefit, and that appellant failed to show any countervailing reason why a disproportionate number of black children were placed in the E.M.R. classes.

****

VI. REHABILITATION ACT

****

Congress was clearly concerned with the misclassification of students as retarded. The Senate Report for the Rehabilitation Act states that "racial and ethnic factors may contribute to misclassification as mentally retarded." S.Rep. No. 93-1297, 93d Cong., 2d Sess. reprinted in 1974 U.S. CODE CONG. & AD. NEWS 6373, 6389. The Senate Report for the Education for All Handicapped Children Act states that "[t]he [Labor and Public Welfare] Committee is deeply concerned about practices and procedures which result in classifying children as having handicapping conditions when, in fact, they do not have such conditions." S.Rep. No. 94-168, 94th Cong., 1st Sess. 26, reprinted in 1975 U.S. CODE CONG. & AD. NEWS 1425, 1450.

The Department of Education adopted almost identical regulations under both of these acts. These regulations require that recipients of federal funds under the acts ensure that:

[t]ests and other evaluation materials have been validated for the specific purpose for which they are used . . . [and] assess specific areas of educational need and not merely those which are designed to provide a single general intelligence quotient.
34 C.F.R. § 104.35(b)(1), (2) and 34 C.F.R. § 300.532(a)(2), (b), originally adopted as 45 C.F.R. § 121a.532(a)(2), (b).

The regulations further provide that evaluation and placement be based on "a variety of sources, including aptitude and achievement tests, teacher recommendations, physical conditions, social or cultural background, and adaptive behavior." 34 C.F.R. § 104.35(c)(1), (2); 35 C.F.R. § 300.533(a)(1), originally adopted as 45 C.F.R. § 121a.533(a)(1), (2). Placement is required to not be based upon a single criterion. 20 U.S.C. § 1412(5)(C); 34 C.F.R. § 300.532(d), originally adopted as 45 C.F.R. § 121a.532(d).

In summary, the Education for All Handicapped Children Act specifically requires that tests and evaluation procedures be free of racial and cultural bias. Both the EAHCA and the Rehabilitation Act require that the tests used for evaluation be validated for the specific purpose for which they are used, and that placement not be based upon a single criterion but on a variety of sources. . . .

****

The district court found that defendants failed to show that the tests were validated for placing black students with scores of 70 or less in E.M.R. classes. The district court noted that very few studies had examined the difference of IQ predictability for black as compared to white populations, and that those studies which had examined this problem found the tests much less valid for blacks than for whites. Further, the district court found that, even assuming the tests were validated for placement of white schoolchildren in E.M.R. classes, such validation for blacks had been generally assumed but not established. For example, the tests had been adjusted to eliminate differences in the average scores between the sexes, but such adjustment was never made to adjust the scores to be equal for black and white children. . . .

****

The district court also found that the appellant did not utilize the variety of information required by statute and regulation to make E.M.R. placements, but relied primarily on the IQ test. This finding also is not clearly erroneous. Testimony showed that school records lacked sufficient evidence of educational history, adaptive behavior, social and cultural background or health history for these factors to have been utilized in placement.

Since the appellant has not shown that these findings are clearly erroneous, we affirm the district court's holding that the defendants violated the provisions of the Rehabilitation Act and the Education for All Handicapped Children Act (1) by not insuring that the tests were validated for the specific purpose for which they are used, and (2) by not using the variety of statutorily mandated evaluation tools.

VII. TITLE VI

Title VI of the Civil Rights Act of 1964, 42 U.S.C. § 2000d, provides that:

No person in the United States shall, on the ground of race, color, or national origin, be excluded from participation in, be denied the benefits of, or be subjected to discrimination under any program or activity receiving federal financial assistance.

Regulations issued under this statutory mandate require that recipients of federal funding may not

utilize criteria or methods of administration which have the effect of subjecting individuals to discrimination because of their race, color, or national origin, or have the effect of defeating or substantially impairing accomplishment of the objectives of the program as respect individuals of a particular race, color, or national origin.
34 C.F.R. 100.3(b)(2), originally adopted as 45 C.F.R. § 80.3(b)(2).

****

A prima facie case is demonstrated by showing that the tests have a discriminatory impact on black schoolchildren. *Board of Education of New York v. Harris*, 444 U.S. 130, 151, 100 S.Ct. 363, 375, 62 L.Ed.2d 275 (1979). Once a plaintiff has established a prima facie case, the burden then shifts to the defendant to demonstrate that the requirement which caused the disproportionate impact was required by educational necessity. *Debra P. v. Turlington*, 644 F.2d 397, 407 (5th Cir. 1981). . . .

Appellees clearly demonstrated the discriminatory impact of the challenged tests. It is undisputed that black children as a whole scored two points lower than white children on the tests, and that the percentage of black children in E.M.R. classes was much higher than for whites. As discussed previously, these test scores were used to place black schoolchildren in E.M.R. classes and to remove them from the regular educational program. The burden therefore shifted to the defendants to demonstrate that the IQ tests which resulted in the disproportionate placement of black children were required by educational necessity.

Appellant argues first that E.M.R. classes are a benefit for, rather than adverse discrimination against, black children, implying that appellees did not even establish a prima facie case. However, the district court found that improper placement in E.M.R. classes has a definite adverse effect, in that E.M.R. classes are dead-end classes which de-emphasize academic skills and stigmatize children improperly placed in them. *Larry P.*, 495 F. Supp. at 941-42. . . .

Appellant next argues that even if the impact is adverse, it is not caused by discriminatory criteria (the IQ tests), but by other nondiscriminatory factors: (1) placement is based on a variety of information and evaluation tools that are non-discriminatory and not solely on the IQ tests; (2) the tests are validated for black schoolchildren, and therefore accurately reflect mental retardation in black children; and (3) blacks have a higher percentage of mental retardation than whites.

Appellant's first two arguments have been discussed in VI, *supra*, and are unavailing. Appellant's third argument is that the disproportionate number of black children in E.M.R. classes is based on a higher incidence of mental retardation in blacks than in whites that is due to poor nutrition and poor medical care brought on by the lower socioeconomic status of blacks. This argument also fails. Appellees showed, and the district court made a finding, that "the overrepresentation of black children in E.M.R. classes cannot be explained away solely on the grounds of the generally lower socio-economic status of black children and their parents." *Id.* at 956. The district court specifically found the testimony of appellant's experts in support of this argument failed to explain why more severe mental retardation does not occur in greater proportions among the poorer sections of the population. In addition, there was testimony from other experts that poor nutrition or medical care during early life does not affect later performance on IQ scores, unless it is a severe malnutrition of a type that is rare in this country. This finding of the district court has not been shown to be clearly erroneous.

Because appellant has failed to show that any of these district court findings were clearly erroneous, the district court did not err in holding that the defendants violated Title VI by utilizing these IQ tests for placement into E.M.R. classes.

****

CONCLUSION

The named plaintiffs were proper class representatives. A three-judge district court pursuant to 28 U.S.C. § 2281 was not required. The district court properly concluded that appellant violated federal statutes. We reverse, however, the court's finding of a federal constitutional violation. The lower court was without jurisdiction to review the state constitutional claims, and accordingly we vacate that portion of the decision below.

The judgment of the district court is AFFIRMED IN PART AND REVERSED IN PART. Costs are awarded to plaintiffs-appellees.

ADDITIONAL COMMENTARY

1. A district's failure to initiate an evaluation, when factors have come to the school's attention, that would have led it to believe a disabling condition existed has been found to be a violation of Section 504. *E.g., Great Valley School District*, 16 E.H.L.R. 107 (OCR 1990). In addition, if delays in evaluation force the parents to seek an appropriate education at a private school, the local district could be required to reimburse the parents for their expenses. See *Gerstmyer v. Howard County Public Schools,* 850 F. Supp. 361 (D. Md. 1994), where the school district was ordered to

pay for private schooling and tutoring. The district had been notified of the need for an evaluation four months before the child entered first grade but did not perform an evaluation until six months after the initial referral.

2. In a suit brought against a school district by a high school graduate for the school's failing to conduct a special education evaluation, the court found a statutory duty to evaluate, but no common law duty to evaluate. Thus, no negligence action can be found; IDEA due process procedures must be used. *Bean v. Conway School District*, 18 I.D.E.L.R. 65 (D.N.H. 1991). See discussion in the section on malpractice.

3. Parents are not required to notify a district that they are seeking an independent evaluation. However, parents do run the risk of having to bear the cost of the evaluation themselves if the independent evaluator does not have the credentials required by the district. *Kerry*, 18 I.D.E.L.R. 527 (O.S.E.R.S. 1991).

4. Students whose primary suspected disability area is speech and language may not need a full battery of assessments (i.e., psychological, adaptive behavior, physical). However, the multidisciplinary team must include a speech-language pathologist who utilizes appropriate instruments for the appraisal of speech and language disorders. In addition, that person is required to make referrals for additional assessments by other evaluators whenever necessary to ensure an appropriate placement decision. See Comment to 34 C.F.R. 300.532.

5. IDEA specifies additional evaluation requirements for students suspected of a learning disability. First, regulations dictate the composition of the multidisciplinary team. That team must include both a regular education teacher and at least one person "qualified to conduct individual diagnostic examinations of children, such as a school psychologist, speech-language pathologist, or remedial reading teacher." 34 C.F.R. 300.540. Second, at least one member of the evaluation team, but not the regular educator, is required to observe the student in the regular classroom or, if the child is not of school age, in a age-appropriate environment. 34 C.F.R. 300.542. Third, the regulations establish criteria for determining that a child exhibits a learning disability. Specifically, a child must demonstrate achievement inconsistent

with his or her age and ability potential in one or more of the following areas:

a. Oral expression
b. Listening comprehension
c. Written expression
d. Basic reading skills
e. Reading comprehension
f. Mathematics calculation
g. Mathematics reasoning

In addition, the deficits noted must not be caused by a visual, hearing, or motor impairment; cognitive disability; emotional disturbance; or environmental, cultural, or social disadvantage. 34 C.F.R. 300.541.

Next, regulations specify that each team member submit a written evaluation report according to particular guidelines. That report must include:

1. *Whether the child exhibits a specific learning disability;*
2. *The basis for making the determination;*
3. *The relevant behavior noted during the observation of the child;*
4. *The relationship of that behavior to the child's academic functioning;*
5. *The educationally relevant medical findings, if any;*
6. *Whether there is a severe discrepancy between achievement and ability which is not correctable without special education and related services; and*
7. *The determination of the team concerning the effects of environmental, cultural, or economic disadvantage.*
34 C.F.R. 300.543.

Finally, team members must indicate in writing whether the conclusion of the group reflects individual determinations of the issue. If an individual disagrees with the group's conclusion, he or she is required to file a minority report stating the disagreements and the basis for those differences. 34 C.F.R. 300.543 (c).

Two practical problems result from these regulations regarding specific learning disabilities. The first involves to what extent the district must employ medical diagnosis in order to rule out the presence of sensory impairments before making a determination of specific learning disabilities. Generally, districts will require that students suspected of learning disabilities have their vision and hearing screened as part of the evaluation. If that screening suggests the need for a full medical evaluation, the parents would be asked to take their child to the appropriate physician for follow-up testing.

The second practical problem also involves the exclusionary provision of the definition of specific learning disabilities. The regulations state that the deficits cannot be attributable to visual, hearing, motor, or emotional impairments. Therefore, for example, it is unclear whether a student with an identified visual impairment may also manifest a learning disability or whether, by definition, dual disabilities of this sort are impossible. Some states and districts employ these regulations literally and conclude that such dual disabilities are definitionally impossible. Other states and districts hold that if the evaluation team can demonstrate that a child is achieving below expectations, even given the presence of another disability, then a determination of learning disabilities as a secondary disability is appropriate.

THE INDIVIDUALIZED EDUCATION PROGRAM (IEP)

The individualized education program (IEP)[68] forms the foundation of the services provided to students with disabilities under IDEA. All aspects of a student's education are both derived from and governed by the IEP's contents. As stated by one court:

> Congress did not attempt to provide detailed substantive content to the concept of an "appropriate" education. Instead, emphasizing the uniqueness of each handicapped child's educational requirements, Congress defined appropriate education as "special education and related services which . . . are provided in conformity with the individualized education program." 20 U.S.C. 1401(18). The IEP is thus the heart of the congressional scheme. It is a document to be developed by parents and educators working together that states the child's present level of performance, the objectives of his program and the services that will achieve them, and "appropriate objective criteria" for determining success.[69]

The IEP requirement of the Individuals with Disabilities Education Act and its implementing regulations have two main parts: the IEP meeting and the IEP document. This combination of meeting and document represents the second mechanism of the IDEA for defining appropriateness for an individual child. The IEP meeting is designed to provide parents and educators with an opportunity to discuss and collaboratively develop an educational program for the student. The IEP document forms the written record of the decisions reached at the meeting. The statute and regulations include stringent procedural requirements for both the IEP meeting and the IEP document to ensure that special education decisions are made collaboratively by people who are knowledgeable both about the individual student's needs and special education. These provisions serve a number of functions:[70]

— The IEP meeting serves as a communication tool between the family and the school and enables them to jointly decide what the child's needs are, what services will be provided, and what the anticipated outcomes may be.

— The IEP process serves as a focus for resolving any differences between the family and the school through the meeting and, when necessary, through the due process procedures made available in IDEA.

— The IEP document sets out in written form a commitment of resources from the school that the group has determined is necessary for the child to gain educational benefits from the services provided.

— The IEP serves as a management tool to ensure that each child is provided the education and services appropriate to his or her special needs.

— The IEP document serves as a monitoring tool that may be used by the state and federal personnel to determine if children with disabilities are actually receiving the free appropriate public education guaranteed to them by IDEA.

- The IEP document serves as an evaluation device to determine the progress made by a child toward his or her goals.

A student must have a valid IEP in place before a school may offer special educational services.[71] This means that the IEP (1) has been developed at a meeting involving all of the required participants, (2) is less than one calendar year old, (3) is regarded by the family and the current school as being appropriate for the child, and (4) will be implemented as written.

The requirement of having an IEP "in effect" also holds true when placing a child in special education for the first time. An appropriate placement for a child cannot be determined until after decisions have been made about the child's needs. Since these decisions are made at an IEP meeting, a district cannot logically provide an appropriate placement and services until after an IEP meeting. The school district must conduct an IEP meeting concerning any child with disabilities within 30 calendar days after it has been determined that the child is in need of special education.[72]

The regulations, however, do not preclude a district from using a "trial placement" or "interim IEPs" as part of the evaluation procedure before the IEP is written. For a placement to be considered a trial placement, there must be an interim IEP developed, the family must agree to the "trial placement" and interim IEP, a specific and short time line not over 30 days must be set forth, and at the end of that time a meeting must be held to finalize the child's IEP.[73]

Every student's IEP must be reviewed at least once a year.[74] This does not mean that every IEP must be reviewed at the *beginning* of each school year—only that it must be reviewed once during the *calendar* year.[75] A child's IEP may be reviewed more often and should be reviewed as often as necessary for the child.

These meetings may be called by the school, including the child's special education teacher, or by the parents, whenever a party believes the current IEP is not appropriate. The district is responsible for setting and conducting all meetings[76] and should act favorably on all reasonable requests for meetings.[77]

The IEP Meeting

Regulations outline the individuals who must be in attendance at an IEP meeting.[78] The list includes:

1. A representative of the public agency
2. The child's teacher
3. One or both of the child's parents
4. The child, where appropriate
5. Other individuals at the discretion of the parent or agency

The school's representative must be a member of the school staff, other than the child's teacher, who is qualified to provide or supervise special education. The school representative should be able to commit the district to providing the resources agreed upon at the IEP meeting. The agency representative does not have to be the same person at every IEP meeting but may vary depending on the nature of the child's disability and the possible resources that will have to be provided for that child.

The child's teacher will also vary depending on the child and his or her disability. For an initial placement meeting, the teacher is generally the teacher in the area of the suspected disability or the child's regular teacher. In addition, a member of the evaluation team or a person familiar with both the evaluation and the procedures used in the evaluation attends the initial IEP meeting.[79] If the child receives services in both special and regular education classes, the teacher in attendance may be both the special education teacher and the regular education teacher(s). To avoid great numbers of participants when the child has more than one regular education teacher, districts often accumulate input from the regular education teachers, which is presented either by a regular education teacher or the child's special education teacher. When a child's regular education teachers do not routinely attend IEP meetings, they should nonetheless be informed of the outcome of the meetings.

At the school's discretion, other individuals at the IEP meeting may include service providers. For example, related service personnel may attend IEP meetings or provide written input without appearing when the child has a need for specific related services. The service provider can offer information regarding the nature, frequency, and amount of services needed by the child. At the initial IEP meeting someone must be present who can knowledgeably interpret the result of the instruments or procedures used to evaluate the child.

One or both of the child's parents are expected to attend and actively participate in the IEP meeting. If a child has no parent, a surrogate parent is appointed to serve that role.[80] It is not uncommon for a child to have parents who do not live in the same household. When one parent has legal custody, ordinarily that parent will have the authority to make educational decisions about the child and will be the parent with whom the school will interact. However, when divorced parents have joint legal custody, it is not clear whether the school must deal with both parents. One of the few cases to raise this issue indicates that although it may burdensome to send notices and documents to both parents, they are both legally entitled to access to school records.[81] It is advisable for the school to interact with both parents and to treat them equally.

The school must take steps to gain parental participation. These steps include notifying the parents early enough before the meeting to allow them to attend and scheduling the meetings at a mutually agreeable time and place.[82] When notifying parents of the meeting, the school "must indicate the purpose, time, and location of the meeting, and who will be in attendance."[83] A meeting may be conducted without a parent present if the school cannot persuade the parent to attend.[84] However, in these situations, the school must have a detailed record of its attempts to arrange the meeting with the parent(s) in attendance.[85] In these situations, the school should use other methods, such as telephone conversations, to include parental participation, even if a parent is not physically at the IEP meeting.[86]

At this point, it may be helpful to note some differences in state implementation of these individualized education programs. Many states utilize only one meeting to accomplish their obligation under IDEA, but other states have determined that two meetings must occur. In the latter situation, at the first meeting, the team presents and discusses the evaluation and considers eligibility. The second team utilizes that information to develop the IEP. When two meetings are employed, districts are required to solicit parental participation in both meetings.

Parents are intended to be active participants in the IEP process and should participate equally in the discussion about the child's needs and the decisionmaking in determining what services the school will provide. The district must do whatever is necessary to ensure that the parents understand and can participate in the meetings. This may include providing an interpreter[87] or allowing parents to tape record the meetings.[88]

Regulations state that the child should attend the IEP meetings when appropriate.[89] This decision is generally left to the parent. The decision should be based on whether the child would be helpful in developing the IEP and whether participation would benefit the child. Generally, this means that only older children would attend IEP meetings, since these children may provide insight and may be mature enough for their perspective and preferences to be fully considered.

The Document

Neither the federal statute nor the regulations prescribe the length or format of an IEP. States and districts have generally developed standard formats of their own. IEPs should be as long as necessary to adequately outline the child's program and services. There are items, however, that must be included. The statute and regulations indicate that, minimally, the IEP must include the following:[90]

— A statement of the present levels of educational performance of such child
— A statement of annual goals, including short-term instructional objectives
— Appropriate objective criteria and evaluation procedures and schedules for determining, on at least an annual basis, whether instructional objectives are being achieved
— A statement of the specific educational services to be provided to such child, and the extent to which such child will be able to participate in regular educational programs
— The projected date for initiation and the anticipated duration of such services
— A statement of the needed transition services for students beginning no later than age 16

The first part of an IEP should describe the child's current status and present level of performance. This narrative will obviously be very different for each child, since it should indicate that child's particular deficits and strengths. The statement should provide an accurate description of the effect of the disability on the child's performance, including both academic and nonacademic areas when appropriate.[91] It is not necessary to cover every area of the child's education; rather, the focus should be on the problems resulting from the child's disability or the way in which the disability interferes with the learning and educational process.[92] Objective measures such as test scores should be used when they are pertinent to program and placement. Whenever such scores are noted, the sig-

nificance of each score should be explained. Each level of performance presented should be directly addressed in the other areas of the IEP: annual goals, short-term objectives, and services to be provided.

The annual goals are statements that describe what the child can reasonably be expected to achieve within one calendar year.[93] Each goal should be addressed in the other areas of the IEP; thus, there should be short-term objectives and a statement of services to be provided to help the child achieve each goal. The goals are used during a review of the IEP to help determine if the child is progressing and whether the services are appropriate.

The short-term objectives are the intermediate steps between the present level of performance and the annual goals.[94] They should be based on the annual goals and provide an observable path with objective milestones toward achievement of the goals.[95] The objectives are not intended to be detailed instructional plans that would include specific methods, activities, and materials to be used. Rather, the objectives should be useful to teachers in developing their instructional plans and to all parties in monitoring progress toward achieving the annual goals. The IEP also must set forth criteria to be used for measuring this progress.[96]

The individualized education program must include all of the services that will be provided to the child, including special education, related services, physical education, vocational education, and transition services.[97] The extent of services to be provided must be set forth so that the level of resources committed is clear to both the family and the school.[98] Once the services have been agreed to, the school is committed to provide them.[99]

The child's program must be implemented without delay once it has been agreed to at the IEP meeting. Generally, it is expected that the child will receive the services outlined in the IEP immediately after the meeting, unless specified in the IEP.[100] Some exceptions to this requirement are obviously allowed, such as when the meeting occurs during or immediately before a vacation period or when a short delay is necessary to work out implementation arrangements.[101]

In addition to noting the time when the program will be implemented and the anticipated duration of services, the IEP must state the extent to which the student will participate in regular education. The regulations, however, do not require a detailed description of goals and objectives for regular education.[102]

Once the child's program is determined, the parent must consent to it before it can be implemented. An IEP is not valid without parental consent. Although signatures are not required by the federal statute or regulations, most districts have the parent sign the IEP document. Signatures are used to provide a record of attendance at the IEP meeting and both parties' commitment to the program.[103] (When a parent is not in attendance at the initial IEP meeting, parental consent to the program still must be acquired through other methods, including telephone conversations, written correspondence, or personal contacts.) A signature on the IEP can constitute consent if the parent has been properly advised and the IEP contains language of consent.[104]

The IEP remains in effect until supplanted by a new valid IEP. A change in the amount of services or placement cannot be made without a new IEP.[105] However, as long as there is no change in the overall amount, some adjustment in scheduling the services may be made by the school without an IEP revision. In some cases, it is possible to make changes in the short-term instructional objectives without an IEP revision. In order to make this change, the school must give the parents prior written notice, including a statement that the school will hold an IEP meeting to discuss the changes if the family requests it and no other changes in the IEP are made. Although parental consent is not technically required to change an IEP, parents may, in effect, not allow any changes that they do not agree with to occur by requesting a due process hearing.[106]

ADDITIONAL COMMENTARY

1. To assist them in participating in the IEP process, parents may bring anyone to the IEP meeting who is familiar with either the education laws or the child's needs. *See Monroe County School District*, 352 E.H.L.R. 168 (OCR 1986), where it was found that the district violated IEP requirements when it requested that a parent's guest leave the IEP meeting.

2. Since IEP meetings are often held at the end of the school year, the current teacher, who is required to attend the meeting, may not actually be the teacher to implement the IEP. Nonetheless, the presence of the new teacher is not required, probably because often the identity is unknown at the time of the meeting.

3. Regulation 34 C.F.R. 300.350 requires the district to provide the special education and related services agreed to in the IEP. However, unless the IEP was inappropriate, the district is not held responsible if the child fails to meet the specified goals. A comment following 34 C.F.R. 300.350 clarifies that an annual goal is not a guarantee by the district, but only a responsibility to make a good faith effort to reach those goals. *See also* Department of Education Interpretation: IEP Purpose and Requirements, 46 Fed. Reg. 5460 (1981), 1 E.H.L.R. 103:43, Questions 44–47.

4. When a child who has been receiving special education moves to another district, the new district must adopt an IEP before the child is placed in a special education program. The new district can consider the child's previous placement and school records in writing a new IEP. *E.g., Rieser*, 211 E.H.L.R. 403 (E.H.A. 1986). Generally, it is expected that the new IEP will be written within one week of the child's enrollment in the new

district. Individualized Education Program, OSEP Policy Paper (May 23, 1980); *E.g.* Case No. Se 86561, 508 E.H.L.R. (S.E.A. Ca. 1986). In addition, the child's former IEP may be implemented until the new district evaluates the child and creates a new IEP. OCR Policy Letter, 211 E.H.L.R. 403 (1986).

5. At least one court has found that minor defects in an IEP will not render it invalid. In *Doe v. Defendant,* the Sixth Circuit Court of Appeals refused to strike an IEP even though the IEP failed to state the student's present level of educational performance and objective evaluation criteria for determining success of the short-term objectives because there was evidence that both the parents and the district were aware of the relevant information. *Doe v. Defendant I*, 898 F.2d 1186 (6th Cir. 1990). *But see Pocatello School District #25*, 18 I.D.E.L.R. 83 (S.E.A. 1991).

6. Whether an IEP should include modification to regular education is a matter of dispute. However, both the Office for Civil Rights and the Office of Special Education Programs have issued compliance letters that stated that regular education modifications must be included in the IEP. *Seneca Highlands (Pa.) Intermediate Unit #9*, 16 E.H.L.R. 180 (OCR 1990); *Schrag*, 18 I.D.E.L.R. 530 (O.S.E.P. 1991).

7. Part of the parents' right to participate in IEP meetings includes their right to tape record meetings at their discretion. *N.W. v. Favolisi*, 131 F.R.D. 654 (D. Conn. 1990). An OSEP informal statement on this issue also includes videotaping. *Conley*, 16 E.H.L.R. 1080 (O.S.E.P. 1990).

8. Transition services infuse the IEP with a longer-range perspective than just the implementation year. The IEP must be designed to assist the student in reaching his or her potential as an adult in the community, responding to the student's needs, "preferences and interests," 20 U.S.C. 1401(a)(19).

9. Recently, a high school student with disabilities filed a § 1983 action against a regular education teacher for refusal to carry out the provisions of the child's IEP, *Doe v. Withers*, 20 I.D.E.L.R. 422 (W.Va. Circuit Court 1993). The student's IEP called for exams to be given orally by the learning disabilities teacher. The history teacher refused to comply even after repeated contacts from the parents and school staff. The student failed the history course. The jury returned a verdict for the student and awarded $5,000 in compensatory damages and $10,000 in punitive damages in addition to attorney's fees.

LEAST RESTRICTIVE ENVIRONMENT

IDEA mandates that children with disabilities will be provided an appropriate education in the least restrictive environment (LRE). Turnbull and Fiedler (1984) state,[107] "The 'least restrictive environment' principle [LRE] cannot be adequately considered except in conjunction with the principle of 'appropriate education.' The two principles are inextricably intertwined." It might be best to say that a child has the right to the least restrictive appropriate placement. This right is derived from the following statutory and regulatory language.

To the maximum extent appropriate, children with disabilities, including children in public or private institutions or other care facilities, are educated with children who are not disabled, and that special classes, separate schooling, or other removal of children with disabilities from the regular educational environment occurs only when the nature or severity of the disability is such that education in regular classes with the use of supplementary aids and services cannot be achieved satisfactorily.[108]

Each public agency shall ensure:

(1) That to the maximum extent appropriate, children with disabilities, including children in public or private institutions or other care facilities, are educated with children who are nondisabled; and

(2) That special classes, separate schooling or other removal of children with disabilities from

the regular educational environment occurs only when the nature or severity of the disability is such that education in regular classes with the use of supplementary aids and services cannot be achieved satisfactorily.[109]

The statute does not use or define the term *least restrictive environment.* The term is not defined in the regulations but is used as a heading for one section.[110] Although not synonymous, other terms are also often used in discussions about this concept, most notably *mainstreaming, inclusion,* and *full integration.*

Full integration and *inclusion* are the most recent terms used in the literature. *Full integration* has been defined variously, including the following:

- *Educating students with disabilities in age-appropriate regular school settings regardless of the degree or severity of their disabling condition*
- *Providing special services within regular schools*
- *Involving students with disabilities in as many academic classes and extracurricular activities as possible*
- *Encouraging social relationships between students with disabilities and students without disabilities*
- *Arranging for students with disabilities to receive their education and vocational training in community environments when appropriate.*[111]

Similarly, *inclusion* or *inclusive schooling* has been defined as "providing all students within the mainstream appropriate educational programs which are challenging and yet geared to their capabilities and needs as well as any support and assistance they and/or their teachers may need to be successful in the mainstream."[112] Stainback and Stainback go on to argue that all students, regardless of disability or severity, "should be included in the mainstream with appropriate programs to support and meet their individual needs." Both of these terms are seen as extensions of the term mainstreaming and reflect a philosophy that finds no rationale for segregating students with special needs.

Mainstreaming is the term most commonly used in conjunction with the concept of least restrictive environment. It is the process of educating children with disabilities in regular educational settings, i.e., in physical proximity with their nondisabled peers. Mainstreaming is often associated with the cascade of services published in the 1960s by M. Reynolds[113] (see Figure 4.1).

Interestingly, when examining case law regarding least restrictive environment, it cannot escape notice that many of the cases, perhaps an overrepresented sample, stem from disputes regarding children with hearing impairments. Not surprisingly, those associated with education of the hearing impaired have been among the most vocal in promoting opposition to the practice of assigning a unitary meaning to the term *least restrictive environment.* As stated by the Commission on the Education of the Deaf, "If LRE [least restrictive environment] is perceived as mainstreaming, the placement process is corrupted and prejudicial from the outset in that every child would be indiscriminately placed in the regular classroom, regardless of what makes sense for that unique individual."[114]

Mainstreaming is a much narrower concept than least restrictive environment. It is simply one application of the least restrictive environment principal. In *Rowley,* the Supreme Court noted that a mainstreamed placement is a preference but not a requirement for every child.

Despite this preference for "mainstreaming" handicapped children—educating them with nonhandicapped children—Congress recognized that regular classrooms simply would not be a suitable setting for the education of many handicapped children. The Act expressly acknowledges that "the nature or severity of the handicap [may be] such that education in regular classes with the use of supplementary aids and services cannot be achieved satisfactorily." The Act thus provides for the education of some handicapped children in separate classes or institutional settings.[115]

Least Mainstreamed

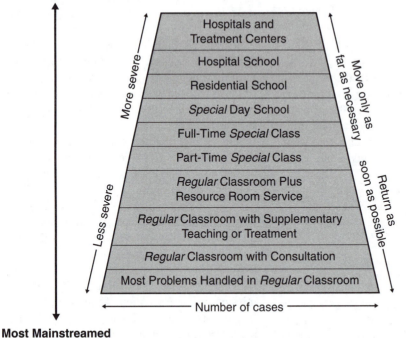

Hospitals and
Treatment Centers

Hospital School

Residential School

Special Day School

Full-Time *Special* Class

Part-Time *Special* Class

Regular Classroom Plus
Resource Room Service

Regular Classroom with Supplementary
Teaching or Treatment

Regular Classroom with Consultation

Most Problems Handled in *Regular* Classroom

More severe

Less severe

Move only as far as necessary

Return as soon as possible

Number of cases

Most Mainstreamed

FIGURE 4.1   A Framework for Considering Some Issues in
Special Education

Source: From "A Framework for Considering Some Issues in Special Education"
by M. C. Reynolds, *Exceptional Children, 28,* 1962, 367–370. Copyright 1962 by
The Council for Exceptional Children. Reprinted with permission.

The comments to the regulations also make it clear that a mainstreamed placement is not mandated for every child.

> The overriding rule in this section is that placement decisions must be made on an individual basis. The section also requires each agency to have various alternative placements available in order to insure that each child with a disability receives an education which is appropriate to his or her individual needs."[116]

Neither is full inclusion mandated for every child under IDEA.[117]

Each district must make available a full continuum of services from which the placement committee makes its decision based on the child's individual needs.[118] Requiring a continuum of alternative placements ensures the availability of an appropriate program for every child with a disability. It also ensures that a child will not be placed in an overly restrictive placement because the district does not have another one available. An appropriate placement must be made available for the child. The requirement is to meet the individual needs of the child and provide him or her with the least restrictive appropriate placement.

Determining which placement is least restrictive for a child is an individual decision; as with determining the appropriate placement, it must be made on an individual basis. In other words, a child should not be placed into a program on the basis of his or her label, precon-

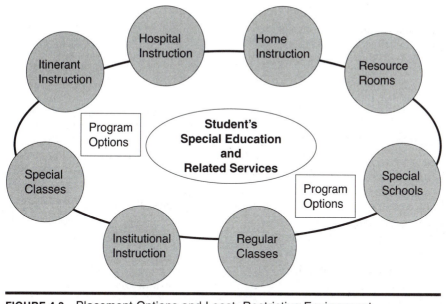

FIGURE 4.2   Placement Options and Least Restrictive Environment

Source: Toward Equality: Education of the Deaf, A Report to the President and the Congress of the United States by the Commission on the Education of the Deaf, February, 1988, p. 32 (B. Griffin, 1987).

ceived notions, or merely on existing programs. What should be considered are the child's needs: emotional, social, physical, psychological, and so on. Figure 4.2[119] attempts to depict the concept of least restrictive environment. The point is that the ordering of least restrictive environments from greatest to least is completely dependent on the individual child. In the abstract, the placements themselves are equivalent.

Still, the federal regulations indicate a clear congressional preference for mainstreaming. This preference is based on the assumption that there are inherent benefits in integration—that students who have disabilities will perform better academically and will have better self-esteem and social adjustments if they are in regular classrooms, and students without disabilities will become more accepting and tolerant of students with disabilities. The preference has its roots in the *Brown v. Board of Education*

notion that separate is inherently unequal, thus there must be some overriding reason to segregate a child with disabilities from his or her peers.

Providing a child who has disabilities with an appropriate education represents one overriding reason. The preference for mainstreaming is secondary to the implementation of an appropriate education. The statute "significantly qualifies the mainstreaming requirement by stating that it should be implemented 'to the maximum extent appropriate' and that it is inapplicable where education in a mainstream environment cannot be achieved satisfactorily."[120] When making a placement decision, the first criteria that must be met is that the placement is appropriate, i.e., reasonably calculated to enable the child to receive educational benefits. Thus, the IEP team cannot select an option that is inappropriate just because it occurs in the presence of nondisabled peers. Equally true, the team cannot select an option that is more segregated because it offers a more than appropriate education.[121] The goal of the placement process is the selection of the least restrictive appropriate placement.

In *Roncker v. Walter*,[122] the court noted three substantial exceptions to IDEA's preference for mainstreaming, or reasons sufficient to segregate: first, when the child "would not benefit from mainstreaming"; second, when "any marginal benefits received from mainstreaming are far outweighed by the benefits gained from services which could not feasibly be provided in the non-segregated setting"; and third, when the child is a substantially disrupting force in the mainstreamed setting.[123]

In *Roncker v. Walter*,[124] the court found that if the particular services that make a more restrictive setting more appropriate can be transported to a less restrictive setting, such a modification is required by the least restrictive environment mandate. Under this portability test, if it has been shown that there is an appropriate mainstreamed placement, it must be shown that what makes the residential placement appropriate cannot be provided in the mainstreamed setting, or the residential placement must be shown to be less restrictive than the mainstreamed placement.

Not all courts adhere to this test. The Fifth Circuit Court of Appeals set forth an alternative in *Daniel R. R. v. State Board of Education*.[125] That court established several factors to consider in determining whether a placement is the least restrictive appropriate option. The first factor to be considered is "whether the state has taken steps to accommodate the handicapped child in regular education." If modifications have been attempted, the court must inquire into whether the efforts are sufficient. However, the court noted that "regular education instructors [are not required] to devote all or most of their time to one handicapped child or to modify the regular education program beyond recognition."[126] Next, the court should consider whether the child benefits from the mainstream instruction. Finally, the court can focus on "the effect the handicapped child's presence has on the regular classroom environment and, thus, on the education that the other students are receiving."[127]

Two more recent cases have applied the *Daniel R. R.* test: *Greer v. Rome* and *Oberti v. Board of Education of the Borough of Clementon School District*.[128] *Greer* found that by limiting the options considered to the regular class with little or no support or a self-contained special education class, the district had failed to consider the "whole range of supplemental aids and services, including resource rooms and itinerant instruction," that may be necessary to allow the child to be placed in a more typical setting.[129] Likewise in *Oberti*, the court determined that the Clementon School District failed to satisfy the first question of the *Daniel R. R.* test that the child in question could not be educated in the regular class. The district did not give adequate consideration to various supplementary aids and services,[130] did not demonstrate that the services in the special class clearly outweighed those available in the regular class, and did not demonstrate convincingly that the disruptions the child caused while in kindergarten would continue in the present situation.

In addition, the Third Circuit Court of Appeals in *Oberti* ruled that IDEA creates a presumption that the child will be placed in the regular classroom, which must be rebutted to adequately justify removal from that setting. Further, the *Oberti* court concluded that burden of proof lies squarely with the school district to demonstrate it has appropriately implemented the law and its presumption. The parents, as challengers of the district, need not prove that the IEP developed by the district is inappropriate. Other courts have held that the burden of proof rests with the party that challenges the ruling of the hearing officer, whether parents or school district.[131]

Finally, in the most recent of these cases, the Ninth Circuit Court of Appeals developed another, yet similar, test for analyzing placements. In *Sacramento City Unified School District v. Rachel H.,*[132] the parents of a child with moderate mental retardation appealed the decision of the district to place their daughter in a regular classroom for one-half the day and a special education class for one-half the day. The Ninth Circuit Court of Appeals held for the parents and adopted the four-part test developed by the lower court. That test considers four factors: (1) the educational benefits available in a regular classroom, supplemented with appropriate aids and services as compared with the educational benefits of a special education classroom; (2) the nonacademic benefits of interaction with children who are not disabled; (3) the effect of the child's presence on the teacher and other children in the classroom; and (4) the cost of mainstreaming the child in a regular classroom.[133]

It may be helpful to think of the process of determining the least restrictive environment as a three-step process:

Step 1: Develop an appropriate program as outlined by the child's IEP.

Step 2: Determine in which settings that program can be implemented.

Step 3: Choose the option that maximizes interaction with nondisabled peers.

Thus, it becomes clear that there are situations in which a mainstreamed placement is neither the least restrictive nor an appropriate placement for a particular child. For some children, a regular school may be very restrictive, whereas a residential or nonmainstreamed option will be less restrictive. "In some instances, a special facility will constitute the least restrictive environment for a particular handicapped child."[134] For these children, the regulations require that other placements be available. The Third Circuit Court of Appeals in *Geis v. Board of Education* put it this way:

As to the requirement that handicapped children be placed in the least restrictive environment possible, we believe that this determination must include consideration of the particular handicap a student has. . . . Current regulations make it even more clear that the goal of placing children in the least restrictive environment does not trump all other considerations; such a setting is selected in light of a pupil's special education needs. For some pupils a residential placement may very well be the least restrictive. Considering S.G.'s language problems, for example, the district court could conclude that a residential placement where sign language is used is the least restrictive environment.[135]

Again, note that *Geis* involved a student with a hearing impairment. Students who are deaf and hearing impaired present probably the most clear example of the possible restrictiveness of the regular classroom. Deafness, unlike any other disability, involves not just a different mode of expressive language but a different mode of receptive language, and, in some cases, a completely different language from English, i.e., American Sign Language. Therefore, a young deaf child placed in a regular classroom may become isolated in a way that a child with another disability would not. In such a case, the child would be limited to probably only one communication partner with whom he or she could fluently converse—his or her interpreter. Obviously, a child placed in a situation where communication is so restricted and peer conversations require adult mediation is not experiencing a "normal" learning environment. Rather, placement in a situation that allows for multiple communication partners of a variety of ages becomes much more "normal" and far less restrictive to the child's overall development. That is not to say, however, that no profoundly deaf child is ever appropriately placed in a mainstreamed setting. Many are. However, those placements must be made with careful attention to the child's individual strengths and weaknesses in order to meet the baseline of appropriateness.

Recently, in recognition of the unique situation of many students with hearing impairments, the United States Department of Education offered clarification of the process school districts should use in developing a free and appropriate public education for students who are hearing impaired. "The secretary believes that the unique communication and related needs of many children who are deaf have not been adequately considered in the development of their IEP's." Therefore, the following factors were identified for consideration in the development of an IEP for a child with a hearing impairment.

1. *Communication needs and child's and family's preferred mode of communication;*

2. *Linguistic needs;*
3. *Severity of hearing loss and potential for using residual hearing;*
4. *Academic level; and*
5. *Social, emotional and cultural needs, including opportunities for peer interactions and communication.*[136]

In conclusion, the least restrictive environment provides just another example of IDEA's requirement that children be treated as unique individuals with differing needs. Those unique learning characteristics necessitate a variety of approaches and a variety of placement opportunities in order for each child to receive a free and appropriate public education.

RONCKER v. WALTER
700 F.2d 1058 (Sixth Circuit 1983)

CONTIE, Circuit Judge.

****

I.

The plaintiff's son, Neill Roncker, is nine years old and is severely mentally retarded. . . . Neill also suffers from seizures but they are not convulsive and he takes medication to control them. No evidence indicates that Neill is dangerous to others but he does require almost constant supervision because of his inability to recognize dangerous situations.

. . . . In the spring of 1979, a conference was held to evaluate Neill's Individual Education Plan (IEP). . . . After evaluating Neill, the school district decided to place him in a county school. Since these county schools were exclusively for mentally retarded children, Neill would have received no contact with non-handicapped children.

****

The Ronckers refused to accept the placement and sought a due process hearing. . . .

II.

****

The first inquiry in the two-step test mandated by *Rowley* [*Board of Ed. of the Hendrick Hudson Central School District v. Rowley*, 458 U.S. 176, 102 S.Ct. 3034 (1982)] is whether the state has complied with the Act's procedural requirements. These requirements clearly have been satisfied in this case. The second inquiry is whether "the individualized educational program developed through the Act's procedures [is] reasonably calculated to enable the child to receive educational benefits?" *Id.* at 3051.

. . . . The present case differs from *Rowley* in two significant ways.

First, this case involves the mainstreaming provision of the Act while *Rowley* involved a choice between two methods for educating a deaf student. In the latter case, the dispute is simply one of methodology and the Supreme Court has emphatically stated that such questions should be left to the states. *Id.* at 3051-52. In the present case, the question is not one of methodology but rather involves a determination of whether the school district has satisfied the Act's requirement that handicapped children be educated alongside non-handicapped children to the maximum extent appropriate. The states accept federal aid in return for compliance with the Act. Since Congress has decided that mainstreaming is appropriate, the states must accept that decision if they desire federal funds.

****

III.

****

The Act does not require mainstreaming in every case but its requirement that mainstreaming be provided to the maximum extent appropriate indicates a very strong congressional preference. The proper inquiry is whether a proposed placement is appropriate under the Act. In some cases, a placement which may be considered better for academic reasons may not be appropriate because of the failure to provide for mainstreaming. The perception that a segregated institution is academically superior for a handicapped child may reflect no more than a basic disagreement with the mainstreaming concept. Such a disagreement is not, of course, any basis for not following the Act's mandate. *Campbell v. Talladega City Bd. of Education*, 518 F. Supp. 47, 55 (N.D. Ala. 1981). In a case where the segregated facility is considered superior, the court should determine whether the services which make that placement superior could be feasibly provided in a non-segregated setting. If they can, the placement in the segregated school would be inappropriate under the Act. Framing the issue in this manner accords the proper respect for the strong preference in favor of mainstreaming while still realizing the possibility that some handicapped children simply must be educated in segregated facilities either because the handicapped child would not benefit from mainstreaming, because any marginal benefits received from mainstreaming are far outweighed by the benefits gained from services which could not feasibly be provided in the non-segregated setting, or because the handicapped child is a disruptive force in the non-segregated setting. Cost is a proper factor to consider since excessive spending on one handicapped child deprives other handicapped children. See *Age v. Bullitt County Schools*, 673 F.2d 141, 145 (6th Cir. 1982). Cost is no defense, however, if the school district has failed to use its funds to provide a proper continuum of alternative placements for handicapped children. The provision of such alternative placements benefits all handicapped children.

In the present case, the district court must determine whether Neill's educational, physical or emotional needs require some service which could not feasibly be provided in a class for handicapped children within a regular school or in the type of split program advocated by the State Board of Education. . . .

****

The judgment of the district court is VACATED and the case is REMANDED for further proceedings consistent with this opinion.

— — — —

LACHMAN v. ILLINOIS STATE BOARD OF EDUCATION
852 F. 2d 290 (Seventh Circuit 1988)

ESCHBACH, Senior Circuit Judge.

Benjamin Lachman is a profoundly deaf seven-year-old child. . . .

****

. . . . Since the time Benjamin became eligible for participation in the RHIP [Regional Hearing Impaired Program] pre-school program, in September 1984, his parents and the school district have disagreed as to the manner in which his education should be facilitated. . . .

I.

The Lachmans believe that Benjamin can best be educated at a neighborhood school near his home, in a regular classroom with the assistance of a full-time cued speech instructor. In contrast, the school district has consistently proposed that all or at least half of Benjamin's school day be spent in a self-contained classroom with other hearing-impaired children. Those self-contained classrooms are located in schools outside Benjamin's neighborhood. . . . The course of education recommended by the school district centers on the use of the total communication approach to educating hearing-impaired children, which relies primarily upon sign language as a means of communication. . . .

****

III.

Examination of the district court opinion reveals that it considered the focal point of the disagreement between the Lachmans and the school district to be a question of whether Benjamin's education can best be facilitated by utilization of the cued speech technique or the total communication concept. The Lachmans dispute that inference by the district court. They perceive the . . . question in this case is whether the challenged IEP fails to satisfy the . . . requirement that "to the maximum extent appropriate" Benjamin, as a handicapped child, be "educated with children who are not handicapped," and that he be removed from the regular classroom environment and placed in a special class only to the extent that "the nature or severity of [his] handicap is such that education in regular classes with the use of supplementary aids and services cannot be achieved satisfactorily." 20 U.S.C. § 1412(5)(B).

****

Rowley [*Board of Ed. of the Hendrick Hudson Central School District v. Rowley*, 458 U.S. 176, 102 S.Ct. 3034 (1982)] makes clear that "once a court determines that the requirements of the Act have been met, questions of methodology are for resolution by the State." 458 U.S. at 208, 102 S.Ct. at 3052. The mainstreaming preference articulated in § 1412(5)(B) is one of the "requirements of the Act" referred to in the above excerpt from *Rowley*. . . .

****

We are convinced that appellants' effort to characterize the sole, true issue in this case as whether the proposed IEP satisfies the § 1412(5)(B) mainstreaming preference is misdirected. Undoubtedly, this case does present a valid question of whether the IEP proposed by the school district and affirmed by the Illinois State Board of Education would result in Benjamin being mainstreamed to the "maximum extent appropriate" as contemplated by § 1412(5)(B). However, on careful examination, it becomes apparent that a determination of whether the IEP proposed for Benjamin provides for mainstreaming to the maximum extent appropriate can be made only within the context of the methodology employed to facilitate his education.

The degree to which a challenged IEP satisfies the mainstreaming goal of the EAHCA simply cannot be evaluated in the abstract. Rather, that laudable policy objective must be weighed in tandem with the Act's principal goal of ensuring that the public schools provide handicapped children with a free appropriate education. . . . A major part of the task of local and state officials in fashioning what they believe to be an effective program for the education of a handicapped child is the selection of the methodology or methodologies that will be employed. "The primary responsibility for formulating the education to be accorded a handicapped child, *and for choosing the educational method most suitable to the child's needs*, was left by the Act to state and local educational agencies in cooperation with the parents or guardians of the child." *Rowley*, 458 U.S. at 207, 102 S.Ct. at 3051 (emphasis supplied) quoted in *Northwest R-1 School District*, 813 F.2d at 164.

The Lachmans' contention that their son can be fully mainstreamed rests squarely on their belief in, and preference for, the cued speech technique. They do not maintain that the fully-mainstreamed placement they seek would be possible without the use of cued speech and the utilization of a cued speech instructor working at Benjamin's side, full-time, in the classroom. Further, appellants do not claim that Benjamin could be mainstreamed to any greater extent than called for in the proposed IEP, if the total communication methodology is utilized. The reasons relied on by the school district for refusing to place Benjamin in a regular classroom full-time focus on its lack of confidence in the cued speech technique as a means for facilitating immediate, full mainstreaming in Benjamin's case. Instead, the school district believes that the total communication concept is the most appropriate way to facilitate Benjamin's early primary education and it has selected that methodology for his IEP.

On the facts of this case, it is clear that the § 1412(5)(B) issue of mainstreaming is subsumed by the parties' disagreement as to methodology. In the absence of the parties' difference of opinion as to that question of educational methodology, there would be no disagreement between them as to the extent of mainstreaming that could presently be achieved for Benjamin. . . .

****

. . . . Given these findings, we conclude that the proposed IEP will provide Benjamin Lachman with a free appropriate public education as required by § 612(1) of the Act. Accordingly, the judgment of the district court AFFIRMED.

(Footnotes omitted.)

DANIEL R. R. v. STATE BOARD OF EDUCATION
874 F.2d 1036 (Fifth Circuit 1989)

GEE, Circuit Judge.

****

Daniel R. is a six year old boy, [a] victim of Downs Syndrome [who] is mentally retarded and speech impaired. By September 1987, Daniel's developmental age was between two and three years and his communication skills were slightly less than those of a two year old. In 1985, Daniel's parents, Mr. and Mrs. R., enrolled him in EPISD's [El Paso Independent School District] Early Childhood Program, a half-day program devoted entirely to special education. . . . Before the 1986–87 school year began, Mrs. R. requested a new placement that would provide association with nonhandicapped children. Mrs. R. wanted EPISD to place Daniel in Pre-kindergarten—a half-day, regular education class. . . .

. . . . Daniel did not participate without constant, individual attention from the teacher or her aide, and failed to master any of the skills Mrs. Norton [the Pre-kindergarten instructor] was trying to teach her students. Modifying the Pre-kindergarten curriculum and her teaching methods sufficiently to reach Daniel would have required Mrs. Norton to modify the curriculum almost beyond recognition. In November 1986, the ARD [Admission, Review, and Dismissal] Committee met again, concluded that Pre-kindergarten was inappropriate for Daniel, and decided to change Daniel's placement. Under the new placement, Daniel would attend only the special education, Early Childhood class; . . .

****

In contrast to the EHA's [now IDEA] vague mandate for a free appropriate public education lies one very specific directive prescribing the educational environment for handicapped children. Each state must establish

procedures to assure that, to the maximum extent appropriate, handicapped children . . . are educated with children who are not handicapped, and that special education, separate schooling or other removal of handicapped children from the regular educational environment occurs only when the nature or severity of the handicap is such that education in regular classes with the use of supplementary aids and services cannot be achieved satisfactorily.

§ 1412(5)(B).

With this provision, Congress created a strong preference in favor of mainstreaming. . . .

By creating a statutory preference for mainstreaming, Congress also created a tension between two provisions of the Act. School districts must both seek to mainstream handicapped children and, at the same time, must tailor each child's educational placement and program to his special needs. §§ 1412(1) and (5)(B). . . .

****

Although Congress preferred education in the regular education environment, it also recognized that regular education is not a suitable setting for educating many handicapped children. *Rowley*, 458 U.S. at 181 n. 4. . . . Thus, the EHA allows school officials to remove a handicapped child from regular education or to provide special education if they cannot educate the child satisfactorily in the regular classroom. § 1412(5)(B). . . . Schools must provide a free appropriate public education and must do so, to the maximum extent appropriate, in regular education classrooms. But when education in a regular classroom cannot meet the handicapped child's unique needs, the presumption in favor of mainstreaming is overcome and the school need not place the child in regular education. . . .

B. DETERMINING COMPLIANCE WITH THE MAINSTREAMING REQUIREMENT

****

Although we have not yet developed a standard for evaluating mainstreaming questions, we decline to adopt the approach that other circuits have taken. . . .

****

Ultimately, our task is to balance competing requirements of the EHA's dual mandate: a free appropriate public education that is provided, to the maximum extent appropriate, in the regular education classroom. As we begin our task we must keep in mind that Congress left the choice of educational policies and methods where it properly belongs—in the hands of state and local school officials. Our task is not to second-guess state and local policy decisions; rather, it is the narrow one of determining whether state and local school officials have complied with the Act. Adhering to the language of EHA, we discern a two part test for determining compliance with the mainstreaming requirement. First, we ask whether education in the regular classroom, with the use of supplemental aids and services, can be achieved satisfactorily for a given child. *See* § 1412(5)(B). If it cannot and the school intends to provide special education or to remove the chid from regular education, we ask, second, whether the school has mainstreamed the child to the maximum extent appropriate. *See id.* A variety of factors will inform each stage of our inquiry; . . . no single factor is dispositive in all cases. Rather, our analysis is an individualized, fact-specific inquiry that requires us to examine carefully the nature and severity of the child's handicapping condition, his needs and abilities, and the schools' response to the child's needs.

In this case, several factors assist the first stage of our inquiry, whether EPISD can achieve education in the regular classroom satisfactorily. At the outset, we must examine whether the state has taken steps to accommodate the handicapped child in regular education. The Act requires states to provide supplementary aids and services and to modify the regular education program when they mainstream handicapped children. *See* § 1401(17), (18), § 1412(5)(B); *Rowley*, 458 U.S. at 189, 102 S.Ct. at 3042, 73 L. Ed. 2d at 701; 34 C.F.R., Part 300, App. C Question 48; *see also* Tex. Admin. Code Tit. 19 § 89.223(a)(4)(C). If the state has made no effort to take such accommodating steps, our inquiry ends, for the state is in violation of the Act's express mandate to supplement and modify regular education. If the state is providing supplementary aids and services and is modifying its regular education program, we must examine whether its efforts are sufficient.

****

Next, we examine whether the child will receive an educational benefit from regular education. This inquiry necessarily will focus on the student's ability to grasp the essential elements of the regular education curriculum. Thus, we must pay close attention to the nature and severity of the child's handicap as well as to the curriculum and goals of the regular education class. . . .

We also must examine the child's overall educational experience in the mainstreamed environment, balancing the benefits of regular and special educa-

tion for each individual child. For example, a child may be able to absorb only a minimal amount of the regular education program, but may benefit enormously from the language models that his nonhandicapped peers provide for him. . . .

Finally, we ask what effect the handicapped child's presence has on the regular classroom environment and, thus, on the education that the other students are receiving. A handicapped child's placement in regular education may prove troublesome for two reasons. First, the handicapped child may, as a result of his handicap, engage in disruptive behavior. "[W]here a handicapped child is so disruptive in a regular classroom that the education of other students is significantly impaired, the needs of the handicapped child cannot be met in that environment. Therefore regular placement would not be appropriate to his or her needs." 34 C.F.R. § 300.552 Comment (quoting 34 C.F.R. Part 104—Appendix, Paragraph 24). Second, the child may require so much of the instructor's attention that the instructor will have to ignore the other student's [sic] needs in order to tend to the handicapped child. The Act and its regulations mandate that the school provide supplementary aids and services in the regular education classroom. A teaching assistant or an aide may minimize the burden on the teacher. If, however, the handicapped child requires so much of the teacher or the aide's time that the rest of the class suffers, then the balance will tip in favor of placing the child in special education.

If we determine that education in the regular classroom cannot be achieved satisfactorily, we next ask whether the child has been mainstreamed to the maximum extent appropriate. The EHA and its regulations do not contemplate an all-or-nothing educational system in which handicapped children attend either regular or special education. Rather, the Act and its regulations require schools to offer a continuum of services. 34 C.F.R. § 300.551. . . . The appropriate mix will vary from child to child and, it may be hoped, from school year to school year as the child develops. If the school officials have provided the maximum appropriate exposure to non-handicapped students, they have fulfilled their obligation under the EHA.

C. EPISD'S COMPLIANCE WITH THE MAINSTREAMING REQUIREMENT

After a careful review of the voluminous administrative record, we must agree with the trial court that

EPISD's decision to remove Daniel from regular education does not run afoul of the EHA's preference for mainstreaming. Accounting for all of the factors we have identified today, we find that EPISD cannot educate Daniel satisfactorily in the regular education classroom. Furthermore, EPISD has taken creative steps to provide Daniel as much access to nonhandicapped students as it can, while providing him an education that is tailored to his unique needs. Thus, EPISD has mainstreamed Daniel to the maximum extent appropriate.

EPISD cannot educate Daniel satisfactorily in the regular education classroom; each of the factors we identified today counsels against placing Daniel in regular education. First, EPISD took steps to modify the Pre-kindergarten program and to provide supplementary aids and services for Daniel—all of which constitute a sufficient effort. . . .

Second, Daniel receives little, if any, educational benefit in Pre-kindergarten. . . .

Third, Daniel's overall educational experience has not been entirely beneficial. As we explained, Daniel can grasp little of the Pre-kindergarten curriculum; the only value of regular education for Daniel is the interaction which he has with nonhandicapped students. Daniel asserts that the opportunity for interaction, alone, is a sufficient ground for mainstreaming him. When we balance the benefits of regular education against those of special education, we cannot agree that the opportunity for Daniel to interact with nonhandicapped students is a sufficient ground for mainstreaming him. Regular education not only offers Daniel little in the way of academic or other benefits, it also may be harming him. . . . Simply put, Daniel is exhausted and, as a result, he sometimes falls asleep at school. Moreover, the record indicates that the stress of regular education may be causing Daniel to develop a stutter.

****

Finally, we agree that Daniel's presence in regular Pre-kindergarten is unfair to the rest of the class. When Daniel is in the Pre-kindergarten classroom, the instructor must devote all or most of her time to Daniel. Yet she has a classroom filled with other, equally deserving students who need her attention. Although regular education instructors must devote extra attention to their handicapped students, we will not require them to do so at the expense of their entire class.

****

. . . . In this case, the trial court correctly concluded that the needs of the handicapped child and the needs of the nonhandicapped students in the Pre-kindergarten class tip the balance in favor of placing Daniel in special education. We thus

AFFIRM.

— — — —

SCHULDT v. MANKATO INDEPENDENT SCHOOL DISTRICT
937 F.2d 1357 (Eighth Circuit 1991)

GIBSON, Circuit Judge.

Nine-year old Erika Schuldt was born with spina bifida, which paralyzed her from the waist down. Erika uses a lightweight wheelchair and her condition requires regular physical therapy, catheterization, and bowel care. The Schuldts live about five blocks from the Roosevelt Elementary School, and when the time came for Erika to go to kindergarten, her parents notified the school district that they wanted Erika to attend Roosevelt.

. . . . On June 16, 1988, Lyle McFarling, Director of Special Education, wrote to the Schuldts informing them that the school district would not modify Roosevelt to make it accessible to Erika. The letter stated:

District 77 is not required to make each of its elementary school buildings accessible for handicapped students if it has an accessible site which offers the same programs that are available at the inaccessible building site.

. . . [W]e are recommending that Erica [sic] attend one of the three totally accessible elementary buildings that we have available in District 77. Washington, Kennedy and Hoover Elementary Schools are all totally accessible buildings and would meet Erica's [sic] needs appropriately.

Unhappy with the school district's response, Erika's parents requested and attended a conference to further discuss where Erika would attend elementary school. After this meeting, McFarling sent the Schuldts a memorandum explaining that although

Roosevelt could be modified to give Erika physical access to the building, the district refused to place her at Roosevelt because even after modification, placement at Roosevelt would still be inferior to placement at one of the school district's three fully handicapped accessible schools.

****

II.

The Schuldts make numerous arguments that the Education for the Handicapped Act requires the school district to modify Roosevelt and make it fully accessible to Erika.

A.

The Schuldts argue that the act requires the school district to place Erika at the school nearest to her home. . . .

The act and regulations promulgated thereunder give the school district discretion in selecting the location where it will educate a handicapped child. Specifically, 34 C.F.R. § 300.552 (1990) provides factors a school district should take into consideration when making its decision about the location of a student's education. The regulation instructs the school district to choose a location based on the student's individualized education program, to choose a location that is as close as possible to the child's home, and unless the child's program requires something else, to choose the location where the child would attend school if he or she were not handicapped. *Id.*

We interpret section 300.552 as directing the school district to locate Erika at a school where her teachers can fully implement her program. The phrase "as close as possible" is not a mandate that the school district place Erika at Roosevelt. . . .

The Schuldts' argument is aimed at forcing the school district to assign Erika to Roosevelt. They contend that Roosevelt is the ideal location for Erika because it would allow her to attend school with her younger siblings, and with other children in her neighborhood. Even assuming that Roosevelt would be the optimum environment for Erika, the Education for the Handicapped Act does not require the school district to provide services which "maximize the potential of each handicapped child commensurate with the opportunity provided other children." *Rowley*, 458 U.S. at 200, 102 S. Ct. at 3048. By

busing Erika to one of several nearby schools, the school district is already providing Erika with a fully integrated public education, thereby meeting its obligation under the act.

B.

The Schuldts also argue that the district court erred because it considered cost to the school district when evaluating the propriety of the school district's decision not to modify Roosevelt. Lyle McFarling testified, on behalf of the school district, that cost was not a factor in his decision to assign Erika to a school other than Roosevelt. The Schuldts argue that this testimony, coupled with the fact that the school district did not submit any evidence of how cost would affect the school district's ability to provide services to other children, should have prevented the district court from considering cost when reaching its decision.

The record does not suggest that the court relied heavily on cost-benefit analysis for its ultimate decision. The court's brief reference to the balancing of costs and benefits only appears once, and that reference is in the court's discussion of whether the Education for the Handicapped Act creates an absolute duty to place a child in the school nearest to that child's home. Slip op. at 12. The court was explaining that distance from a child's home is not the determining factor, but only one of several factors a school district must consider when deciding whether a child's placement complies with the act and its regulations. *Id.*

The district court opinion cited this court's opinion in *A.W. v. Northwest R-1 School District*, 813 F.2d 158 (8th Cir. 1987), in which we stated that a court may "consider both cost to the local school district and benefit to the child," *id.* at 163, when evaluating the school district's placement decision. Slip op. at 12. The district court was entitled to rely on *A.W.* as a matter of law. Lyle McFarling's testimony that cost was not a consideration did not prevent the district court from recognizing that the cost of modifying Roosevelt would have implications on the school district's ability to provide other services. *See A.W.*, 813 F.2d at 163.

****

While it is true that the school district did not introduce extensive evidence of the impact the costs of structural modifications would have on the overall budget, the Schuldts themselves introduced substantial testimony on that issue. Moreover, the district court did not need such specific evidence to know that the total funds available to the school district are limited, and it is axiomatic that funds spent modifying Roosevelt must, of necessity, mean a reduction of funds available for other education related needs.

The Schuldts also cite *New Mexico Association for Retarded Citizens v. New Mexico*, 678 F.2d 847, 855 (10th Cir. 1982), for the proposition that "[s]chool districts are required to modify existing programs where the 'financial burden would not be excessive' and the modifications would benefit the child." Brief for Appellants at 24, *Schuldt v. Mankato Indep. School Dist.*, No. 77 (No. 90-5146MN). They claim that "[t]he test for excessiveness is whether the modifications would 'jeopardize the overall viability of the educational system.'" *Id.* (citation omitted).

****

The underlying premise of the Schuldts' claim,

which we reject, is that Roosevelt is the only school to which the school district can assign Erika and still be in compliance with the law. *New Mexico* does not go so far. The *New Mexico* court stated: "[M]odification of existing programs *may* be required where the financial burden would not be excessive *and the accommodation would enable handicapped children to realize the benefits of the State's educational program.*" *New Mexico*, 678 F.2d at 855 (emphasis added). Even if *New Mexico* were on point, this language does not mandate that school districts *must* structurally modify *all* of their school buildings to accommodate physically handicapped children when those children are already receiving an appropriate public education. The Schuldts' argument on this issue is without merit.

****

For the foregoing reasons, we affirm the decision of the district court.

(Footnotes omitted.)

SACRAMENTO CITY UNIFIED SCHOOL DISTRICT v. RACHEL H.
14 F.3d 1398 (Ninth Circuit), *cert. denied*, 129 L.Ed. 2d 813 (1994)

SNEED, Circuit Judge:
****

I. FACTS AND PRIOR PROCEEDINGS

Rachel Holland is now 11 years old and is mentally retarded. She was tested with an I.Q. of 44. She attended a variety of special education programs in the [Sacramento City Unified School] District from 1985–89. Her parents sought to increase the time Rachel spent in a regular classroom and in the fall of 1989, they requested that Rachel be placed full-time in a regular classroom for the 1989–90 school year. The District rejected their request and proposed a placement that would have divided Rachel's time between a special education class for academic subjects and a regular class for non-academic activities such as art, music, lunch, and recess. The district court found that this plan would have required moving Rachel at least six times each day between the two classrooms. *Holland*, 786 F. Supp. at 876. The Hollands instead enrolled Rachel in a regular kindergarten class at the Shalom School, a private school.

Rachel remained at the Shalom School in regular classes and at the time the district court rendered its opinion was in the second grade.

The Hollands and the District were able to agree on an Individualized Education Program ("IEP") for Rachel. Although the IEP is required to be reviewed annually, see 20 U.S.C. § 1401a(20)(B), because of the dispute between the parties, Rachel's IEP has not been reviewed since January 1990.

The Hollands appealed the District's placement decision to a state hearing officer pursuant to 20 U.S.C. § 1415(b)(2). They maintained that Rachel best learned social and academic skills in a regular classroom and would not benefit from being in a special education class. The District contended Rachel was too severely disabled to benefit from full-time placement in a regular class. The hearing officer concluded that the District had failed to make an adequate effort to educate Rachel in the regular class pursuant to the IDEA. . . .

The district appealed this determination to the district court. . . . The court affirmed the decision of the hearing officer that Rachel should be placed full-time in a regular classroom.

In considering whether the District proposed an appropriate placement for Rachel, the district court examined the following factors: (1) the educational benefits available to Rachel in a regular classroom, supplemented with appropriate aids and services, as compared with the educational benefits of a special education classroom; (2) the non-academic benefits of interaction with children who were not disabled; (3) the effect of Rachel's presence on the teacher and other children in the classroom; and (4) the cost of mainstreaming Rachel in a regular classroom.

1. Educational Benefits

The district court found the first factor, educational benefits to Rachel, weighed in favor of placing her in a regular classroom. . . . The court noted that theDistrict's evidence focused on Rachel's limitations but did not establish that the educational opportunities available through special education were better or equal to those available in a regular classroom. Moreover, the court found that the testimony of the Hollands' experts was more credible because they had more background in evaluating children with disabilities placed in regular classrooms and that they had a greater opportunity to observe Rachel over an extended period of time in normal circumstances. The district court also gave great weight to the testimony of Rachel's current teacher, Nina Crone, whom the court found to be an experienced, skillful teacher. Ms. Crone stated that Rachel was a full member of the class and participated in all activities. Ms. Crone testified that Rachel was making progress on her IEP goals: She was learning one-to-one correspondence in counting, was able to recite the English and Hebrew alphabets, and was improving her communication abilities and sentence lengths.

The district court found that Rachel received substantial benefits in regular education and that all of her IEP goals could be implemented in a regular classroom with some modifications to the curriculum and with the assistance of a part-time aide.

2. Non-Academic Benefits

The district court next found that the second factor, non-academic benefits to Rachel, also weighed in favor of placing her in a regular classroom. The court noted that the Hollands' evidence indicated that Rachel had developed her social and communications skills as well as her self-confidence from placement in a regular class, while the District's evidence tended to show that Rachel was not learning from exposure to other children and that she was isolated from her classmates. . . . The court found the testimony of Rachel's mother and her current teacher to be the most credible. . . .

3. Effect on the Teacher and the Children in the Regular Class

The district court next addressed the issue of whether Rachel had a detrimental effect on others in her regular classroom. The court looked ar two aspects: (1) whether there was detriment because the child was disruptive, distracting, or unruly, and (2) whether the child would take up so much of the teacher's time that the other students would suffer from lack of attention. The witnesses of both parties agreed that Rachel followed directions and was well-behaved and not a distraction in class. The court found the most germane evidence on the second aspect came from Rachel's second grade teacher, Nina Crone, who testified that Rachel did not interfere with her ability to teach the other children and in the future would require only a part-time aide. Accordingly, the district court determined that the third factor, the effect of Rachel's presence on the teacher and other children in the classroom weighed in favor of placing her in a regular classroom.

4. Cost

Finally, the district court found that the District had not offered any persuasive or credible evidence to support its claim that educating Rachel in a regular classroom with appropriate services would be significantly more expensive than educating her in the District's proposed setting.

The District contended that it would cost $109,000 to educate Rachel full-time in a regular classroom. This figure was based on the cost of providing a full-time aide for Rachel plus an estimated $80,000 for school-wide sensitivity training. The court found that the District did not establish that such training was necessary. Further, the court noted that even if such training were necessary, there was evidence from the California Department of Education that the training.could be had at no cost. Moreover, the court found it would be inappropriate to assign the total cost of the training to Rachel when other children with disabilities would benefit. In addition, the court concluded that evidence did not suggest that Rachel required a full-time aide.

In addition, the court found the District should have compared the cost of placing Rachel in a special class of approximately twelve students with a full-time special education teacher and two full-time aides and the cost of placing her in a regular class with a part-time aide. The District provided no evidence of this cost comparison.

****

By inflating the cost estimates and failing to address the true comparison, the District did not meet its burden of proving that regular placement would burden the District's funds or adversely affect the services available to other children. Therefore, the court found that the cost factor did not weigh against mainstreaming Rachel.

The district court concluded that the appropriate placement for Rachel was full-time in a regular second grade classroom with some supplemental services and affirmed the decision of the hearing officer.

****

IV. DISCUSSION

****

B. Mainstreaming Requirements of the IDEA

1. The Statute

The IDEA provides that each state must establish:
[Procedures to assure that, to the maximum extent appropriate, children with disabilities . . . are educated with children who are not disabled, and that special classes, separate schooling, or other removal of children with disabilities from the regular educational environment occurs only when the nature or severity of the disability is such that education in regular classes with the use of supplementary aids and services cannot be achieved satisfactorily . . .
20 U.S.C. § 1412(5)(B).

This provision sets forth Congress' preference for educating children with disabilities in regular classrooms with their peers . . .

****

3. Test for Determining Compliance with the IDEA's Mainstreaming Requirement

We have not adopted or devised a standard for determining the presence of compliance with 20 U.S.C. § 1412(5)(B). The Third, Fifth, and Eleventh Circuits use what is known as the *Daniel R. R.* test. *Oberti* [v. Board of Education], 995 F. 2d [1204] at 1215; *Greer* [v. Rome City School District], 950 F.2d [688] at 696; *Daniel R. R.* [v. State Board of Education], 874 F. 2d [1036] at 1048. The Fourth, Sixth and Eighth Circuits apply the *Roncker* test. *Devries v. Fairfax County Sch. Bd.*, 882 F.2d 876, 879 (4th Cir. 1989); *A. W. v. Northwest R-1 Sch. Dist.*, 813 F.2d 158, 163 (8th Cir.), *cert. denied*, 484 U.S. 847, 108 S. Ct. 144, 98 L.Ed. 2d 100 (1987); *Roncker v. Walter*, 700 F. 2d 1058, 1063 (6th Cir.), *cert. denied*, 464 U.S. 864, 104 S. Ct. 196, 78 L. Ed. 2d 171 (1983).

Although the district court relied principally on *Daniel R. R.* and *Greer*, it did not specifically adopt the *Daniel R. R.* test over the *Roncker* test. Rather, it employed factors found in both lines of cases in its analysis. The result was a four-factor balancing test in which the court considered (1) the educational benefits of placement full-time in a regular class; (2) the non-academic benefits of such placement; (3) the effect Rachel had on the teacher and children in the regular class; and (4) the costs of mainstreaming Rachel. This analysis directly addresses the issues of appropriate placement for a child with disabilities under the requirements of 20 U.S.C. § 1412(5)(B). Accordingly, we approve and adopt the test employed by the district court.

4. The District's Contentions on Appeal

The District strenuously disagrees with the district court's findings that Rachel was receiving academic and non-academic benefits in a regular class and did not have a detrimental effect on the teacher or other students. It argues that the court's findings were contrary to the evidence of the state Diagnostic Center and that the court should not have been persuaded by the testimony of Rachel's teacher, particularly her testimony that Rachel would need only a part-time aide in the future. The district court, however, conducted a full evidentiary hearing and made a thorough analysis. The court found the Holland's evidence to be more persuasive. Moreover, the court asked Rachel's teacher extensive questions regarding Rachel's need for a part-time aide. We will not disturb the findings of the district court.

The District is also not persuasive on the issue of cost. . . .

****

We affirm the judgement of the district court. While we cannot determine what the appropriate placement is for Rachel at the present time, we hold that the determination of the present and future appropriate placement for Rachel should be based on the principles set forth in this opinion and the opinion of the district court.

AFFIRMED

(Footnotes omitted.)

ADDITIONAL COMMENTARY

1. The Office for Special Education and Rehabilitative Services (OSERS) issued a letter which summarizes least restrictive environment issues, 18 I.D.E.L.R. 213 (1991):

   The LRE provisions contained in Part B require that all children with disabilities, regardless of the nature or severity of their disability, must be educated, wherever possible, with children who are not disabled, and that "special classes, separate schooling or other removal of [children with disabilities] from the regular educational environment occurs only if the nature or severity of the [disability] is such that education in regular classes, even with the use of supplementary aids and services, cannot be achieved satisfactorily." 34 C.F.R. § 300.550(b)(1)-(2); see also 20 U.S.C. § 1412(5)(B).

   Part B also requires that each child's placement must be based upon his or her individualized education program (IEP), must be determined at least annually, and must be in the school or facility as close as possible to the child's home. See 34 C.F.R. § 300.552(a)(1)-(3). Further, unless the IEP of a child who is disabled specified another arrangement, "the child is to be educated in the school or facility he or she would attend if not [disabled]." See 34 C.F.R. § 300.552(c).

   Therefore, under Part B, a determination of what constitutes the least restrictive educational placement must be based upon the individual needs of each child, as described and specified in his or her IEP. Placement cannot be based solely on such factors as the category of the child's disability, the availability of appropriate staff, administrative convenience, or the configuration of the service-delivery system.

   Part B recognizes, however, that children with disabilities may need to be educated in various types of settings in order to meet their unique educational needs. For this reason, Part B requires public agencies to make available to all students with disabilities a continuum of alternative placements, or a range of placement options, to meet the needs of these students for special education and related services. See 34 C.F.R. § 300.551(a). The options on this continuum include "instruction in regular classes, special classes, special schools, home instruction, and instruction in hospitals and institutions." 34 C.F.R. § 300.551(b)(1). Further the options on the continuum of alternative placements must be made available to the extent necessary to implement each child's IEP. See 34 C.F.R. § 300.552(b).

2. Regulations require that "each child's educational placement . . . is as close as possible to the child's home; . . . unless the IEP of a child with a disability requires some other arrangement, the child is educated in the school which he or she would attend if nondisabled." 34 C.F.R. 300.552. However, the primary concern remains that of providing an appropriate placement. Thus, if the neighborhood school cannot provide an appropriate education, the child need not be placed there. Further, since a district is not obligated to duplicate a program at a child's neighborhood school, the child may be required to attend a school further from home to receive specific educational services. *Barnett v. Fairfax County School Board,* 927 F.2d 146 (4th Cir. 1991); *Schuldt v. Mankato Independent School District,* No. 77, 937 F.2d 1357 (8th Cir. 1991); *Plano Independent School District, Texas,* 18 I.D.E.L.R. 1275 (1992); *Royal Oak Public Schools, Michigan,* 19 I.D.E.L.R. 194 (1992).

3. Leonard is a fifth-grade student who has been identified as having mental retardation (MR) and severe emotional disturbance (SED). After a reevaluation, the district proposed a change in his placement from a special education school to a "self-contained MR/SED" class. His mother re-

fused this placement because it did not provide opportunities for interactions with peers. While awaiting outcomes, Leonard's placement included an "EMR class" (educable mentally retarded) with mainstreaming and the segregated school. The court held that the segregated school placement would provide an academic benefit for Leonard; he could not benefit from the EMR class because of the nature of his emotional disability. However, the district and the intermediate school unit should make a "good faith effort" to provide mainstreaming for Leonard. *Liscio v. Woodland Hills School District*, 734 F. Supp. 689 (W.D. Pa. 1989).

4. Two brothers with hearing impairments, ages 11 and 13 years, had attended a private school for students with hearing impairments since they were quite young. The school district proposed a change to a mainstreamed public school program for students with hearing impairments. The court held that "public education and mainstreamed education were not intended to be mandated for every handicapped child." For these two students, a mainstreamed education was not least restrictive, i.e., "it is far better to prepare the handicapped to function in society . . . via special schools . . . rather than mainstreaming a youngster now with the possibility of producing an adult who might have to rely on social services." *Visco v. School District of Pittsburgh*, 684 F. Supp. 1310 (W.D. Penn. 1988).

5. James is a child with a hearing impairment. His school district proposed a placement in a segregated program for children with hearing impairments. This placement was founded on a belief that placement in a less segregated environment would be appropriate only after James's speech became more intelligible. The Court of Appeals held that the board's proposed placement was not inappropriate because of the "mainstreaming policy." Severity of handicap is a consideration. *Briggs v. Board of Education of the State of Connecticut*, 882 F.2d 688 (2nd Cir. 1989).

6. For an excellent discussion of theories and methods of inclusion, see L. Brown, P. Schwartz, A. Udvari-Solner, E. Kampschroer, F. Johnson, J. Jorgensen, and L. Gruenewald, "How Much Time Should Students with Severe Intellectual Disabilities Spend in Regular Education Classrooms and Elsewhere?" *Journal of Association for Persons with Severe Handicaps, 16,* (1991): 39–47.

7. For a discussion of the ties between the civil rights movement and IDEA, particularly the roots of the concept of least restrictive environment, see P. Strain and B. Smith, *Global Educational and Social Forces Affecting Preschool Mainstreaming.* Policy and Practice in Early Childhood Special Education Series (Pittsburgh: Allegheny-Singer Research Institute, 1991), p. 274.

8. Two other terms used in this area are *normalization* and *regular education initiative.* Leaders in the field of special education, such as Wolf Wolfensberger, Burton Blatt, and others, have advocated normalization for persons with disabilities. As defined by Bengt Nirje (1969), "The normalization principle means making available to [persons with disabilities] patterns and conditions of everyday life which are as close as possible to the norms and patterns of the mainstream of society. Wolfensberger defines it as 'establishing or maintaining personal behaviors and characteristics which are as culturally normative as possible'" (Symposium on "'Normalization': The Normalization Principle—Implications and Comments," *British Journal of Mental Subnormality, 16* (1970): 62.)

Regarding the "regular education initiative," Madeleine Will, Assistant Secretary of Special Education and Rehabilitative Services, said in her November 1986 Report to the Secretary of Education:

> *The Office of Special Education and Rehabilitative Services is committed to increasing the educational success of children with learning problems. OSERS challenges states to renew their commitment to serve these children effectively. The heart of this commitment is the search for ways to serve as many of the children as possible in the regular classroom by encouraging special education and other special programs to form a partnership with regular education. The objective of the partnership for special education and the other special programs is to use their knowledge and expertise to support regular education in educating children with learning problems. (p. 20)*

9. The LRE mandate also applies to preschool students with disabilities. Consideration must then

be made for mainstreaming preschoolers with disabilities when the district does not provide programs for nondisabled preschoolers. The district is not required to initiate preschool programs just to provide mainstreaming opportunities. Comment, 34 C.F.R. 300.552 (1990). However, if the district does not operate preschools, it must pursue alternative methods for integration such as integrating preschoolers with disabilities into other publicly operated preschools or into private preschools, or locating the preschool in a regular elementary school. As with school-age children, a preschooler's IEP must indicate the extent to which the child is to participate in regular education.

RELATED SERVICES

One of the most controversial and possibly most expensive aspects of IDEA is its related services mandate. The statutory definition of *related services* is:

> [T]ransportation, and such developmental, corrective, and other supportive services (including speech pathology and audiology, psychological services, physical and occupational therapy, recreation, including therapeutic recreation and social work services, counseling services, including rehabilitation counseling, and medical services, except that such medical services shall be for diagnostic and evaluation purposes only) as may be required to assist a child with a disability to benefit from special education, and includes the early identification and assessment of disabling conditions in children.[137]

The regulations do little more than list additional examples of possible services, e.g., "school health services, social work services in schools, and parent counseling and training."[138] It is clear that this listing is not intended to be exhaustive, but is meant only to provide examples of possible services. As stated in the comments to the regulations:

> The list of related services is not exhaustive and may include other developmental, corrective, or supportive services (such as artistic and cultural programs, art, music, and dance therapy), if they are required to assist a child with a disability to benefit from special education.[139]

Recent amendments added assistive technology devices and services[140] and transition services[141] to the statute. Although not included in the definition of special education or related services, assistive technology[142] and transition services[143] can be required to be included as related services if needed. In essence, related services could be virtually anything needed by the child to benefit from special education;[144] only medical services and individually prescribed equipment are excluded. The responsibility of the district is to provide those services to students with disabilities that are necessary for them to benefit from their special education.

In *Irving Independent School District v. Tatro*,[145] the Supreme Court devised a three-part test to determine whether a school district is required to provide a particular service to a student as a related service: (1) the child must be "handicapped" so as to require special education, (2) the service must be necessary for the child to benefit from his or her special education, and (3) it must be determined if the service falls within an exclusion, i.e., medical or individually prescribed equipment.

In *Tatro*, the Court emphasized that the child must be "handicapped" under IDEA before he or she can be eligible for related services. "In the absence of a handicap that requires special education, the need for what otherwise might qualify as a related service does not create an obligation under the Act."[146] Thus, a student who may need some counseling services but does not require other special educational services is not "handicapped" and does not qualify for related services. This is consistent with a comment to the regulations that states:

The definition of "special education" is a particularly important one under these regulations, since a child does not have a disability under this part unless he or she needs special education. . . . The definition of related services also depends on this definition, since a related service must be necessary for a child to benefit from special education. Therefore, if a child does not need special education, there can be no "related services," and the child [because without a disability] is not covered under the Act.[147]

There is one exception to this requirement. When a state defines a related service, e.g., speech therapy, as special education, and the child is classified as educationally disabled in that area, e.g., speech impaired, that related service must be provided to the child regardless of whether the child requires other special education. In this instance, the related service itself constitutes the "special education."[148] The regulations defining the term *special education* address this point:

[Special education] includes speech pathology, or any other related service, if the service consists of specially designed instruction, at no cost to the parents, to meet the unique needs of a child with a disability, and is considered special education rather than a related service under State standards.[149]

There seems to be a substantial amount of controversy over whether a service is actually necessary for a child to receive educational benefits. To show necessity usually requires a showing that the services are an integral part of the other educational services provided. In other words, it must be shown that the services are made necessary by the disabling condition and concomitant educational program:

— Is the service necessary for the student to gain access to or remain in the special program?
— Is the service necessary to resolve other needs for the student before educational efforts will be successful?

— Is the service necessary for the student to make meaningful progress on the identified goals?

An increasing body of litigation revolves around the issue of exclusions—primarily whether a service is a medical service for evaluation purposes, a health service, or an ongoing medical treatment (only the latter is excluded from the related service mandate). Thus, disputes arise about whether the medical service is relevant to determining a proper classification or educational placement. The question of whether a service is a medical service or a health service has proved troublesome. In *Tatro*, the Supreme Court drew the distinction, simplistically, on the qualification of the service provider, thus services that must be provided by a physician are necessarily medical services. However, since then, the distinction seems to be drawn on the complexity, frequency, and emergency nature of the services provided.[150]

Another area of frequent litigation involves the related service of transportation. This is logical since transportation is the most common related service offered. It can be required as necessary for the child to receive benefits from the primary special education—a child cannot benefit from special education provided at a school site unless he or she can get to the school site. Additionally, it can be required as necessary for the child to receive benefits from other related services provided, such as transportation to therapy. The school must provide transportation even if the child is not receiving services within the school district boundaries, e.g., if the child is attending a special day school or a residential school outside of the district.[151]

The question of who must provide related services often raises concerns, particularly in the areas of counseling and psychotherapy. A comment to the regulations states:

There are certain kinds of services that might be provided by persons from varying professional backgrounds and with a variety of operational titles, depending upon requirements in individual States. For example, counseling services might be provided by social workers, psychologists, or guidance counselors; and psychological testing might be done by qualified psychological examiners, psychometrists, or psychologists, depending upon State standards.[152]

It appears, then, that for most services, the service provided is dictated by state statutes and regulations. However, when psychological services are provided by a psychiatrist, some courts have held the service to then fall in the category of medical services, excluded by the statute.[153] This issue is further complicated when it is not clear whether the psychological services are necessary to the child's educational or medical needs. If the services are primarily designed to address a medical need, they are not related services.[154] This situation also occurs in the situation of students who are in need of drug therapy. Again, if it is determined that the drug-treatment program is needed for a medical, rather than educational, purpose, it is not a related service under IDEA.[155]

IRVING INDEPENDENT SCHOOL DISTRICT v. TATRO
468 U.S. 883, 104 S. Ct. 3371, 82 L. Ed. 2d 664 (1984)

Chief Justice BURGER delivered the opinion of the Court.

I.

****

Amber Tatro is an 8-year-old girl born with a defect known as spina bifida. As a result, she suffers from orthopedic and speech impairments and a neurogenic bladder, which prevents her from emptying her bladder voluntarily. Consequently, she must be catheterized every three or four hours to avoid injury to her kidneys. In accordance with accepted medical practice, clean intermittent catheterization (CIC), a procedure involving the insertion of a catheter into the urethra to drain the bladder, has been prescribed. The procedure is a simple one that may be performed in a few minutes by a layperson with less than one hour's training.

In 1979 petitioner, *Irving Independent School District*, agreed to provide special education for Amber, who was then three and one-half years old. In consultation with her parents, who are respondents here, petitioner developed an individualized education program for Amber under the requirements of the Education of the Handicapped Act, . . . 20 U.S.C. §§ 1401(19), 1414(a)(5) [now IDEA]. The individualized education program provided that Amber would attend early childhood development classes and receive special services such as physical and occupational therapy. That program, however, made no provision for school personnel to administer CIC.

****

The issue in this case is whether CIC is a "related service" that petitioner is obliged to provide to Amber. We must answer two questions: first, whether CIC is a "supportive servic[e] . . . required to assist a handicapped child to benefit from special education"; and second, whether CIC is excluded from this definition as a "medical servic[e] serving purposes other than diagnosis or evaluation."

A.

The Court of Appeals was clearly correct in holding that CIC is a "supportive servic[e] . . . required to assist a handicapped child to benefit from special education." It is clear on this record that, without having CIC services available during the school day, Amber cannot attend school and thereby "benefit from special education." CIC services therefore fall squarely within the definition of a "supportive service."

As we have stated before, "Congress sought primarily to make public education available to handicapped children" and "to make such access meaningful." *Board of Education of Hendrick Hudson Central School District v. Rowley*, 458 U.S. 176, 192, 102 S. Ct. 3034, 3043, 73 L. Ed. 2d 690

(1982). A service that enables a handicapped child to remain at school during the day is an important means of providing the child with the meaningful access to education that Congress envisioned. The Act makes specific provision for services, like transportation, for example, that do no more than enable a child to be physically present in class *see* S. Rep. No. 94-168, p.38 (1975), U.S. Code Cong. & Admin. News 1975, p.1425; 121 Cong. Rec. 19483-19484 (1975) (remarks of Sen. Stafford). Services like CIC that permit a child to remain at school during the day are no less related to the effort to educate than are services that enable the child to reach, enter, or exit the school.

We hold that CIC services in this case qualify as a "supportive servic[e] . . . required to assist a handicapped child to benefit from special education."

B.

We also agree with the Court of Appeals that provision of CIC is not a "medical servic[e]," which a school is required to provide only for purposes of diagnosis or evaluation. *See* 20 U.S.C. § 1401(17). We begin with the regulations of the Department of Education, which are entitled to deference. *See, e.g., Blum v. Bacon*, 457 U.S. 132, 141, 102 S.Ct. 2344, 2361, 72 L.Ed. 2d 728 (1982). The regulations define "related services" for handicapped children to include "school health services," 34 C.F.R. § 300.13(a) (1983), which are defined in turn as "services provided by a qualified school nurse or other qualified person," § 300.13(b)(4). Thus, the Secretary has determined that the services of a school nurse otherwise qualifying as a "related service" are not subject to exclusion as a "medical service," but that the services of a physician are excludable as such.

This definition of "medical services" is a reasonable interpretation of congressional intent. Although Congress devoted little discussion to the "medical services" exclusion, the Secretary could reasonably have concluded that it was designed to spare schools from an obligation to provide a service that might well prove unduly expensive and beyond the range of their competence. From this understanding of congressional purpose, the Secretary could reasonably have concluded that Congress intended to impose the obligation to provide school nursing services.

Congress plainly required schools to hire various specially trained personnel to help handicapped children, such as "trained occupational therapists, speech therapists, psychologists, social workers and other appropriately trained personnel." S.Rep. No. 94-168, *supra*, at 33, U.S. Code Cong. & Admin. News 1975, p.1457. School nurses have long been a part of the educational system, and the Secretary could therefore reasonably conclude that school nursing services are not the sort of burden that Congress intended to exclude as a "medical service." By limiting the "medical services" exclusion to the services of a physician or hospital, both far more expensive, the Secretary has given a permissible construction to the provision.

****

To keep in perspective the obligation to provide services that relate to both the health and educational needs of handicapped students, we note several limitations that should minimize the burden petitioner fears. First, to be entitled to related services, a child must be handicapped so as to require special education. *See* 20 U.S.C. § 1401(1); 34 C.F.R. § 300.5 (1983). In the absence of a handicap that requires special education, the need for what otherwise might qualify as a related service does not create an obligation under the Act. *See* 34 C.F.R. § 300.14, Comment (1) (1983).

Second, only those services necessary to aid a handicapped child to benefit from special education must be provided, regardless how easily a school nurse or layperson could furnish them. For example, if a particular medication or treatment may appropriately be administered to a handicapped child other than during the school day, a school is not required to provide nursing services to administer it.

Third, the regulations state that school nursing services must be provided only if they can be performed by a nurse or other qualified person, not if they must be performed by a physician. *See also, e.g., Department of Education of Hawaii v. Katherine D.*, 727 F.2d 809 (CA9 1983).

Finally, we note that respondents are not asking petitioner to provide *equipment* that Amber needs for CIC. Tr. of Oral Arg. 18-19. They seek only the *services* of a qualified person at the school.

We conclude that provision of CIC to Amber is not subject to exclusion as a "medical service," and we affirm the Court of Appeals' holding that CIC is a "related service" under the Education of the Handicapped Act.

— — — —

GRANITE SCHOOL DISTRICT v. SHANNON M.
787 F. Supp. 1020 (U.S. District Court, District of Utah 1992)

SAM, District Judge.

****

II. FACTS

For purposes of this action, the parties have stipulated to the following facts. Shannon is a six-year old student who attended kindergarten classes at Granite's Orchard Elementary during the 1989–90 school year. She suffers from congenital neuromuscular atrophy and severe scoliosis and is confined to a motorized wheelchair. Shannon is classified as "orthopedically impaired" under the Act [IDEA]. She breathes through a tracheotomy tube in her windpipe, which must be suctioned to loosen mucous and reduce the chances of a potentially life-threatening mucous plug. Shannon also receives her food through a nasogastric tube, which the nurse attends to. Shannon's nurse typically suctions Shannon's tracheostomy tube five times during a three-hour school day, including the bus ride. In spite of suctioning, Shannon's tracheostomy tube occasionally gets a mucous plug. Shannon cannot breathe until the plug is broken up or the tracheostomy tube is changed. When a plug occurs, Shannon's caretaker uses saline solution, tries to suction, and then changes the tube if the first two do not work. Sometimes, Shannon needs an ambu bag (a portable ventilator) to open her lungs if her color is bad and she is not getting enough oxygen. Shannon needs someone available in case she has problems with respiration, suctioning, her nasogastric tube, pain or positioning. Granite has a "do not resuscitate" order from Shannon's doctor stating that heroic measures are not to be used if Shannon should suffer cardiac arrest. In 1991, Shannon was scheduled to start first grade, which consists of a seven-hour day. . . .

III. DISCUSSION

The issue before the court is whether the health care, which Shannon needs in order to attend school, must be provided by Granite as part of her free appropriate public education. More specifically, the court must decide whether full time nursing care for Shannon is a supportive service required by the Act, or whether it is a medical service excluded under the Act. The question is one of law, which the court reviews de novo.

****

Shannon contends that Granite is required by the Act to provide, as a "related service," the full-time nursing care which she needs in order to attend school. In essence, Shannon argues that she needs tracheostomy care to attend school and she needs to attend school to benefit from her special education.

Granite's position is that the law requires it to provide Shannon with a basic floor of opportunity which she receives through home-bound instruction, rather than maximization of Shannon's potential, which she seeks through full-time nursing care in the classroom. Granite further claims that the type of care that Shannon is requesting is not required under the Act because full time nursing care is a medical service, beyond diagnosis or evaluation, and is thus excluded under the Act.

2. A Basic Floor of Opportunity—Sufficient Supportive Services to Benefit from Education

****

To keep in perspective the obligation to provide services that relate to both the health and educational needs of handicapped students, we note several limitations that should minimize the burden petitioner fears. First, to be entitled to related services, a child must be handicapped so as to require special education.

****

Second, only those services necessary to aid a handicapped child to benefit from special education must be provided, regardless [of] how easily a school nurse or layperson could furnish them. . . .

Third, the regulations state that school nursing services must be provided only if they can be performed by a nurse or other qualified person, not if they must be performed by a physician. See 34 C.F.R. §§ 300.13(a), (b)(4), (b)(10) (1983).
Tatro, 468 U.S. at 894, 104 S. Ct. at 3378.

Instructive authority is also found in *Thomas v. Cincinnati Bd of Ed.*, 918 F.2d 618 (6th Cir. 1990), in which the Sixth Circuit ruled that a child who required tracheostomy and gastrostomy tube care could gain reasonable benefits from five hours of weekly home instruction even though the school-based program might provide more related services. . . . The court reasoned that:

> Although it appears that Emily may receive fewer related services at home than at the SMI program, we are not deciding which placement would be more advantageous to Emily's development, only whether the revised IEP will enable her to benefit. All the experts agreed that Emily would benefit educationally from the revised IEP providing for additional home instruction and, indeed, plaintiff does not contend that this IEP is not appropriate, only that it is not as good as the SMI program. . . . Since there is no dispute over whether the revised IEP will enable Emily to benefit educationally, we conclude that the school district has satisfied the Act's substantive provisions.
> *Id.* at 627.

3. Medical Services Exclusion

****

The specific holding of *Tatro* is that CIC service is a supportive service not subject to the medical services exclusion of the Act. The court does not read *Tatro* to stand for the proposition that all health services performed by someone other than a licensed physician are related services under the Act regardless of the amount of care, expense, or burden on the school system and, ultimately, on other school children.

Other courts interpreting *Tatro* have found Shannon's asserted interpretation, based on the physician-non-physician provider, too narrow. The court concurs with the analysis and authorities set forth in *Clovis Unified School Dist. v. California Office of Adm. Hearings*, 903 F.2d 635 (9th Cir. 1990). That case involved, inter alia, the issue of whether the school was required by the Act to pay for care of an emotionally disturbed child in a psychiatric hospital as a related service. . . .

A number of District Courts have faced this issue and have concluded that the "licensed physician" distinction is inadequate as a sole criterion for determining when services fall under the medical exclusion from liability. In *Max M. v. Thompson*, 592 F. Supp. 1437 (N.D. Ill. 1984), the District Court held that psychotherapy, a recognized related service under the Act, does not become excluded as a medical service merely because it is provided by a psychiatrist—a licensed physician—rather than by a psychologist. We agree with the reasoning of this opinion, and with its rejection of an arbitrary classi-

fication of services based solely on the licensed status of the service provider. If a licensed physician may provide related services without their becoming instantly "medical," we believe that by the same token a program clearly aimed at curing an illness—whether mental or physical—does not become instantly "related" when it can be implemented by persons other than licensed physicians.

The post-*Tatro* case of *Detsel v. Board of Education of Auburn*, 637 F. Supp. 1022 (N.D.N.Y. 1986), *aff'd* 820 F.2d 587 (2d Cir.), *cert. denied*, 484 U.S. 981, 108 S. Ct. 495, 98 L. Ed. 2d 494 (1987), is even more on point. There a district court found that intensive life support service necessary to maintain a child in school fell outside the "related services" mandated by the Act. . . . Applying the principles of *Tatro*, the court found that holding the school district responsible for the provision of such "extensive, therapeutic health services" would be contrary to the rationale of the medical services exclusion in the Act, based as it is upon relieving schools of the obligation to provide services calculated to be unduly expensive. *Id.*

. . . . [S]ervices which must be provided by a licensed physician, other than those which are diagnostic or evaluative, are excluded and that school nursing services of a simple nature are not excluded. In reaching this decision the Court considered the extent and nature of the services performed, not solely the status of the person performing the services.

****

The court is of the view that the basic floor of opportunity, as required by the Act, has been provided to Shannon. In the court's opinion, Shannon's IEP confers some educational benefit on her. No evidence to the contrary has been presented. The Act and the controlling case authority require that a child with a disability be provided with sufficient supportive services to enable the child to benefit from instruction. This Granite has done. The court, therefore, is of the opinion and finds that Granite has complied with the law. . . .

The court acknowledges the preference of Congress, manifest in the Act, to mainstream children with disabilities into the regular classroom. However, the Act also provides for the child's removal from regular classes if the child's education cannot be achieved satisfactorily. 20 U.S.C. § 1412(5)(B). The harsh reality of Shannon's case is that she requires the full-time care of at least a licensed practical nurse because of the constant possibility of a mucous plug in the tracheostomy tube. Such a plug is common, occurring a number of times each day. Without the appropriate care, Shannon's disability becomes life threatening. The record reflects that Granite's three school nurses must serve 75,000 children in more than ninety schools and, therefore, are not reasonably available to provide Shannon with constant care. The cost to Granite of providing Shannon with constant nursing care is estimated at $30,000 a year. The expense of providing Shannon's requested care would undoubtedly take money away from other programs. The court's decision must be tempered by paramount concern for Shannon's safety and by the Act's principle goal of providing a free appropriate public education for all handicapped children. . . . Accordingly, the court is further of the opinion and finds that Shannon's mainstreaming cannot be "achieved satisfactorily."

As an additional basis for its ruling that Granite is not required by Federal law to provide Shannon with the requested care, the court is also of the opinion and finds that the constant nursing/tracheostomy care requested by Shannon falls within the medical services exclusion of the Act, and, therefore, it is not

a service that Granite must provide as a matter of federal law. The court rejects the narrow construction of the medical services exclusion of the Act based on the licensed physician distinction asserted by Shannon. Shannon's reliance on *Tatro* is misplaced. The differences between the level of care required in *Tatro* and the care required by Shannon are significant. The child in *Tatro* did not require constant monitoring. The CIC procedure, which the child would soon be able to perform for herself, could be performed by a layperson a few times a day. In contrast, Shannon requires constant care to monitor and clear her tube. . . .

****

. . . . [T]he court concludes that the Act does not require Granite to provide Shannon with full-time nursing/tracheostomy care as a supportive service. The court further concludes that Shannon cannot satisfactorily be mainstreamed or educated with children who are not disabled. The services requested by Shannon are also found not to be a related service under the medical services exclusion of the Act.

. . . . Granite's motion for summary judgment is GRANTED.

(Footnotes omitted.)

▬ ▬ ▬ ▬

HURRY v. JONES
734 F.2d 879 (First Circuit 1984)

COFFIN, Circuit Judge.

****

George Hurry (George) suffers from cerebral palsy and a degree of mental retardation, and is confined to a wheelchair by spastic quadriplegia. He has attended various special education programs in the Providence area. Until January 1976 the City of Providence provided him with door-to-door bus transportation to and from school. By January of 1976, however, George had reached a weight of 160 pounds, and the bus drivers deemed it unsafe to continue to carry him up and down the steep concrete steps that led from his front door to the street. Mr. and Mrs. Hurry began to transport George to and from school in their van.

Starting in June 1976 Mr. Hurry held a position that required him to work until 5:15 p.m. each day.

Because Mrs. Hurry could not lift George from the van and carry him up the steps without her husband's aid, he had to wait in the van for several hours each day until Mr. Hurry left work. He frequently missed school when the weather was too hot or too cold to permit him to wait in the van. George began to complain of pain in his legs from the long periods he spent in the van. In December of 1977, Mr. and Mrs. Hurry stopped transporting him to school; . . .

. . . . By October 29, 1979, the parties had agreed on an Individual Educational Program for George that provided him with transportation to and from school and obviated the need for injunctive relief. . . . [T]he Hurrys pursued claims for damages for the period during which George attended school only if they were able to transport him and for the period during which he did not attend school at all.

****

The decision of the district court awarding the Hurrys $5,750.00 as reimbursement for transportation expenses and the decision denying their application for attorney's fees are affirmed. The decision awarding George Hurry $8,796.00 under the EAHCA and $5,000.00 under the Rehabilitation Act is reversed. The parties will bear their own costs on appeal.

BAILEY ALDRICH, Senior Circuit Judge (dissenting in part).

I concur in those portions of the opinion that deny recovery, but cannot in the part ordering reimbursement for transportation. . . . I first consider the merits, vis., that in spite of a regulation calling for transportation of handicapped children from and to their street-level front door, defendants have been charged with additional burdens due to the fact that plaintiffs' front door was twelve damaged steps above the street.

The district court found,

Bus drivers for the school department would carry George from the front door of his home down approximately twelve steps to the street level and into the bus. By January of 1976, however, George had gained weight and was so heavy (160 lbs.) that the bus drivers would no longer carry him. In addition to the child being overweight, the concrete steps were steep and cracked in some places, making it somewhat unsafe for anyone to attempt to carry George down to the street (Emphasis suppl.) (560 F. Supp., ante, at 503).

****

The underlying statute, Education for All Handicapped Children Act (EAHCA), 20 U.S.C. §§ 1413 (a)(4)(B) and 1401(17), required furnishing, simply, "transportation." The Rhode Island regulations, which the court quoted, and considered, spelt this out, one with respect to transportation generally,

("door to door") and one specifically with regard to assistance, manifestly defining what was meant by "door."

1.0 Responsibility—All handicapped children who need special transportation as a related service and as determined by the evaluation process and described in the I.E.P. shall be provided such service. It shall include free transportation to and from the home (door to door, if necessary) to the educational program in which he/she is enrolled. . . .

2.0 Transportation Needs of Handicapped Children.

2.1.2 A minimum of one aide assigned to each bus. Such aide, in addition to providing general care and supervision of all handicapped children on such bus, shall also provide assistance (from street level entrance of dwelling) to such children lacking the mobility to leave the home and board transportation vehicles, and shall further assist such children in debarking the vehicle and entering the school. . . .
(Emphasis suppl.) (Id. at 506-07).

The district court found these regulations "clear," and that, in failing to arrange for George's reaching the street level, defendants "ignored their obvious duty." I find them clear, but just the reverse. In my opinion "street level" means exactly what it says, and the court, although recognizing, ante, that the door was above the street level, excised from the regulation, without even discussion, precisely what had caused all the difficulties.

My brethren feel that because defendants did not attack it, the district court's interpretation is the law of the case. Before reaching that question, I must first consider whether the ruling was wrong. I believe it plainly so. . . .

****

I must dissent.
(Footnotes omitted.)

— — — —

McNAIR v. OAK HILLS LOCAL SCHOOL DISTRICT
872 F.2d 153 (Sixth Circuit 1989)

JOINER, Senior District Judge.

On October 3, 1985, James, Mary and Kelly McNair (McNair) filed a complaint against the Oak Hills Local School District, the Oak Hills Board of

Education, and Louis Cardimone, Superintendent of the Oak Hills School District (collectively referred to as Oak Hills), under the Education of the Handicapped Act (EHA), 20 U.S.C. §§ 1400, *et seq.* [now IDEA]. The McNairs sought, among other things, a determination that Oak Hills had to provide their child, Kelly, with transportation to and from St. Rita's School for the Deaf, a private school. . . .

****

. . . . [T]he relevant underlying facts of this case:
. . . .

2. Kelly McNair has a hearing impairment which qualifies her for a free, appropriate, public education under P.L. 94-142 [now IDEA].
3. Kelly McNair is currently enrolled at St. Rita's, a non-public school.
4. The Oak Hills School District was willing to provide Kelly McNair with an appropriate education at Frost Elementary School.
5. Kelly McNair was placed at St. Rita's by her parents.
6. Mr. and Mrs. McNair are paying the tuition charges at St. Rita's.

****

The McNairs want Oak Hills to provide transportation for Kelly to and from St. Rita's as a related service under the EHA. They will succeed only if they establish that which § 1400(c) requires:

(1) that the child is handicapped;
(2) that transportation is a related service;
(3) that the related service is designed to meet the unique needs of the child caused by the handicap; and
(4) the school district must be responsible under the EHA and its regulations for providing the related services under the particular circumstances of the case at hand.

In the instant case, the parties have stipulated that Kelly is handicapped under the EHA because of her hearing impairment. The second requirement is also satisfied, as the service at issue in this case is transportation to and from school, and this is by statute made a related service under the EHA. 20 U.S.C. § 1401(17); . . . The third requirement of the statute, the showing that the related services are "designed to meet . . . unique needs" of the child is not met in this case. The parties have stipulated that Kelly's handicap does not require any special transportation needs, therefore, she could utilize the same transportation service as a non-handicapped child. The need for transportation, although a related service, is no more unique to Kelly because she is deaf than it would be if she were not deaf. Since the statute specifically requires a relationship between the related service and the unique needs of the child, the third requirement under the EHA has not been satisfied, and the Act does not require Oak Hills to provide Kelly with transportation to St. Rita's.

****

The court is not reaching any determination as to whether a school district in a situation similar to the instant one would have to provide the related service to the child if it was designed to meet that child's unique needs. In other words, because the third requirement set out above was not satisfied, the court reaches no conclusion as to the final requirement. We leave that for another court on another day. All we hold today is that when a child is voluntarily placed in a private school, a public school district need not provide a related service to that child under the EHA if that particular service is not designed to meet the unique needs of the child.

****

AFFIRMED.
(Footnotes omitted.)

ADDITIONAL COMMENTARY

1. In *Maurits v. Board of Education of Hartford County*, 555 E.H.L.R. 364 (D. Md. 1983), a child with hemophilia was judged to not be entitled to physical therapy as a related service since he received no special education nor was he educationally disabled. However, the question remains whether some services may need to be provided by the district pursuant to Section 504, *e.g.,* *Bement Community School District #5*, 353 E.H.L.R. 383 (OCR 1989). The Office for Civil Rights has ruled that the Section 504 requirement that schools provide a free appropriate public education (FAPE) requires schools to provide related services to students who are handicapped under Section 504, but not eligible as disabled under IDEA. According to OCR, this result is

required by the nondiscrimination mandates and may be enforced by OCR. 16 E.H.L.R. 1177 (OCR 1990); *also West Chester Area School District*, 18 I.D.E.L.R. 802 (S.E.A. PA 1992). See Chapter 3 on Section 504 for additional discussion.

2. A hearing-impaired student was not entitled to transportation as a related service since the transportation was not necessary to address the hearing impairment. *McNair v. Oak Hills Local School District*, 872 F.2d 153 (6th Cir. 1989). However, an earlier Office for Civil Rights ruling stated that types of services may not be restricted to students with certain disabilities, *e.g.*, transportation may not be limited only to mobility impaired students. 352 E.H.L.R. 541 (OCR 1987).

3. A service may be necessary for a student's education even though the service has to be provided to another person. For example, the regulations use parent counseling as an example of a related service. In *Stacey G. v. Pasadena Independent School District*, 695 F.2d 949 (5th Cir. 1983), the court ordered the school to provide parent training and counseling necessary to avoid a residential placement for the student. *Also Dole*, 211 E.H.L.R. 399 (O.S.E.R.S. 1986). In *Cohen v. Dade County School Bd.*, 450 So. 2d 1238 (Fl. App. 1984), the district was required to pay for transportation for the family to visit a child in a residential placement.

4. The regulations provide recreation as one example of related services. Recreation is further defined as including (a) assessment of leisure function, (b) therapeutic recreation services, (c) recreation programs in school and community agencies, and (d) leisure education. 34 C.F.R. 300.16(9). *E.g.*, a request for scouting as a recreational service. *Franklin #5 School District*, 506 E.H.L.R. 387 (S.E.A. 1985).

5. Computers are often requested as an auxiliary aid. *E.g., San Francisco Unified School District*, 507 E.H.L.R. 416 (S.E.A. 1985); *Hamilton*, 213 E.H.L.R. 269 (O.S.E.R.S. 1989). One can assume that the inclusion of assistive technology will increase the focus on this area. *Lambert*, 18 IDELR 1039 (OSEP 1992). In many cases, the IEP team may determine it is necessary for the child to have

a computer at home also. *Schrag*, 18 I.D.E.L.R. 627 (OSEP 1991).

6. Courts have determined that because of establishment of religion concerns, some services may not be provided on the grounds of parochial schools. However, in *Zobrest v. Catalina Foothills School District*, 113 S. Ct. 2462 (1993), the Supreme Court held that providing a sign-language interpreter by the public school district in a parochial school posed no violation of the First Amendment. This will be discussed *supra* in connection with placement at private schools.

7. Just as parents can be reimbursed for unilateral placement of a child if found to be necessary, so can they be reimbursed for expenses incurred in providing related services that are later found to be necessary and not provided by the school. Here again, the parents must show that the services the district offered were not appropriate and the services they procured were. *E.g., Doe v. Defendant I*, 898 F.2d 1186 (6th Cir. 1990), involving tutorial services for a student with learning disabilities, the parent was not reimbursed for private tutorial services because it was not shown that the volunteer services offered by the district were inappropriate.

8. A school district was held responsible for the costs of a student's related services provided during a hospitalization, even though the student was not determined to be eligible for special education until her release. This was because the district should have known the student was eligible but had failed to act for an unreasonable amount of time. *Barnett*, 18 I.D.E.L.R. 1235 (OSEP 1992).

9. Transition services will become of increasing significance to schools. The district's responsibilities in this area are very broad. The services must be provided in an outcome-oriented process, implying progress and results. If appropriate, the IEP must set out relevant interagency linkages and responsibilities. These agencies, such as State Departments of Vocational Rehabilitation, must be listed and their roles described. Further, the M-team must be reconvened to identify alternative strategies if the agency fails to provide services. 20 U.S.C. 1401(a)(19).

RESIDENTIAL PLACEMENTS

The placement of a child with disabilities in a residential school has been the subject of much controversy and litigation. The regulations state that residential placements for educational purposes may be necessary. Each public agency shall ensure that a continuum of alternative placements is available to meet the needs of children with disabilities for special education and related services.[156] Clearly, the state and the local school district may not have policies precluding residential placements.[157]

Most litigation in this area surrounds the question of when a residential placement is necessary. Generally, the parents and school are on opposite sides of the fence, sometimes parents urging residential placement and sometimes the district promoting the residential placement. A second issue in this area is the question of when a residential placement is for educational purposes or for other purposes, e.g., medical.

Under the *Rowley* standard of appropriateness, a school need only provide a child with a program from which he or she derives educational benefits. If the traditional public school is providing such a program, i.e., if the child is progressing, or it is expected that the child will progress, there is an appropriate placement option without having to look at a residential placement. If the mainstreamed program is not appropriate, the team should look at what components make the residential placement appropriate to determine if these elements are "portable."

In other words, could those program components be delivered in a conventional classroom with adaptations? If so, that setting would be considered least restrictive and residential placement would not be justified. However, as with any determination of the least restrictive environment, if a residential placement meets the appropriate standard and a mainstreamed setting does not, then residential placement would be required. It should be stressed that there must be some reason to remove a child from a conventional setting and that such rationale must have its locus in the provision of programming necessary to appropriately address an individual child's needs. As with all placement decisions, residential placement must be made on an individual basis and must be based on the IEP and evaluation team's recommendations.

When Are Residential Placements Necessary?

When It Is the Only Appropriate Placement. A residential placement is required when it is "the only educational placement reasonably calculated to enable [the child] to receive educational benefits."[158] Residential placements may be required when the student with disabilities needs constant care or instruction. Constant instruction is generally considered to be necessary when the student's needs dictate that the approach used must be consistent in both the student's school and home environment. If the student's home environment cannot provide the needed immersion,[159] consistency, and follow through, or if it does not provide the child with sufficient support, a residential placement may be required. Two examples of this may be when a child is severely and profoundly disabled and when the basic educational goals are for the child to develop self-sufficiency.[160] A child may not progress outside of a residential placement, indicating the need for greater attention and time to help the child develop. A second example may be when a child has severe behavior problems and needs consistent and constant intervention to deal with the behaviors.[161] Once again, such a child may not progress outside of the residential placement, indicating the need for more constant and consistent attention that can be provided in a residential facility.[162]

When It Is the Least Restrictive Option. Sometimes for a child there are other appropriate options, unlike the preceding examples, but a residential placement is the least restrictive option for a particular child. These occur in two ways: when the child is precluded from a more mainstreamed environment and when the mainstreamed environment is actually more restrictive for a particular child.

A student whose behavior has become so violent that it becomes a danger to himself or herself or to others may require a more restrictive environment than the mainstream school. The regulations to Section 504 indicate that when this happens, the needs of the child with disabilities cannot be met in the mainstreamed school. These regulations are also quoted in a comment to the least restrictive regulations in IDEA. Thus, a school may be justified in moving a child to a more restrictive setting.[163] However, a residential placement may also be necessary when the child is violent outside of the school. In *Walker v. Cronin*,[164] a court ordered a residential placement for a child over the school's objections. The parent's request for a residential placement had been denied, and while awaiting a hearing on the issue, the child became more violent. This prompted the parent to unilaterally place the child in a residential facility; her decision was upheld by the court.[165]

In some situations, most notably those children who are blind and profoundly hearing impaired, a residential placement may become the least restrictive appropriate option. In these situations, most particularly when the child is an adolescent or when the child has previously been in a residential setting, courts have found that the child's need for interaction and peers makes the residential placement a less restrictive environment. The residential placement is less restrictive because it gives the child a more "normal" life—constant interaction with peers, no need for tutoring, and access to extracurricular activities. This sometimes is also true for younger children. In *Grkman v. Scanlon*,[166] the court granted a residential placement against the school's protests to a hearing-impaired child who had previously been in a residential facility for preschool and had reached school age.[167]

Another example of when a residential placement may be the least restrictive educational setting for a child who is hearing impaired relates to language development. For any child, language learning is dependent on ready access to language and multiple communication partners, including peers. A profoundly deaf youngster may be hindered from adequate language development if he or she was placed in a regular classroom where the only person with whom he or she could readily communicate was a sign-language interpreter. In that situation, a residential school, in which the child would be surrounded by children and adults who sign may represent a more "normal" language learning environment and therefore would constitute the least restrictive environment for him or her.

Educational Placements

Under IDEA, a school is only responsible for a residential placement when the primary reason for the placement is educational. This is much like some of the related services issues—i.e., is the residential placement necessary for the child's educational progress and is the placement a medical or educational placement? Court opinions of these are varied, which probably reflects the complexity of the cases, individuals, and rationales for private residential placements. The most common court analysis is that when all of the student's needs are so intertwined and interrelated that they cannot be separated, the school district is responsible for providing the residential placement. The court in *Kruelle v. New Castle School District*,[168] sets forth this analysis:

Analysis must focus, then, on whether full-time placement may be considered necessary for educational purposes, or whether the residential placement is a response to medical, social or emotional problems that are segregable from the learning process. . . . One of the early cases to grapple with this issue, North v. Dist. of Columbia Bd. of Educ., 471 F. Supp. 136 (D.D.C. 1979) . . . is almost indistinguishable on the facts from the present case. It also involved the same issue: whether placement was required for emotional problems and was therefore the responsibility of the parents or social service agencies or whether full-time placement was a necessary ingredient for learning. The North court enjoined the school board from denying a sixteen-year old multiply handicapped epileptic free placement in a residential academic program because it found the social, emotional, medical and educational problems to be so intertwined "that realistically it is not possible for the court to perform the Solomon-like task of separating them." 471 F. Supp. at 141. However, as later cases demonstrate, the claimed inextricability of medical and educational grounds for certain services does not signal court abdication from decision-making in difficult matters. Rather, the unseverability of such needs is the very basis for holding that the services are an essential prerequisite for learning.[169]

But in *Field v. Haddonfield Board of Education*,[170] the court found that an emotionally disturbed child's placement in a residential drug and alcohol facility was not an educational but a medical placement. This is consistent with a Department of Education policy letter on the issue, which states:

If a residential program is necessary to provide FAPE then it must be made available. If a child is addicted and handicapped, public agencies are only required to provide the aspects of the child's program that would enable the child to receive FAPE. If a service is required solely to treat the child's addiction and is not required to provide FAPE, then the public agency is not required to provide the service or to provide it at no cost.[171]

However, when it is clear that the student's need for a residential placement does not arise out of the need to educate but, rather, arises out of other noneducational needs, the school district is not responsible for the residential component of the placement. In some states, once the child is moved out of the district, the school is not responsible for any part of the child's education. One must recognize that, in reality, this decision is not an easy one to make. Although it may be possible in some situations to determine whether a student's social, medical, and educational problems may be distinguished, situations exist such that "all of the student's needs are so intimately intertwined that realistically it is not possible for the court to perform the Solomon-like task of separating them." In this situation, the court ordered the school district to pay for the residential placement.[172]

ST. LOUIS DEVELOPMENTAL DISABILITIES TREATMENT CENTER PARENTS ASSOCIATION v. MALLORY

591 F. Supp. 1416

(U.S. District Court, Western District of Missouri 1984)

HUNTER, Senior District Judge.

This case, tried to the Court without a jury, presents a challenge to a portion of Missouri's system of providing special education to the handicapped. At issue are the special schools and facilities in Missouri that serve the more profoundly and severely handicapped children of the State. These special schools are attended only by handicapped children.

The plaintiffs posit that the separate nature of the schools prevents the handicapped children who attend them from progressing as they would if they attended a typical, local public school. The defendants, on the other hand, view the special schools as a necessary component of a special education system because not all handicapped children can benefit educationally from attending a regular, neighborhood school.

****

. . . . [T]he plaintiffs do not seek the closing of all special schools that serve only the handicapped. They do not challenge the State School for the Blind nor the State School for the Deaf. The plaintiffs' efforts are directed at the State Schools for the Severely Handicapped, the State Schools and Hospitals administered by the Department of Mental Health, and the separate schools maintained by the two special school districts. Again, the Court emphasizes that the issue presented is not whether any of the individual plaintiffs have been mistakenly placed in a special school, but whether the defendants' special education system which utilizes separate schools violates any of the statutory or constitutional provisions alleged.

****

III. LEAST RESTRICTIVE ENVIRONMENT

The plaintiffs next contend that the children placed in the special schools and facilities are denied an education in the least restrictive environment. The focus of this portion of the plaintiffs' claim is on the defendants' continuum of alternative educational settings. The plaintiffs' maintain that the Education Act's least restrictive environment provision mandates that handicapped children be educated in either regular classrooms or separate classrooms in regular schools. They further maintain that the defendants' placement continuums which include special schools are not required by the Act and inconsistent with the least restrictive provision.

Neither Section 1412(5)(B) nor any other provision of the Education Act indicates a congressional intent to eliminate separate or other facilities for the handicapped children who need them to benefit educationally. The definition of "special education" calls for the delivery of publicly funded education services in a classroom, hospital, institutional setting, or at the child's home. 20 U.S.C. § 1401(16). The hospital, institution and home settings are all settings separated from nonhandicapped children in public schools. Moreover, the "classroom" setting is generic. It is not limited to local public school classrooms, but speaks of classroom settings without limitation. Furthermore, the placement provision, Section 1412(5)(B), recognizes the need for separate educational settings both explicitly and implicitly.

The section acknowledges that some handicapped children will not be able to receive a satisfactory education in a "regular educational environment" and will need to be placed in "special classes, separate schooling" or otherwise removed from the regular school setting. Unless Congress intended to repeat itself, special classes and separate schooling must mean two distinct education placements. Even if separate schooling does not mean separate schools, which this Court believes that it does, the phrase "other removal from the regular education environment" indicates a recognition of the appropriateness of separate settings for some children. After all, Section 1412(5)(B) does not mandate that all handicapped children be educated along side [sic] nonhandicapped children. It only requires that educational agencies, to the "maximum extent appropriate," place handicapped children in regular classrooms. The implication is that some handicapped children will not be able to be educated in a regular school environment. Moreover, two other sections of the Education Act indicate that Congress did not intend to foreclose separate alternative educational settings. Section 1414(d) authorizes the state to provide direct educational services to handicapped children in settings separate from public schools in certain circumstances.

****

The regulations accompanying the Education Act are consistent with this view. Beyond stating a presumption in favor of a regular classroom placement, Congress left it to the Secretary to promulgate regulations to ensure that each child is appropriately placed. Crucial to the present issue, the regulations require that each state have a continuum of alternative placements available. The continuum must include the alternative placements listed in Section 300.13 of the regulations: regular classes, special classes, special schools, home instruction and instruction in hospitals and institutions. 34 C.F.R. § 300.552(b). Section 300.552(b) further requires that the full continuum of settings be available for the placement of each child, in line with his unique needs. *See also* 34 C.F.R. §§ 300.360-361. The defendants each have a continuum of alternative educational settings that complies with the regulations. Mo. Rev. Stat. § 162.725(1); State Plan 1984-86 at A29; R. Werner at Vol. 13.

****

CONCLUSION

Based on the foregoing discussion, this Court concludes that the special educational programs and the separate facilities of the defendants, considered systematically, do not violate the statutory or constitutional provisions relied upon by the plaintiffs. . . . (Footnotes omitted.)

— — — —

VISCO v. SCHOOL DISTRICT OF PITTSBURGH
684 F. Supp. 1310
(U.S. District Court, Western District of Pennsylvania 1988)

ROSENBERG, District Judge

****

. . . Jennifer Visco, age 13, . . . and Rene Visco, age 11, . . . are hearing impaired. Both children reside with their mother in the School District for the City of Pittsburgh.

Jennifer and Rene . . . attend DePaul Institute, a private school that specializes in educating the hearing-impaired. . . . Jennifer and Rene have both progressed from grade to grade at DePaul and both are good students.

In the fall of 1981, the School District evaluated Rene and Jennifer and produced an Individualized Educational Plan (IEP) for each student. Based on each child's IEP, the School District recommended that Jennifer should be placed in a special program for the hearing-impaired at the Liberty School and that Rene should be placed in a different program for the hearing-impaired at the Beechwood School. The Liberty School and the Beechwood School have programs for the hearing impaired developed by the State . . . .

Visco rejected both proposals. . . .

Visco . . . claims that the city schools, Liberty and Beechwood, do not have teachers who possess the functional abilities and communications skills that her children specifically need as deaf children living in a deaf household. The . . . plaintiff's complaint . . . is that the School District's programs for the hearing-impaired at the Liberty School and Beechwood School do not provide a "free appropriate education" for her children as guaranteed by the Education of the Handicapped Act of 1975. 20 U.S.C. Section 1401 *et seq.* (hereinafter referred to as the EHA or the Act). The plaintiff contends that because she and her children comprise a deaf household, there is little emphasis on speech and lip reading [sic] at home. This results in a particular need by her children to learn and practice speech, language and lip reading in the school setting so that her children can learn to function as ordinary adults in society. Plaintiff believes the oral-aural program at DePaul is "appropriate" for her children because it heavily stresses these skills in *all* classroom and recreational activities, as opposed to the programs offered at the Liberty and Beechwood Schools. The Beechwood and Liberty programs emphasize *sign language* instead of oral-aural communication for most classroom and recreational interaction. . . . In other words, plaintiff contends that since she is hearing-impaired and relies on sign language to communicate with her children at home, school is the only place where Jennifer and Rene can learn and practice oral language and lip reading—skills that are absolutely essential for a hearing-impaired individual to function in society.

****

The Act defines a "free appropriate public education" as special education and related services which:

(A) have been provided at public expense, under public supervision and directions, and without charge,

(B) meet the standards of the State educational agency,

(C) include an appropriate preschool, elementary, or secondary school education in the State involved, and

(D) are provided in conformity with the individualized education program required under section 1414(a)(5) [of this title].
20 U.S.C. Section 1401(18).

****

The question before this court is, therefore, how to interpret the Act in order to provide a free appropriate public education for Jennifer and Rene Visco, specifically. Individualization must be the touchstone for the analysis; this value is reflected in the IEP requirement of the Act mandated by Congress.

****

In reviewing the Congressional preference of mainstreaming, much debate has ensued over whether the "least restrictive environment" referred to in the Act is synonymous with mainstreaming. Clearly, mainstreaming is a means, not an end. Mainstreaming's function is to prepare a handicapped individual to function as a normal adult in society; it is *not* a goal in and of itself. . . .

****

. . . . Furthermore, the regulations for the EHA plainly state "[i]n selecting the least restrictive environment, consideration is given to any potential harmful effect on the child or on the quality of services he or she needs." 34 C.F.R. Section 300.552(d) (1987). . . . A fair reading of this regulation makes the least restrictive environment a function of potential harmful effect and the quality of services. Therefore, in determining a "free appropriate education" under the Act, it is necessary to consider the individual requirements of the child or children in question along with the potential harm a program may present. It follows that the decision of whether or not to move a child from one program to another is arrived at by balancing the possible benefits against the potential harm for the particular child in question.

The EHA, along with the accompanying regulations and the policies behind the Act must be applied to the facts of this case. Jennifer has attended DePaul Institute since age 3-1/2 years and Rene since the age of 1-1/2 years, and both children have progressed from grade to grade easily. . . . Once a student is making good progress in a particular program, a change must be viewed with a great degree of cau-

tion. In balancing the potential benefits against the potential harms, even if the benefits and the harms were to weigh equally, the child in question should not be moved from one program to another.

****

Mastery of language skills is vital to an adult in our society. The program at DePaul allows a hearing-impaired youngster to enter the tenth grade as any other pupil. It makes no sense to move Jennifer and Rene, risking loss of fundamental language skills which will prepare them for 10th grade, with the only possible benefit being several years of "mainstreaming"; . . . Nescient educational mainstreaming defeats the very purpose for which mainstreaming was conceived. The ultimate goals is to adequately prepare individuals for the mainstream of life.

The instant case poses a particularly compelling illustration of this because Jennifer has only 2 years to go at DePaul and Rene has 4; after which, both Jennifer and Rene will be able to enter high school as any other 10th grader. To interrupt their studies with a different method of teaching in order to "mainstream" Jennifer and Rene for such a short period of time is definitely not worth risking the acquisition of language skills both children need to function as high school students as well as adults in society.

****

. . . [T]he petition of the plaintiff is hereby granted and it is hereby ordered and directed:

that the plaintiff children, Jennifer and Rene, shall continue to remain as students at DePaul Institute until their graduations;

****

(Footnotes omitted.)

— — — —

FIELD v. HADDONFIELD BOARD OF EDUCATION
769 F. Supp. 1313
(U.S. District Court, District of New Jersey 1991)

GERRY, Chief Judge:

****

. . . . During the 1988–89 school year Daniel was a tenth grade student who was classified as emotionally disturbed. In particular, Daniel has expressive and attention disorders, and has a tendency to become

frustrated because of his inability to express himself and because of very low self esteem. . . . Pursuant to Daniel's individualized educational program ("IEP"), Daniel attended classes as a day student at the Alternative School in Cherry Hill, New Jersey for half a day, and the Haddonfield Memorial High School ("HMHS") for the other half. As a result of disciplinary and other problems encountered at the Alternative School, Daniel's parents sought to have Daniel enrolled full-time at HMHS. . . .

****

On January 13, 1989, Daniel was suspended from HMHS as a result of an altercation he had with a teacher. At that time, the child study team recommended that Daniel be placed as a day student at the Yale School in Cherry Hill, a special education school for emotionally disturbed children. The Fields responded that they did not consider Yale appropriate because of the level of the program. Rather, after consulting with . . . an educational consultant, the Fields sought to have Daniel placed in a residential, twenty-four hour per day placement. . . .

****

At a settlement conference on September 27, 1989, placement at the Yale School appeared to be the most viable resolution. On October 11, 1989, however, the parties were informed that Daniel was denied admission to the Yale School. On October 13, 1989, after visiting the Mill Creek School, the Fields determined that that school was an acceptable placement, and Daniel was enrolled immediately.

****

By February of 1990, Daniel's behavior at the Mill School was deteriorating. He was inattentive in class, verbally abusive to teachers, unmotivated, and doing poor academically. One day, Daniel was discovered showing a bottle of Valium to other students. The school immediately convened a "crisis meeting" with Daniel's parents. During that meeting, Daniel admitted taking the Valium from his mother, and also admitted to smoking marijuana and occasional drinking.

The possession of drugs on campus is grounds for automatic suspension from Mill Creek. Mill Creek advised both the Board and Daniel's parents that Daniel was expelled and that he would have to attend a residential substance abuse program in order to be readmitted to Mill Creek. Mill Creek recommended the Strecker program, also part of the Institute of Pennsylvania Hospital, and stated that Daniel could remain in school if he attended that program. Sandra Schoenholtz, assistant director of Mill Creek, opined that Daniel's possession of drugs may have been part of a larger problem, his emotional disturbance, and that his behavior and performance in school were linked together.

Plaintiffs asked the Board whether they would pay for the substance abuse program at Strecker, and whether it wished to look at other programs. . . .

****

B. THE STRECKER PROGRAM AND THE "MEDICAL SERVICES" EXCLUSION

The core issue presented by plaintiffs' appeal of the second due process petition is whether Daniel's placement in the Strecker substance abuse program was a "related service" or rather whether the program was an excluded "medical service." A "free appropriate public education" to which Daniel is entitled includes special education and related services. 20 U.S.C. § 1401(18). . . .

****

. . . . Under the regulations, medical services which must be provided by the school district are those "services provided by a licensed physician to determine a child's medically related handicapping condition which results in the child's need for special education and related services." 34 C.F.R. § 300.13 (b)(4) (1990).

Where a child's education is adversely affected by substance abuse, successful completion of a substance abuse program can be expected to increase the effectiveness of the child's educational program. In this case, after being found possessing Valium and admitting to drinking alcohol and smoking marijuana, Daniel's expulsion from Mill Creek appeared to be based on several related grounds. Daniel's advisor, Sandra Shoenholtz who is an assistant director at Mill Creek, testified that one of Mill Creek's "cardinal rules" was that possession of drugs was grounds for automatic expulsion. T.157-58. Moreover, Ms. Shoenholtz testified that a student's drug use is usually a manifestation of a deeper emotional or social problem. . . . In fact, after Daniel completed the Strecker program, he initially demonstrated improved behavior in school.

However, the fact that a particular program may benefit a classified child's special education program clearly does not ipso facto compel the conclusion that that program is a "related service" and thus a school district responsibility under the EHA. . . .

****

Although we have found no case on point dealing with a substance abuse program, we conclude under the facts of this case that the services performed at the Strecker program constitute medical services for which the plaintiffs [the parents] must bear the cost under the EHA. According to the hospital brochure that describes the Strecker program, the program operates under the recognition that drug dependency is a disease, and treatment is geared with this in mind. . . . The brochure describes the procedures which all patients are given upon admission:

- a complete medical evaluation by a specialist in internal medicine
- a psychosocial assessment of the patient's home environment that focuses on family, friends and work factors
- a diagnostic assessment by a psychiatrist who becomes the patient's private, attending physician, and continues to work with him or her on a daily basis throughout the treatment process. Upon discharge, patients can continue seeking the Institute psychiatrist as an outpatient, . . .
- The Strecker Program also provides skilled medical services for detoxification, and for clinical management of other physical or emotional problems, if needed.

Id. at Pa 140.

****

Moreover, although Mill Creek may have "required" Daniel to attend a substance abuse program as a condition for his continued enrollment at the school, this is not to say that a substance abuse program was "required to assist the child to benefit from special education." 20 U.S.C. § 1401(17); *see Anrig*, 651 F. Supp. at 431. Although the Strecker program addressed some of Daniel's emotional problems as a "dual diagnosis" program, the testimony and records reveal that the program provided intensive therapy for Daniel's underlying psychiatric disorders, which included psychiatric counselling, numerous physical evaluations as well as medication. *See* P. App. at Pa 41-134 (Strecker medical records); T. 190 (testimony of Ms. Schoenholtz). Strecker provided medical treatment which Mill Creek could not, as an educational institution, provide. *See* T.190-91. . . . Compare *Taylor v. Honig*, 910 F.2d 627 (9th Cir. 1990) (residential program was "related service" where handicapped child's program developed through IEP by the school system), with *Clovis*, 903 F.2d at 644-45 (residential program was excluded "medical service" where handicapped child's pro-

gram developed by a medical team supervised by a licensed physician).

The "[a]nalysis . . . focus[es] . . . on whether full-time placement may be considered necessary for educational purposes, or whether the residential placement is a response to medical, social or emotional problems that are segregable from the learning process." *Kruelle v. New Castle County School Dist.*, 642 F.2d 687, 693 (3d Cir. 1981). Here, Strecker provided treatment which was clearly "segregable," from, though beneficial to, Daniel's learning process. For instance, although Mill Creek's educational program was integrated with the Strecker program, Mill Creek personnel is not involved in the patient's daily therapy sessions conducted by the psychiatrist, nor other group sessions such as Alcoholics Anonymous and Narcotics Anonymous. . . .

Although school districts are not required to pay for non-diagnostic or non-evaluative medical services, the school must provide educational services to students who are confined to a hospital. 20 U.S.C. § 1401(16). Strecker's standard billing policy is consistent with this requirement. The patient is billed for the treatment administered at Strecker while the school district is separately billed for the educational component offered through Mill Creek (for those patients who, like Daniel, were enrolled in Mill Creek). . . .

****

Finally, we note that our conclusion is not inconsistent with the Department of Education's Policy letter of April 18, 1988. In that advisory opinion, an inquiry was made as to a school district's responsibility for a child who becomes handicapped as a result of drug addiction. The Office of Special Education Programs had previously determined that addiction itself is not considered to be a handicapping condition covered by the EHA. The Secretary responded that

[i]f a residential program is necessary to provide FAPE [a fair (sic) appropriate public education] then it must be made viable. If a child is addicted and handicapped, public agencies are only required to provide the aspects of the child's program that would enable the child to receive FAPE. If a service is required solely to treat the child's addiction and is not required to provide FAPE, then the public agency is not required to provide the service or to provide it at no cost.
213 E.H.L.R. 133-34 (Supp. 1988).

The Board has fulfilled its obligation under the EHA by providing for Daniel's education through the Mill Creek program. However, the Fields must pay for Daniel's enrollment in the Strecker program since we find that that program renders medical services within the meaning of 20 U.S.C. section 1401(17). Accordingly, we will affirm the ALJ's determination.

****

(Footnotes omitted.)

ADDITIONAL COMMENTARY

1. The need for structure may be a determinative factor in a residential placement. In *Grand Prairie Independent School District v. Douglas*, 506 E.H.L.R. 240 (S.E.A. Tx. 1984), the hearing officer found that a residential placement was not necessary. The child was autistic and needed a strict structure in order to make educational benefits. However, it was decided that the requirement of structure needed after school hours could be met by home intervention and family counseling. This would allow the child to remain in a day-school placement and reside with his family at home. *See also Abrahamson v. Herschman*, 701 F.2d 223 (1st Cir. 1983).

2. It is important to remember that even when a student is placed in an out-of-district residential facility, it is still the district's obligation to evaluate the student and develop the IEP.

3. The cost of a residential placement—which typically includes tuition, room and board, and transportation for student and parent—can sometimes reach staggering annual sums. Nonetheless, if deemed to be the least restrictive appropriate option for a student, or agreed to in settlement between the parents and the school, the cost alone is not sufficient to overturn the placement. In *In re Smith*, 17 E.H.L.R. 520 (11th Cir. 1991), the court found that the district court had erred by overturning a residential placement agreement solely because of cost (in excess of $150,000 annually).

4. In *Mark Z. v. Mountain Brook Board of Education*, 792 F. Supp. 1228 (N.D. Ala. 1992), the court held that when comparing two residential placements, one public and one private, that provide essentially equal programs, the public facility represents the least restrictive environment.

CHANGES IN PLACEMENT

The IDEA regulations state:

Written notice . . . must be given to the parent of a child with a disability a reasonable time before the public agency:

(1) Proposes to initiate or change the identification, evaluation, or educational placement of the child or the provision of a free appropriate public education, or

(2) Refuses to initiate or change the identification, evaluation, or educational placement of the child or the provision of a free appropriate public education of the child.[173]

Additionally, the regulations require that during the pendency of a dispute the child must remain in his or her current placement, i.e., the child must "stay put."[174] As a practical matter, this means that if the district wishes to alter a student's program, an IEP team must be convened, and the parents must agree to the alteration. The parents then have an opportunity to challenge the proposal through a due process hearing during which no change in placement can take place. Thus, the proposal of a change in placement is a significant step in that it requires a change in the IEP and triggers due process guarantees.

When Is a Change a Change?

The phrase *change in placement* has generated a number of hearings and cases recently. It seems easiest to determine what constitutes a change in placement by what the courts have said it is not. In the context of disciplinary issues,[175] the courts have said that a change in placement is one that significantly alters the student's educational experience. This general standard has also been accepted in determining when an alteration is a "change in placement" for other purposes, e.g., "a change of educational placement requires, at a minimum a fundamental change in, or elimination of, a basic element of an education program."[176] The important element is whether the change is likely to affect the student's learning in some significant way. As stated by one court:

> The question of what constitutes a change in educational placement is, necessarily, fact specific. . . . The touchstone in interpreting [IDEA's] section 1415 has to be whether the [change of placement] decision is likely to affect in some significant way the child's learning experience.[177]

In *DeLeon v. Susquehanna Community School District*,[178] a child's transportation arrangements were changed, resulting in a slight increase in travel time from school to home. The court found that this was not likely to cause a significant change in the child's learning experience; therefore, it was not a change in placement. However, in a different situation, a transportation change was found to be a change in placement. There, the child was switched from use of a regular education bus to a special education bus.[179]

Clearly, where the change eliminates or alters a major component of the program, a change in placement (for which the parents can seek review) has taken place. For example, when the change substantially alters the frequency or extent of services provided, a change in placement has occurred,[180] or when the services provided are altered, a change has occurred. One OCR decision found that even promoting a special education child one grade level with his peers necessitated the procedural requirements of IDEA.[181]

Changes That Do Not Trigger the Stay-Put Provision

Courts have found no change in placement if all components of a child's program are retained but relocated. This is true, sometimes, when a child is moved from one location to another,[182] but it is difficult to retain all components and merely move one child. It is much more often that courts have found no change in placement when an entire program is moved from one location to another. Here, it is easier to retain all major components of the program and merely shift locations.[183]

Further, in the latter situation, where an entire program is moved, courts have found that a change in placement has occurred but the stay-put provisions are not applicable. In *Tilton v. Jefferson County Board of Education*,[184] a day-treatment program was closed for budgetary reasons. Students were transferred to an alternative program, but it operated only 180 days a year rather than year-round like the previous program. The court found a change in placement because the programs were not comparable. However, the court found that since the program was closed for purely budgetary reasons, the stay-put provision was not triggered. This appears logical only when one considers that there really was no program in which the students could remain—there was no way to enforce the stay-put provision.

Graduation

Because it terminates a student's special education services, graduation is a change in placement. In *Stock v. Massachusetts Hospital School*,[185] the Supreme Court of Massachusetts held that the graduation of a student with disabilities constituted a change in placement and thus would trigger all procedural protections. In addition, the stay-put provision applies; the student may not be graduated during the pendency of a hearing on the issue.[186]

The common question regarding graduation is not when parents want to delay graduation, but when students with disabilities have been denied graduation. A district is not required to award a diploma to a student who has not fulfilled all of its graduation requirements, even though the student may have completed his or her IEP requirements. The parents must, however, be told during the IEP process that successful completion of the IEP will not result in the student receiving a regular diploma.[187] These cases usually arise in context of a minimum competency examination as part of a graduation requirement. The use of minimum competency examinations has been upheld as long as they are a valid examination of skills and students have been given an adequate opportunity to prepare themselves for the exam.

DeLEON v. SUSQUEHANNA COMMUNITY SCHOOL DISTRICT
747 F.2d 149 (Third Circuit 1984)

BECKER, Circuit Judge.

****

This appeal presents the question whether a change in the method of transporting a seriously handicapped child to a special education facility can be considered a change in "educational placement" within the meaning of the Education of All Handicapped Children Act, 20 U.S.C. § 1415(e)(3) ("EHA") (now IDEA). . . .

During the 1982–83 school year, appellant Mania DeLeon, Lorin's mother, transported Lorin to school in her own car. [The district paid her $75.91 per day for this transportation arrangement.]. . .

In March 1983, an IEP was agreed on for Lorin for the 1983–84 school year. This IEP did not specify the mode of transportation. In early August 1983, the District solicited bids for a combined transportation run involving Lorin and several other children in special education programs. The other children attended the Lourdesmont School, which was located about two miles from Clarks Summit. The DeLeons bid on the "combined run," and also objected to Lorin's inclusion in the run. The DeLeons were not the low bidders and were not awarded the contract. When the school year started, they refused to allow Lorin to be transported with the other children, in spite of the fact that Lorin would be driven directly to school in the morning and would only have to make one brief stop in the afternoon to pick up the other children.

The DeLeons objected to the combined run on the ground that the increase in transportation time on the trip home would be detrimental to Lorin's education. . . .

II.

The threshold question is whether the change in Lorin's method of transportation amounts to a change in "educational placement." Section 1415(b)(2) entitles parents to "an impartial due process hearing" with regard to any complaint presented to a school district concerning the treatment of their special education child. Subsection (e)(3) of the same section provides that "[d]uring the pendency of any proceedings conducted pursuant to this section . . . the child shall remain in the then-current educational placement . . . ." If the change in transportation which the District has sought to impose on Lorin is not a "change in educational placement" within the meaning of subsection (e)(3), then the District was free to proceed with the change before completing the mandated due process hearing. If, however, there was a change in educational placement, the actions of the District may have violated the EHA.

****

Unfortunately, the two leading cases on the subject involve an entirely different problem: whether a decision concerning the closing of a facility, which by definition involves not only the interests of a large number of children but also a substantial fiscal policy question for the school district, should be outside the hearing requirement of section 1415(b)(2) and the "stay put" provision of section 1415(e)(3), because the questions involved are broad "policy" decisions rather than individual choices concerning particular children.[188]

****

It is clear that the "stay put" provision does not entitle parents to the right to demand a hearing before a minor decision alters the school day of their children. The touchstone in interpreting section 1415 has to be whether the decision is likely to affect in some significant way the child's learning experience. In some areas it may be possible to draw bright lines: for instance, replacing one teacher or aide with another should not require a hearing before the change is made. On the other hand, there are areas where such bright lines will be impossible to draw.

We believe that transportation services is such an area. Under some circumstances, transportation may have a significant effect on a child's learning experience. Minor changes in the daily transportation routine, however, will not generally have such an impact on the child's learning experience, even when the child is severely handicapped. In this case, transportation by a parent was replaced with transportation by a stranger, and transportation alone was replaced with transportation as part of a group of children. There was also a slight increase, of approximately ten minutes, in the length of time to be spent in transit, but only on the way home from school.

****

III. CONCLUSION

Since the change in Lorin's method of transportation does not amount to a change in "educational placement" within the meaning of the EHA, the District did not violate that Act by making the change without prior due process procedures. The DeLeons, therefore, have not established a claim for relief against the school district.

Accordingly, the judgment of the district court will be affirmed.

****

(Footnotes omitted.)

— — — —

CRONIN v. BOARD OF EDUCATION
OF THE EAST RAMAPO CENTRAL SCHOOL DISTRICT
689 F. Supp. 197
(U.S. District Court, Southern District of New York, 1988)

WARD, District Judge.

****

BACKGROUND

Bruce Cronin is twenty years of age . . . and has been classified as emotionally disabled by the School District.

In 1985, the Committee on the Handicapped ("COH") determined that Bruce was eligible to attend the vocational training program at Boces in addition to classes at the Karafin School, which he had been attending since 1979 when he was first placed there by the School District. The Boces course was a "mainstream" course not designed primarily for handicapped children. . . . In March 1987, plaintiffs were notified that the COH had determined to graduate Bruce at the end of the 1986–87 school year pending completion of the requirements for graduation. Having received a letter on March 30, 1987 from Boces stating that Bruce should continue in the Boces program for another year, the Cronins on April 1987 requested an impartial hearing officer be appointed to resolve the conflict. On April 30, 1987, the Cronins were informed that Bruce had met all of his graduation requirements and would be graduated.

****

. . . [T]he threshold question is whether the determination to graduate Bruce constitutes a change in educational placement that when challenged would trigger the protection of the stay-put provision of the Act [now IDEA]. If Bruce's graduation is not a change in educational placement within the meaning of the EHA, then the School District was free to graduate Bruce. If, however, Bruce's graduation is a change in educational placement, then the School District should have permitted Bruce to remain in the Boces program, his undisputed "current placement," until the completion of all proceedings under the EHA.

The EHA nowhere defines the phrase "change in placement," *see Honig v. Doe*, . . . 108 S. Ct. 605, nor does the statute's structure or legislative history provide any guidance as to whether graduation of a handicapped student would constitute . . . such a change. . . . "The touchstone in interpreting section 1415 has to be whether the decision is likely to affect in some significant way the child's learning experience." *DeLeon v. Susquehanna Community School Dist.*, 747 F.2d 149, 153 (3rd Cir. 1984).

Courts have found that an expulsion of a handicapped student constitutes a "change in placement" within the meaning of the EHA. *Doe v. Maher*, 793 F.2d 1470, 1482 (9th Cir. 1986), *aff'd in part, modified in part,*—U.S. —,108 S.Ct. 592, 98 L. Ed. 2d 686 (1988); . . .

****

Because graduation is similar to long-term suspensions and expulsions in that it results in total exclusion of a child from his or her educational placement, graduation would appear to be a "change in educational placement" implicating the mandatory procedural safeguards of the EHA. Although this is an issue of first impression in the federal courts, a Massachusetts court has held that graduation is a change in educational placement under the Act.

In *Stock v. Massachusetts Hosp. School*, 467 N.E.2d 448, 453, 392 Mass. 205 (1984), *cert. denied*, 474 U.S. 844, 106 S. Ct. 132, 88 L. Ed. 2d 109 (1985), the Supreme Judicial Court of Massachusetts stated that it was "obvious . . . that graduation, because it will cause the termination of a student's participation in special education programs, can hardly be characterized as anything other than a change in placement." The court went on to point out that "[n]o change in placement seems quite so serious nor as worthy of parental involvement and procedural protections as the termination of placement in special education programs."

This Court finds the reasoning of *Stock* to be persuasive. There is no question that the termination of an individual child's educational program inherent in a graduation will significantly affect a child's learning process. Unless the child is immediately placed by his parents or guardians into another program following graduation, the child will be receiving no instruction at all. Accordingly, this Court holds that the decision to graduate a handicapped child is a "change in educational placement" under the EHA that triggers all of the procedural protections of the Act.

Having found that graduation is a "change in educational placement," the Court concludes that Bruce's removal from the Boces program by graduation during the pendency of the administrative proceedings violated the stay-put provision of the EHA. Therefore, the Court orders that the School District immediately reinstate Bruce to the Boces program during the pendency of these proceedings, unless school officials and Bruce's parents agree on a satisfactory alternative arrangement.

****

(Footnotes omitted.)

— — — —

DEBRA P. v. TURLINGTON
564 F. Supp. 177
(U.S. District Court, Middle District of Florida 1983; affirmed 730 F.2d 1405 (5th Cir. 1984))

CARR, District Judge.

In 1978, the Florida Legislature . . . required public school students in the State of Florida to pass a functional literacy examination in order to receive a state high school diploma. Fla. Stat. § 232.246(1)(b). Shortly after its enactment, Florida high school students filed a class action challenging the constitutionality of the literacy test requirement. This Court found that the test violated both the equal protection and due process clauses of the Constitution and enjoined its use as a diploma sanction until the 1982–83 school year. *Debra P. v. Turlington*, 474 F. Supp. 244 (M.D. Fla. 1979). On appeal, the Fifth Circuit Court of Appeals affirmed many of this Court's findings. *Debra P. v. Turlington*, 644 F.2d 397 (5th Cir. 1981). However, the appellate court remanded the case for further factual findings on two key issues.

Specifically, this Court was directed to make further findings on whether or not the functional literacy test, the Florida Student State Assessment Test, Part II (SSAT-II), covers material actually taught in Florida's classrooms. . . . In addition, the Court of Appeals requested this Court to reexamine the "role and effect of the 'vestiges' of past discrimination" upon twelfth grade black students. . . .

****

The SSAT-II is a test of a student's ability to successfully apply basic communications and mathematics skills to everyday life situations. *See* Fla. Stat. § 232.246(1)(b); Fla. Admin. Code Rule 6A-1.942(2)(a). The test covers 24 basic skills. Of these, 11 are designated as communications skills and 13 are designated as mathematics skills.

****

The Court of Appeals has upheld the denial of a diploma to these students to long as the "test is a fair test of that which was taught.". . . The Court reasoned that "[i]f the test is not fair, it cannot be said to be rationally related to a state interest" and therefore it would be violative of the Equal Protection Clause. In other words, the SSAT-II is only constitutional if it is instructionally valid.

****

. . . [E]vidence suggests, the resolution of the instructional validity issue depends both on whose experts are believed and on what sort of proof is required. With regard to the former, it is important to understand that the instructional validity issue, and the related concept of minimum competency testing, are relatively new and highly controversial subjects which seem to have polarized the educational community. Thus, in large part, this Court has been called upon to settle not only a legal argument but also a professional dispute. At times, the distinction between these two spheres has blurred. The experts for both sides spoke in terms of "fairness," "adequacy" and "sufficiency." Yet, these terms are not necessarily synonymous with constitutionality. As noted in a law review article cited frequently by the appellate court, any judicial decision on this issue "will reflect only the minimum standards essential to fairness under our legal system. Policymakers must meet, but are not limited to, the minimum standards in pursuing the goal of educational equity for students.". . . In other words, even though the defendants might have implemented a much more equitable program, their actions might still pass constitutional muster.

But, what does the Constitution require in this instance? It may not be fair to expect students with differing interests and abilities to learn the same material at the same rate, but is it unconstitutional? Similarly, it may be inequitable that some students, through random selection, are assigned to mediocre teachers while others are given excellent instructors, but does this inequity rise to the level of a constitutional violation?

These questions lead to other issues concerning the appropriate burden of proof. The plaintiffs argue that the defendants have not carried their burden because they have not attempted to follow students throughout their entire careers. They also assert that there is insufficient evidence of what actually goes on in the classrooms. But, absent viewing a videotape of every student's school career, how can we know what really happened to each child? Even assuming that such videotapes were available, how could the Court decide, in constitutional terms, which students received appropriate instruction and which did not? Suppose that there is one student who never encountered a teacher who taught the SSAT-II skills, or a teacher who taught the skills well, should the entire test be declared invalid? What if the number of students were 3,000 rather than 1?

It is necessary to consider these questions in order to appreciate the dilemma confronted by this Court. Instructional validity is an elusive concept. Moreover, unlike some of the other claims made by the plaintiffs at the first trial, the instructional validity issue strikes at the heart of the learning and teaching process. It also lends itself to individualized determinations rather than objective treatment.

Instructional validity is a subpart of content validity which together with curricular validity, insures that a test covers matters actually taught. As the Court of Appeals noted, and as this Court previously found, the SSAT-II is a "good test of what the students should know.". . . That is, the subjects tested parallel the curricular goals of the State. To this end, the Department of Education publishes minimum performance standards and also "periodically examine[s] and evaluate[s] procedures, records, and programs in each district to determine compliance with law and rules established by the state board.". . . Thus, although the individual districts are still somewhat autonomous, they no longer have the authority to decide that they will not teach certain minimum skills. . . . In the same vein, the Department of Education, the individual districts, and the separate schools are required to submit annual reports of how well school instructional programs are helping students acquire minimum performance skills. In sum, since at least 1979, school administrators and teachers have been well aware of the minimum performance standards imposed by the State and their duty to teach these skills.

The districts also receive funding from the State to remediate students who need special educational assistance in order to master the basic skills. . . . Each district school board is also required to establish pupil progression plans to insure that students are not promoted without consideration of each student's mastery of basic skills. . . . The State has also established uniform testing standards for grades 3, 5, 8 and 11 to monitor the acquisition of basic skills by students statewide.

These legislative requirements bolster the conclusion that the SSAT-II is, at least, curricularly valid. They lend support to the opinions of the defendants' experts that the SSAT-II is instructionally valid. It is clear from the survey results that the terms of the Educational Accountability Act are not just hollow words found in a statute book. Rather, the district reports, teacher surveys, and site visit audits, as interpreted by the defendants' experts, all indicate that the directives of the Act are a driving force in all of Florida's public schools.

****

For the reasons stated above, and based on a review of the evidence presented by both sides, the Court finds that the defendants have carried their burden of proving by the preponderance of the evidence that the SSAT-II is instructionally valid and therefore constitutional. Although the instruction offered in all the classrooms of all the districts might not be ideal, students are nevertheless afforded an adequate opportunity to learn the skills tested on the SSAT-II before it is used as a diploma sanction.

****

As noted earlier, deciding that the SSAT-II is a fair test of that which is taught in the Florida public schools does not end this Court's inquiry. The Court must still decide whether or not the State should be enjoined from imposing the diploma sanction because the vestiges of past purposeful discrimination have an unconstitutional impact on black high school students.

No one disputes the fact that the SSAT-II failure rate among black students is disproportionately high. Of the three thousand twelfth grade students who have not passed the test, about 57% are black even though blacks only constitute about 20% of the entire student body. While these statistics are alarming, they do not, standing alone, answer the constitutional question this Court must confront.

In order for this Court to continue to prohibit the State from using the SSAT-II as a diploma sanction, the disproportionate failure rate among today's high school seniors must be found to have been caused by past purposeful segregation or its lingering effects. If the disparate failure of blacks is not due to the present effects of past intentional segregation or if the test is necessary to remedy those effects, then the four year injunction entered in 1979 can not be extended.

****

The mere fact that black students are not doing as well as white students on the test does not direct a different result. . . . Indeed, as long as past purposeful segregation remains part of our collective memory, its vestiges will, sadly, remain with us, not only in our schools, but in every aspect of our lives.

****

Twelve years have passed since the Florida public schools became physically unitary. Since that time, the State of Florida has undertaken massive efforts to improve the education of all of its school children. The SSAT-II is an important part of those efforts. Its use can be enjoined only it is perpetuates the effects of past school segregation or if it is not needed to remedy those effects. . . . Applying this standard to the facts presented at both the 1979 and 1983 trials, the Court finds that the injunction should not be extended. The State of Florida may deny diplomas to the members of the Class of 1983 who have not passed the SSAT-II.

(Footnotes omitted.)

ADDITIONAL COMMENTARY

1. In *Anderson v. District of Columbia*, 877 F.2d 1018 (D.C. Cir. 1989), the court held that the student may remain in the then current placement only until the trial court proceedings are completed. The court held that the stay-put provision did not entitle the student to remain in a private school at public expense pending the review by the appeals court of a district court decision that upheld proposed public school placements. *See also Spindler*, 18 I.D.E.L.R. 1038 (OSEP 1992). A court ruling becomes a student's then current educational placement for stay-put purposes if a subsequent IEP can not be agreed upon.

2. In *Joshua B. v. New Trier Township High School District 203*, 770 F.Supp. 431 (N.D. Ill. 1991), the court held that the stay-put provision did not apply because the student's current educational placement was at an out-of-state residential facility through a unilateral action of his parents. Thus, no public agency had ever determined the student's need for special education nor an appropriate placement.

3. A child's IEP from a previous district is his then current IEP for purposes of stay-put when he moves to a new district and the parents and school district can not agree on a new IEP. *Lyons v. Town of Yarmouth*, 18 I.D.E.L.R. 671 (D. Me. 1992).

4. In *Pueblo City School District #60*, 17 E.H.L.R. 535 (OCR 1990), the Office for Civil Rights found no violation in the district's policy of excluding student from competing for graduation with honors when their programs did not satisfy the graduation requirements.

PRIVATE SCHOOLS

A perennial issue in special education is what services a child is entitled to when the parent has chosen to enroll the child in a private school. In this category, the following are not included: situations involving unilateral placement of children in private school for purposes of receiving special services, district placement in a private school, and the private schools' obligations under Section 504. These are discussed in other sections. Rather, under exploration is the question of the district's responsibility to provide services in support of the nonspecial education received by a child who is enrolled by his or her parent in private regular education facility. The additional question of the constitutional constraints placed on this situation will also be explored.

Private Schools and Special Education

Children who attend private schools may still be entitled to receive special education from their public school district. IDEA requires the following:

To the extent consistent with the number and location of children with disabilities in the State who are enrolled in private elementary and secondary schools, provision is made for the participation of such children in the program assisted or carried out under this subchapter by providing for such children special education and related services.[189]

Although the district and the state have an obligation to offer each child with a disability with a publicly supervised free appropriate education, a parent does not have to accept a placement in the public facility or program offered by the district. Parents can choose to enroll their children in a private program instead. At this point, the Department of Education has determined that the parents have waived their children's right to a free appropriate education.[190] Also at this point, the district only has the obligation to provide the private school children with "a genuine opportunity for equitable participation" in special education services.[191] This interpretation is derived from the general regulations involving state administered programs. Those regulations, in part, state the following:

> A subgrantee [i.e., an indirect recipient of federal funds] shall provide students enrolled in private schools with a genuine opportunity for equitable participation in accordance with the requirements in Reg. 76.652-76.662 and in the authorizing statute and implementing regulations for a program.[192]

To be comparable, services must be comparable in quality, scope, and opportunity.[193] This standard has yet to be fleshed out by rulings or litigation.

It seems necessary to point out, however, that this is a rather narrow interpretation of the IDEA regulations on this issue. The regulations regarding private placement of children in private schools are as follows:

> As used in this part, "private school children with disabilities" means children with disabilities enrolled in private schools or facilities other than children with disabilities covered under Regs. 300.400-300.402.
>
> The State educational agency shall insure that:
>
> (a) To the extent consistent with their number and location in the State, provision is made for the participation of private school children with disabilities in the program assisted or carried out under this part by providing them with special education and related services; and
>
> (b) The other requirements in 34 CFR 76.651-76.662 [of EDGAR] are met.
>
> Each [local educational agency] shall provide special education and related services designed to meet the needs of private school children with disabilities residing in the jurisdiction of the agency.[194]

The regulations give no guidance as to where the services are to be provided, and answers to letters of inquiry indicate that service at either the private or public school site would be acceptable.[195] Two requirements must, however, be considered. First, it would seem most typical that service in the child's primary school location may be mandated by the least restrictive environment provisions. Second, if necessary services are provided off the school site, typically transportation to and from the service would be a mandated related service.[196]

Parochial School Students

Providing services to parochial school students involves the added complications of the constraints on state action required by the Establishment Clause. The First Amendment provides the "Congress shall make no law respecting an establishment of religion."[197] *Lemon v. Kurtzman*[198] is the cornerstone of modern establishment of religion analysis. In this case, the Court struck down a statute that provided salary supplements for teachers in private schools, salary reimbursements for private school teachers, and instructional materials. The Court consolidated previous analyses and developed what is now accepted as the analysis for determining whether a challenged practice effects an establishment of religion. Under the *Lemon* test, a questioned program or practice passes scrutiny if (1) it has a secular legislative purpose, (2) the primary effect neither advances nor inhibits religion, and (3) the program does not foster an excessive entanglement between government and religion.[199] This analysis has been applied over the last 20 years. The Courts have been strict in their interpretations in cases involving K–12 settings, applying a high standard of separation between church and state. Table 4.1 summarizes the outcome of Supreme Court cases.

It is generally stated that the wall of separation must be high because of the impressionability of the young children involved.[200] The Supreme Court in *Edwards v. Aguillard* explained this protectiveness:

> *The Court has been particularly vigilant in monitoring compliance with the Establishment Clause*

TABLE 4.1 Supreme Court Cases Involving Services to Religious K–12 Schools

PRACTICES UPHELD AS CONSTITUTIONAL	PRACTICES FOUND UNCONSTITUTIONAL
Everson v. Board of Education, 330 U.S. 1 (1947). Public school may provide transportation to students to and from private sectarian schools.	*McCollum v. Board of Education*, 333 U.S. 203 (1948). Public school may not provide release time for religious instruction on public school property.
Zorach v. Clauson, 343 U.S. 306 (1952). Public school may provide release time for students to attend religious classes off public school premises.	*Lemon v. Kurtzman*, 403 U.S. 602 (1971). State programs which allowed state officials to supplement salaries of private school teachers and to pay for secular textbooks and instructional materials found unconstitutional.
Board of Education v. Allen, 392 U.S. 236 (1968). State law requiring schools to lend textbooks to parochial school students free of charge was upheld.	*Levitt v. Committee for Public Education and Religious Liberty*, 413 U.S. 472 (1973). State statute that provided for reimbursement of private schools for expenses related to the administration, grading, compiling, and reporting of tests, which could be internally prepared, found unconstitutional.
Meek v. Pettenger, 421 U.S. 349 (1975). Lending of textbooks without charge to children attending private schools upheld.	
Wolman v. Walter, 433 U.S. 229 (1977). Portions of a state statute authorizing the loan of secular textbooks to parochial school students, authorizing the supplying of standardized tests and scoring services, providing for speech and hearing diagnostic services in the parochial school, and providing for therapeutic services at a neutral site were upheld.	*Sloan v. Lemon*, 413 U.S. 825 (1973). State statute which provided for reimbursement of tuition paid by parents to send their children to private schools found unconstitutional.
	Meek v. Pittenger, 421 U.S. 349 (1975). Direct loan of instructional materials and equipment to private schools held unconstitutional. The provision of counseling, testing, psychological services, speech and hearing therapy, teaching and related services for exceptional children to students enrolled in private schools at the private schools found unconstitutional.
Committee for Public Education and Religious Liberty v. Regan, 444 U.S. 646 (1980). State statute which provided for cash reimbursement to parochial schools to cover the cost of administering and grading state prepared tests upheld.	
Mueller v. Allen, 463 U.S. 388 (1983). State law that allowed taxpayers to deduct educational expenses, public or private, in computing their state income tax liability upheld.	*Wolman v. Walter*, 433 U.S. 229 (1977). Provisions of a state law authorizing the provision of instructional materials and equipment and unrestricted transportation and services for field trips for parochial school students found unconstitutional.
Board of Education of Westside Community Schools v. Mergens, 110 S. Ct. 2356 (1990). Equal Access Act, which allows student initiated religious clubs to meet on school premises if other noncurriculum related student clubs are allowed to meet on the premises was upheld.	*Aguilar v. Felton*, 473 U.S. 402 (1985). Using federal funds to send public school teachers into parochial schools for Chapter I instruction found unconstitutional.
	School District of Grand Rapids v. Ball, 473 U.S. 373 (1985). Paying parochial school teachers to teach parochial school students secular subjects on the premises of the private school and in paying public school teachers to teach supplemental courses at parochial school sites found unconstitutional.
Lamb's Chapel v. Center Moriches Union Free School District, 113 S. Ct. 2141 (1993). Allowing the use of school premises by a church to show a film series did not violate the Establishment Clause.	
Zobrest v. Catalina Foothills School District, 113 S. Ct. 2462 (1993). Providing the services of a sign language interpreter under IDEA to an eligible deaf student enrolled at a Catholic high school did not violate the Establishment Clause.	*Lee v. Weisman*, 112 S. Ct. 2649 (1992). Clergy led invocations and benedictions at graduation ceremony found unconstitutional.
	Board of Education of Kiryas Joel Village School District v. Grumet, 114 S. Ct. 2481 (1994). State law which created a public school district serving only members of the Satmar Hasidic sect found unconstitutional.

in elementary and secondary schools. Families entrust public schools with the education of their children, but condition their trust on the understanding that the classroom will not purposely be used to advance religious views that may conflict with the private beliefs of the student and his or her family. Students in such institutions are impressionable and their attendance is involuntary. The State exerts great authority and coercive power through mandatory attendance requirements, and because of the students' emulation of teachers as role models and the children's susceptibility to peer pressure. Furthermore, "[t]he public school is at once the symbol of our democracy and the most pervasive means for promoting our common destiny. In no activity of the State is it more vital to keep out divisive forces than in its schools."[201]

The increased protectiveness can be seen by the language used by the courts in applying the *Lemon* test in the K–12 setting. In these cases, the courts have adopted the language of "impermissible symbolic links" between church and state.[202] The effect is that it is more likely that a violation of the establishment clause will be found when creating a perception of endorsement of religion and those doing the perceiving are children of impressionable years.

> *Our cases have recognized that the Establishment Clause guards against more than direct, state-funded efforts to indoctrinate youngsters in specific religious beliefs. Government promotes religion as effectively when it fosters a close identification of its powers and responsibilities with those of any—or all—religious denominations as when it attempts to inculcate specific religious doctrines. If this identification conveys a message of government endorsement or disapproval of religion, a core purpose of the establishment clause is violated. . . . Our school aid cases have recognized a sensitivity to the symbolic impact of the union of church and state.*

Under these standards, it is clear that a state cannot provide direct aid to a parochial K–12 school, since it gives the appearance of fostering a relationship between church and state.

However, it is sometimes difficult to determine what constitutes direct aid and if it gives the appearance of fostering a relationship between church and state.

For purposes of understanding how services can be constitutionally provided to parochial school students, three Supreme Court cases must be reviewed. First, in *Meek v. Pittenger,*[203] the Court struck down the state's attempt at directly providing auxiliary services (including "therapeutic services") and instructional equipment to parochial schools. The Court found these provisions had an unconstitutional primary effect of advancing religion by affording substantial and direct aid to sectarian schools. In *Wolman v. Walter,*[204] the Court upheld a program that provided parochial school students with textbooks, diagnostic services on private school grounds, standardized testing and scoring, and therapeutic and remedial services on neutral sites. The Court held that the diagnostic services to be provided on the parochial school site did not violate the establishment clause, noting

> *that providing diagnostic services on the non-public school premises will not create an impermissible risk of the fostering of ideological view. It follows that there is not need for excessive surveillance, and there will not be impermissible entanglement.*[205]

The services upheld in *Meek* were distinguished from those struck down in *Wolman* by showing the services in *Wolman* were to be provided on a neutral site. The Court noted the following:

> *The fact that a unit on a neutral site on occasion may serve only sectarian pupils does not provide the same concerns that troubled the Court in Meek. The influence on therapist's behavior that is exerted by the fact that he serves a sectarian pupil is qualitatively different from the influence of the pervasive atmosphere of a religious institution. The dangers perceived in Meek arose from the nature of the institution, not from the nature of the pupils.*[206]

Aguilar v. Felton[207] involved New York City's use of federal funds to provide the required comparable services to private school students under Chapter 1.[208] Public school teachers were sent to provide services on parochial school sites but were given instructions to avoid involvement with religious activities, to keep religious material out of their classrooms, and to minimize their contact with the private school personnel. The Court struck the program, finding that it would require "a permanent and pervasive state presence in the sectarian schools receiving aid" to ensure that only secular instruction was taking place.[209]

Witters v. Washington Department of Services for the Blind[210] involved a blind student who was pursuing a Bible studies degree at a Christian college. The state denied the student financial aid under a state vocational rehabilitation assistance program, believing that to do otherwise would violate the Establishment Clause. The Supreme Court disagreed, finding that since the funds went directly to the student, not the institution, there was no impermissible endorsement of religion. This case is similar to the K–12 tuition tax deduction case in which the Court found that since the deduction was given to all students and was given to the students rather than the institutions, the Establishment Clause was not violated when the students used the benefit to attend parochial schools.[211]

Since these cases, schools and the courts have continued to try to provide services to parochial school students without violating the Establishment Clause. It appears that intermittent services or diagnostic services can be provided on the parochial school site; ongoing services must be provided in a neutral location. There is a split in the cases as to whether these services when provided in a mobile unit, must be provided off of the school premises.[212]

The issue becomes more difficult when the services to be provided must be with the child at all times, e.g, aides and interpreters. In *Zobrest v. Catalina Foothills School District*,[213] this question was put before the United States Supreme Court. Focusing on *Mueller* and *Witters*, the five-member majority reasoned that through IDEA the state merely provides a benefit equally to all children, thereby creating no link between church and state. The state provides the same service, sign-language interpreter service, to all eligible students with disabilities regardless of where they attend school. However, this decision also rested on the particularized nature of the role of the sign-language interpreter. The Court concluded that an interpreter serves as a neutral conduit of information and "neither adds to nor subtracts from"[214] the message, religious or otherwise, being conveyed in the Catholic school. However, it is unknown whether any other related service comprises a similarly mechanical service so as to escape Establishment Clause violation.

Another unanswered question related to the issue of placing public employees in private sectarian schools concerns what school districts must do rather than what they may do. *Zobrest* established only that public monies under IDEA *may* be used to provide the services of a sign-language interpreter in a parochial setting. However, in *Goodall v. Stafford County School Board*,[215] the Fourth Circuit Court of Appeals concluded that statutory language does not require such services to be provided.[216] It found that as long as a school district makes an appropriate program available and stands ready to provide that education if the child re-enrolls in the public system, it has met its obligation under the law. The Supreme Court did not rule on any statutory issue in *Zobrest*, and thus the question remains unresolved.

AGUILAR v. FELTON
473 U.S. 402, 105 S. Ct. 3232 (1985)

Justice Brennan delivered the opinion of the Court.

I. A.

The program at issue in this case, originally enacted as Title I of the Elementary and Secondary Education Act of 1965, authorizes the Secretary of Education to distribute financial assistance to local educational institutions to meet the needs of educationally deprived children from low-income families. The funds are to be appropriated in accordance with programs proposed by local educational agencies and approved by state educational agencies. 20 U.S.C. § 3805(a). "To the extent consistent with the number of educationally deprived children in the school district of the local educational agency who are enrolled in private elementary and secondary schools, such agency shall make provisions for including special educational services and arrangements . . . in which such children can participate." § 3806(a). . . .

Since 1966, the City of New York has provided instructional services funded by Title I to parochial school students on the premises of parochial schools. . . .

The programs conducted at these schools include remedial reading, reading skills, remedial mathematics, English as a second language, and guidance services. These programs are carried out by regular employees of the public schools (teachers, guidance counselors, psychologists, psychiatrists and social workers) who have volunteered to teach in the parochial schools. . . .

****

II.

In *School Districts of the City of Grand Rapids v. Ball, ante.* p.—, the Court has today held unconstitutional under the Establishment Clause two remedial and enhancement programs operated by the Grand Rapids Public School District, in which classes were provided to private school children at public expense in classrooms located in and leased from the local private schools. The New York programs challenged in this care are very similar to the programs we examined in *Ball.* In both cases, the publicly funded programs provide not only professional personnel, but also all materials and supplies necessary for the operation of the programs. Finally, the instructors in both cases are told that they are public school employees under the sole control of the public school system.

****

In *Lemon v. Kurtzman,* 403 U.S. 602 (1971), the Court held that the supervision necessary to ensure that teachers in parochial schools were not conveying religious messages to their students would constitute the excessive entanglement of church and state. . . . Similarly, in *Meek v. Pittenger,* 421 U.S. 349 (1975), we invalidated a state program that offered, *inter alia,* guidance, testing, remedial and therapeutic services performed by public employees on the premises of the parochial schools. *Id.,* at 352-353. As in *Lemon,* we observed that though a comprehensive system of supervision might conceivably prevent teachers from having the primary effect of advancing religion, such a system would inevitably lead to an unconstitutional administrative entanglement between church and state.

The prophylactic contacts required to ensure that teachers play a strictly nonideological role, the Court held [in Lemon], necessarily give rise to a constitutionally intolerable degree of entanglement between church and state. Id., at 619. The same excessive entanglement would be required for Pennsylvania to be "certain," as it must be that . . . personnel do not advance the religious mission of the church-related schools in which they serve. Public Funds for Public Schools v. Marburger, 358 F. Supp. 29, 40-41, aff'd, 417 U.S. 961. Id., at 370.

****

The critical elements of the entanglement proscribed in *Lemon* and *Meek* are thus present in this case. First, as noted above, the aid is provided in a pervasively sectarian environment. Second, because assistance is provided in the form of teachers, ongoing inspection is required to ensure the absence of a religious message. Cf. *Lemon,* 403 U.S., at 619, with *Tilton, supra,* at 668, and *Roemer, supra,* at 765. In short, the scope and duration of New York's Title I program would require a permanent and pervasive State presence in the sectarian schools receiving aid.

****

III.

Despite the well-intentioned efforts taken by the City of New York, the program remains constitutionally flawed owing to the nature of the aid, to the institution receiving the aid, and to the constitutional principles that they implicate—that neither the State nor Federal Government shall promote or hinder a particular faith or faith generally through the advancement of benefits or through the excessive entanglement of church and state in the administration of those benefits.

Affirmed.

(Footnotes omitted.)

— ▬ ▬ ▬

PULIDO v. CAVAZOS
934 F.2d 912 (Eighth Circuit 1991)

GIBSON, Circuit Judge.

Once again the constitutionality of certain provisions of Chapter 1 of Title I of the Education Consolidation and Improvement Act of 1981, 20 U.S.C. §§ 2701-3386 (1988), providing remedial education to low income students in parochial schools is before this court. Rudy Pulido, John M. Swomley and G. Hugh Wamble filed a suit to challenge the use of mobile and portable classrooms to provide remedial services to educationally deprived children enrolled in private schools and the formula for allocating the cost of such services between private and public schools. . . .

****

The contract between Blue Hills and the Department of Education requires that all facilities used to provide Chapter 1 services be "religiously neutral." The mobile classroom units used to provide Chapter 1 services consist of vans and recreational vehicles that have been modified for use as classrooms. The portable units consist of trailers and prefabricated buildings modified for use as classrooms. During the 1988–89 school year, mobile and portable units were used at 104 sites in Missouri. When feasible, Blue Hills parks the units on public streets, on other public property, or on private property not owned by the private school or any related religious organization. In some instances, however, Blue Hills has not been able to park units at such places because they were either unsafe or unavailable. In those instances, Blue Hills parks the units on private school property— typically on a parking lot, driveway or playground. At 19 of the sites using mobile and portable units, Blue Hills was not able to park the units off the parochial school property, and at those sites, Blue Hills used 18 mobile units and one portable unit to provide Chapter 1 services. When Blue Hills parks units on parochial school property, they are parked as far as possible from the school buildings. The Department of Education has advised Blue Hills "to investigate every other possibility before parking mobile units on property that is owned by the school."

Pulido challenged the parking of units both on and off the premises of parochial schools as an unconstitutional establishment of religion. . . .

****

A statute or governmental action is consistent with the establishment clause of the first amendment if: (1) it has a secular legislative purpose; (2) its principal or primary effect is neither to advance nor inhibit religion; and (3) it does not foster excessive government entanglement with religion. *Lemon v. Kurtzman*, 403 U.S. 602, 612-13, 91 S. Ct. 2105, 2111-12, 29 L. Ed. 2d 745 (1971). . . .

****

A.

We first consider the constitutionality of providing Chapter 1 services to parochial school students in mobile and portable units parked on public property.

Pulido contends that providing Chapter 1 services in mobile and portable units parked on public property adjacent to parochial schools violates both the primary effect and excessive entanglement elements of the *Lemon* test. The Secretary and parochial school parents argue that the Supreme Court decision in *Wolman* [*v. Walter,* 433 U.S. 229 (1977)] specifically approves using mobile and portable units parked on public property to provide Chapter 1 services to parochial school students. . . . *Wolman* states:

> [W]e hold that providing therapeutic and remedial services at a neutral site off the premises of the nonpublic schools will not have the impermissible effect of advancing religion. Neither will there be any excessive entanglement arising from supervision of public employees to insure that they maintain a neutral stance. It can hardly be said that the supervision of public employees performing public functions on public property creates an excessive entanglement between church and state.
> *Id.* at 248 . . . .

This reasoning is fully applicable to the mobile and portable units parked on public property and provides a strong basis for affirming the district court's judgment on this issue. . . .

B.

Pulido argues that providing Chapter 1 services in units parked both on and off the parochial school premises is unconstitutional because providing services in these locations has the primary effect of advancing religion and does so in three ways. First, he claims that providing Chapter 1 services in mobile and portable units impermissibly advances religion because the services are not provided in religiously neutral locations, and that the units are merely "annexes" of the parochial schools. Second, he argues that providing Chapter 1 services in units parked on the property of and adjacent to parochial schools creates a "symbolic union" between church and state. He says that the units are "physically and educationally identified with the functions of the nonpublic school," as evidenced by religious artifacts on the outside of parochial schools and the fact that most parochial schools are located "on a campus" that also includes a church, rectory, and, in some instances, a convent. Third, he argues that the services have the primary effect of advancing religion because the services are a direct aid to religion. We consider these arguments in turn.

-1-

****

Here, we are convinced that the services are provided in a religiously neutral atmosphere and the units do not operate as "annexes" of the parochial schools. The mobile and portable units are separate

from the parochial school buildings and classrooms. . . .

Indeed, the mobility of the units does much to establish their religious neutrality and to answer Pulido's arguments that the units operate as "annexes" of the parochial schools and are physically and educationally identified with the functions of the parochial schools. . . . The mobile units do not remain on the parochial school property. Although one portable unit remains parked on parochial school property during the school year, it is removed during the summer. The units are only placed on the parochial school property as a last resort and are parked as far as possible from the parochial school building. . . .

-2-

Pulido next argues that providing Chapter 1 services in units parked on the property of or near parochial schools creates a "symbolic union" between church and state. Impermissible advancement may occur when the government "fosters a close identification of its powers and responsibilities with those of any—or all—religious denominations." *Ball*, 473 U.S. at 389, 105 S. Ct. at 3225.

****

. . . . The fact that Blue Hills removes the units from the parochial school and public property once the Chapter 1 classes are over demonstrates the lack of a "symbolic union" between the parochial school and the government both in the eyes of the students and the public. . . . By receiving the instruction in a classroom, different from their parochial school classroom and outside of their parochial school building, and from a religiously neutral instructor who is different than their parochial school instructor, the children should "discern the crucial difference between the religious school classes and the 'public school' classes." *Ball*, 473 U.S. at 391, 105 S. Ct. at 3226.

-3-

Pulido also contends that the use of the mobile and portable units, both on and off the property of the parochial schools, results in government aid to religion and thus has the primary effect of advancing religion. . . .

These facts do not add up to describe a program that has the primary effect of advancing religion. . . .

Both private and public school students are eligible for Chapter 1 services if they are educationally deprived and reside in a qualifying low income area. *See* 20 U.S.C. § 2724; 34 C.F.R. § 200.50 (1990). The Supreme Court has stated that the fact that the remedial services are provided only to religious school students does not mean that the services impermissibly advance religion or breed political conflict as long as the services are provided at a "neutral site." *Wolman*, 433 U.S. at 247-48, 97 S. Ct. at 2605-06. . . .

****

C.

Pulido next argues that providing Chapter 1 services in units on the property of or near parochial schools results in excessive government entanglement between church and state. Specifically, Pulido complains that there is "extensive daily contact" between the parochial and the Blue Hills' staffs. Pulido points to evidence that the staffs discuss various subjects, including the skills taught in the parochial and Chapter 1 classrooms, scheduling of the Chapter 1 program, and the progress and eligibility of students for the Chapter 1 program. Pulido complains that these contracts amount to excessive entanglement in violation of the establishment clause.

****

. . . . We are satisfied that every effort has been made to ensure that no entanglement occurs between the staffs. Blue Hills supervisory staff monitor all aspects of the Chapter 1 program and regularly visit the mobile and portable units and the leased space. Blue Hills does not monitor or inspect the private schools, and likewise, the private schools do not monitor or supervise the Chapter 1 program. We are satisfied that there is no excessive entanglement between the church and state.

****

The use of the mobile and portable units to provide Chapter 1 services is a "practical response to the logistical difficulties of extending needed and desired aid to all children of the community." *Wolman*, 433 U.S. at 247 n. 14. . . . The Supreme Court has clearly held that parochial school students may receive Chapter 1 services, that these students are entitled to receive "comparable services," and that these services cannot be provided in parochial school classrooms. Pulido puts forth no feasible alternative for providing "comparable" Chapter 1 services to parochial school students in Missouri. . . .

Thus, we affirm the district court's ruling that the use of mobile and portable units off the premises of parochial school property is constitutional, but reverse the district court's ruling that the use of such units on the parochial school property is unconstitutional.

****

(Footnotes omitted.)

— — — —

ZOBREST v. CATALINA FOOTHILLS SCHOOL DISTRICT
113 S. Ct. 2462 (1993)

Chief Justice REHNQUIST delivered the opinion of the Court.

Petitioner James Zobrest, who has been deaf since birth, asked respondent school district to provide a sign-language interpreter to accompany him to classes at a Roman Catholic high school in Tucson, Arizona, pursuant to the Individuals with Disabilities Education Act (IDEA), 20 U.S.C. § 1400 *et seq.*, and its Arizona counterpart Ariz. Rev. Stat. Ann. § 15-761 *et seq.* (1991 and Supp. 1992). The United States Court of Appeals for the Ninth Circuit decided, however, that provision of such a publicly employed interpreter would violate the Establishment Clause of the First Amendment. We hold that the Establishment Clause does not bar the school district from providing the requested interpreter.

James Zobrest attended grades one through five in a school for the deaf, and grades six through eight in a public school operated by respondent. While he attended public school, respondent furnished him with a sign-language interpreter. For religious reasons, James' parents (also petitioners here) enrolled him for the ninth grade in Salpointe Catholic High School, a sectarian institution. . . .

Petitioners instituted this action in the United States District Court for the District of Arizona under

20 U.S.C. § 1415(e)(4)(A), . . . Petitioners asserted that the IDEA and the Free Exercise Clause of the First Amendment require respondent to provide James with an interpreter at Salpointe, and that the Establishment Clause does not bar such relief. The complaint sought a preliminary injunction and "such other and further relief as the Court deems just and proper." The District Court denied petitioners' request for a preliminary injunction, finding that the provision of an interpreter at Salpointe would likely offend the Establishment Clause. . . . The court thereafter granted respondent summary judgment, on the ground that "[t]he interpreter would act as a conduit for the religious inculcation of James—thereby, promoting James' religious development at government expense." . . . "That kind of entanglement of church and state," the District Court concluded, "is not allowed." *Ibid.*

The Court of Appeals affirmed by a divided vote, 963 F.2d 1190 (CA9 1992), applying the three-part test announced in *Lemon v. Kurtzman,* 403 U.S. 602, 613 (1971). It first found that the IDEA has a clear secular purpose: "to assist States and Localities to provide for the education of all handicapped children." 963 F.2d, at 1193 (quoting 20 U.S.C. § 1400(c)). Turning to the second prong of the *Lemon* inquiry, though, the Court of Appeals determined that the IDEA, if applied as petitioners proposed, would have the primary effect of advancing religion and thus would run afoul of the Establishment Clause. "By placing its employee in the sectarian school," the Court of Appeals reasoned, "the government would create the appearance that it was a 'joint sponsor' of the school's activities." 963 F.2d, at 1194-1195. This, the court held, would create the "symbolic union of government and religion" found impermissible in *School Dist. of Grand Rapids v. Ball,* 473 U.S. 373, 392 (1985). In contrast, the dissenting judge argued that "[g]eneral welfare programs neutrally available to all children," such as the IDEA, pass constitutional muster, "because their benefits diffuse over the entire population." 963 F.2d, at 1199 (Tang, J., dissenting). We granted certiorari, 506 U.S. (1992), and now reverse.

****

We have never said that "religious institutions are disabled by the First Amendment from participating in publicly sponsored social welfare programs." *Bowen v. Kendrick,* 487 U.S. 589, 609 (1988). For if the Establishment Clause did bar religious groups from receiving general government benefits, then "a church could not be protected by the police and fire departments, or have its public sidewalk kept in repair." *Widmar v. Vincent,* 454 U.S. 263, 274-275 (1981) (internal quotation marks omitted). Given that a contrary rule would lead to such absurd results, we have consistently held that government programs that neutrally provide benefits to a broad class of citizens defined without reference to religion are not readily subject to an Establishment Clause challenge just because sectarian institutions may also receive an attenuated financial benefit. Nowhere have we stated this principle more clearly than in *Mueller v. Allen,* 463 U.S. 388 (1983), and *Witters v. Washington Dept. of Services for Blind,* 474 U.S. 481 (1986), two cases dealing specifically with government programs offering general educational assistance.

In *Mueller,* we rejected an Establishment Clause challenge to a Minnesota law allowing taxpayers to deduct certain educational expenses in computing their state income tax, even though the vast majority of those deductions (perhaps over 90%) went to parents whose children attended sectarian schools. *See* 463 U.S., at 401; . . . Two factors, aside from States' traditionally broad taxing authority, informed our decision. . . . We noted that the law "permits all parents—whether their children attend public school or private—to deduct their children's educational expenses." 463 U.S., at 398. . . . We also pointed out that under Minnesota's scheme, public funds become available to sectarian schools "only as a result of numerous private choices of individual parents of school-age children," thus distinguishing *Mueller* from our other cases involving "the direct transmission of assistance from the State to the schools themselves." 463 U.S., at 399.

Witters was premised on virtually identical reasoning. In that case, we upheld against an Establishment Clause challenge the State of Washington's extension of vocational assistance, as part of a general state program, to a blind person studying at a private Christian college to become a pastor, missionary, or youth director. Looking at the statute as a whole, we observed that "[a]ny aid provided under Washington's program that ultimately flows to religious institutions does so only as a result of the genuinely independent and private choices of aid recipients." 474 U.S., at 487. The program, we said, "creates no financial incentive for students to undertake sectarian education." *Id.,* at 488. We also remarked that, much like the law in *Mueller*, "Washington's program is 'made available generally without regard to the sectarian nonsectarian, or public-nonpublic nature of the institution benefited.'" *Witters, supra*, at 487. . . . In light of these factors, we held that Washington's program—even as applied to a student who sought state assistance so that he could become a pastor—would not advance religion in a manner inconsistent with the Establishment Clause. *Witters, supra*, at 489.

That same reasoning applies with equal force here. The service at issue in this case is part of a general government program that distributes benefits neutrally to any child qualifying as "handicapped" under the IDEA, without regard to the "sectarian-nonsectarian, or public-nonpublic nature" of the school the child attends. By according parents freedom to select a school of their choice, the statute ensures that a government-paid interpreter will be present in a sectarian school only as a result of the private decision of individual parents. In other words, because the IDEA creates no financial incentive for parents to choose a sectarian school, an interpreter's presence there cannot be attributed to state decisionmaking. Viewed against the backdrop of *Mueller* and *Witters*, then the Court of Appeals erred in its decision. When the government offers a neutral service on the premises of a sectarian school as part of a general program that "is in no way skewed towards religion," *Witters, supra*, at 488, it follows under our prior decisions that provision of that service does not offend the Establishment Clause. *See Wolman v. Walter*, 433 U.S. 229, 244 (1977). Indeed, this is an even easier case than *Mueller* and *Witters* in the sense that, under the IDEA, no funds traceable to the government ever find their way into sectarian schools' coffers. The only indirect economic benefit a sectarian school might receive by dint of the IDEA is the handicapped child's tuition—and that is, of course, assuming that the school makes a profit on each student; that, without an IDEA interpreter, the child would have gone to school elsewhere; and that the school, then, would have been unable to fill that child's spot.

Respondent contends, however, that this case differs from *Mueller* and *Witters*, in that petitioners seek to have a public employee physically present in a sectarian school to assist in James' religious education. In light of this distinction, respondent argues that this case more closely resembles *Meek v.*

Pittenger, 421 U.S. 349 (1975), and *School Dist. of Grand Rapids v. Ball*, 473 U.S. 373 (1985). In *Meek*, we struck down a statute that, inter alia, provided "massive aid" to private schools—more than 75% of which were church related—through a direct loan of teaching material and equipment. 421 U.S., at 364-365. The material and equipment covered by the statute included maps, charts, and tape recorders. *Id.*, at 355. According to respondent, if the government could not place a tape recorder in a sectarian school in *Meek*, then it surely cannot place an interpreter in Salpointe. The statute in *Meek* also authorized state-paid personnel to furnish "auxiliary services"—which included remedial and accelerated instruction and guidance counseling—on the premises of religious schools. We determined that this part of the statute offended the First Amendment as well. *Id.*, at 372. *Ball* similarly involved two public programs that provided services on private school premises; there, public employees taught classes to students in private school classrooms. 473 U.S., at 375. We found that those programs likewise violated the Constitution, relying largely on *Meek*. 473 U.S., at 386-389. According to respondent, if the government could not provide educational services on the premises of sectarian schools in *Meek* and *Ball*, then it surely cannot provide James with an interpreter on the premises of Salpointe.

Respondent's reliance on *Meek* and *Ball* is misplaced for two reasons. First, the programs in *Meek* and *Ball*—through direct grants of government aid—relieved sectarian schools of costs they otherwise would have borne in educating their students. *See Witters, supra*, at 487 ("[T]he State may not grant aid to a religious school, whether cash or in kind, where the effect of the aid is 'that of a direct subsidy to the religious school' from the State") (quoting *Ball, supra*, at 394). For example, the religious schools in *Meek* received teaching material and equipment from the State, relieving them of an otherwise necessary cost of performing their educational function. 421 U.S., at 365-366. "Substantial aid to the educational function of such schools," we explained, "necessarily results in aid to the sectarian school enterprise as a whole," and therefore brings about "the direct and substantial advancement of religious activity." *Id.*, at 366. So, too, was the case in *Ball*: The programs challenged there, which provided teachers in addition to instructional equipment and material, "in effect subsidize[d] the religious functions of the parochial schools by taking over a substantial portion of their responsibility for teaching secular subjects." 473 U.S., at 397. "This kind of direct aid," we determined, "is indistinguishable from the provision of a direct cash subsidy to the religious school." *Id.*, at 395. The extension of aid to petitioners, however, does not amount to "an impermissible 'direct subsidy'" of Salpointe. *Witters*, 474 U.S., at 487. For Salpointe is not relieved of an expense that it otherwise would have assumed in educating its students. . . . Handicapped children, not sectarian schools, are the primary beneficiaries of the IDEA; to the extent sectarian schools benefit at all from the IDEA, they are only incidental beneficiaries. . . .

Second, the task of a sign-language interpreter seems to us quite different from that of a teacher or guidance counselor. Notwithstanding the Court of Appeals' intimations to the contrary, *see* 963 F.2d, at 1195, the Establishment Clause lays down no absolute bar to the placing of a public employee in a sectarian school. Such a flat rule, smacking of antiquated notions of "taint," would indeed exalt form over substance. Nothing in this record suggests that a sign-language interpreter would do more than accurately interpret whatever material is presented to the class as a whole. In fact, ethical guidelines require interpreters to "transmit everything that is said in exactly the same way it is intended." App. 73. James' parents have chosen of their own free will to place him in a pervasively sectarian environment. The sign-language interpreter they have requested will neither add to nor subtract from that environment, and hence the provision of such assistance is not bared by the Establishment Clause.

The IDEA creates a neutral government program dispensing aid not to schools but to individual handicapped children. If a handicapped child chooses to enroll in a sectarian school, we hold that the Establishment Clause does not prevent the school district from furnishing him with a sign-language interpreter there in order to facilitate his education. The judgment of the Court of Appeals is therefore

Reversed.

JUSTICE BLACKMUN, with whom JUSTICE SOUTER joins, . . .

****

. . . . Until now, the Court never has authorized a public employee to participate directly in religious indoctrination. Yet that is the consequence of today's decision.

****

At Salpointe, where the secular and the sectarian are "inextricably intertwined," governmental assistance to the educational function of the school necessarily entails governmental participation in the school's inculcation of religion. A state-employed sign-language interpreter would be required to communicate the material covered in religion class, the nominally secular subjects that are taught from a religious perspective, and the daily Masses at which Salpointe encourages attendance for Catholic students. In an environment so pervaded by discussions of the divine, the interpreter's every gesture would be infused with religious significance. Indeed, petitioners willingly concede this point: "That the interpreter conveys religious messages is a given in the case." Brief for Petitioners 22. By this concession, petitioners would seem to surrender their constitutional claim.

The majority attempts to elude the impact of the record by offering three reasons why this sort of aid to petitioners survives Establishment Clause scrutiny. First, the majority observes that provision of a sign-language interpreter occurs as "part of a general government program that distributes benefits neutrally to any child qualifying as 'handicapped' under the IDEA, without regard to the 'sectarian-nonsectarian, or public-nonpublic' nature of the school the child attends.". . . Second, the majority finds significant the fact that aid is provided to pupils and their parents, rather than directly to sectarian schools. As a result, "[a]ny aid . . . that ultimately flows to religious institutions does so only as a result of the genuinely independent and private choices of aid recipients." . . . quoting *Witters v. Washington Department of Services for the Blind*, 474 U.S. 481, 487 (1986). And, finally, the majority opines that "the task of a sign-language interpreter seems to us quite different from that of a teacher or guidance counselor.". . . .

But the majority's arguments are unavailing. As to the first two, even a general welfare program may have specific applications that are constitutionally forbidden under the Establishment Clause. . . . For example, a general program granting remedial assistance to disadvantaged schoolchildren attending public and private, secular and sectarian schools alike would clearly offend the Establishment Clause insofar as it authorized the provision of teachers. *See Aguilar v. Felton*, 473 U.S. 402, 410 (1985); *Grand*

Rapids School District v. Ball, 473 U.S. 373, 385 (1985); *Meek v. Pittenger*, 421 U.S. 349, 371 (1975). Such a program would not be saved simply because it supplied teachers to secular as well as sectarian schools. Nor would the fact that teachers were furnished to pupils and their parents, rather than directly to sectarian schools, immunize such a program from Establishment Clause scrutiny.... The majority's decision must turn, then, upon the distinction between a teacher and a sign-language interpreter.

"Although Establishment Clause jurisprudence is characterized by few absolutes," at a minimum "the Clause does absolutely prohibit government-financed or government-sponsored indoctrination into the beliefs of a particular religious faith." *Grand Rapids*, 473 U.S., at 385.... In keeping with this restriction, our cases consistently have rejected the provision by government of any resource capable of advancing a school's religious mission. Although the Court generally has permitted the provision of "secular and nonideological services unrelated to the primary, religion-oriented educational function of the sectarian school," *Meek*, 421 U.S., at 364, it has always proscribed the provision of benefits that afford even "the opportunity for the transmission of sectarian views," *Wolman*, 433 U.S., at 244.

Thus, the Court has upheld the use of public school buses to transport children to and from school, *Everson v. Board of Education*, 330 U.S. 1 (1947), while striking down the employment of publicly funded buses for field trips controlled by parochial school teachers, *Wolman*, 433 U.S., at 254. Similarly, the Court has permitted the provision of secular textbooks whose content is immutable and can be ascertained in advance, *Board of Education v. Allen*, 392 U.S. 236 (1968), while prohibiting the provision of any instructional materials or equipment that could be used to convey a religious message, such as slide projectors, tape recorders, record players, and the like, *Wolman*, 433 U.S., at 249. State-paid speech and hearing therapists have been allowed to administer diagnostic testing on the premises of parochial schools, *Wolman* 433 U.S., at 241-242, whereas state-paid remedial teachers and counselors have not been authorized to offer their services because of the risk that they may inculcate religious beliefs, *Meek*, 421 U.S., at 371.

These distinctions perhaps are somewhat fine, but "lines must be drawn." *Grand Rapids*, 473 U.S., at 398 (citation omitted). And our cases make clear that

government crosses the boundary when it furnishes the medium for communication of a religious message. If petitioners receive the relief they seek, it is beyond question that a state-employed sign-language interpreter would serve as the conduit for petitioner's religious education, thereby assisting Salpointe in its mission of religious indoctrination....

Witters, supra, and *Mueller v. Allen*, 463 U.S. 388 (1983), are not to the contrary. Those cases dealt with the payment of cash or a tax deduction, where governmental involvement ended with the disbursement of funds of lessening of tax. This case, on the other hand, involves ongoing, daily, and intimate governmental participation in the teaching and propagation of religious doctrine. When government dispenses public funds to individuals who employ them to finance private choices, it is difficult to argue that government is actually endorsing religion. But the graphic symbol of the concert of church and state that results when a public employee or instrumentality mouths a religious message is likely to "enlis[t]—at least in the eyes of impressionable youngsters—the powers of government to the support of the religious denomination operating the school." *Grand Rapids*, 473, U.S., at 385. And the union of church and state in pursuit of a common enterprise is likely to place the imprimatur of governmental approval upon the favored religion, conveying a message of exclusion to all those who do not adhere to its tenets.

Moreover, this distinction between the provision of funds and the provision of a human being is not merely one of form. It goes to the heart of the principles animating the Establishment Clause. As Amicus Council on Religious Freedom points out, the provision of a state-paid sign-language interpreter may pose serious problems for the church as well as for the state. Many sectarian schools impose religiously based rules of conduct, as Salpointe has in this case. A traditional Hindu school would be likely to instruct its students and staff to dress modestly, avoiding any display of their bodies. And an orthodox Jewish yeshiva might well forbid all but kosher food upon its premises. To require public employees to obey such rules would impermissibly threaten individual liberty, but to fail to do so might endanger religious autonomy. For such reasons, it long has been feared that "a union of government and religion tends to destroy government and to degrade religion." *Engel v. Vitale*, 370 U.S. 421, 431 (1962).

The Establishment Clause was designed to avert exactly this sort of conflict.

III.

The Establishment Clause "rests upon the premise that both religion and government can best work to achieve their lofty aims if each is left free from the other within its respective sphere." *McCollum v. Board of Education*, 333 U.S. 203, 212 (1948). To this end, our cases have strived to "chart a course that preserve[s] the autonomy and freedom of religious bodies while avoiding any semblance of established religion." *Walz v. Tax Commission*, 397 U.S. 664, 672 (1970). I would not stray, as the Court does today, from the course set by nearly five decades of Establishment Clause jurisprudence. Accordingly, I dissent.
(Footnotes omitted.)

ADDITIONAL COMMENTARY

1. In *Dreher v. Amphitheater Unified School District*, 797 F. Supp. 753 (D.Ariz. 1992), the court found that the district had fulfilled its obligation by offering an appropriate placement at the Arizona School for the Deaf and Blind. The parents rejected the offer and unilaterally placed the student in a private facility. They then sought reimbursement for the costs of speech therapy. The court found that although the student should have a genuine opportunity to participate in special education and related services, that offer had been rejected. Therefore, the district was not obligated to pay for the related services at the private institution.

2. Providing services to children in the isolated sect of Satmar Hasidism has been the subject of much litigation. The Satmar are an orthodox Jewish sect; a major tenet of their religion is to draw boundaries between themselves and the rest of society. Their primary language is Yiddish; their dress is distinctive. They also practice gender segregation during public events, such as school. In *Parents Association of P.S. 16 v. Quinones*, 803 F.2d 1235 (2nd Cir. 1986), the court found an establishment clause violation in the district's practice of segregating the Hasidic students in one section of the public school and providing services consistent with their religion. In *Board of Education of Monroe-Woodbury v. Wieder*, 72 N.Y.2d 174 (1988), the court held that the students did not have a right to public educational services within their private schools—but neither was the district forced to offer services only at a public school. Following this, the legislature created a school district whose boundaries were equivalent to the boundaries of the Hasidim. The Supreme Court recently considered this law and found it a violation of the Establishment Clause (*Board of Education of Kiryas Joel School District v. Grumet*, 114 S. Ct. 2481 (1994)). Interestingly, in separate concurrences, Justices O'Connor and Kennedy suggested that the Court should reexamine its ruling in *Aguilar v. Felton*, 473 U.S. 402 (1985), which they reasoned had motivated the passage of New York's improper state law in *Kiryas Joel*.

3. The court in *Felter v. Cape Girardeau Public School District*, 810 F.Supp. 1062 (E.D. Mo. 1993), found no Establishment Clause violation in transporting a special education student from the sidewalk outside the parochial school to the public school for special education classes.

4. In *Pulido v. Cavazos*, 934 F.2d 912 (8th Cir. 1991), *Barnes v. Cavazos*, 966 F.2d 1056 (6th Cir. 1992), and *Board of Education of Chicago v. Alexander*, 983 F.2d 745 (7th Cir. 1993), the court upheld the Department of Education's decision to take the additional costs of providing services to parochial schools off the top of the state's federal allocation.

DUE PROCESS PROCEDURES

The IEP is said to be the heart of IDEA. Following that analogy, the due process protections are the soul (or, if the IEP is the engine, the due process protections are the wheels on which the entire statute rides). One of the primary concepts within IDEA is full parental participation.

In order to make this a reality, the statute provides the due process procedures to assure parental participation and to provide parties a mediation to resolve disputes. In *Rowley,* the Supreme Court indicated that considerable reliance should be placed on the procedures set forth in the statute to ensure that students are provided with appropriate placements.[217] The procedures are important to a student's placement and the hearing mechanism. The procedural protections of IDEA are pervasive from identification to placement. The statute and regulations specify every procedural step along the way. At points along the path, where parents and the district may disagree, the opportunity for a due process hearing exists to resolve the conflict. Figure 4.3 shows a flowchart that includes time frames of the procedural steps within IDEA.

The purpose of the hearing is to resolve disputes between the school and the parent(s) of the child with the disability. These disputes generally fall into the following categories: identification, evaluation, placement, the components of a free appropriate public education, and related services.

The hearing itself is a fact-finding administrative procedure. It is judicial in nature and run like an informal court proceeding. It is conducted by an impartial hearing officer who must examine the evidence presented and make determinations of fact and law. Both parties are expected to present witnesses and evidence and may rebut evidence and cross-examine witnesses. This is the primary avenue of relief available for parties with an IDEA concern and the exclusive channel to the court system. Both parties must pursue this administrative remedy, unless futile to do so, before taking the action into the regular judicial channels. Additionally, the Supreme Court in *Smith v. Robinson*[218] held that not only must administrative procedures be exhausted, but an IDEA claim may not be attached to another action, e.g., a Section 504 complaint in order to avoid the administrative process.

There are other administrative avenues that may be pursued. These, however, do not lead to judicial review. If the concern involves Section 504 issues, a party can ask the Office for Civil Rights (OCR) in the region for an opinion on the issue.[219] Since one way of complying with Section 504 is fulfilling obligations under IDEA, many issues overlap. It is important to note here that this administrative remedy does exist; however, its appeal route does not lead to court. The only available remedy is that a school's failure to comply with OCR may lead to the revocation of federal funds.

For issues that are procedural in nature under IDEA, a party may file an EDGAR complaint with the state education agency (SEA). The Education Department General Administrative Regulations (EDGAR) are administrative requirements that apply to most programs controlled by the federal Department of Education. There are specific regulations for implementing IDEA.[220] The EDGAR regulation requires a complaint procedure to resolve procedural issues under IDEA. The minimum complaint procedure must include a mechanism to investigate and resolve a complaint within 60 days, which may be appealed to the Secretary of Education.[221] Any individual or organization may file an EDGAR complaint if they believe a public agency responsible for providing special education has violated a state or federal law or regulation controlling these programs. The complaint may be based on an alleged violation affecting one child or a group of children; it may allege an incident that is a violation or a systemic violation throughout the agency. The important distinctions between EDGAR complaints and due process hearings is that EDGAR complaints deal only with procedural issues; the appeal route is to the Office of Special Education Programs (OSEP) within the Department of Education; and the only remedy is an opinion from OSEP or the state education agency that the district or school is not in compliance with statutes and/or regulations.

Federal Statute Number
34 CFR 300.

Inform parent prior to referral
Referral
Receipt of referral
Notice of receipt of referral (with rights)
Notice of intent to evaluate (with rights)   .504 (a)(1)
Consent for replacement evaluation   .504 (b)
Parental consent obtained

Due Process Hearing Possible
• Identification

M-team evaluation
  Invite parents to meeting
  Examine data
  Document criteria for disabling condition
  Document need for special education
M-team report(s) sent to parents (with rights)

Due Process Hearing Possible
• Evaluation

Invitation to IEP meeting (with rights)   .345 (a)&(b)
IEP meeting   .345 (c)
Notice of placement (with rights)   .504 (a)
Parental consent for initial placement   .504 (b)(1)
Placement

Due Process Hearing Possible
• Placement
• Components of FAPE and
  related services

Annual review of IEP   .343 (d)
Annual notice of placement (with rights)   .552 (a)(1)
Notice of reevaluation (with rights)   .504 (a)(1)

3-year reevaluation   .534 (b)

M-team evaluation
  Invite parents to meeting
  Examine data
  Document criteria for disabling condition
  Document need for special education
  Recommendations for related services
M-team report(s) sent to parents (with rights)
Invitation to IEP meeting (with rights)   .345 (a)&(b)
IEP meeting   .343 (c)

Notice of placement (with rights)   .504 (a)

90 DAYS   30 DAYS   ASAP   3 YEARS   90 DAYS   30 DAYS

FIGURE 4.3   IDEA Process from Referral to Placement (Showing a Two-Meeting Process)

Initiating a Hearing

The due process hearing is set up either by the school or the state education agency, depending on state law.[222] The hearing must be conducted by an impartial hearing officer and must comply with the federal time lines. Recognizing that time is of the essence, these time lines are quite short. In an attempt to provide continuity for the child, during the pendency of the hearing the child must "stay-put" in the then current educational placement. The actual route of the hearing process may vary from state to state. Once the process has been concluded, the issue, of course, can be appealed to a trial court in the regular judicial system.

When a parent and school disagree concerning educational matters, either party may initiate a "due process hearing."[223] The parent of a child with disabilities or the parent of a child whom the parent believes to have a disability may initiate a hearing, as described in this regulation, if the parent disagrees with either of the following:

1. A proposal by a local school district or a proposal by another public agency operation an education program to initiate or change the identification, evaluation, or educational placement of the child or the provision of a free appropriate public education to the child; or
2. A refusal by a local school district or a proposal by another public agency operating an educational program to initiate or change the identification, evaluation, or educational placement of the child or the provision of a free appropriate public education to the child.

A local school district or other public agency operating an educational program may initiate a hearing, as described in this regulation, if the parents of a disabled child or of a child whom the school district believes to be disabled have refused or otherwise failed to consent to the conduct of the identification, evaluation, or educational placement of the child or the provision of a free appropriate public education to the child. Upon receipt of a notice of appeal or a decision of the school district to appeal, the school district (or the SEA in some states) must arrange for a hearing. The date and time of the hearing must be agreed to and a hearing officer must be selected. The hearing must be conducted and a decision rendered within 45 days of the notice of appeal.

Hearing Officer

The due process hearing must be conducted by an impartial hearing officer. The hearing officer may not be employed by the public agency involved in the education of the child and may not have any other apparent conflict of interest in regard to the hearing.[224] This has been interpreted to prohibit state education agency employees from serving as hearing officers, both in states where there is a single and double layer of hearings.[225] Additionally, there is some evidence to support the prohibition of local school district employees serving as hearing officers, even in other districts.[226] The courts are divided as to whether the superintendent of the state education agency (SEA) may serve within the hearing process.[227]

The qualifications of hearing officers vary from state to state, depending on state statute and regulations. Typically, they fall within any one of three categories, or combinations thereof: attorneys, certified special education teachers, and/or those who have completed state training.

Preparing for a Hearing

Figure 4.4 is a checklist of tasks that should be performed by the various parties involved in a hearing.

A. School Personnel
  1. Prepare the child's records (a copy must be given to the parents and the hearing officer).
  2. Obtain agreement from an appropriate person to serve as the hearing officer.
  3. Study and become familiar with the hearing process as developed in the local district or state or county residential facility.
  4. Decide who will serve as the spokesperson (representative) for the school district.
  5. Determine persons who will give testimony for the school presentation.
  6. Anticipate parents' questions and prepare appropriate responses.
  7. Make staff members available for questioning on parent request.
  8. Prepare an opening statement.
  9. Develop the school case in detail for presentation.
  10. Contact all parties several days before the hearing as a final check on arrangements.
  11. After the hearing, check arrangements with recorder regarding the number of transcripts, delivery to all parties, date of delivery, etc.
  12. On receipt of decision, determine if the school district will appeal the decision.
  13. On decision to appeal, notify parents and file appropriate appeal with the state superintendent of public instruction.
  14. If the parent appeals, furnish the state superintendent of public instruction with necessary information and materials.

B. Parents
  1. Contact an agency or a knowledgeable individual for assistance in assessing the disagreement with the school and for help in preparing for the hearing.
  2. Meet with the agency representative or person selected.
  3. Determine if you have an appropriate basis for a hearing.
  4. Notify the school of your request for a hearing.
  5. Study and become familiar with the hearing procedure in your state and local school district.
  6. Develop a general plan for presenting your case.
  7. Decide who will be your spokesperson (representative) at the hearing.
  8. Request a copy of your child's school records.
  9. Decide what evidence you will present at the hearing.
  10. Anticipate questions that you as a parent may be asked and prepare responses.
  11. Request the attendance of any specific school persons you wish to question.
  12. Anticipate the school's case and prepare to cross-examine witnesses.
  13. Select and contact any expert witnesses you wish to testify on your behalf.
  14. Decide on an open or closed hearing.
  15. Prepare an opening statement.
  16. Check with your witnesses several days prior to the hearing to make sure all arrangements are clear.
  17. When available, review the hearing transcript.
  18. On receipt of the decision, determine if you wish to appeal.
  19. If the decision is to appeal, send the letter of appeal to the state superintendent of public instruction with a copy to the local school district.

C. Hearing Officer
  1. Request a copy of the parents' request for a hearing and the hearing notice.
  2. Set a date, time, and place for the hearing that are mutually agreeable to all parties. Notify the parties of the hearing arrangements and their rights.
  3. Arrange for a stenographer to make a written transcript of the hearing.
  4. Refrain from discussing the nature of the hearing with anyone.
  5. Obtain information regarding the hearing procedure from persons familiar with the process.
  6. Determine if you can remain unbiased in your role as the hearing officer. If not, disqualify yourself.
  7. Become familiar with state and federal rules and laws as they relate to the hearing process.
  8. Become familiar with official state, local district, and/or state or county residential facility plans for the delivery of special education programs and services.
  9. Determine if the school has made proper arrangements for the hearing.
  10. Send both parties a written outline of the procedure you will follow in carrying out the hearing.
  11. On arrival at the hearing site, check to see if arrangements are to your satisfaction.
  12. Following the hearing, make sure you have correct address information for sending the hearing decision to both parties.
  13. Find out from the stenographer how soon you will receive the transcript.
  14. Be sure you have all exhibits or that they will be appended to transcript.
  15. Prepare the written decision and transmit to both parties in keeping with state and local time restrictions.
  16. Return all hearing material to state education agency's office.

FIGURE 4.4 Special Education Hearing Checklist

Hearing Procedures

The parties to the hearing have a right to counsel and traditional due process rights to present evidence, confront and cross-examine witnesses, compel attendance of witnesses, and obtain verbatim records of the hearing.[228] Either party may prohibit the production of any evidence that has not been disclosed to that party at least five days before the hearing.[229] The hearing officer's decision must be in writing and must include written findings of fact.[230]

The hearing officer must reach a final decision within 45 days after receipt of the request for a hearing.[231] In the states that provide for a hearing at the local level, the losing party may usually appeal to the state education agency.[232] For those states with a state-level administrative appeal route, appeals of the hearing officer may be taken to this second-level review, and that decision must be rendered within 30 days of receipt of a request for review.[233] With either route, the decision of the final administrative review may be appealed by filing a civil action in either state or federal court.[234]

In sum, any party to a hearing has the right to:

— Be accompanied and advised by counsel and by individuals with special knowledge or training with respect to the problems of children with disabilities.
— Present evidence and confront, cross-examine, and compel the attendance of witnesses.
— Prohibit the introduction of any evidence at the hearing that has not been disclosed to that party at least five (5) days before the hearing.
— Request in writing to the hearing officer an extension of time for rendering a final decision upon a showing of good cause.
— Obtain a written or electronic verbatim record of the hearing.
— Obtain written finding of facts and decisions.
— Receive a copy of the hearing officer's decision not later than 45 days after the request for the hearing.

— Appeal the findings of the hearing to the state education agency and/or to a federal or state civil court.

Parents involved in hearings have the additional right to:

— Have the child who is the subject of the hearing present.
— Open the hearing to the public.
— Be informed of free or low-cost legal and other relevant services.
— Have hearings involving oral arguments held at a reasonably convenient time and place.
— Receive, under specific conditions, reasonable attorney's fees, if they prevail.

Even though more and more parties are being represented at administrative hearings by attorneys, the parties should understand the process. They may also have to educate their attorney in this area of law or interview extensively to find an attorney with expertise in special education law.

Figure 4.5 presents a flow chart of a typical procedure. In this example, the state has a two-level system and no mediation option.

Judicial Review

IDEA specifically provides that either party may initiate a lawsuit in federal or state civil court.[235] The statute states:

In any [such] action . . . the court shall receive the records of the administrative proceedings, shall hear additional evidence at the request of a party, and, basing its decision on the preponderance of the evidence, shall grant such relief as the court determines is appropriate.[236]

The stated standard, preponderance of the evidence, would imply that the court should take new evidence in *de novo* proceedings. This is the standard of review used by some courts, specifically those in the First, Third, Sixth, Seventh, and Ninth Circuits.[237] Traditionally, how-

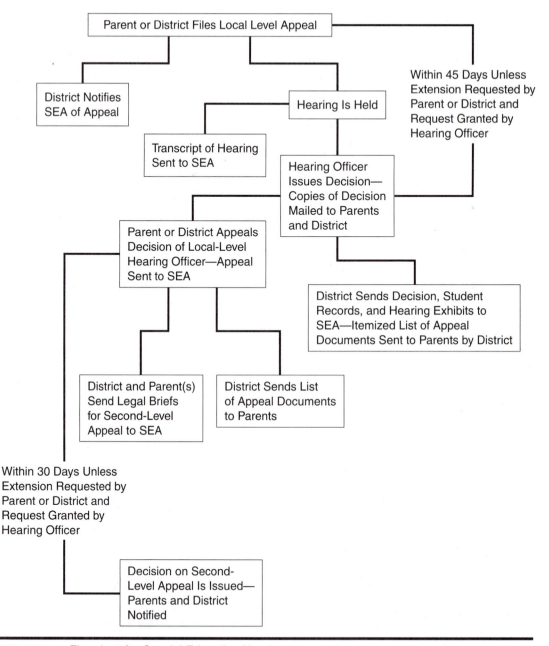

FIGURE 4.5 Flowchart for Special Education Hearing

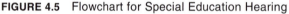

ever, when a court reviews an administrative decision, it defers to the decisions of the administrative officer and, acting in an appellate posture, overturns a decision only if clearly erroneous. This posture also has been used by courts, specifically the Second Circuit.[238]

The Supreme Court in *Rowley* stated that the court's purpose was to determine whether the school had complied with the procedural requirements and to determine whether the IEP was reasonably calculated to enable the child to receive educational benefits. It cautioned, however, that although the court should render its decision based on the stated standard of preponderance of the evidence, this was not "an invitation to the courts to substitute their own notions of sound educational policy for those of school authorities which they review." Further, the Court stated that the reviewing court should receive the records of the hearing officer and that this "carries with it the implied requirement that due weight shall be given to these proceedings."[239] Thus, it appears that some deference should be given to the administrative decision.

SMITH v. ROBINSON
468 U.S. 992, 104 S. Ct. 3457 (1984)

Justice BLACKMUN delivered the opinion of the Court.

****

I.

The procedural history of the case is complicated, but it is significant to the resolution of the issues. Petitioner Thomas F. Smith, III (Tommy), suffers from cerebral palsy and a variety of physical and emotional handicaps. When this proceeding began in November 1976, Tommy was 8 years old. In the preceding December, the Cumberland School Committee had agreed to place Tommy in a day program at Emma Pendleton Bradley Hospital in East Providence, R.I., and Tommy began attending that program. In November 1976, however, the Superintendent of Schools informed Tommy's parents, who are the other petitioners here, that the School Committee no longer would fund Tommy's placement because, as it construed Rhode Island law, the responsibility for educating an emotionally disturbed child lay with the State's Division of Mental Health, Retardation and Hospitals (MHRH).

Petitioners took an appeal from the decision of the Superintendent to the School Committee. In addition, petitioners filed a complaint under 42 U.S.C. § 1983 in the United States District Court for the District of Rhode Island against the members of the School Committee, asserting that due process required that the Committee comply with "Article IX—Procedural Safeguards" of the regulations adopted by the State Board of Regents regarding Education of Handicapped Children (Regulations) and that Tommy's placement in his program be continued pending appeal of the Superintendent's decision.

****

Resolution of this dispute requires us to explore congressional intent, both in authorizing fees for substantial unaddressed constitutional claims and in setting out the elaborate substantive and procedural requirements of the EHA [now IDEA], with no indication that attorney's fees are available in an action to enforce those requirements. . . .

****

B.

We have little difficulty concluding that Congress intended the EHA to be the exclusive avenue through which a plaintiff may assert an equal protection claim to a publicly financed special education. The EHA is a comprehensive scheme set up by Congress to aid the States in complying with their constitutional obligations to provide public education for handicapped children. Both the provisions of the statute and its legislative history indicate that Congress intended handicapped children with constitutional claims to a free appropriate public education to pursue those claims through the carefully tailored administrative and judicial mechanism set out in the statute.

In the statement of findings with which the EHA begins, Congress noted that there were more than 8,000,000 handicapped children in the country, the special education needs of most of whom were not being fully met. 20 U.S.C. §§ 1400(b)(1), (2), and (3). Congress also recognized that in a series of "landmark court cases," the right to an equal education opportunity for handicapped children has been established. S. Rep. No. 94-168, p. 6 (1975). *See also id.*, at 13 ("It is the intent of the Committee to establish and protect the right to education for all handicapped children and to provide assistance to the States in carrying out their responsibilities under State law and the Constitution of the United States to provide equal protection of the laws"). The EHA was an attempt to relieve the fiscal burden placed on States and localities by their responsibility to provide education for all handicapped children. 20 U.S.C. §§ 1400(b)(8) and (9). At the same time, however, Congress made clear that the EHA is not simply a funding statute. The responsibility for providing the required education remains on the States. S. Rep. No. 94-168, at 22. And the Act establishes an enforceable substantive right to a free appropriate public education. *See Board of Education v. Rowley*, 458 U.S. 176 (1982). *See also* 121 Cong. Rec. 37417 (1975) (statement of Sen. Schweiker: "It can no longer be the policy of the Government to merely establish an unenforceable goal requiring all children to be in school. [The bill] takes positive necessary steps to insure that the rights of children and their families are protected"). Finally, the Act establishes an elaborate procedural mechanism to protect the rights of handicapped children. The procedures not only ensure that hearings conducted by the State are fair and adequate. They also effect Congress' intent that each child's individual educational needs be worked out through a process that begins on the local level and includes ongoing parental involvement, detailed procedural safeguards, and a right to judicial review. §§ 1412(4), 1414(a)(5), 1415. *See also* S. Rep. No. 94-168, at 11-12 (emphasizing the role of parental involvement in assuring that appropriate services are provided to a handicapped child); *id.*, at p. 22; *Board of Education v. Rowley*, 458 U.S., at 208-209.

In light of the comprehensive nature of the procedures and guarantees set out in the EHA and Congress' express efforts to place on local and state educational agencies the primary responsibility for developing a plan to accommodate the needs of each individual handicapped child, we find it difficult to believe that Congress also meant to leave undisturbed the ability of a handicapped child to go directly to court with an equal protection claim to a free appropriate public education. Not only would such a result render superfluous most of the detailed procedural protections outlined in the statute, but, more important, it would run counter to Congress' view that the needs of handicapped children are best accommodated by having the parents and the local education agency work together to formulate an individualized plan for each handicapped child's education. No federal district court presented with a constitutional claim to a public education can duplicate that process.

We do not lightly conclude that Congress intended to preclude reliance on § 1983 as a remedy for a substantial equal protection claim. . . . Nevertheless, § 1983 is a statutory remedy and Congress retains the authority to repeal it or replace it with an alternative remedy. The crucial consideration is what Congress intended. . . .

In this case, we think Congress' intent is clear. Allowing a plaintiff to circumvent the EHA administrative remedies would be inconsistent with Congress' carefully tailored scheme. The legislative history gives no indication that Congress intended such a result. . . . We conclude, therefore, that where the EHA is available to a handicapped child asserting a right to a free appropriate public education, based either on the EHA or on the Equal Protection Clause of the Fourteenth Amendment, the EHA is the exclusive avenue through which the child and his parents or guardian can pursue their claim.

****

V.

The judgment of the Court of Appeals is affirmed.

It is so ordered.

(Footnotes omitted.)

— — — —

ROGERS v. BENNETT
873 F.2d 1387 (Eleventh Circuit 1989)

TJOFLAT, Circuit Judge:

In this case, the Georgia State Board of Education and two local school districts challenge the jurisdiction of the United States Department of Education's Office of Civil Rights to investigate parental complaints concerning the education of their handicapped children. . . .

I.

The dispute between the appellants and the Office of Civil Rights (the OCR) centers on the proper interpretation of section 504 of the Rehabilitation Act of 1973, . . . 29 U.S.C. § 794 . . . and on the intended interplay between section 504 and the Education of the Handicapped Act, 20 U.S.C. §§ 1400-1485 (1982 & Supp. IV 1986). We therefore briefly sketch the relevant provisions of these acts on the facts giving rise to the parties' dispute.

****

The EHA is comprehensive in scope, providing for the federal funding of local special education programs, . . . In exchange for these funds, states agree to adhere to federal regulations regarding the education of the handicapped. In 1975, Congress amended the EHA to provide a specific, exclusive administrative procedure by which parents can challenge the adequacy of the educational programs designed for their children. . . .

In the period between the original enactment of the EHA and its amendment in 1975, Congress passed the Rehabilitation Act of 1973. . . . The main purpose of the Rehabilitation Act was to provide funding for the vocational rehabilitation of handicapped individuals. *See id.,* § 2, 87 Stat. at 357. A miscellaneous provision at the end of the Act, however, also provided handicapped individuals with general protection against discrimination, . . .

Significantly, section 504 only prevents discrimination against the handicapped; unlike the EHA, it does not require that states devote extra resources to meeting the needs of handicapped individuals. . . . To implement the provisions of section 504, the Department of Education (the Department) issued regulations that prohibit state and local officials from discriminating against the handicapped in the provision of a free and appropriate public education to school-aged children. *See* 34 C.F.R. § 104.33 (1988). These regulations are administered by the OCR.

Two parallel procedures enforce these antidiscrimination regulations. First, parents are afforded certain procedural rights in a dispute with a local educational authority regarding the education of their handicapped children. *See id.* § 104.36. Upon exhausting these procedures, aggrieved parents can take advantage of the remedial provisions of Title VI

of the Civil Rights Act of 1964, 42 U.S.C. §§ 2000d 1, 2000d 2 (1982), and bring suit in federal court to remedy the alleged violation of section 504. *See* 29 U.S.C. § 794a(a)(2) (1982). . . .

As a second enforcement mechanism for section 504, the Department promulgated certain regulations that authorized it to conduct reviews of state and local educational institutions to assure compliance with the provisions of section 504. *See* 34 C.F.R. §§ 104.61, 100.7 (1988). The OCR initiates these compliance reviews on a periodic basis or in response to information that indicates a possible failure to comply with section 504. *See id.* § 100.7(a), (c). A parental complaint is the typical source of such information. If the state or local educational institution fails or refuses to cooperate with the OCR's investigation, the Department of Education may seek to effect the institution's compliance with 34 C.F.R. § 100.7 by initiating proceedings to terminate federal financial assistance to that institution. *See id.* § 100.8.

Acting in response to several parental complaints under section 504, the OCR initiated individual investigations of the special education programs in Chatham County (Georgia), DeKalb County (Georgia), and of the State of Georgia's Department of Education. Both the administrators of the county special education programs and officials in the Georgia Department of Education refused to cooperate with the OCR's investigation. As a result, the OCR began administrative proceedings to terminate federal funding of these three institutions' handicapped programs.

In response to these administrative proceedings, the Georgia State Board of Education and the DeKalb and Chatham County school districts brought suit against the United States Department of Education in federal district court, alleging that the OCR was acting beyond its jurisdiction in investigating parental complaints concerning the educational opportunities available to handicapped students in the Georgia programs.

****

II. B.

We next examine whether the OCR is *plainly* without jurisdiction to investigate state special education programs under section 504 in response to a parent's complaint. In arguing that the OCR is without jurisdiction, the appellants make two arguments worthy of discussion.

****

When section 504 was originally enacted, it contained no language expressly authorizing the promulgation of implementing regulations. As a result, the Department initially refused to promulgate regulations implementing section 504, believing the section to be self-executing. . . . Congress, however, clarified its intent in the legislative history accompanying the Rehabilitation Act Amendments of 1974, Pub. L. No. 93-516, 88 Stat. 1617. The report accompanying that Act indicates that Congress intended federal agencies to implement section 504 by means of appropriate regulations: . . .

. . . . The Report also indicates that Congress envisioned that the Department would coordinate the promulgation of these regulations. . . .

Faced with this evidence regarding the intent of Congress, the President issued Executive Order No. 11,914. That Order provided in relevant part:

****

Section 1. The Secretary of Health, Education, and Welfare shall coordinate the implementation of section 504 of the Rehabilitation Act of 1973, as amended, hereinafter referred to as section 504, by all Federal Departments and agencies empowered to extend Federal financial assistance to any program or activity. . . .

Sec. 2. In order to implement the provisions of section 504, each Federal department and agency empowered to provide Federal financial assistance shall issue rules, regulations, and directives, consistent with the standards and procedures established by the Secretary of Health, Education, and Welfare.

****

Based on this information regarding the Congressional and executive interpretation of section 504, we conclude that the OCR is not *plainly* outside its jurisdiction when it investigates the Georgia special education programs pursuant to 34 C.F.R. § 100.7 (1988).

In their second attack on the OCR's jurisdiction

to investigate the Georgia programs, appellants contend that the OCR's powers under section 504 were restricted by the Supreme Court's decision in *Smith v. Robinson*, 468 U.S. 992, 104 S.Ct. 3457, 82 L. Ed. 2d 746 (1984). In *Robinson*, parents of handicapped children brought suit against the Rhode Island Commissioner of Education, protesting the commissioner's decision denying responsibility for their children's education. They complained that the commissioner's decision violated the EHA, section 504 of the Rehabilitation Act, and the fourteenth amendment. After an extensive discussion of the relationships between the statutes and constitutional provision involved, the Supreme Court held that the enforcement mechanisms provided by the EHA were the exclusive method by which *parents* could challenge state denial of educational benefits to handicapped children. *See id.* at 1009, 104 S. Ct. at 3467.

Robinson leads us to conclude that in the ordinary case, a *parent's* private remedy under EHA is exclusive. In the instant case, however, the parent is not bringing a suit against the appellants; instead, the federal government itself is investigating the Georgia programs—albeit in response to a parental complaint. We do not believe that such federal supervisory action is plainly precluded by the EHA's detailed scheme for the processing of parental complaints. Thus, in examining the interrelation between section 504 of the Rehabilitation Act of 1973 and the 1975 amendments to the EHA, we conclude that law may allow—and Congress and the President may have intended—two overlapping, complementary schemes of enforcement: one exercised by private litigants through the provisions of the EHA, the other provided by the Department's supervisory investigations of state programs as authorized under the regulations implementing section 504. We therefore conclude that the OCR's exercise of supervisory powers over the Georgia special education programs is not *plainly* outside of the agency's jurisdiction.

****

(Footnotes omitted.)

— ■ — ■ — ■ — ■

DOYLE v. ARLINGTON COUNTY SCHOOL BOARD
953 F.2d 100 (Fourth Circuit 1991)

[After rejecting the public school program as inappropriate, the parents of a student with profound learning disabilities filed suit seeking private school

placement for their 14-year-old daughter. The hearing officer ruled in favor of the parents. The state review officer reversed that ruling after reevaluating the credibility of one witness. The federal district court affirmed the review officer's decision and the parents appealed.]

WIDENER, Circuit Judge.

OPINION

. . . . They argue on appeal that the district judge erred in not recusing himself, that the district court did not give proper deference to the actual finding of the hearing officer, and that there were substantive and procedural violations of the Individuals with Disabilities Education Act (IDEA). 20 U.S.C. §§ 1400-1485. We find no error on the question of recusal. However, we are of opinion the district court committed reversible error in not considering the administrative findings. Therefore, the district court judgment is vacated and the case is remanded with instructions that the district court give "due weight" to the administrative findings. . . .

****

[W]e must determine what level of deference should be given to the administrative findings. Generally, in reviewing state administrative decisions in IDEA cases, courts are required to make an independent decision based on a preponderance of the evidence, while giving due weight to state administrative proceedings. *Hendrick Hudson Dist. Bd. of Educ. v. Rowley*, 458 U.S. 176, . . . (The reviewing court "makes a bounded, independent decision— 'bounded by the administrative record and additional evidence, and independent by virtue of being based on a preponderance of the evidence before the court.'") (quoting *Town of Burlington v. Massachusetts Dep't of Educ.*, 736 F.2d 773, 791 (1st Cir. 1984), *aff'd sub nom. Burlington School Comm. v. Massachusetts Dep't of Educ.*, 471 U.S. 359, 105 S. Ct. 1996, 85 L. Ed. 2d 385 (1985).

The statements we have just quoted have come about by virtue of the plan for administrative and judicial review of decisions of local school boards with respect to the education of handicapped children. 20 U.S.C. § 1415(b)(2) provides in general that when parents or guardians have a complaint with respect to a decision under the statutes, they are entitled to an impartial due process hearing conducted by the state education agency or by the local education agency, as determined by state law, which shall not be conducted by an employee of the agency involved. Section 1415(c) provides that if any such

hearing is conducted by the local education agency, an aggrieved party has a right to appeal to the state education agency which shall conduct an impartial review. The officer conducting such review shall make an independent decision. Section 1415(e)(2) provides that a party aggrieved by an administrative decision of the state agency may bring an action in the United States district or a state court of competent jurisdiction, in which case the court "shall receive the records of the administrative proceedings, shall hear additional evidence at the request of a party, and, basing its decision on the preponderance of the evidence, shall grant such relief as the court determines is appropriate.". . .

With this system for administrative and judicial review in mind, the question is how we apply the due weight requirement of *Rowley*. The local hearing officer in this case examined the historical facts with respect to disability with some care, as well as the statutory requirements. The reviewing officer for the State Board of Education did not do the same but stated that he would have found the same facts on the same evidence. The only point on which the local and state hearing officers differed in any consequence was in the credibility of one of the witnesses for the plaintiffs. . . . That witness was a Dr. Solomon, who was a teacher at the Lab School and had observed Mairin's current class at the Lab School as well as the proposed class at Nottingham. She testified that Mairin was one of the most, if not the most, complex learning disabled children she had ever encountered and that, in her opinion, a highly individualized program such as Lab's was the only methodology which would suffice for Mairin. Without saying any reason . . . , the reviewing officer concluded that Dr. Solomon saw her role as that of an advocate and found her testimony not to be credible. While it is true that by statute and regulation the reviewing officer is required to make an independent decision, we are of opinion that his reason for discrediting a witness who he had not seen or heard testify, in the face of the crediting of that same witness by a hearing officer who had seen and heard the witness testify, is so far from the accepted norm of a fact-finding process designed to discover truth that we think the due weight which should be accorded the decision of the reviewing fact-finding officer depending on that credibility decision is none. . . .

The First and District of Columbia Circuits have examined the question of due weight. In *Town of*

Burlington, the court criticized the district court for having given the administrative findings the prima facie effect of a master's findings. That court familiarly stated that fact-findings are not binding on the court even if supported by the traditional substantial evidence test. The court also stated that "weight due the administrative findings of fact must be left to the discretion of the trial court" and that the trial court "must consider the findings carefully and endeavor to respond to the hearing officer's resolution of each material issue." Apparently, the First Circuit would require such a response by the district court, both to findings of fact and conclusions of law of the hearing officer. 736 F.2d at 791-792. In *Kerkam v. McKenzie*, 862 F.2d 884 (D.C. Cir. 1988), the court took the district court to task for its unexplained preference for the conclusions of those who opposed the hearing officer's view and stated that it remanded "for the district court to directly tackle the issue of whether the plaintiffs' showing is enough to overcome the hearing officer's conclusion that the program offered at Mamie D. Lee was 'appropriate' as that term is used in §1412(1)." 862 F.2d at 889. Since the Supreme Court had held in *Rowley* that whether or not a program is appropriate is a matter of fact, we think the holding of *Kerkam* is very close to, if not directly,

one that findings of fact by a hearing officer made in a regular manner and with evidentiary support are entitled to presumptive validity, otherwise there would be nothing to overcome. The District of Columbia Circuit thus would give greater validity than does the First Circuit to the administrative fact-finding of the hearing officer or officers.

More in line with the view of the District of Columbia Circuit, we think that findings of fact by the hearing officers in cases such as these are entitled to be considered prima facie correct, akin to the traditional sense of permitting a result to be based on such fact finding, but not requiring it. . . .

****

On remand, the district court must reconsider its decision and give due weight to the state administrative findings. The court should address each such relevant factual finding made by the hearing officer and explain why, under the due weight standard, it has chosen to accept or not accept that finding. The judgment of the district court is

AFFIRMED IN PART, VACATED IN PART, AND REMANDED WITH INSTRUCTIONS.

****

(Footnotes omitted.)

ADDITIONAL COMMENTARY

1. In a study involving satisfaction with the special education due process hearing mechanism, Goldberg and Kuriloff reported that parties' perceptions of fairness and accuracy of the process are highly correlated with being successful in the outcome (S. Goldberg and P. Kuriloff, "Evaluating the Fairness of Special Education Hearings," *Exceptional Children, 57,* (1991): 546–555. However, whether they won or lost, parties in the study indicated that the procedure was followed correctly and they understood the process. This, however, does not necessarily equate to a perception of fairness. As stated by the authors of that study:

   When justice is defined as the existence of a strong, reliable, predictive relationship between effectively using the elements of due process and gaining a favorable outcome, due process hearings appear to be achieving one goal Congress intended when it mandated them in special education disputes

   (Kuriloff, 1985). But this kind of objective fairness is not all Congress had in mind. It also wanted to ensure that parents could participate in crucial educational decisions about their children, and to come away feeling they had been fairly treated (Friendly, 1975; Neal & Kirp, 1985). The findings of this study add support to earlier, largely anecdotal evidence (Kirp & Jensen, 1983) that special education hearings do not achieve this more subjective form of fairness. (p. 553; see original text for internal references)

2. *The Education of Students with Disabilities: Where Do We Stand?* A Report to the President and Congress of the United States (Washington, DC: National Council on Disability, 1989) contains some findings relating to parents' needs in and perceptions of due process hearing.

   Finding 6:
   There is a perception that the outcomes of due process hearings are biased in favor of the schools.

Parents who testified before the Council reported feelings of intimidation with respect to actually utilizing due process procedures. They described feeling vulnerable and a perception that they do not have an equal chance when up against a school system with an array of professionals and a seemingly endless supply of resources. There is some research that supports the parents' position. For example, less than 1% of parents of students with disabilities have actually been involved in litigation at the State level according to the National Association of State Directors of Special Education (1985). This may be due to the perception that they would not have an equal chance against the school system, or it may be because many parents do not know their rights or are satisfied with the outcome of the process. Moreover, the most frequently cited figure for parent success regarding hearing outcomes is 33% (Sacken, 1988).

Finding 9:

There is a paucity of attorneys with expertise in special education law available to represent parents.

Witnesses who appeared before the Council decried what they described as the absence of a sufficient number of attorneys with expertise in special education law available to assist them. Deborah Mattison of the Michigan Protection and Advocacy System reported that 40% of the annual requests for assistance to the Michigan Protection and Advocacy System are from those seeking assistance in the special education arena. Mary Tatro reported that in Texas the Protection and Advocacy System only takes cases that will affect a large number of children. "Right now," Mrs. Tatro said, "when parents call me and say 'Who was your attorney? We need an attorney.' I say, 'there aren't any.'" (see original document for internal references)

3. Some states implement a mediation procedure, although this cannot automatically extend the 45-day time restriction. In those states where mediation is offered, it appears that parties are satisfied in the process because it is faster, cheaper, less adversarial, and the decision making stays within the power of the immediate parties. *See* Ninth Annual Report to Congress on the Implementation of the Education of the Handicapped Act, Dispute Resolution, 1987.

4. Note that the statute does not provide information regarding the rules of evidence, burden of proof, and statute of limitations. Thus, states are free to set forth applicable standards and rules of their own.

5. In *W.G. v. Target Range School Dist.*, 960 F.2d 1479 (9th Cir. 1992), the court highlighted the importance of procedural correctness. There, the court found a denial of a student's rights under IDEA where the district failed to ensure attendance of all necessary parties at IEP meetings. The district was then ordered to reimburse the parents for the costs of a unilateral placement.

6. The Third Circuit Court of Appeals ruled recently that exhaustion of administrative remedies is not necessary in an emergency situation if exhaustion would cause irreparable harm (either mental or physical damage) to the child with disabilities. In such a situation, the parents must present sufficient evidence of irreparable harm to invoke the exception to the principle of exhaustion (*Kimninos v. Upper Saddle River Board of Education*, 13 F. 3d 775 (3rd Cir. 1994)).

7. In *Family and Children's Center, Inc. v. School City of Mishawaka*, 13 F. 3d 1052 (7th Cir. 1994), the court ruled that a private child-care facility for children with emotional disabilities had standing to bring action under IDEA. The center had physical but not legal custody of the children placed there by state and local child welfare agencies.

REMEDIES FOR VIOLATIONS

IDEA contains an elaborate system for resolving disputes over a student's educational program. What is not spelled out specifically, however, is exactly what remedies parties have when it is determined that the statute has been violated. The statute clearly grants the parties the right to enter into court to resolve the dispute, but it is unclear as to what the result of the litigation may be. The statute states:

Any party aggrieved by the findings and decision . . . shall have the right to bring a civil action with respect to the complaint presented. . . . In any action brought under this paragraph the court . . .

shall grant such relief as the court determines is appropriate.[240]

Prior to 1984, many parents sought remedies and attorneys' fees under Section 504[241] or Section 1983 of the Civil Rights Act.[242] However, this ended when, in *Smith v. Robinson,*[243] the U.S. Supreme Court determined that IDEA provides the exclusive appellate route and remedies for violation of a child's right to a free appropriate education. Parties have sought various forms of remedies under IDEA: injunctions, damages, reimbursement, compensatory education, and attorneys' fees.

Injunctions

The most logical remedy under a statute such as IDEA is to require the state or school district to provide that which is guaranteed by the statute. This would procedurally require an injunction—an order requiring specified actions. Thus, the court orders the school to provide the free appropriate education as it has been defined in the litigation. An injunction is also appropriate to enforce the provisions of the IEP as agreed upon by the parties.[244] This situation is analogous to a court ordering the adherence to the provisions of a contract. In *Kantak v. Liverpool Central School District,*[245] the court ordered that the district carry through with the program agreed to by the parents as offered by a hearing officer. The court found this was an enforceable agreement between the state and parents.[246]

Damages

There are many court decisions on whether parties may be granted monetary damages under IDEA. The majority of courts that have dealt with the issue of general damage awards have ruled that damages are not available.[247] The rationale for denying a damage award is that the statute does not include an implied private right of action for damages since it expressly provides for other forms of relief. Additionally, damage awards are seen as inconsistent with the goals of the statute. IDEA is seen as a funding statute, intended to fund and grant rights to students with disabilities, not implement a mechanism for monetary relief when an appropriate education has not been given. These courts have concluded that a monetary damage award would not assist students with disabilities. In fact, one court noted concern that it might potentially harm programming for students with disabilities if schools feared monetary liability for incorrect placements.[248]

Reimbursement

The Supreme Court has drawn a distinction between a general damage award and reimbursement for a parent's out-of-pocket expenses for tuition and related services. In *School Committee of Burlington v. Department of Education of Massachusetts,*[249] the Supreme Court held that parents are entitled to reimbursement for expenses incurred in a unilateral placement when it is finally determined that the unilateral placement was the only appropriate placement choice. In other words, if it is ultimately determined that the placement the school district offered is not appropriate under the statute, the parents are entitled to reimbursement. In making this ruling, the Court noted that reimbursement was not a general damage award but instead "merely requires the Town to belatedly pay expenses that it should have paid all along and would have borne in the first instance had it developed a proper IEP."[250] This, in some cases, may be very expensive for school districts when the parents have chosen a costly unilateral placement for their child. For example, in *Ash v. Lake Oswego,*[251] the district was ordered to reimburse the parents for a placement in a private school in Japan and the related service of transportation to and from the placement.

Generally, reimbursement for tuition and related services is only granted in those circumstances that warrant a unilateral placement, e.g., when no appropriate placement is offered by the school, when a child's health is endangered, or when the district's conduct in the proceedings is egregious. The Supreme Court indicated that reimbursement, even when no appropriate placement was offered, was not automatic. The court should assess the equities and circumstances involved when making this determination. As a result, some courts have only granted reimbursement for the period following notification to the school that the parents were not satisfied with the IEP.[252] Other courts have only allowed reimbursement if parents have investigated other alternatives.[253]

A recently resolved question in this area is whether schools must reimburse parents for unilateral appropriate placements when the school does not meet state certification requirements. This was the situation in *Florence County School District v. Carter.*[254] Here, the parents were granted reimbursement for tuition when the school district failed to offer a timely placement for the child, and the parents unilaterally placed the child in a private school. The court reasoned that the delay was unreasonable and the fault of the district. The private school was not certified and yet the school district was ultimately responsible for tuition reimbursement. Extending the logic presented in *Burlington,*[255] the Court concluded that the procedural requirements of IDEA control the actions of the school, not the parents. When a district fails to offer a free appropriate public education, parents are, in effect, forced to act. In such situations, "[p]arents' failure to select a program known to be approved by the State in favor of an unapproved option is not by itself a bar to reimbursement."[256]

Compensatory Education

Compensatory education is another possible remedy for a district's violation of IDEA. It, too, is an appropriate remedy when it is deter-

mined that a child has not received an appropriate education. To remedy or make up for the progress lost, rather than awarding a monetary sum, courts have instead ordered the district or the state to provide the child with an appropriate education and services past the statutory cut-off age.

The rationale for awarding compensatory education was set out by the Eighth Circuit:

Like the retroactive reimbursement in Burlington, imposing liability for compensatory educational services on the defendants "merely requires [them] to belatedly pay expenses that [they] should have . . . paid all along." Here, as in Burlington, recovery is necessary to secure the child's right to a free appropriate public education. We are confident that Congress did not intend the child's entitlement to a free education to turn upon her parents' ability to "front" its costs.[257]

This remedy, however, is not without controversy. Some courts have found this remedy to not be available under the statute.[258] Others reason that if reimbursement is available to parents who can afford to pay for tuition, then, by analogy, compensatory education should be available to students who received an inappropriate education while awaiting the conclusion of litigation. Allowing compensatory education as a form of remedy is the majority position to date.[259]

Attorneys' Fees

Regarding attorneys' fees, the Supreme Court in 1984[260] held that IDEA contained no provision for recovery of attorneys' fees and parties could not claim attorneys' fees using Section 504 only as a litigation vehicle. Congress responded in 1986 by enacting the Handicapped Children's Protection Act. This amendment, in part, states:

In any action or proceeding brought under this subsection, the court, in its discretion, may award reasonable attorneys' fees as part of the costs to the parents or guardian of a child or youth with a disability who is the prevailing party.[261]

Congress, however, incorporated several limitations on the granting of fees. Fees must be based on comparable rates for similar legal services, but may not include any multiplier assessed for unusual or difficult cases.[262] Fees may not be awarded for services performed after a parent's rejection of a written settlement offer if the final relief gained through the process is not more favorable than the settlement offer.[263] Fees may be reduced if the parent "unreasonably protracted" the controversy.[264]

Since its enactment, several recurring issues have risen. First, there is always the question of who is a prevailing party. The courts have generally adopted the U.S. Supreme Court's definition of a prevailing party used in Section 1983 actions: "if the defendant, under pressure of the lawsuit, alters his conduct (or threatened conduct) towards the plaintiff that was the basis for the suit, the plaintiff will have prevailed."[265] Stated more generally, the question is whether the parents prevailed on a significant issue in the action, or changed the status quo, even though they may not have gotten exactly what they originally requested.[266] This is true even if the district orders changes, even procedural, different from those originally complained about by the parent.[267]

Next, the statute's provision is for an award of fees to a prevailing party "in any action or proceeding." Thus, it is generally held that fees may be awarded, not just for litigation, but for *statutorily required* administrative hearings.[268] Some courts have even granted fees for time spent at IEP meetings,[269] other prehearing work,[270] expert witness fees,[271] and posthearing monitoring costs.[272] A majority of the circuits allow a parent who has prevailed at the administrative level to bring an independent action in court to recover fees.

The statute specifies that "the court" may award fees; the question then arises whether a "hearing officer" has the authority to do so. The prevalent authority is that a hearing officer may not make such an award.[273] The parents, if they believe they have prevailed, must file an action in either state or federal court to recover fees.

SCHOOL COMMITTEE OF THE TOWN OF BURLINGTON, MASSACHUSETTS v. DEPARTMENT OF THE COMMONWEALTH OF MASSACHUSETTS
471 U.S. 359, 105 S. Ct. 1996, 85 L. Ed. 2d 385 (1985)

Justice REHNQUIST delivered the opinion of the Court.

****

In the spring of 1979, Michael [Panico] attended the third grade of Memorial School, a public school in Burlington, Mass., under an IEP calling for individual tutoring by a reading specialist for one hour a day and individual and group counselling. Michael's continued poor performance and the fact that Memorial School was not equipped to handle his needs led to much discussion between his parents and Town school officials about his difficulties and . . . his future schooling. . . .

In late June, the Town presented the Panicos with a proposed IEP for Michael for the 1979–1980 academic year. It called for placing Michael in a highly structured class of six children with special academic and social needs, located at another Town public school, the Pine Glen School. On July 3, Michael's father rejected the proposed IEP . . . .

Meanwhile the Panicos received the results of the latest expert evaluation of Michael by specialists at Massachusetts General Hospital, who opined that

Michael's "emotional difficulties are secondary to a rather severe learning disorder characterized by perceptual difficulties" and recommended "a highly specialized setting for children with learning handicaps ... such as the Carroll school," a state-approved private school for special education located in Lincoln, Mass. App. 26, 31. Believing that the Town's proposed placement of Michael at the Pine Glen School was inappropriate in light of Michael's needs, Mr. Panico enrolled Michael in the Carroll School in mid-August at his own expense, and Michael started there in September.

The BSEA held several hearings during the fall of 1979, and in January 1980 the hearing officer decided that the Town's proposed placement at the Pine Glen School was inappropriate and that the Carroll School was "the least restrictive adequate program within the record" for Michael's educational needs. The hearing officer ordered the Town to pay for Michael's tuition and transportation to the Carroll School for the 1979–1980 school year, including reimbursing the Panicos for the expenditures on these items for the school year to date.

****

.... We granted certiorari, 469 U.S. 1071 ... (1984), only to consider the following two issues: whether the potential relief available under § 1415 (e)(2) includes reimbursement to parents for private school tuition and related expenses, and whether § 1415(e)(3) bars such reimbursement to parents who reject a proposed IEP and place a child in a private school without the consent of local school authorities. We express no opinion on any of the many other views stated by the Court of Appeals.

Congress stated the purpose of the Act in these words:

to assure that all handicapped children have available to them ... a free appropriate public education which emphasizes special education and related services designed to meet their unique needs [and] to assure that the rights of handicapped children and their parents or guardians are protected.
20 U.S.C. § 1400(c).

****

The modus operandi of the Act is the already mentioned "individualized educational program." The IEP is in brief a comprehensive statement of the educational needs of a handicapped child and the specially designed instruction and related services to

be employed to meet those needs. § 1401(19). The IEP is to be developed jointly by a school official qualified in special education, the child's teacher, the parents or guardian, and, where appropriate, the child. In several places, the Act emphasizes the participation of the parents in developing the child's educational program and assessing its effectiveness. *See* §§ 1400(c), 1401(19), 1412(7), 1415(b)(1)(A), (C), (D), (E), and 1415(b)(2); 34 CFR § 300.345 (1984).

Apparently recognizing that this cooperative approach would not always produce a consensus between the school officials and the parents, and that in any disputes the school officials would have a natural advantage, Congress incorporated an elaborate set of what it labeled "procedural safeguards" to insure the full participation of the parents and proper resolution of substantive disagreements.... The parents are further entitled to "an impartial due process hearing," which in the instant case was the BSEA hearing, to resolve their complaints.

The Act also provides for judicial review in state or federal court to "[a]ny party aggrieved by the findings and decision" made after the due process hearing. The Act confers on the reviewing court the following authority:

[T]he court shall receive the records of the administrative proceedings, shall hear additional evidence at the request of a party, and, basing its decision on the preponderance of the evidence, shall grant such relief as the court determines is appropriate.
§ 1415(e)(2).

The first question on which we granted certiorari requires us to decide whether this grant of authority includes the power to order school authorities to reimburse parents for their expenditures on private special education for a child if the court ultimately determines that such placement, rather than a proposed IEP, is proper under the Act.

We conclude that the Act authorizes such reimbursement. The statute directs the court to "grant such relief as [it] determines is appropriate." The ordinary meaning of these words confers broad discretion on the court. The type of relief is not further specified, except that it must be "appropriate." Absent other reference, the only possible interpretation is that the relief is to be "appropriate" in light of the purpose of the Act. As already noted, this is principally to provide handicapped children with "a free appropriate public education which emphasizes special education and related services designed to meet their unique needs." The Act contemplates that such education will be provided where possible in regular public schools. . . . The Act also provides for placement in private schools at public expense where this is not possible. . . . In a case where a court determines that a private placement desired by the parents was proper under the Act and that an IEP calling for placement in a public school was inappropriate, it . . . seems clear beyond cavil that "appropriate" relief would include a prospective injunction directing the school officials to develop and implement at public expense an IEP placing the child in a private school.

If the administrative and judicial review under the Act could be completed in a matter of weeks, rather than years, it would be difficult to imagine a case in which such prospective injunctive relief would not be sufficient. As this case so vividly demonstrates, however, the review process is ponderous. A final judicial decision on the merits of an IEP will in most instances come a year or more after the school term covered by that IEP has passed. In the meantime, the parents who disagree with the proposed IEP are faced with a choice: go along with the IEP to the detriment of their child if it turns out to be inappropriate or pay for what they consider to be the appropriate placement. If they choose the latter course, which conscientious parents who have adequate means and who are reasonably confident of their assessment normally would, it would be an empty victory to have a court tell them several years later that they were right but that these expenditures could not in a proper case be reimbursed by the school officials. . . .

In this Court, the Town repeatedly characterizes reimbursement as "damages," but that simply is not the case. Reimbursement merely requires the Town to belatedly pay expenses that it should have paid all along and would have borne in the first instance had it developed a proper IEP. Such a post hoc determination of financial responsibility was contemplated in the legislative history:

If a parent contends that he or she has been forced, at the parent's own expense, to seek private schooling for the child because an appropriate program does not exist within the local educational agency responsible for the child's education and the local educational agency disagrees, that disagreement and the question

of who remains financially responsible is a matter to which the due process procedures established under [the predecessor to § 1415] appl[y].
S. Rep. No. 94-168, p. 32 (1975), U.S. Code Cong. & Admin. News 1975, pp. 1425, 1456 (emphasis added).

****

Regardless of the availability of reimbursement as a form of relief in a proper case, the Town maintains that the Panicos have waived any right they otherwise might have to reimbursement because they violated § 1415(e)(3), which provides:

During the pendency of any proceedings conducted pursuant to [§ 1415], unless the State or local educational agency and the parents or guardian otherwise agree, the child shall remain in the then current educational placement of such child . . . .

We need not resolve the academic question of what Michael's "then current educational placement" was in the summer of 1979, which both the Town and the parents had agreed that a new school was in order. For the purposes of our decision, we assume that the Pine Glen School, proposed in the IEP, was Michael's current placement and, therefore, that the Panicos did "change" his placement after they had rejected the IEP and had set the administrative review in motion. In so doing, the Panicos contravened the conditional command of § 1415(e)(3) that "the child shall remain in the them current educational placement."

****

We do not agree with the Town that a parental violation of § 1415(e)(3) constitutes a waiver of reimbursement. The provision says nothing about financial responsibility, waiver, or parental right to reimbursement at the conclusion of judicial proceedings. Moreover, if the provision is interpreted to cut off parental rights to reimbursement, the principal purpose of the Act will in many cases be defeated in the same way as if reimbursement were never available. As in this case, parents will often notice a child's learning difficulties while the child is in a regular public school program. If the school officials disagree with the need for special education or the adequacy of the public school's program to meet the child's needs, it is unlikely they will agree to a interim private school placement while the review process runs its course. Thus, under the Town's reading of § 1415(e)(3), the parents are forced to leave the child in what may turn out to be an inappropriate educational placement or to obtain the appropriate placement only by sacrificing any claim for reimbursement. The Act was intended to give handicapped children both an appropriate education and a free one; it should not be interpreted to defeat one or the other of those objectives.

****

This is not to say that § 1415(e)(3) has no effect on parents. While we doubt that this provision would authorize a court to order parents to leave their child in a particular placement, we think it operates in such a way that parents who unilaterally change their child's placement during the pendency of review proceedings, without the consent of state or local school officials, do so at their own financial risk. If the courts ultimately determine that the IEP proposed by the school officials was appropriate, the parents would be barred from obtaining reimbursement for any interim period in which their child's placement violated § 1415(e)(3). This conclusion is supported by the agency's interpretation of the Act's application to private placements by the parents:

(a) If a handicapped child has available a free appropriate public education and the parents choose to place the child in a private school or facility, the public agency is not required by this part to pay for the child's education at the private school or facility. . . .

(b) Disagreements between a parent and a public agency regarding the availability of a program appropriate for the child, and the question of financial responsibility, are subject to the due process procedures under [§ 1415].
34 CFR § 300.403 (1984).

We thus resolve the questions on which we granted certiorari; . . . We do think that the court was correct in concluding that "such relief as the court determines is appropriate," within the meaning of § 1415(e)(2), means that equitable considerations are relevant in fashioning relief.

The judgment of the Court of Appeals is Affirmed.

(Footnotes omitted.)

— — — —

FLORENCE COUNTY SCHOOL DISTRICT FOUR v. CARTER
114 S. Ct. 361 (1993)

Justice O'CONNOR delivered the opinion of the Court.

. . . .

I.

Respondent Shannon Carter was classified as learning disabled in 1985, while a ninth grade student in a school operated by petitioner Florence County School District Four. School officials met with Shannon's parents to formulate an individualized education program (IEP) for Shannon, as required under IDEA. . . . The IEP provided that Shannon would stay in regular classes except for three periods of individualized instruction per week, and established specific goals in reading and mathematics of four months' progress for the entire school year. Shannon's parents were dissatisfied, and requested a hearing to challenge the appropriateness of the IEP. . . . Both the local educational officer and the state educational agency hearing officer rejected Shannon's parents' claim and concluded that the IEP

was adequate. In the meantime, Shannon's parents had placed her in Trident Academy, a private school specializing in educating children with disabilities. Shannon began at Trident in September 1985 and graduated in the spring of 1988.

Shannon's parents filed this suit in July 1986, claiming that the school district had breached its duty under IDEA to provide Shannon with a "free appropriate public education," § 1401(a)(18), and seeking reimbursement for tuition and other costs incurred at Trident. . . . The court held that the school district's proposed educational program and the achievement goals of the IEP "were wholly inadequate" and failed to satisfy the requirements of the Act. . . . The court further held that "[a]lthough [Trident Academy] did not comply with all of the procedures outlined in [IDEA],". . . Shannon's education was "appropriate" under IDEA, and that Shannon's parents were entitled to reimbursement of tuition and other costs. . . .

The Court of Appeals for the Fourth Circuit affirmed. 950 F.2d 156 (1991). . . .

****

II.

****

As this case comes to us, two issues are settled: 1) the school district's proposed IEP was inappropriate under IDEA, and 2) although Trident did not meet the § 1404(a)(18) requirements, it provided an education otherwise proper under IDEA. This case presents the narrow question whether Shannon's parents are barred from reimbursement because the private school in which Shannon enrolled did not meet the § 1401(a)(18) definition of a "free appropriate education." We hold that they are not, because § 1401 (a)(18)'s requirements cannot be read as applying to parental placements.

Section 1401(a)(18)(A) requires that the education be "provided at public expense, under public supervision and direction." Similarly, § 1401(a) (18)(D) requires schools to provide an IEP, which must be designed by "a representative of the local educational agency," 20 U.S.C. § 1401(a)(20) (1988 ed., Supp. IV), and must be "establish[ed]," "revise[d]," and "review[ed]" by the agency, § 1414(a)(5). These requirements do not make sense in the context of a parental placement. In this case, as in all *Burlington* [*School Committee of Burlington v. Department of Education*, 471 U.S. 359] reimbursement cases, the parents' rejection of the school district's proposed IEP is the very reason for the parents' decision to put their child in a private school. In such cases, where the private placement has necessarily been made over the school district's objection, the private school education will not be under "public supervision and direction." Accordingly, to read the § 1401(a)(18) requirements as applying to parental placements would effectively eliminate the right of unilateral withdrawal recognized in *Burlington*. Moreover, IDEA was intended to ensure that children with disabilities receive an education that is both appropriate and free. *Burlington, supra*, at 373. To read the provisions of § 1401(a)(18) to bar reimbursement in the circumstances of this case would defeat this statutory purpose.

Nor do we believe that reimbursement is necessarily barred by a private school's failure to meet state education standards. . . . Indeed, the school district's emphasis on state standards is somewhat ironic. As the Court of Appeals noted, "it hardly seems consistent with the Act's goals to forbid parents from educating their child at a school that provides an appropriate education simply because that school lacks the stamp of approval of the same public school system that failed to meet the child's needs in the first place." 950 F.2d, at 164. Accordingly, we disagree with the Second Circuit's theory that "a parent may not obtain reimbursement for a unilateral placement if that placement was in a school that was not on [the State's] approved list of private" schools. *Tucker*, 873 F.2d, at 568 (internal quotation marks omitted). Parents' failure to select a program known to be approved by the State in favor of an unapproved option is not itself a bar to reimbursement.

Furthermore, although the absence of an approved list of private schools is not essential to our holding, we note that parents in the position of Shannon's have no way of knowing at the time they select a private school whether the school meets state standards. South Carolina keeps no publicly available list of approved private schools, but instead approves private school placements on a case-by-case basis. In fact, although public school officials had previously placed three children with disabilities at Trident, see App. to Pet. for Cert. 28a, Trident had not received blanket approval from the State. South Carolina's case-by-case approval system meant that Shannon's parents needed the cooperation of state officials before they could know whether Trident was state-approved. As we recognized in Burlington, such cooperation is unlikely in cases where the school officials disagree with the need for the private placement. 471 U.S., at 372.

III.

The school district also claims that allowing reimbursement for parents such as Shannon's puts an unreasonable burden on financially strapped local educational authorities. The school district argues that requiring parents to choose a state-approved private school if they want reimbursement is the only meaningful way to allow States to control costs; otherwise States will have to reimburse dissatisfied parents for any private school that provides an education that is proper under the Act, no matter how expensive it may be.

There is no doubt that Congress has imposed a significant financial burden on States and school districts that participate in IDEA. Yet public educational authorities who want to avoid reimbursing parents for the private education of a disabled child can do one of two things: give the child a free appropriate public education in a public setting, or place the child in an appropriate private setting of the State's choice. This is IDEA's mandate, and school officials who conform to it need not worry about reimbursement claims.

Moreover, parents who, like Shannon's, "unilaterally change their child's placement during the pendency of review proceedings, without the consent of the state or local school officials, do so at their own financial risk." *Burlington, supra*, at 373-374. They are entitled to reimbursement only if a federal court concludes both that the public placement violated

IDEA, and that the private school placement was proper under the Act.

Finally, we note that once a court holds that the public placement violated IDEA, it is authorized to "grant such relief as the court determines is appropriate." 20 U.S.C. § 1415(e)(2). Under this provision, "equitable considerations are relevant in fashioning relief," *Burlington*, 471 U.S., at 374, and the court enjoys "broad discretion" in so doing, *id.*, at 369. Courts fashioning discretionary equitable relief under IDEA must consider all relevant factors, including the appropriate and reasonable level of reimbursement that should be required. Total reimbursement will not be appropriate if the court determines that the cost of the private education was unreasonable.

Accordingly, we affirm the judgment of the Court of Appeals.

— ■ — ■ — ■ — ■ —

LESTER H. v. GILHOOL
916 F.2d 865 (Third Circuit 1990)

NYGAARD, Circuit Judge.

****

I.

The plaintiff, Lester H., is a profoundly retarded twelve-year-old with severe behavioral problems. Lester began his education within the school district in the fall of 1983. But even before Lester entered school, the District Director of Special Education determined that the School District could not provide an appropriate special education program for him .... The School District, Lester's mother and the Delaware County Intermediate Unit ("IU") agreed that Lester should be placed at the Summit School, a special education day-facility, for that academic year.... Octavia P., Lester's mother, signed a Notice of Recommended Assignment ("NORA") consenting to the Summit School placement. He remained at Summit throughout the year and progressed with his Individualized Education Program ("IEP").....

The next fall, Lester's behavior deteriorated significantly. In October 1984, the Director, Summit

officials and Lester's teacher concluded that Summit could no longer provide an appropriate education for Lester and they recommended that he be placed in a residential program.... Nevertheless, Lester remained at Summit during the 1984–85 school year because the School District limited its efforts to place him to only one approved school, the Elwyn Institute, and one unapproved school, the Don Guanella School. Both schools rejected him.... Lester was finally removed from Summit in August, 1985. Lester's mother signed a NORA consenting to in-home instruction while her child awaited appropriate residential placement.... The School District then developed an in-home IEP for the 1985–86 academic year which provided Lester with only five hours of instruction per week. This IEP began on November 11, 1985 and, with revisions, continued until late June, 1986....

For the majority of Lester's home-bound instruction period, the School District did not request residential placement for him. In April, 1986, the School District applied to the Devereux Foundation and the Wordsworth Academy. Both schools rejected Lester. Finally, after prodding by Lester's counsel and the

Pennsylvania Department of Education ("DoE"), the School District re-applied to Elwyn. Lester was admitted to Elwyn's Extended School Year day program in June, 1986 and his mother signed a NORA consenting to this placement. . . . He lasted only 34 days at Elwyn and was returned to in-home instruction. . . .

During August and September, 1986, the School District applied to four schools. All four schools rejected Lester. . . . Lester's counsel then petitioned the Chief of the Bureau of Special Education of the DoE requesting that he assist in locating an appropriate special education program for Lester. . . . In response DoE required the School District to provide it with a status report and suggested that the Director apply to the AuClair School, an out-of-state facility located in Bear, Delaware. . . . Lester was admitted and has attended AuClair since January 21, 1987, and is making slow but satisfactory progress.

****

Lester moved for a preliminary injunction requiring that he be immediately placed in a residential special education program. The motion was denied as moot when AuClair admitted Lester. . . . The district court held a trial on the remaining issue in the spring of 1988 and entered a declaratory judgment order on November 9, 1989, awarding Lester 2-1/2 years of compensatory education to extend beyond age 21. . . .

****

V.

The next issue is whether the compensatory education granted by the district court is proper relief. Our inquiry and the scope of review are two-tiered. First, we consider whether Congress empowered the courts to grant a compensatory remedy under 20 U.S.C. § 1415(e)(2). We exercise plenary review over this question. . . . Second, if the remedy is available, we review to see whether the district court abused its discretion by granting the remedy to Lester. 20 U.S.C. § 1415(e)(2).

An aggrieved party may seek relief in federal court. 20 U.S.C. § 1415(e)(1). The court may award whatever relief "[it] determines is appropriate,". . .

****

The School District argues that the [Supreme] Court in *Honig, supra* relied upon section 1412(2)

(B) to deny equitable relief to persons over age 21. The *Honig* Court concluded that Doe, age 24, was "no longer entitled to the protections and benefits of the EHA, which limits eligibility to disabled children between the ages of three and 21." *Honig*, 108 S. Ct. at 601, citing 20 U.S.C. § 1412(2)(B). The Court reasoned that Doe could no longer claim injunctive relief because the Act did not cover him. *Honig*, 108 S. Ct. at 601. In *Board of Educ. of E. Windsor Regional School Dist. v. Diamond*, 808 F.2d 987, 991 (3d Cir. 1986), we wrote that Section 1412(2)(B) requires a state "to provide a 'free appropriate education' to every disabled child." Thus, under Section 1415(e)(2), a district court is empowered to provide a remedy for individual handicapped children who are deprived of that right.

The crucial difference between *Honig* and Lester's case is the nature of the relief. In *Honig*, Doe was only asking that the Court make the District comply with the Act in the future. But, as an adult (i.e., someone over age 21), Doe had no right to demand that the District comply with the Act either presently or in the future. The Act only gives minors the right to education. Lester, in contrast, is only requesting a remedy to compensate him for rights the district already denied him. He has the right to ask for compensation because the School District violated his statutory rights while he was still entitled to them.

****

. . . . In *Burlington*, the Supreme Court held that tuition reimbursement constitutes appropriate relief under the EHA because it "merely requires the Town to belatedly pay expenses that it should have paid all along and would have borne in the first instance had it developed a proper IEP." 471 U.S. at 370-71, 105 S. Ct. at 2003. Furthermore, tuition reimbursement addresses "[a] child's right to a *free* appropriate public education," and satisfies the congressional intent to provide relief which remedies the deprivation of that right. *Burlington*, 471 U.S. at 370, 105 S. Ct. at 2003 (emphasis in original).

Miener v. State of Missouri, 800 F.2d 749 (8th Cir. 1986) extended this rationale to compensatory education, adding that the School District "should [not] escape liability for [educational] services simply because [the parent] was unable to provide them in the first instance. . . . We are confident that Congress did not intend the child's entitlement to a *free* education to turn upon her parent's ability to 'front' its costs." *Miener*, 800 F.2d at 753. The *Miener* court reasoned that compensatory education, like tuition reimbursement, cures the deprivation of a handicapped child's statutory rights, thus providing a remedy which Congress intended to make available. 800 F.2d at 753; . . . .

We conclude that Congress empowered the courts to grant a compensatory remedy. Furthermore, we conclude that Congress, by allowing the courts to fashion an appropriate remedy to cure the deprivation of a child's right to a free appropriate public education, did not intend to offer a remedy only to those parents able to afford an alternative private education. The only question remaining then is whether the court abused its discretion by granting 30 months of compensatory education to Lester beyond age 21. We conclude that it did not.

The School District had no reason to delay a proper placement for Lester. It knew before he entered the school system that it could not provide an appropriate educational program for him. Stipula-tions at P 13, app. at 37. The court found that the District "should have known or could have ascertained from the approved schools list that there were at least six Pennsylvania schools" suitable for Lester, and that it could have "applied promptly" to each of them. App. at 10. Furthermore, the district court specifically found that the School District "should have known the identity of AuClair and other out-of-state schools or should have ascertained their identity" before it did, and that Lester was harmed by their failure to do so. App. at 13. For sixteen months the School District failed to apply on Lester's behalf for admission to any school, and during the thirty months of inappropriate placement, Lester regressed. Because of this, we hold that the district court did not abuse its discretion when it fashioned this remedy for Lester. The court's award merely compensates Lester for what everyone agrees was an inappropriate placement from 1984 through January, 1987 and belatedly allows him to receive the remainder of his free and appropriate public education.

****

(Footnotes omitted.)

▬ ▬ ▬ ▬

MITTEN v. MUSCOGEE COUNTY SCHOOL DISTRICT
877 F.2d 932 (Eleventh Circuit 1989)

HOEVELER, District Judge.

****

Paige Mitten is a severely handicapped twelve-year-old child suffering from cerebral palsy, partial blindness and mental retardation. She cannot sit alone, walk, crawl or feed herself, nor is she toilet trained. Paige and her family moved from Texas to Muscogee County in 1985. Paige had been attending public schools in Texas, where the school system had developed an individualized education plan ("IEP") for her. She had last been evaluated in February 1984.

The Muscogee County School District refused to permit Paige to enter the public school system. The District also failed to develop a new IEP for her or to implement the old one. Instead, the District recommended residential placement at the Department of Human Resources Columbus Service Center (the "Center"). . . . [T]he school district decided to develop a permanent IEP by November 12, 1985.

Paige's parents requested a due process hearing . . . . At the hearing, the regional hearing officer determined that the school district had failed to provide a timely hearing and had failed to provide free and appropriate education as required under the EHA. . . .

The School District appealed. The state hearing officer sustained the decision of the regional hearing officer. After the passage of the HCPA [Handicapped Children's Protection Act] in 1986, and based upon its retroactive enforcement date, the parents sought an administrative award of attorneys' fees and costs. The state hearing officer concluded that the parents could not petition administratively for such an award, but must seek relief from the federal court.

****

DISCUSSION

Congress enacted the Handicapped Children's Protection Act, 20 U.S.C. section 1415(e)(4)(B) as an amendment to the Education of the Handicapped Act ("EHA"), 20 U.S.C. section 1415(e)(4), in August 1986. On its face, the statute provides attorneys fees to the prevailing party in administrative actions. It provides that

> In any action or proceeding brought under this subsection, the court, in its discretion may award reasonable attorneys fees as part of the costs to the parents or guardian of a handicapped child or youth who is the prevailing party.
> 20 U.S.C. section 1415(e)(4)(B). . . .

****

The term "action or proceeding" under the Act includes administrative hearings and appeals. *Unified School Dist. No. 259 v. Newton*, 673 F. Supp. 418, 420 (D. Kan. 1987). . . . The district court's reliance upon *Rolison v. Biggs*, 660 F. Supp. 875 (D. Del. 1987) is misplaced. The weight of authority is contrary to the *Biggs* decision. *See, e.g., Arons v. New Jersey State Bd. of Educ.*, 842 F.2d 58 (3d Cir. 1988) (the HCPA permits recovery of attorney's fees to the prevailing party at both the judicial and administrative levels); *Neisz v. Portland Pub. School Dist.*, 684 F. Supp. 1530 (D. Or. 1988) (costs and attorney's fees incurred by handicapped student's parents in a successful administrative challenge to the school district's determination were recoverable under the HCPA); *Burpee v. Manchester School Dist.*, 661 F. Supp. 731 (D.N.H. 1987) (permitting recovery of attorney's fees at the administrative level); *Kristi W. v. Graham Ind. School Dist.*, 663 F. Supp. 86 (M.D. Tex. 1987).

Appellees contend that administrative hearings are brought under subsection (b) of the statute rather than subsection (e) and, therefore, "any action or proceeding brought under this subsection" does not refer to administrative proceedings. However, the legislative history of the 1986 amendments to the EHA explicitly addresses this problem and states that

> Section 2 of the bill amends section 615(e)(4) of EHA to permit a court, in its discretion, to award reasonable attorneys' fees, costs and expenses to the parents or guardian of a handicapped child or youth who is the prevailing party in an action or proceeding (a due

> process hearing or a state level review) brought under Part B of EHA.
> H.R. Rep. No. 99-296, 99th Cong., 2nd Sess. (1985) at 5. . . .

Thus, if the appellants can establish that they were the prevailing parties in their administrative challenge to the school district's determination, they may recover their attorney's fees and costs in pursuing that challenge. This issue involves construction of the term "prevailing parties" under the Act. The appellants contend that the trial court erred in misconceiving their primary objectives and denying them attorneys fees and costs under the EHA. The district court found that the parents were not the prevailing parties in the administrative hearings because they failed to achieve their primary objective, which according to the court, was to have Paige placed in the local school system. The appellants contend that they were the prevailing parties because they achieved the most significant relief they sought, which was to ensure that Paige received a free and appropriate education. . . .

[T]he statute's legislative history addresses this problem by explicitly requiring that the term "prevailing" party" be given the same meaning it was given by the United States Supreme Court, in *Hensley v. Eckerhart*, 461 U.S. 424, 103 S. Ct. 1933, 76 L. Ed. 2d 40 (1983), which employed the significant relief standard. . . .

****

Second, the district court mistakenly applied the wrong standard in determining that substantively the parents were not the prevailing party because they did not achieve what the court determined was the primary objective. The legislative history indicates that the correct standard is the significant relief standard. Even if we assume that the parents' primary objective was to have Paige enrolled in the local public school, it seems clear that they wanted their child to have appropriate education. While the situs may be important, certainly the fundamental objective is the training and education of the child. In this quest the parents prevailed. The regional hearing officer determined that the child should have that which constituted a "free and appropriate education." This was the significant relief sought, and the lower court was in error in determining otherwise.

****

. . . . The district court found that because the hearing officer left Paige at the Center rather than placing her in a day school as her parents requested, Paige's placement at the Center was tantamount to providing her with the "free and appropriate education" mandated by the EHA. This conclusion, however, overlooks the fact that although Paige was permitted to stay at the Center, her educational program there was completely revamped. Originally, Paige was not provided with an educational plan at the Center. Neither were licensed teachers provided for her. The hearing officer directed the Center to provide her with eight hours of instruction by licensed teachers during the school day. Thus, the hearing officer can hardly be said to have found the school district's provisions for Paige appropriate.

****

The judgment of the district court is REVERSED and this case is REMANDED to the district court for a determination of the amount of reasonable attorneys' fees to be awarded to the appellants.
(Footnotes omitted.)

ADDITIONAL COMMENTARY

1. Circuits that have denied general damage awards include *Colin K. v. Schmidt*, 715 F.2d 1 (1st Cir. 1983); *Hudson v. Wilson*, 828 F.2d 1059 (4th Cir. 1987); *Hall v. Knott County Board of Education*, 941 F.2d 402 (6th Cir. 1991); *Anderson v. Thompson*, 658 F.2d 1205 (7th Cir. 1981); *Miener v. Missouri*, 673 F.2d 969 (8th Cir. 1982); and *Powell v. Defore*, 699 F.2d 1078 (11th Cir. 1983). The Fifth Circuit has granted damages in *Jackson v. Franklin County School Board*, 806 F.2d 623 (5th Cir. 1986) and *Boxall v. Sequoia Union High School District*, 464 F. Supp. 1104 (N.D. Cal. 1979).

2. Circuits that have allowed an independent action to recover attorneys' fees include *Moore v. District of Columbia*, 907 F.2d 165 (D.C. Cir. 1990); *McSomebodies v. Burlingame Elementary School District*, 886 F.2d 1558 (9th Cir. 1989); *Mitten v. Muscogee County School District*, 877 F.2d 932 (11th Cir. 1989); *Duane M. v. Orleans Parish School Board*, 861 F.2d 115 (5th Cir. 1988); *Eggers v. Bullitt County School District*, 854 F.2d 892 (6th Cir. 1988); and *Counsel v. Dow*, 849 F.2d 731 (2nd Cir. 1988).

3. In *Reed v. Oakland Unified School District*, 15 E.H.L.R. 441:368 (N.D. Cal. 1989), the parents were found to be prevailing parties for purposes of recovering attorneys' fees even though they did not receive exactly the relief they originally sought. The parents had originally requested additional speech therapy; in the final analysis, the student's placement was changed and she received some additional services.

   Two Circuit Courts of Appeals have also recently wrestled with the definition of prevailing party with regard to attorneys' fees. In *Brown v. Griggsville Unit School District No. 4*, 12 F. 3d 781 (7th Cir. 1993), the court held that parents were not prevailing parties even though the school district ultimately offered placement in a program the parents had tried to effect through the hearing process. The court ruled that the district's placement offer was motivated by changed in the child's performance and not a result of the actions taken by his parents.

   The Fourth Circuit also declined to recognize the parents as prevailing parties in *S-1 and S-2 v. State Board of Education of North Carolina*, 21 F. 3d 49 (4th Cir. 1994). That court ruled "[t]he fact that a lawsuit may operate as a catalyst for post-litigation changes in the defendant's conduct cannot suffice to establish plaintiffs as a prevailing party" (at 51).

4. Parents are eligible for reimbursement for an independent evaluation if the district cannot demonstrate the appropriateness of its own evaluation at a due process hearing. *E.g., Mullen v. District of Columbia*, 16 E.H.L.R. 792 (D.C. 1990). *In re Christopher B.*, 401 E.H.L.R. 313 (S.E.A. 1989). *See* discussion in eligibility section.

5. In *Dellmuth v. Muth*, 491 U.S. 223, 109 S. Ct. 2397 (1989), the Supreme Court held that the Eleventh Amendment barred reimbursement against a state. This holding prohibited parents from obtaining a monetary award from the state, not school districts. The decision was made moot as a result of the Education of the Handicapped Amendments of 1990. Congress amended the statute to clearly abrogate state

immunity under IDEA. As a result, states are not immune from monetary damage awards under the Eleventh Amendment for violations occurring after October 30, 1990. *Joshua B. v. New Trier Township High School District*, 203, 770 F.Supp. 431 (N.D.Ill. 1991).

6. One court has held that a person can be awarded compensatory education, even if the person commences the action after the student has reached the age of 21. *Cocores v. Portsmouth School District*, 18 I.D.E.L.R. 461 (D.N.H. 1991); *Murphy v. Timberlane Regional School District*, 18 I.D.E.L.R. 58 (D.N.H. 1991).

7. In *Mylo v. Baltimore County Board of Education*, 18 I.D.E.L.R. 346 (4th Cir. 1991), the court upheld sanctions against a parent for not complying with court orders, but such was not grounds for dismissing the IDEA claim against the district.

8. In *Todd D. v. Andrews*, 933 F.2d 1576 (11th Cir. 1991), the court made it clear that if the local district is unable to effect an appropriate placement, the burden rests on the state to do so. In this case, the student's needs dictated services in a regional or state center. It then became the duty of the state to develop interagency agreements necessary to implement the placement. This was also the result in *Cordero v. Pennsylvania Department of Education*, 795 F.Supp. 1352 (M.D. Pa 1992), where the court ordered that the state department work with the other state agencies to ensure that students receive an appropriate education under IDEA.

9. In an unusual case from West Virginia, a judge allowed a high school student to carry forth a suit against a history teacher for damages under Section 1983, *Doe v. Withers*, 20 I.D.E.L.R. 422 (W.Va. Circuit Court 1993). The teacher had refused to implement the student's IEP requirement that tests be presented orally by the learning disabilities teacher. This refusal continued even after repeated contacts by the parents and school staff. Finding that the teacher's actions violated the student's rights, the jury returned a verdict of $5,000 in compensatory damages and $10,000 in punitive damages. The student was also awarded attorney's fees.

10. A school district's failure to produce an acceptable IEP or file an administrative proceeding during two years while at an impasse with the parents entitled the student to compensatory education services in *Murphy v. Timberlane Regional School District,* 22 F. 3d 1186 (1st Cir. 1994). The court held that IDEA placed an affirmative obligation on the district to protect a child's right to an appropriate education even in the face of the parents' intransigence. The court also adopted a six-year limitations period for compensatory education claims.

11. In *E. M. v. Millville Board of Education,* 849 F. Supp. 312 (D. N.J. 1994), the court ruled that mediation was an "action or proceeding" within the meaning of the attorney fee provision of IDEA; therefore, parents were entitled to recover expenses incurred during the mediation process.

12. Parents of four students with disabilities filed a class action to challenge the school district's denial of year-round programming in *Hoeft v. Tucson Unified School District,* 967 F.2d 1298 (9th Cir. 1992). None of the parents had filed individual due process complaints nor an Education Department General Administrative Regulations (EDGAR) complaint. They maintained, in part, that they were exempted from the exhaustion of administrative remedies because they sought a court-ordered injunction, relief unavailable under IDEA. The court reasoned that allowing such an argument to stand would flood courts with cases claiming an exhaustion exception simply by virtue of requesting an injunction. Rather, they concluded that the individual relief to the children was the actual result sought by the parents and that IDEA's administrative remedies were sufficient to effect those ends.

ENDNOTES

1. 169 Wis. 231 (1919).

2. For a detailed historical analysis of the education of cognitively disabled children, see M. L. Hutt & R. G. Gibby, *The Mentally Retarded Child* (Boston: Allyn and Bacon, 1965).

3. 347 U.S. 483 (1954).

4. P.L. 89-750.

5. P.L. 91-230.

6. Pennsylvania Association for Retarded Citizens v. Pennsylvania, 334 F. Supp. 1257 (E.D. Pa. 1971), 343 F. Supp. 279 (E.D. Pa. 1972); Mills v. Bd. of Educ., 348 F. Supp. 866 (D.D.C. 1972).

7. 334 F. Supp. 1257 (E.D. Pa. 1971), 343 F. Supp. 279 (E.D. Pa. 1972).

8. 343 F. Supp. at 307.

9. 348 F. Supp. 866 (D.D.C. 1972).

10. P.L. 93-380 (1974).

11. P.L. 94-142, 42 U.S.C. 1401 *et seq.*

12. The state of New Mexico did not originally accept federal funding under the EAHCA. It did so after litigation involving the question of whether the state violated Section 504 by declining the money. New Mexico ARC v. New Mexico, 495 F. Supp. 391 (D.N.M. 1980), rev'd 678 F.2d 847 (10th Cir. 1982).

13. 34 C.F.R. 300.1 *et seq.*

14. Turnbull, H. R., & Turnbull, H. *Free Appropriate Public Education: Law and Implementation* (Denver: Love Publishing Company, 1978).

15. 20 U.S.C. 1412 (2) (B).

16. 20 U.S.C. 1401(a)(1).

17. According to the federal government's National Center for Education Statistics (Statistical Analysis Report, May 1994), for the 100 largest school districts in the United States, the average percentage of the total student body who had individualized education programs (IEPs) during the 1991–92 school year equaled 10.4%. Of those 100 districts, the East Baton Rouge Parish School District had the lowest proportion of students served under IDEA (3.7% or 2,242 students) and the Boston School District had the highest (18.7% or 11,422 students).

18. This is discussed further in the section on related services and provision of services under Section 504.

19. Humboldt Unified School District, 18 I.D.E.L.R. 28 (OCR 1991).

20. 875 F.2d 954 (1st Cir. 1989).

21. 875 F.2d at 962.

22. 753 F.2d 1397 (7th Cir. 1985).

23. Case No. SE-53-81, 506 E.H.L.R. 240 (1984).

24. *Gramm*, 17 E.H.L.R. 216 (O.S.E.R.S. 1990).

25. 20 U.S.C. 1401 (a)(16).

26. 20 U.S.C. 1401 (a)(18).

27. 34 C.F.R. 104.33(b).

28. 458 U.S. 176, 102 S.Ct. 3034 (1982).

29. 102 S. Ct. at 3042.

30. 102 S.Ct. at 3051.

31. 102 S. Ct. at 3049.

32. *E.g.,* E. M. Gallegos, "Beyond *Board of Education v. Rowley*: Educational Benefit for the Handicapped?" *American Journal of Education, 97*(3) (1989): 258–259.

33. 20 U.S.C. 1401(a)(18)(B).

34. 102 S.Ct. at 3047–48.

35. California—Pink v. Mt. Diablo Unified School Dist., 738 F.Supp. 345 (N.D. Cal. 1990). Massachusetts—David D. v. Dartmouth School Comm., 775 F.2d 411 (1st Cir. 1985). Michigan—Barwacz v. Michigan Dep't. of Educ., 674 F. Supp. 1296 (W.D. Mich. 1987). New Jersey—Bd. of Educ. of East Windsor v. Diamond, 808 F.2d 987 (3rd Cir. 1986); Geis v. Bd. of Educ. of Parsippany Troy Hills, 774 F.2d 575 (3rd Cir. 1985) (standard altered after case). North Carolina—Harrell v. Wilson Cty Schools, 58 N.C. App. 260, 293 S.E.2d 687 (1982).

36. 471 U.S. 359, 105 S. Ct. 1996 (1985). The idea of reimbursement to parents for tuition is discussed fully in the section on remedies.

37. *E.g.,* Tucker v. Bay Shore Union Free School Dist., 873 F.2d 563 (2nd Cir. 1989); Schimmel v. Spillane, 819 F.2d 477 (4th Cir. 1987). For the opposite result, *see e.g.,* Carter v. Florence County School Dist., 950 F.2d 156 (4th Cir. 1991) *aff'd* 114 S. Ct. 361 (1993); Alamo Heights Ind. School Dist. v. State Bd. of Educ., 790 F.2d 1153 (5th Cir. 1986); Shirk v. Dist. of Columbia, 756 F. Supp. 31 (D.D.C. 1991); Carrington v. Comm. of Educ. 535 N.E.2d 212 (Mass. App. 1989).

38. 114 S. Ct. 361 (1993).

39. Schimmel v. Spillane, 819 F.2d 477 (4th Cir. 1987).

40. 950 F.2d at 162.

41. 20 U.S.C. 1401 (16).

42. *E.g.,* Bonnie Ann F. v. Calallen School District, 835 F. Supp. 340 (S. D. Tex. 1993); Gregory K. v. Longview School Dist., 811 F.2d 1307 (9th Cir. 1987); Hawaii v. Katherine D., 727 F.2d 809 (9th

Cir. 1984); Springdale v. Grace, 693 F.2d 41 (8th Cir. 1982).

43. *See Timothy W.* and discussion in the section entitled Eligibility.

44. Russell v. Jefferson School Dist., 609 F. Supp. 605 (N.D. Cal. 1985).

45. Age v. Bullitt County Public Schools, 673 F.2d 141 (6th Cir. 1982).

46. Kruelle v. New Castle Cty School Dist., 642 F.2d 687 (3rd Cir. 1981); Colin K. v. Schmidt, 536 F. Supp. 1375 (D.R.I. 1982); Johnson v. Lancaster-Lebanon Intermediate Unit 13, 757 F. Supp. 606 (E.D. Pa. 1991); Chris D. v. Montgomery Cty Bd. of Educ., 753 F. Supp. 922 (M.D. Ala. 1990).

47. Polk v. Central Susquehhanna Inte. Unit 16, 853 F.2d 171 (3rd Cir. 1988); Burke Cty Bd. of Educ. v. Denton, 895 F.2d 973 (4th Cir. 1990); Martin v. School Bd. of Prince George Cty, 348 S.E.2d 857 (Va. App. 1986).

48. 34 C.F.R. 300.550.

49. Clevenger v. Oak Ridge School Bd., 744 F.2d 514, 517 (6th Cir. 1984); *see also* A.W. v. Northwest R-1 School Dist., 813 F.2d 158 (8th Cir. 1987).

50. 34 C.F.R. 300.128; 300.220.

51. 211 E.H.L.R. 276 (O.S.E.P. Policy Letter 1980).

52. 34 C.F.R. 300.500.

53. 34 C.F.R. 300.504(a).

54. 34 C.F.R. 300.505.

55. 34 C.F.R. 300.500.

56. Lumberton (MS) Public School, 18 I.D.E.L.R. 33 (1991); Philadelphia School District, 18 I.D.E.L.R. 931 (1992); Cobb County (GA) School District, 19 I.D.E.L.R. 29 (1992).

57. 34 C.F.R. 300.532.

58. Tauton (MA) School District, 16 E.H.L.R. 128 (1989).

59. Manchester (NH) School District, 18 I.D.E.L.R. 425 (1990).

60. 34 C.F.R. 300.503(a)(1).

61. *Doushty*, 16 E.H.L.R. 1363 (O.S.E.R.S. 1990).

62. 34 C.F.R. 300.503(b).

63. 34 C.F.R. 300.503 (c); T. S. v. Board of Education of the Town of Ridgefield, 10 F. 3d 87 (2nd Cir. 1993).

64. 20 U.S.C.A. 1412(5)(C).

65. 34 C.F.R. 300.534.

66. 34 C.F.R. 300.504 comment 1.

67. B.E.H. Policy Letter, 211 E.H.L.R. 187 (1980).

68. 20 U.S.C. 1401(20). 34 C.F.R. 300.340 defines *individualized education program* as "a written statement for a child with a disability that is developed and implemented in accordance with § 300.341-300.350."

69. Campbell v. Talladega County Bd. of Educ., 518 F. Supp. 47, 52 (N.D. Ala. 1981).

70. Dept. of Educ. Interpretation: IEP Purpose and Requirements, 46 Fed. Reg. 5460 (1981), specifically Parts a–f.

71. 34 C.F.R. 300.342(1). Spielberg v. Henrico County Pub. Schools, 853 F.2d 256 (4th Cir. 1988). A district's decision to transfer a child from private to public school may not occur before the IEP on which the change of placement is based has been properly developed.

72. 34 C.F.R. 300.343(c) (1988).

73. *Boney*, 18 I.D.E.L.R. 37 (O.S.E.P. 1991).

74. 34 C.F.R. 300.343(d).

75. *See* comments to 34 C.F.R. 300.343: "Meetings may be held any time throughout the year, as long as IEPs are in effect at the beginning of each school year."

76. 34 C.F.R. 300.344(b) (1988).

77. Dept. of Educ. Interpretation: IEP Purpose and Requirements, 46 Fed. Reg. 5460 (1981), 1 E.H.L.R. 103:43.

78. 34 C.F.R. 300.344.

79. 34 C.F.R. 300.344(b) (1988).

80. 20 U.S.C. 1415(b)(1)(B).

81. Fay v. S. Colonie Cent. School Dist., 802 F.2d 21 (2nd Cir. 1986).

82. 34 C.F.R. 300.345.

83. 34 C.F.R. 300.345(b).

84. *E.g., School Administrative Dist. #56*, 18 I.D.E.L.R. (S.E.A. Me. 1991).

85. 34 C.F.R 300.345(d) states:

A meeting may be conducted without a parent in attendance if the public agency is unable to convince the parents that they should attend. In this case the public agency must have a record of its attempts to arrange a mutually agreed on time and place such as:

(1) Detailed records of telephone calls made or attempted and the results of those calls.

(2) Copies of correspondence sent to the parents and any responses received, and

(3) Detailed records of visits made to the parent's home or place of employment and the results of those visits.

86. *See* Case No. 85-0470, 507 E.H.L.R. 251 (S.E.A. Mass. 1985).

87. 34 C.F.R. 300.345(e) (1988).

88. E.H. & H.H. v. Tirozzi, 735 F. Supp. 53 (D.C. Conn. 1990). Here, the court granted the parent's request to tape record the meetings over the objection of the special education teacher. This parent had difficulty understanding English; her request was based on her need to review the meeting at home with a dictionary to fully understand the proceedings.

89. 30 C.F.R. 300.344 (a)(4).

90. 20 U.S.C. 1401(a)(20) (1993); *also* 34 C.F.R. 300.346 (1993).

91. For a general discussion, *see* Dept. of Educ. Interpretation: IEP Purpose and Requirements, 46 Fed. Reg. 5450 (1981), 1 E.H.L.R. 103:43, question 36.

92. Case No. 11, 508 E.H.L.R. 32 (S.E.A. N.Y. 1987).

93. For a general discussion, *see* Dept. of Educ. Interpretation: IEP purpose and Requirements, 46 Fed. Reg. 5460 (1981), 1 E.H.L.R. 103:43, question 38.

94. *Id.*, question 39.

95. *Cullman County Pub. Schools*, 508 E.H.L.R. (S.E.A. Ala. 1986).

96. 34 C.F.R. 300.346(a)(5) (1993).

97. By a 1990 amendment transition services must be provided to all students with disabilities beginning no later than age 16, but should begin earlier when appropriate, 20 U.S.C. 1401 (a)(20)(d).

98. *Winston County School Dist.*, 352 E.H.L.R. 66 (OCR 1986).

99. *Dysart Unified School Dist.*, 311 E.H.L.R. 32 (OCR 1986).

100. 34 C.F.R. 300.342 (2). *E.g., Sinclair*, 211 E.H.L.R. 335 (E.H.A. 1984); *Sikeston (Mo.) R-VI*, 16 E.H.L.R. 467 (OCR 1990).

101. *See* comments to 34 C.F.R. 300, 342.

102. BEH Policy Letter, 211 E.H.L.R. 119 (1979). Parental consent is required for an initial special education placement. 34 C.F.R. 300.504(b)(ii) (1990). *See* Dept. of Educ. Interpretation: IEP Purpose and Requirements, 46 Fed. Reg. 5460 (1981), 1 E.H.L.R. 103:43, question 29.

103. *Schrag*, 16 E.H.L.R. 800 (O.S.E.P. 1990).

104. Policy Letter, 16 E.H.L.R. 800 (O.S.E.P. 1990); 34 C.F.R. 300.500 (a) states:

> *Consent means that: (1) The parent has been fully informed of all information relevant to the activity for which consent is sought. . . . (2) The Parent understands and agrees in writing to the carrying out of the activity for which his or her consent is sought, and the consent describes that activity. . . . (3) The parent understands that the granting of consent is voluntary . . . and may be revoked at any time.*

105. Case No. SE 86622, 508 E.H.L.R. 253 (S.E.A. Cal. 1986). A difference in classification cannot be unilaterally made by the district. *In the matter of a nine-year-old handicapped student,* 16 E.H.L.R. 538 (S.E.A. Tenn. 1990).

106. 34 C.F.R. 300.506 (1988); 34 C.F.R. 300.513 (1988). In addition, the stay-put provision requires that the child remain in the last valid IEP during the pendency of review.

107. H. R. Turnbull and C. R. Fiedler, *Judicial Interpretation of the Education for All Handicapped Children Act,* ERIC Clearinghouse on Handicapped and Gifted Children (Reston, VA: Council for Exceptional Children, 1984), p. 11.

108. 20 U.S.C. 1412(5)(B).

109. 34 C.F.R. 300.550.

110. 34 C.F.R. 300.550–34 C.F.R. 300.556.

111. *See* S. Lehr, *Purposeful Integration . . . Inherently Equal* (Boston: Technical Assistance for Parents Program, 1987).

112. S. Stainback, "Inclusive Schooling," in W. Stainback (Ed.), *Support Networks for Inclusive Schools: Interdependent Integrated Education* (Baltimore, MD: Paul H. Brookes, 1990).

113. Reynolds, M. C. "A Framework for Considering Some Issues in Special Education," *Exceptional Children, 28* (1962): 367–370.

114. *Toward Equality: Education of the Deaf,* A Report to the President and the Congress of the United States by the Commission on the Education of the Deaf, February, 1988, p. 31.

115. 458 U.S. at 181, fn. 4.

116. Comment to 34 C.F.R. 300.552.

117. Frost, 18 IDELR 594 (OSERS 1991).

118. 34 C.F.R. 300.551.

119. *Toward Equality: Education of the Deaf,* A Report to the President and the Congress of the United States by the Commission on the education of the Deaf, February, 1988, p. 32 (B. Griffin, 1987).

120. A.W. v. Northwest R-1 School Dist., 813 F.2d 158, 163 (8th Cir. 1987), *cert. denied*, 108 S. Ct. 144 (1987).

121. Springdale School Dist. #50 v. Grace, 693 F.2d 41 (8th Cir. 1982).

122. 700 F.2d 1058 (6th Cir. 1983).

123. *Roncker*, 700 F.2d at 1063.

124. 700 F.2d 1058 (6th Cir. 1983).

125. 874 F.2d 1036 (5th Cir. 1989).

126. *Daniel R.*, 874 F.2d at 1048.

127. *Daniel R.*, 874 F.2d at 1048.

128. Greer v. Rome, 950 F.2d 688 (11th Cir. 1991); Oberti v. Bd. of Educ. of the Borough of Clementon School Dist., 995 F.2d 1204 (3rd Cir. 1993).

129. Greer, 950 F.2d at 696.

130. *See also,* Mavis v. Sobol, 839 F. Supp. 968 (N.D. N.Y. 1993).

131. *See* Roland M. v. Concord Committee, 910 F.2d 983 (1st Cir. 1990); Bd. of Educ. of Community Consolidated School Dist. No. 21 v. Illinois State Bd. of Educ., 938 F.2d 712 (7th Cir. 1991); M. R. by R. R. v. Lincolnwood Bd. of Educ., 843 F. Supp. 1236 (N.D. Ill. 1994); Kerkum v. McKenzie, 862 F.2d 884 (D.C. Cir. 1988).

132. 14 F. 3d 1398, (9th Cir.), *cert. denied,* 129 L.Ed. 2d 813 (1994).

133. 14 F. 3d at 1400.

134. Taylor v. Bd. of Educ. of Copake-Taconic Hills, 649 F. Supp. 1253, 1258 (N.D.N.Y. quoted with approval in Lachman v. Illinois State Bd. of Educ., 852 F.2d 290, 295 (7th Cir. 1988).

135. Geis v. Bd. of Educ., 774 F.2d 575, 583 (3rd Cir. 1985).

136. Notice of Policy Guidance, 19 I.D.E.L.R. 463 (OSEP 1992).

137. 20 U.S.C. 1401(a)(17)(1991).

138. 34 C.F.R. 300.16(a); 34 C.F.R. 300.16(b).

139. 34 C.F.R. 300.16, Note.

140. 20 U.S.C. 1401(a)(25), (26).

141. 20 U.S.C. 1401 (a)(19).

142. The regulations, 34 C.F.R. 300.16, and the statute, 20 U.S.C. 1401(a)(25), define *assistive technology device* as "any item, piece of equipment or product system whether acquired commercially off the shelf, modified, or customized, that is used to increase, maintain, or improve the functional capabilities of children with disabilities."

143. Transition services include "post-secondary education, vocational training, integrated employment (including supported employment), continuing and adult education, adult services, independent living, or community participation." 20 U.S.C. 1401 (a)(19).

144. *Note also* that the components of room and board plus transportation to and from a residential placement can also be considered a "related service." As aptly put by one court, "That residential placement as sought by Douglas and Christopher may be available as a 'related service' under the Act is indisputable; . . . if residential placement is necessary in order for Douglas and Christopher to receive any educational benefits from special education, then under the EHA, the District must pay for the cost of that placement." Christopher T. v. San Francisco Unified School Dist., 553 F.Supp. 1107 (N.D. Cal. 1982). Residential placements are discussed in the section on specific placement issues.

145. 104 S. Ct. 3371 (1984).

146. 104 S. Ct. at 3378.

147. 34 C.F.R. 300.17, Note 1.

148. *See* EHA Policy Letter, 213 E.H.L.R. 273 (1989); Holmes v. Sobol, 690 F. Supp. 154 (W.D. N.Y. 1988); Vergason, 18 I.D.E.L.R. 538 (OSERS 1991).

149. 34 C.F.R. 300.17(2).

150. *E.g.,* Detsel v. Bd. of Educ. of Auburn, 820 F.2d 587 (2nd Cir. 1987); Bevin H. v. Wright, 666 F. Supp. 71 (W.D. Pa. 1987); Macomb County Intermediate School District v. Joshua S., 715 F.Supp. 824 (E.D. Mich. 1989); Granite School District v. Shannon M., 787 F.Supp. 1020 (D. Utah 1992).

151. Alamo Heights Ind. School Dist. v. State Bd. of Educ., 790 F.2d 1153 (5th Cir. 1986); Pinkerton v. Moye, 509 F. Supp. 107 (W.D. Va. 1981); Cohen v. School Bd. of Dade Cty, 450 So. 2d 1238 (Fla. App. 1984).

152. 34 C.F.R. 300.16 Comment.

153. *Compare* Max M. v. Thompson, 592 F. Supp. 1437 (N.D. Ill. 1984) to Darlene L. v. Illinois State Bd. of Educ., 568 F. Supp. 1340 (N.D. Ill. 1983).

154. *E.g.,* Clovis Unified School Dist. v. California Office of Admn. Hearings, 903 F.2d 635 (9th Cir. 1990).

155. *E.g.,* Field v. Haddonfield Bd. of Educ., 769 F. Supp. 1313 (D. N.J. 1991).

156. 34 C.R.F. 300.551(a). 34 CRF 300.302 states: "If placement in a public or private residential program is necessary to provide special education and related services to a child with a disability, the program, including non-medical care and room and board, must be at no cost to the parents of the child. Comment. This requirement applies to placements which are made by public agencies for educational purposes.

157. *See* Cordero by Bates v. Pennsylvania Department of Education, 795 F. Supp. 1352 (M.D. Pa. 1992). The court found state limitations on private school placement and funding violated the state's responsibility under IDEA to ensure a full continuum of placement alternatives. Riley v. Ambach, 508 F. Supp. 1222 (E.D. N.Y. 1980), 559 E.H.L.R. 180 (1982). Commissioner's actions eliminated residential schools as an option for learning disabled children. The court found it inappropriate to so limit placement options and enjoined the commissioner's actions.

158. Martin v. School Bd. of Prince George Cty, 348 S.E.2d 857, 864 (Va. App. 1986).

159. Dewalt v. Burkholder, 3 E.H.L.R. 551:550 (E.D. Va. 1980).

160. *E.g.*, Capello v. D.C. Bd. of Educ., 669 F.Supp. 14 (D.D.C. 1987).

161. *E.g.*, Cremeans v. Fairland Local School District, 633 N.E. 2d (Ohio App. 4 Dist. 1993); Hines v. Pitt Co. Bd. of Educ., 497 F.Supp. 403 (E.D.N.C. 1980).

162. *Note* that in Brown v. School Bd. of Henrico Cty, 18 I.D.E.L.R. 670 (Va. App. 1992) after the parents had gained a court decree mandating a residential placement, the court later found the residential placement to be inappropriate because the child refused to attend and the parents acquiesced in the child's actions.

163. *See* discipline section infra.

164. 438 N.E.2d 582 (Ill. App. 1982).

165. For a similar situation, *see* Taylor v. Honig, 910 F.2d 627 (9th Cir. 1990), where the court upheld the parent's unilateral out-of-state residential placement because the school had offered an inappropriate placement and the child had attacked the parent while awaiting a hearing of the issue.

166. 528 F. Supp. 1032 (W.D. Pa. 1981).

167. *See* also Dallas Ind. School Dist., 501 E.H.L.R. 101 (S.E.A. 1979), where the hearing officer used the child's difficulty in adjusting to new situations to demonstrate that continued private school placement was less restrictive environment.

168. 642 F.2d 687 (3rd Cir. 1981).

169. 642 F. Supp. at 693-694.

170. 769 F. Supp. 1313 (D.N.J. 1991).

171. 213 E.H.L.R. 133 (OSEP 1988).

172. North v. D.C. Bd. of Educ., 471 F. Supp. 136 (D.D.C. 1979).

173. 34 C.F.R. 300.504.

174. During the pendency of any proceedings, "unless the state or local educational agency and the parents or guardian otherwise agree the child shall remain in the then current educational placement of such child," 20 U.S.C. 1415(e)(3); 35 C.F.R. 300.513.

175. *See* Chapter 5 for discussion of change in placement as it relates to school disciplinary action.

176. Lunceford v. District of Columbia, 745 F.2d 1577 (D.C. Cir. 1984).

177. DeLeon v. Susquehanna Community School Dist., 747 F.2d 149, 153 (3rd Cir. 1984).

178. *Id.*

179. Greenbrier City School Dist., 16 E.H.L.R. 616 (OCR 1990).

180. St. Mary's City Public Schools, 18 I.D.E.L.R. 1044 (OCR 1991).

181. Bristol School Dist., 17 E.H.L.R. 298 (OCR 1990).

182. *E.g.*, Cohen v. Bd. of Educ., 454 N.Y.S.2d 630 (1982).

183. *E.g.*, Brown v. D.C. Bd. of Educ. (D.D.C. 1985); Concerned Parents and Citizens v. New York, 629 F.2d 751 (2nd Cir. 1980).

184. 705 F.2d 800 (6th Cir. 1983).

185. 467 N.E.2d 448 (1984).

186. Cronin v. Bd. of Educ. of the East Ramapo Central School Dist., 689 F. Supp. 197 (S.D.N.Y. 1988).

187. *E.g.*, Special School Dist. of St. Louis Cty, 16 E.H.L.R. 307 (OCR 1990).

188. In *Concerned Parents v. New York City Board of Education*, 629 F.2d 751, 754 (2d Cir. 1980), the court dealt with this problem by holding that because the children previously enrolled at a school which was closing were transferred to similar, although less "innovative," programs in other schools, the transfers did not affect the "general educational program in which a child . . . is enrolled," and thus were not changes in educational placement. Were we to apply the Second Circuit's holding in the present context, the change involved would clearly fall outside the ambit of the "stay put" provision. In *Tilton v. Jefferson County Board of Education*, 705 F.2d 800 (6th Cir. 1983), the court was also confronted with a school closing, but distinguished *Concerned Parents* on the grounds that "the programs at alternative schools are not comparable" to the program at the facility being closed. *Id.* at 804. The court went on to hold that, in spite of the fact that a "change in educational placement" was taking place, section 1415(e) (3) would not apply to "forestall implementation of a fiscal policy decision." The court in *Tilton* believed that Congress had not intended to interfere with such decisions, traditionally the concern of local school officials, by requiring hearings at which parents, concerned solely with their own child's program, could interfere with resource allocation decisions designed to provide the best possible education for all of the children of a district. *Id.* A heavy judicial hand in that kind of case, possibly requiring school districts to raise substantial funds by taxation or transfer of appropriations, raises substantial and sensitive separation of powers problems. *See generally* G. Frug, *The Judicial Power of the Purse*, 126 U. Pa. L. Rev. 715 (1978). [Taken from original opinion.]

189. 20 U.S.C. 1413(a)(4)(A).

190. OSERS Policy Letter, 17 E.H.L.R. 523 (1991); O.S.E.P. Policy Letter, 211 E.H.L.R. 414 (1987).

191. OSERS Policy Letter, 17 E.H.L.R. 523 (1991); O.S.E.P. Policy Letter, 213 E.H.L.R. 268 (1989).

192. 34 C.F.R. 76.651(a)(1).

193. 34 C.F.R. 76.654.

194. 34 C.F.R. 300.450–.452.

195. BEH Policy Letter, 211 E.H.L.R. 110 (1979); O.S.E.P. Policy Letter, 213 E.H.L.R. 123 (1988).

196. *See* McNair v. Oak Hills Local School Dist., 872 F.2d 153 (6th Cir. 1989).

197. U.S. Const. amend. I. This provision has been made applicable to the states through the Fourteenth Amendment, Cantwell v. Connecticut, 310 U.S. 296 (1940).

198. 403 U.S. 602, 91 S. Ct. 2105 (1971).

199. Lemon v. Kurtzman, 91 S. Ct. at 2111 (1971).

200. *E.g.,* Wallace v. Jaffree, 105 S. Ct. 2479, 2492 n. 51; Grand Rapids v. Ball, 105 S. Ct. 3216, 3226; Edwards v. Aguillard, 107 S. Ct. 2573, 2577.

201. *Edwards*, 107 S. Ct. at 2577.

202. *See* Lynch v. Donnelly, 465 U.S. 668, 104 S. Ct. 1355 (O'Connor, J., concurring).

203. 421 U.S. 349 (1975).

204. 433 U.S. 229 (1977).

205. 433 U.S. at 244.

206. *Wolman*, 433 U.S. at 247-248.

207. 473 U.S. 402 (1985).

208. 20 U.S.C. 2701 *et seq.*

209. *Aguilar*, 473 U.S. at 403.

210. 474 U.S. 481 (1986).

211. Mueller v. Allen, 463 U.S. 388 (1983).

212. Compare Walker v. San Francisco Unified School Dist., 761 F. Supp. 1463 (N.D. Cal. 1991) with Pulido v. Cavazos, 934 F.2d 912 (8th Cir. 1991); Exon, 213 E.H.L.R. 125 (OSERS 1988).

213. 113 S. Ct. 2462 (1993).

214. 113 S. Ct. at 2468.

215. 930 F.2d 363 (4th Cir. 1991), *cert. denied*, 112 S. Ct. 188 (1991).

216. In *Goodall*, the court based its conclusion on the following regulation, 34 C.F.R. 300.403: If a child with a disability has FAPE (free appropriate public education) available and the parents choose to place the child in a private school or facility, the public agency is not required by this part to pay for the child's education at the private school or facility. However, the public agency shall make services available to the child as provided under Sections. 300.450–300.452.

217. *Rowley*, 102 S. Ct. 3034 (1982).

218. 468 U.S. 992, 104 S. Ct. 3457 (1984).

219. This is discussed in detail in the chapter on Section 504.

220. 34 C.F.R. 76.1, *et seq.*

221. 34 C.F.R. 76.781.

222. 20 U.S.C. 1415(b)(2).

223. 34 C.F.R. 300.506.

224. 34 C.F.R. 300.507.

225. *See, e.g.*, Grymes v. Madden, 672 F.2d 321 (3rd 1982); Colin K. v. Schmidt, 715 F.2d 1 (1st Cir. 1983); Robert M. v. Benton, 634 F.2d 1139 (8th Cir. 1980).

226. Mayson v. Teague, 749 F.2d 652 (11th Cir. 1984).

227. Compare, *e.g.*, Victoria L. v. Dist. School Bd., 741 F.2d 369 (11th Cir. 1984); Robert M. v. Benton, 634 F.2d 1139 (8th Cir. 1980).

228. 20 U.S.C. 1415(d); 34 C.F.R. 300.508.

229. 34 C.F.R. 300.508(a)(3).

230. 20 U.S.C. 1415(d); 34 C.F.R. 300.508. Parents have a right to a free verbatim record of the hearing, Policy Letter, 17 E.H.L.R. 357 (1990).

231. 34 C.F.R. 300.512.

232. 20 U.S.C. 1415(c); 34 C.F.R. 300.510.

233. 34 C.F.R. 300.512.

234. 34 C.F.R. 300.511.

235. 20 U.S.C. 1415(e).

236. 20 U.S.C. 1415(e)(2).

237. Lachman v. Illinois State Bd., 852 F.2d 290 (7th Cir. 1988); Gregory K. v. Longview School, 811 F.2d 1307 (9th Cir. 1987); Roncker v. Walter, 700 F.2d 1058 (6th Cir. 1983); Doe v. Anrig, 692 F.2d 800 (1st Cir. 1982); Kruelle v. New Castle Cty School Dist., 642 F.2d 687 (3rd Cir. 1981).

238. Karl v. Bd. of Educ. of Geneseo Central School

Dist., 736 F.2d 873 (2nd Cir. 1984); Briggs v. Bd. of Educ., 882 F.2d 688 (2nd Cir. 1989).

239. 102 S. Ct. at 3051.

240. 20 U.S.C. 1415(e)(2) (1990).

241. 29 U.S.C.A. 794(a).

242. 42 U.S.C.A. 1983.

243. 468 U.S. 992, 104 S. Ct. 3457 (1984).

244. One court has held that Section 1983 is an appropriate avenue of relief to enforce a hearing officer's decision in IDEA. Reid v. Lincolnshire-Prairie View School Dist., 765 F.Supp. 965 (N.D. Ill. 1991).

245. 16 E.H.L.R. 643 (N.D. N.Y. 1990).

246. *See also* Blazejewski v. Bd. of Educ. of Allegheny Central School Dist., 560 F. Supp. 701 (W.D. N.Y. 1983).

247. *But see* Boxall v. Sequoia Union High School Dist. 464 F. Supp. 1104 (N.D. Cal. 1979).

248. Anderson v. Thompson, 658 F.2d 1205, 1213 (7th Cir. 1981).

249. 471 U.S. 359, 105 S. Ct. 1996 (1985).

250. 105 S. Ct. at 2003.

251. 766 F. Supp. 852.

252. *E.g.,* Lewisville Ind. School Dist. v. Brooke P., 16 E.H.L.R. 1313 (E.D. Tex. 1990); *also* Ash v. Lake Oswego, 766 F. Supp. 852.

253. *E.g.,* Alamo Heights Ind. School Dist. v. State Bd. of Educ., 790 F.2d 1153 (5th Cir. 1986).

254. 114 S. Ct. 361 (1993).

255. 471 U.S. 359 (1985).

256. *Carter,* 114 S. Ct. at 364.

257. Meiner v. Missouri, 800 F.2d 749, 750 (8th Cir. 1986).

258. *E.g.,* Alexopulos v. San Francisco Unified School Dist., 817 F.2d 551 (9th Cir. 1987), Natrona Cty School Dist. No. 1 v. McKnight, 764 P.2d 1039 (Wyo. 1988).

259. Burr v. Ambach, 441 E.H.L.R. 314, 863 F.2d 1071 (2nd Cir. 1988); vacated and remanded Sobol v. Burr, 109 S. Ct. 3209 (1989), *reaff'd* Burr v. Sobol, 888 F.2d 258 (2nd Cir. 1989); Lester H. v. Gilhool, 916 F.2d 865 (3rd Cir. 1990); Jefferson County Bd. of Educ. v. Breen, 853 F.2d 853 (11th Cir. 1988); LesterH. v. Carroll, 16 E.H.L.R. 10 (E.D. Pa. 1989); Meiner v. Missouri, 800 F.2d 749 (8th Cir. 1986).

260. Smith v. Robinson, 468 U.S. 992, 104 S. Ct. 3457 (1984).

261. 20 U.S.C. 1415(e)(4)(B).

262. 20 U.S.C. 1415(e)(4)(C).

263. 20 U.S.C. 1415(e)(4)(D).

264. 20 U.S.C. 1415 (e)(4)(F).

265. Hewitt v. Helms, 482 U.S. 755 (1987); Howey v. Tippecanoe School Corp., 734 F.Supp. 1485 (N.D. Ind. 1990).

266. *E.g.,* Mitten v. Muscogee Cty School Dist., 877 F.2d 932 (11th Cir. 1989); Joiner v. Dist. of Columbia, 16 E.H.L.R. 424 (D.C. 1990); Borgna v. Binghamton City School Dist., 18 I.D.E.L.R. 121 (N.D. N.Y. 1991);

267. Krichinsky v. Knox County Schools, 963 F.2d 847 (6th Cir. 1992).

268. 1986 U.S. Code Cong. and Admin. News 1804.

269. Medford v. Dist. of Columbia, 691 F. Supp. 1473 (D. D.C. 1988).

270. Shelly C. v. Venus Indep. School Dist., 878 F.2d 862 (5th Cir. 1989), *but see* Rollison v. Biggs, 656 F.Supp. 1204 (D. Del. 1987).

271. Aranow v. District of Columbia, 791 F.Supp. 318 (D. D.C. 1992).

272. Mason v. Kaagan, 18 I.D.E.L.R. 732 (D. Vt. 1992).

273. Mathern v. Campbell Co. Children's Ctr., 674 F. Supp. 816 (D. Wyo. 1987); Rapid City School Dist. 51-4 v. Vahle, 733 F. Supp. 1364 (W.D. S.D. 1990).

CHAPTER 5

DISCIPLINE

INTRODUCTION

The Fourteenth Amendment to the U.S. Constitution demands that a state, or any entity that is a part of a state, not deny a person of life, liberty, or property unless due process has been afforded.[1] In order to determine if the due process guarantees are triggered, one must first determine if the state has attempted to deny a person of life, liberty, or property. Although education is not a constitutional right,[2] a student does have a property interest in education.[3] In addition, some disciplinary sanctions may implicate a liberty interest. Thus, the due process clause is often triggered in student disciplinary situations.

The concept of constitutional due process contains two components: substantive and procedural due process. *Substantive due process* encompasses the basic concept of fairness; the state may deny a person of life, liberty, or property only for reasons that are considered fair or legitimate. In school disciplinary situations, the requirement generally is that the state's action must be reasonably related to a legitimate state interest or pass a basic test of reasonableness.[4] Usually, the state's interest in disciplinary situations is to maintain order in the school or to protect students. Thus, in order to pass this test, all a school must show is that its rules are reasonably related to these purposes. Substantive due process can be violated when the school's actions are unreasonable in terms of being without grounds or unreasonable in severity. For example, in *Slocum v. Holton Board of Education,*[5] the student argued that the district's policy of reducing letter grades for students who failed to attend after-hours study sessions

when they had a specified number of absences was not rational. The second type of substantive due process argument, unreasonable severity, can be found in recent cases involving corporal punishment. Courts have found that substantive due process violations may have occurred when students were subjected to unreasonably severe corporal punishment.[6]

The concept of *procedural due process* deals with an individual's interests in ensuring that a correct decision be made before a life, liberty, or property interest is diminished by state action. As such, the concept has evolved to require greater procedures when an interest of greater magnitude is being denied. For example, the procedures required before the state can inflict capital punishment are much greater than for the revocation of a business license. This is also true in school situations: The greater the interest, the more elaborate the procedures must be before that interest can be denied.[7]

SCOPE OF AUTHORITY

The general rule regarding the scope of a school's authority is that it extends only to conduct that has an effect on the school.[8] This concept can be explained in terms of substantive due process; if the behavior does not affect the school, the school does not have a reasonable basis to control it. In other words, regulation of behavior that does not affect the school cannot be rationally related to the state's legitimate interests of maintaining the order and discipline of the school. However, this does not mean that schools cannot regulate behavior off schoolgrounds. It only means that to do so, the behavior has to be shown to affect the schools.

For example, in *Smith v. Little Rock School District*,[9] the court upheld an expulsion of a student who had been charged with murder. The alleged act did not occur on school premises, but the student's presence in the school constituted a potential harm for himself and others. Thus, the court found that the school had the authority to institute sanctions against the student since the alleged murder had an effect on the school. The more common recent cases deal with schools' attempts to prohibit the use of alcohol and drugs. These rules must be carefully written to include only behavior that has an effect on the school. Thus, a student cannot be punished by the school for the use of alcohol or drugs regardless of location or time.[10] However, a school can prohibit the use of drugs at school or at school-sponsored activities or may punish students for being at school or school-sponsored activities while under the influence of alcohol or drugs.

CORPORAL PUNISHMENT

Corporal punishment is usually defined as any form of physical discipline.[11] Historically, it has been practiced in the public schools across the United States. Unless prohibited by state statute, it is generally accepted that schools may use reasonable corporal punishment on students.[12] The bulk of litigation involves whether the punishment in question was inflicted reasonably. To determine reasonableness, courts generally look to the nature of the offense, the punishment inflicted, and the age and size of the student. However, many states now prohibit corporal punishment.

In 1977, the Supreme Court[13] held that the infliction of reasonable corporal punishment on students did not violate the Eighth Amendment prohibition of cruel and unusual punishment. A new constitutional argument is developing. In a number of circuits, the courts have found that unreasonable corporal punishment may violate

a student's right to substantive due process.[14] In addition, unreasonable corporal punishment, or unauthorized corporal punishment, places the school personnel at risk of both civil and criminal penalties.[15]

REMOVAL FROM EXTRACURRICULAR ACTIVITIES

Suspension or expulsion from extracurricular activities is another common student disciplinary sanction. The courts have found that due process protections do not apply since no liberty or property interests are implicated. There are numerous cases in which students have challenged their removal from extracurricular activities either due to eligibility requirements or as a penalty for inappropriate behavior.[16] The courts have been very consistent in ruling that a student does not have a property interest in participating in extracurricular activities, either athletic[17] or nonathletic.[18] Nor does the suspension provide a sufficient liberty interest violation as to warrant the application of due process protections since stigma alone (e.g., embarrassment related to suspension from a team), without a concomitant loss of a property interest, will not trigger the application of due process protections. As such, the courts have consistently upheld school districts' actions in suspending or expelling students from extracurricular activities.

IN-SCHOOL SUSPENSIONS

Recognizing that removing students entirely from the school environment may provide them with reinforcement rather than negative consequences for inappropriate behavior, many schools have turned to the practice of *in-school suspensions*. The question then becomes whether due process guarantees attach to this disciplinary sanction and, if so, what process is due a student before an in-school suspension can be implemented. Whether due process is required appears to be dependent on how long the suspension is to last and whether the student is being deprived of an education during the time of the suspension. Courts, however, disagree on whether deprivation of an education means being deprived of classroom instruction or being deprived of the opportunity to engage in educational activities during school time.[19] Courts have also found that the use of an in-school suspension implicates the student's property and liberty interest, but it is *de minimis,* and, as such, no due process procedures are necessary. One court analogized this to other forms of minor classroom discipline and stated, "Teachers should be free to impose minor forms of classroom discipline . . . without being subjected to the strictures of due process scrutiny."[20]

OUT-OF-SCHOOL SUSPENSIONS

Most of what is discussed in terms of procedural due process for short-term suspensions is derived from the landmark case of *Goss v. Lopez.*[21] In that case, nine students were suspended by the school principal for 10 days; no prior hearing was given. The case made its way to the United States Supreme Court. There, the Court determined that due process protections did apply because the students' property interests to an education were denied and their liberty interests in terms of reputation were damaged. It then turned to the question of how much process was due. The Court determined for a suspension of 10 days or less, a student should be granted, at a minimum, (1) an oral notice of the changes, (2) an explanation of the evidence against him or her, and (3) if the student disagreed, he or she should be granted an opportunity to refute the evidence.

The Court specifically determined that there need be no delay between the notice and the "hearing." Also, it specifically excluded formal procedures such as representation by counsel and presentation and cross-examination of witnesses. Finally, it noted that in emergency situations even this minimal hearing could be suspended and handled after the emergency

subsided. The Court determined that this minimal "hearing" was sufficient since, although the students' property and liberty interests were implicated, the extent of the deprivation was relatively minor. Thus, the state was required only to provide minimal due process for a minimal deprivation.

EXPULSIONS

In definitional terms, the only difference between an out-of-school suspension and an expulsion is length of time. An *expulsion* is removal from school for a period of time that exceeds 10 days. Courts have consistently ruled that more process must be afforded before a student can be removed from school for an extended period of time.

Procedural due process is a flexible concept. As the deprivation increases, so does the extent of due process required to fulfill constitutional mandates. However, procedural due process can be broken down into three basic components: notice, opportunity to be heard, and a decision based on the merits. Each of these components becomes more complex as the possible penalty involved becomes more severe. The benchmark in terms of minimum is the *Goss*-type hearing in which the notice may be oral, the opportunity to be heard may be immediate and informal, and the decision may be made by the accuser immediately after the opportunity to be heard. The minimum procedures for an expulsion are not as definite because there is no Supreme Court authority on the issue. Additionally, most states set forth statutory procedures for expelling students that provide elaborate processes; these certainly provide adequate due process to pass constitutional analysis. Each of the 50 states' procedures will not be reviewed here, but a general overview of minimal requirements will be covered.

The student, and possibly the student's parents, must be notified in writing that the school intends to expel the student. The notice must be sufficiently specific to inform the student of the charges and evidence against him or her. It should include:

1. The intent to expel the student
2. The specific charges against the student
3. The rule under which the charges are being brought
4. The evidence supporting the charges
5. The date, time, and place of the hearing
6. The procedures that will be followed at the hearing
7. The notification of the student's rights at the hearing[22]

Sufficient time should be given between the notice and the hearing to give the student an opportunity to prepare a defense. The cases do not present a uniform period of time required. A period as short as 4 days has been upheld, but a 40-day period was determined to be too long. Most districts rely on a fixed time in the state expulsion statute or state department of education regulations.

The core of due process is a fair hearing—the opportunity to be heard.[23] In expulsion cases, this hearing may be open or closed, at the discretion of the student. The student has the right to be heard and to present evidence at the hearing. Although the student does not have most of the constitutional protections afforded by criminal proceedings—the right to remain silent, double jeopardy, the right to counsel—the proceeding should be conducted with an eye toward fundamental fairness. The student should be given a description of the evidence that will be presented against him or her and be given an opportunity to refute it. The student should also be given assistance in his or her defense, including use of an attorney to the same extent used by the school. The decision, which should be based on the evidence presented and be made by an impartial body, should be given to the student in writing shortly after the hearing. Many states offer an administrative appeal route. If the state or district has an appeal route, the student should be informed of his or her rights to an appeal upon notification of the outcome of the hearing.

GOSS v. LOPEZ
419 U.S. 565, 95 S. Ct. 729, 42 L. Ed. 2d 725 (1975)

Justice WHITE delivered the Opinion of the Court.

****

I.

Ohio law, Rev. Code Ann. § 3313.64 (1972), provides for free education to all children between the ages of six and 21. Section 3313.66 of the Code empowers the principal of an Ohio public school to suspend a pupil for misconduct for up to 10 days or to expel him. In either case, he must notify the student's parents within 24 hours and state the reasons for his action. . . .

The nine named appellees, each of whom alleged that he or she had been suspended from public high school in Columbus for up to 10 days without a hearing pursuant to § 3313.66, filed an action under 42 U.S.C. § 1983 against the Columbus Board of Education and various administrators of the CPSS [Columbus Public School System]. The complaint sought a declaration that § 3313.66 was unconstitutional in that it permitted public school administrators to deprive plaintiffs of their rights to an education without a hearing of any kind, in violation of the procedural due process component of the Fourteenth Amendment. It also sought to enjoin the public school officials from issuing future suspensions pursuant to § 3313.66. . . .

****

II.

At the outset, appellants [school officials] contend that because there is no constitutional right to an education at public expense, the Due Process Clause does not protect against expulsions from the public school system. This position misconceives the nature of the issue and is refuted by prior decisions. The Fourteenth Amendment forbids the State to deprive any person of life, liberty, or property without due process of law. Protected interests in property are normally "not created by the Constitution. Rather, they are created and their dimensions are defined" by an independent source such as state statutes or rules entitling the citizen to certain benefits. Board of Regents v. Roth, 408 U.S. 564, 92 S. Ct. 2701, 2709, 33 L. Ed. 2d 548 (1972). . . .

****

Here, on the basis of state law, appellees plainly had legitimate claims of entitlement to a public education. Ohio Rev. Code Ann. §§ 3313.48 and 3313.64 (1972 and Supp. 1973) direct local authorities to provide a free education to all residents between five and 21 years of age, and a compulsory-attendance law requires attendance for a school year of not less than 32 weeks. Ohio Rev. Code Ann. § 3321.04 (1972). . . . Having chosen to extend the right to an education to people of appellees' class generally, Ohio may not withdraw that right on grounds of misconduct absent, fundamentally fair procedures to determine whether misconduct has occurred. . . . The authority possessed by the State to prescribe and enforce standards of conduct in its schools, although concededly very broad, must be exercised consistently with constitutional safeguards. Among other things, the State is constrained to recognize a student's legitimate entitlement to a public education as a property interest which is protected by the Due Process Clause and which may not be taken away for misconduct without adherence to the minimum procedures required by that Clause.

The Due Process Clause also forbids arbitrary deprivations of liberty. "Where a person's good name, reputation, honor, or integrity is at stake because of what the government is doing to him," the minimal requirements of the Clause must be satisfied. *Wisconsin v. Constantineau*, 400 U.S. 433, 437, 91 S. Ct. 507, 510, 27 L. Ed. 2d 515 (1971); *Board of Regents v. Roth, supra*, 408 U.S. at 573, 92 S. Ct. at 2707. School authorities here suspended appellees from school for periods of up to 10 days based on charges of misconduct. If sustained and recorded, those charges could seriously damage the students' standing with their fellow pupils and their teachers as well as interfere with later opportunities for higher education and employment. It is apparent that the claimed right of the State to determine unilaterally and without process whether that misconduct has occurred immediately collides with the requirements of the Constitution.

III.

"Once it is determined that due process applies, the question remains what process is due." *Morrissey v. Brewer*, 408 U.S., at 481, 92 S. Ct., at 2600. We turn to that question, fully realizing as our cases regularly do that the interpretation and application of the Due Process Clause are intensely practical matters and that "(t)he very nature of due process negates any concept of inflexible procedures universally applicable to every imaginable situation." *Cafeteria Workers v. McElroy*, 367 U.S. 886, 895, 81 S. Ct. 1743, 1748, 6 L. Ed. 2d 1230 (1961). . . .

"[T]here can be no doubt that at a minimum they require that deprivation of life, liberty or property by adjudication be preceded by notice and opportunity for hearing appropriate to the nature of the case." . . . At the very minimum, therefore, students facing suspension and the consequent interference with a protected property interest must be given some kind of notice and afforded some kind of hearing. "Parties whose rights are to be affected are entitled to be heard; and in order that they may enjoy that right they must first be notified." *Baldwin v. Hale*, 1 Wall, 223, 233, 17 L. Ed. 531 (1864).

. . . . The student's interest is to avoid unfair or mistaken exclusion from the educational process, with all of its unfortunate consequences. The Due Process Clause will not shield him from suspensions properly imposed, but it disserves both his interest and the interest of the State if his suspension is in fact unwarranted. The concern would be mostly academic if the disciplinary process were a totally accurate, unerring process, never mistaken and never unfair. . . . The risk of error is not at all trivial, and it should be guarded against if that may be done without prohibitive cost or interference with the educational process.

****

We do not believe that school authorities must be totally free from notice and hearing requirements if their schools are to operate with acceptable efficiency. Students facing temporary suspension have interests qualifying for protection of the Due Process

Clause, and due process requires, in connection with a suspension of 10 days or less, that the student be given oral or written notice of the charges against him and, if he denies them, an explanation of the evidence the authorities have and an opportunity to present his side of the story. The Clause requires at least these rudimentary precautions against unfair or mistaken findings of misconduct and arbitrary exclusion from school.

There need be no delay between the time "notice" is given and the time of the hearing. In the great majority of cases the disciplinarian may informally discuss the alleged misconduct with the student minutes after it has occurred. We hold only that, in being given an opportunity to explain his version of the facts at this discussion, the student first be told what he is accused of doing and what the basis of the accusation is. . . . Since the hearing may occur almost immediately following the misconduct, it follows that as a general rule notice and hearing should precede removal of the student from school. We agree with the District Court, however, that there are recurring situations in which prior notice and hearing cannot be insisted upon. Students whose presence poses a continuing danger to persons or property or an ongoing threat of disrupting the academic process may be immediately removed from school. In such cases, the necessary notice and rudimentary hearing should follow as soon as practicable, as the District Court indicated.

In holding as we do, we do not believe that we have imposed procedures on school disciplinarians which are inappropriate in a classroom setting. Instead we have imposed requirements which are, if anything, less than a fair-minded school principal would impose upon himself in order to avoid unfair suspensions. . . .

We stop short of construing the Due Process Clause to require, countrywide, that hearings in connection with short suspensions must afford the student the opportunity to secure counsel, to confront and cross-examine witnesses supporting the charge, or to call his own witnesses to verify his version of the incident. Brief disciplinary suspensions are almost countless. To impose in each such case even truncated trial-type procedures might well overwhelm administrative facilities in many places and, by diverting resources, cost more than it would save in educational effectiveness. Moreover, further formalizing the suspension process and escalating its formality and adversary nature may not only make it too costly as a regular disciplinary tool but also destroy its effectiveness as part of the teaching process.
****

We should also make it clear that we have addressed ourselves solely to the short suspension, not exceeding 10 days. Longer suspensions or expulsions for the remainder of the school term, or permanently, may require more formal procedures. Nor do we put aside the possibility that in unusual situations, although involving only a short suspension, something more than the rudimentary procedures will be required.

IV.

The District Court found each of the suspensions involved here to have occurred without a hearing, either before or after the suspension, and that each suspension was therefore invalid and the statute unconstitutional insofar as it permits such suspensions without notice or hearing. Accordingly, the judgment is

Affirmed.
(Footnotes omitted.)

— — — —

GARCIA v. MIERA
817 F. 2d 650 (Tenth Circuit 1987)

LOGAN, Circuit Judge.

****

In 1982 Garcia was a nine-year-old student in the third grade at the Penasco Elementary School in Penasco, New Mexico. On February 10, 1982, defen-dant-appellee Theresa Miera, the school principal, summoned Garcia to her office for hitting a boy who had kicked her. Miera instructed Garcia to go to her chair to be paddled. . . .

Miera responded by calling defendant J.D. Sanchez, a teacher at the school, for assistance.

Sanchez held Garcia upside down by her ankles while Miera struck Garcia with a wooden paddle. *Id.* at 105. The paddle "was split right down the middle, so it was two pieces, and when it hit, it clapped [and] grabbed." *Id.* at 165. Miera hit Garcia five times on the front of the leg between the knee and the waist. *Id.* at 277-78. After the beating, Garcia's teacher, Ruth Dominez, "noticed blood coming through [Garcia's] clothes," *id.* at 106, and, on taking Garcia to the restroom, was shocked to see a "welt" on Garcia's leg. *Id.* at 268. The beating made a two-inch cut on her leg, *id.* at 176, that left a permanent scar. *Id.* at 145. . . .

The second beating at issue occurred on May 13, 1983. Miera summoned Garcia to her office for saying that defendant Judy Mestas has been seen kissing a student's father, Denny Mersereau, on a school bus during a recent field trip and that Mestas had sent love letters to Mersereau through his son.

Miera proceeded to strike Garcia two times with the paddle on the buttocks. Garcia then refused to be hit again. Miera responded by calling defendant Edward Leyba, an administrative associate at the school. Leyba pushed Garcia toward a chair over which she was to bend and receive three additional blows. Garcia and Leyba struggled and Garcia hit her back on Miera's desk, from which she suffered back pains for several weeks. R. I, 106, 150-52. Garcia then submitted to the last three blows. The beating caused severe bruises on Garcia's buttocks, which did not stop hurting for two to three weeks. *Id.* at 160. The report of the school nurse indicates that as a result of the beating Garcia's "buttocks [were] bright red with [a] crease across both." *Id.* at 109. Dr. Albrecht, a physician who treated Garcia, stated: "I've done hundreds of physicals of children who have had spankings . . . and I have not seen bruises on the buttocks as Teresita had, from routine spankings . . . [T]hey were more extensive, deeper bruises. . . ." *Id.* at 271. Betsy Martinez, a nurse who examined Garcia, stated that if a child had received this type of injury at home she "would have called [the police department's] Protective Services." *Id.* at 270. . . .

I.

We first consider whether corporal punishment of a school child, in any degree of excessiveness, can violate substantive rights under the Due Process Clause. Despite the Supreme Court's explicit disclaimer that it was deciding that issue in *Ingraham v. Wright*, 430 U.S. 651, 97 S. Ct. 1401, 51 L. Ed. 2d 711 (1977), we believe that *Ingraham* requires us to hold that, at some point, excessive corporal punishment violates the pupil's substantive due process rights. . . .

Although the *Ingraham* opinion focuses on procedural due process, it discusses the history of corporal punishment in the law and applies a balancing test between the child's interest in personal security and the traditional view that a school may need to be able to impose "limited" or "reasonable" corporal punishment: "[T]here can be no deprivation of substantive rights as long as disciplinary corporal punishment is within the limits of the common-law privilege." 430 U.S. at 676, 97 S. Ct. at 1415. Relying upon the adequacy of state criminal and tort remedies for excessive punishment, the low incidence of abuse, and impracticality, the court held that "the Due Process Clause does not require notice and a hearing prior to the imposition of corporal punishment in the public schools, as that practice is authorized and limited by the common law." *Id.* at 682, 97 S. Ct. at 1418.

Although *Ingraham* makes clear that ordinary corporal punishment violates no substantive due process rights of school children, by acknowledging that corporal punishment implicates a fundamental liberty interest protected by the Due Process Clause, we believe that opinion clearly signaled that, at some degree of excessiveness or cruelty, the meting out such punishment violates the substantive due process rights of the pupil.

****

The Fourth Circuit in *Hall v. Tawney*, 621 F.2d 607 (4th Cir. 1980), a case closely analogous to the one before us, found a substantive due process right to be free of brutal, demeaning and excessive paddling by public school officials. . . .

****

. . . .

As in the cognate police brutality cases, the substantive due process inquiry in school corporal punishment cases must be whether the force applied caused injury so severe, was so disproportionate to the need presented, and was so inspired by malice or sadism rather than a merely careless or unwise excess of zeal that it

amounted to a brutal and inhumane abuse of official power literally shocking to the conscience.
Hall, *621 F.2d at 613.*

****

We thus envision three categories of corporal punishment. Punishments that do not exceed the traditional common law standard of reasonableness are not actionable; punishments that exceed the common law standard without adequate state remedies violate procedural due process rights; and finally, punishments that are so grossly excessive as to be shocking to the conscience violate substantive due process rights, without regard to the adequacy of state remedies.

****

Applying this standard to the instant case, we hold that, at least by the time of the second beating, the law was clearly established that excessive corporal punishment could deny substantive due process. . . .

****

. . . . We think a reasonably competent legal advisor to a school district should have realized that egregious invasions of a student's personal security would be unconstitutional. "It does not require a constitutional scholar to conclude that a nude search

of a thirteen-year-old child is an invasion of constitutional rights of some magnitude." *Doe v. Renfrow*, 631 F.2d 91, 92-93 (7th Cir. 1980), *cert. denied*, 451 U.S. 1022, 101 S. Ct. 3015, 69 L. Ed. 2d 395 (1981).

****

The threshold for recovery on the constitutional tort for excessive corporal punishment is high. But the allegations with respect to the first beating, that this nine-year-old girl was held up by her ankles and hit several times with a split board of substantial size on the front of her legs until they bled—supported by evidence of a permanent scar—are sufficient. The allegations with respect to the second beating, that the punishment was severe enough to cause pain for three weeks—supported by pictures of the injured buttocks, an affidavit from an examining doctor that in his long experience he had not seen bruises like that from routine spankings, and an affidavit from an examining nurse that if a child had received this type of injury at home she would have reported it as child abuse—are also sufficient. These claims may not survive the crucible of the trial, but they overcome defendants' motion for summary judgment.

REVERSED and REMANDED for further proceedings consistent herewith.

(Footnotes omitted.)

ADDITIONAL COMMENTARY

1. In 1992, 21 states prohibited the practice of corporal punishment in schools. Alaska, 1989, Alaska Stat. § 11.81.430 (1990); California, 1986, Cal. Educ. Code § 49000 (1991); Connecticut, 1989, Conn. Gen. Stat. § 53A-18 (1990); Hawaii, 1973, Haw. Rev. Stat. § 298-16 (1990); Iowa, 1989, Iowa Code § 280.21 (1989); Kentucky, 1991, Ky. Rev. Stat. § 503.110 (1991); Massachusetts, 1972, Mass. Ann. Laws Ch. 71 § 37G (1991); Maine, 1975, Me. Rev. Stat. t. 17-a § 106 (1989); Michigan, 1988, Mich. Comp. Laws § 380.1312 (1991); Minnesota, 1989, Minn. Stat. § 127.45 (1990); Nebraska, 1988, Neb. Rev. Stat. § 79-4,140 (1989); New Hampshire, 1983, N.H. Rev. Stat. Ann. § 627:6 (1990); New Jersey, 1967, N.J. Rev. Stat. § 18a:6-1 (1990); New York, 1985, N.Y. Penal Law § 35.10 (1991); North Dakota, 1989, N.D. Cent. Code § 15-47-47 (1989); Oregon, 1989, Or. Rev. Stat. § 339.250(8)

(1989); Rhode Island, 1983; South Dakota, 1990, S.D. Codified Laws § 13-32-2 (1991); Vermont, 1984, Vt. Stat. Ann. t. 16 § 1161a (1990); Virginia, 1989, Va. Code § 22.1-279.1 (1991); Wisconsin, 1988, Wis. Stat. § 118.31 (1989–1990).

2. A tragic example of excessive discipline found to be a violation of substantive due was presented in *Waechter v. School District 14*, 773 F. Supp. 1005 (W.D. Mich 1991). The child died after he was required to perform a 350-yard sprint in less than two minutes, as a disciplinary measure. The court found that the teacher's actions were disproportionate to the circumstance and constituted a substantive due process violation.

3. Mandatory punishments may be upheld if there is a rational relationship between the punishment and the offense and if the requisite procedural safeguards are in place. For example, a school district rule setting forth a mandatory expulsion

for students possessing a weapon in school was upheld. *Mitchell v. Bd. of Trustees of Oxford Municipal School District*, 625 F.2d 660 (5th Cir. 1980).

4. In the case of a student with an emotional disorder who was expelled for carrying a loaded handgun to school, the court granted summary judgment to the school on the parents' due process claims. The court found that the expulsion procedures provided for adequate prior notice, representation by counsel, an unbiased tribunal, and an opportunity to present evidence; that the denial of an opportunity to cross-examine several witnesses did not sufficiently prejudice the student's case because his own confession had not been rebutted in the record; and that the district was not required to provide a complete transcript of the expulsion hearing. *Carey v. Maine School Administrative District #17*, 754 F.Supp. 906 (D. Me 1990).

5. In *Palmer v. Merluzzi*, 868 F.2d 90 (3rd Cir. 1989), a student challenged the imposition of a 10-day academic suspension and a 60-day athletic suspension because he was not given a notice of charge and a supporting statement of penalties. However, the court held that since the possible sanctions were listed in general student publications, the student had sustained no violation of his due process rights.

6. In an expulsion proceeding, a student may not have the right to directly cross-examine witnesses. This has been the case when the school relied on the assistant principal's examination of an anonymous informant and it was necessary to keep that informant anonymous due to fear of retaliation. *Paredes v. Curtis*, 864 F.2d 426 (6th Cir. 1988). See also *Jones v. Board of Trustees of Pascagoula Municipal Separate School District*, 524 So.2d 968 (Miss. 1988).

SPECIAL ISSUES IN SPECIAL EDUCATION DISCIPLINE

In dealing with discipline of students with disabilities, the first question that must be addressed is whether the behavior involved is a manifestation of the student's disability. Stated in another way, one must first determine if there is a nexus between the behavior in question and the disability. Students cannot be disciplined for a behavior that is a manifestation of their disability.[24] To do so would merely be disciplining the disability or imposing penalties on students because they are disabled.[25]

Although the courts have stated this requirement in different ways, the basic requirement is:

> There must be a determination of whether the child's behavior was caused by his handicap. To do otherwise would be to expel a child for behavior over which he may have little or no control. This would hardly be a fair result or one in keeping with the purposes of the EAHCA [Education for All Handicapped Children Act].[26]

Making a determination of which behaviors are related to a disability is frequently difficult. Clearly, this requirement is not limited to only those students who have been identified as seriously emotionally disturbed.[27] It is equally clear that this is not limited to those students who may not be "capable of understanding rules and regulations or right from wrong."[28] The Ninth Circuit, in an attempt to establish guidelines for identifying a nexus between a child's behavioral problems and disability, refers to

> conduct that is caused by, or has a direct substantial relationship to, the child's handicap. Put another way, a handicapped child's conduct is covered by this definition only if the handicap significantly impairs the child's behavioral controls. Although this definition may, depending on the circumstances, include the conduct of handicapped children who possess the raw capacity to conform their behavior to prescribed standards, it does not embrace conduct that bears only an attenuated relationship to the child's handicap.[29]

The determination of a nexus should be made by a "specialized and knowledgeable group of persons."[30] The Individuals with Disabilities Education Act (IDEA) contains the requirement that the education of each student who has a disability must be directed by an individualized education program (IEP) team. The requirement of a "specialized and knowledgeable group of persons" in the field seems to imply members of the IEP team. The Office for Civil Rights (OCR) has outlined what a manifestation determination should include:

> [T]he determination must be based on the kind of information necessary to a competent professional decision . . . . [T]he information considered would include psychological evaluation data related to behavior . . . . The relevant data would be recent enough to afford an understanding of the child's current behavior . . . . [T]he causation determination is not . . . simply a reflection of the child's special education classification (for example, that he is classified "learning disabled," not "behavior disordered)." It is not a determination of whether she knew right from wrong or that she knew her behavior was wrong. It is not sufficient that the procedure satisfies legal requirements for the suspension of nonhandicapped children.[31]

Since a determination of whether the behavior is related to the disability apparently must be made by the IEP team, it appears that some of the due process provisions of IDEA would come into play.[32] Thus, parents must be given adequate notice of and purpose for the IEP meeting to ensure their participation in the decision-making process. If there is a disagreement as to whether the behavior is a manifestation of the disability, one must assume that IDEA procedures and requirements would have to be followed until some resolution was reached.[33]

Schools' disciplinary policies should reflect this required difference in treatment so that administrators can be certain that the initial inquiry into the nexus is made before further decisions on discipline occur.[34] From a practical standpoint, it would be best to have a discussion concerning a student's potential inappropriate behaviors, and whether those behaviors are related to the disability, during an IEP meeting before the student has actually engaged in those behaviors. This avoids a delay in convening a meeting to determine if a particular behavior is related to a student's disabling condition.[35]

If there is a nexus between the behavior and the disability, then the behavior should be addressed through an individualized behavior program developed as a part of the IEP, rather than applying the disciplinary measures used for the general student population. The Office for Civil Rights (OCR) suggests that even if the behavior is related to the disability, the same disciplinary tools may be employed; only the procedure has to vary.

> If the process followed includes an MDT (multidisciplinary IEP team) determination that the action is appropriate and consistent with meeting the student's educational needs, then the provision of 34 C.F.R. 104.33 would appear to be satisfied. . . . [T]he decision should be an education based judgment, not merely an automatically imposed sanction under the general student disciplinary procedures that would apply to nonhandicapped students who commit similar offenses.[36]

Thus, the IEP team may employ typical disciplinary methods if such methods have been found to be appropriate for the student in a particular situation. In addition, if the behavior is not related to the disability, regular procedures can be employed in most instances. Courts have held that students with disabilities are subject to general disciplinary rules for unrelated behaviors that result in corporal punishment and short-term suspensions.[37] Also, the Office for Civil Rights has issued the opinion that students may be subject to in-school suspensions.[38]

If the discipline to be effected would constitute a change in placement for an IDEA student, IDEA procedures must be followed rather than regular disciplinary procedures for the school. This is because any change in placement necessitates an IEP change. Although the statute does not specifically define the term *change in placement,* the Supreme Court in *Honig v. Doe* accepted a "greater than 10 days" definition used by the Department of Education.[39]

> *The Department of Education has adopted the position first espoused in 1980 by its Office of Civil Rights that a suspension of up to 10 school days does not amount to a "change in placement" prohibited by 1415(e)(3). The EHA nowhere defines the phrase "change in placement," nor does the statute's structure or legislative history provide any guidance as to how the term applies to fixed suspensions. Given this ambiguity, we defer to the construction adopted by the agency charged with monitoring and enforcing the statute. . . . [We] believe the agency correctly determined that a suspension in excess of 10 days does constitute a prohibited change in placement.[40]*

Since removing a child from his or her current placement for a period greater than 10 days is considered a change in placement, IDEA procedures must be followed. See Figure 5.1. This is true regardless of the relationship between the behavior and the disabling condition. The change in the IEP must conform to the requirements on notice and parental consent. In essence, a new IEP must be agreed upon that would continue to provide the student with an appropriate education, but the location for receiving education would be altered. For example, a student may be placed in a more structured school or receive home-bound instruction if either placement would provide the student with an appropriate education. The main point to keep in mind is that the student cannot be denied his or her rights to an appropriate education under IDEA because of behavior problems. The school continues to have the obligation to provide students an education and must find a placement that would continue to do so in spite of the problem behaviors. The school may not cease services to an IDEA student for reasons of his or her behavior.[41]

One must then determine what constitutes a "change in placement" under IDEA. A change in placement triggers the stay-put provisions of IDEA. A disciplinary action that does not constitute a change in placement does not implicate due process or the stay-put provision. In these situations, the school must only concern itself with not disciplining a child solely because of his or her disability, and otherwise make certain that children with disabilities are treated the same as children without disabilities. Unfortunately, there is no litmus test of what constitutes a change in placement.

In *Honig v. Doe*,[42] the Supreme Court held only that a suspension of 10 or more consecutive schooldays amounts to a change in placement. The Office of Special Education Program (OSEP) has not given specific guidance as to what else will be a change in placement, but has warned schools that possibly "repeated discipline problems indicate that services being provided to a particular child should be reviewed or changed."[43] OCR has attempted to resolve these questions in a post-*Honig* memo. It has stated that a series of suspensions which cumulatively total more than 10 days constitutes a change in placement if the result is a pattern of exclusion.[44] OCR offers the following factors to consider: "The length of each suspension, the proximity of the suspensions to one another, and the total amount of time the child is excluded from school."[45]

What happens in the interim when there is a disagreement about the placement of the student so a new placement is not readily apparent? It was previously believed that a student who presented a danger to self or others would be removed from the current educational placement pending a resolution of the situation. For example, in *Jackson v. Franklin County School Board*,[46] the court stated that "schools have discretion to alter a handicapped student's placement when he endangers himself or others and threatens to disrupt a safe school environment."[47] The court, however, recognized that this unilateral change in placement could not continue indefinitely.[48] The Supreme Court disagreed with this interpretation and ruled that the stay-put requirement in IDEA[49] did not include

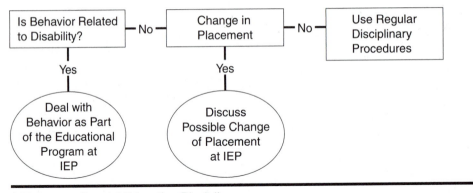

FIGURE 5.1 Special Education Discipline

any exception for removal of even a dangerous student during the pendency of IDEA proceedings.[50]

Recognizing that this may prove frustrating for educational personnel, the Court did offer some suggestions for dealing with these situations. First, the Court noted that IDEA does allow for interim placements on which the school and the parents can agree.[51] Second, school districts are not precluded from using less drastic disciplinary techniques during the interim, such as short-term suspensions or in-school suspensions.[52] Finally, the Court suggested that a school could seek legal redress when the parents will not agree to removal of a truly dangerous student. "[I]n those cases in which the parents of a truly dangerous child adamantly refuse to permit any change in placement, the 10-day respite gives school officials an opportunity to invoke the aid of the courts."[53]

It was also suggested that if the school can prove the futility of the administrative process, it should go directly into court to seek an injunction for the removal of the child.[54] However, it was noted that there is a presumption against removal that the school can overcome only "by showing that maintaining the child in his or her current placement is substantially likely to result in injury either to himself or herself, or to others."[55]

In response to public concerns about school safety, Congress amended IDEA in 1994 to permit a school district to place a child with disabilities in an interim alternative placement for up to 45 days if that child brings a weapon to school. Under this new provision, if parents file a due process complaint, the child would remain in the alternative placement while proceedings are pending unless the parents and the school agree otherwise.[56]

S-1 v. TURLINGTON
635 F.2d 342 (Fifth Circuit 1981)

HATCHETT, Circuit Judge.

****

FACTS

Plaintiffs, S-1, S-2, S-3, S-4, S-5, S-6, and S-8, were expelled from Clewiston High School, Hendry

County, Florida, in the early part of the 1977–78 school year for alleged misconduct. Each was expelled for the remainder of the 1977–78 school year and for the entire 1978–79 school year, the maximum time permitted by state law. All of the plaintiffs were classified as either educable mentally retarded (EMR), mildly mentally retarded, or EMR/dull normal. It is undisputed that the expelled plaintiffs were accorded the procedural protections required by *Goss v. Lopez*, 419 U.S. 565, 95 S. Ct. 729, 42 L. Ed. 2d 725 (1975). Except for S-1, they were not given, nor did they request, hearings to determine whether their misconduct was a manifestation of their handicap. Regarding S-1, the superintendent of Hendry County Schools determined that because S-1 was not classified as seriously emotionally disturbed, his misconduct, as a matter of law, could not be a manifestation of his handicap.

****

Plaintiffs initiated this case alleging violations of their rights under the Education for All Handicapped Children Act (EHA) [now IDEA], 20 U.S.C. § 1401-1415, and section 504 of the Rehabilitation Act of 1973, 29 U.S.C. § 794.

. . . . The children in this suit are clearly handicapped within the meaning of both section 504 and the EHA. The parties agree that a handicapped student may not be expelled for misconduct which results from the handicap itself. It follows that an expulsion must be accompanied by a determination as to whether the handicapped student's misconduct bears a relationship to his handicap. . . .

Defendant local officials argue that they complied with section 504. As support for their position, they state that they determined, in the expulsion proceedings, that the plaintiffs were capable of understanding rules and regulations or right from wrong. They also assert that they found, based upon a psychological evaluation, that plaintiffs' handicaps were not behavioral handicaps (as it would be if plaintiffs were classified as seriously emotionally disturbed), thereby precluding any relationship between the misconduct and the applicable handicap. We cannot agree that consideration of the above factors satisfies the requirement of section 504. A determination that a handicapped student knew the difference between right and wrong is not tantamount to a determination that his misconduct was or was not a manifestation of his handicap. . . . Essentially, what the school officials assert is that a handicapped student's misconduct can never be a symptom of his handicap, unless he is classified as seriously emotionally disturbed. . . .

[S]uch a generalization is contrary to the emphasis which Congress has placed on individualized evaluation and consideration of the problems and needs of handicapped students.

****

With regard to plaintiff S-1, the trial court found that the school officials entrusted with the expulsion decision determined at the disciplinary proceedings that S-1's misconduct was unrelated to his handicap. The trial court, however, held that this determination was made by school board officials who lacked the necessary expertise to make such a determination. The trial court arrived at this conclusion by holding that an expulsion is a change in educational placement. Under 45 CFR § 121a.533(a)(3) and 45 CFR § 84.35(c)(3), evaluations and placement decisions must be made by a specialized and knowledgeable group of persons.

The trial court's finding presents the novel issue in this circuit whether an expulsion is a change in educational placement, thereby invoking the procedural protections of both the EHA and section 504 of the Rehabilitation Act. . . .

. . . . We find the reasoning of the district court in *Stuart v. Nappi*, 443 F. Supp. 1235 (D. Conn. 1978), persuasive. In *Stuart*, a child was diagnosed as having a major learning disability caused by either a brain disfunction or a perceptual disorder. She challenged the use of disciplinary proceedings which, if completed, would have resulted in her expulsion for participating in a schoolwide disturbance. The trial court held that the proposed expulsion constituted a change in educational placement, thus requiring the school officials to adhere to the procedural protections of the EHA. In so holding, the court stated:

> The right to an education in the least restrictive environment may be circumvented if schools are permitted to expel handicapped children (without following the procedures prescribed by the EHA). . . . An expulsion has the effect not only of changing a student's placement, but also of restricting the availability of alternative placements. . . .

We agree with the district court in *Stuart*, and therefore hold that a termination of educational services, occasioned by an expulsion, is a change in educational placement, thereby invoking the procedural protections of the EHA. . . .

The school officials point out that a group of persons entrusted with the educational placement decision could never decide that expulsion is the correct placement for a handicapped student, thus insulating a handicapped student from expulsion as a disciplinary tool. They further state that Florida law does not contemplate this result because expulsion is specifically provided for under Florida law as a disciplinary tool for all students. . . . We . . . find that expulsion is still a proper disciplinary tool under the EHA and section 504 when proper procedures are utilized and under proper circumstances. We cannot, however, authorize the complete cessation of educational services during an expulsion period.

State defendants focus their attention on the fact that, with the exception of S-1, none of the expelled plaintiffs raised the argument, until eleven months after expulsion. . . . The EHA, section 504, and their implementing regulations do not prescribe who must raise this issue. In light of the remedial purposes of these statutes, we find that the burden is on the local and state defendants to make this determination. Our conclusion is buttressed by the fact that in most cases, the handicapped students and their parents lack the wherewithal either to know or to assert their rights under the EHA and section 504.

****

CONCLUSION

Accordingly, we hold that under the EHA, section 504, and their implementing regulations: (1) before a handicapped student can be expelled, a trained and knowledgeable group of persons must determine whether the student's misconduct bears a relationship to his handicapping condition; (2) an expulsion is a change in educational placement thereby invoking the procedural protections of the EHA and section 504; (3) expulsion is a proper disciplinary tool under the EHA and section 504, but a complete cessation of educational services is not; . . . In the circumstances, the trial judge did not abuse his discretion in entering the injunction.

AFFIRMED.
(Footnotes omitted.)

— — — —

HONIG v. DOE
484 U.S. 305, 108 S. Ct. 592, 98 L. Ed. 2d 686 (1988)

[*Note:* The dispute regarding respondent Doe was declared moot since he was 24 years old at the time of this appeal. Respondent Smith was 20 years old and still entitled to relief from the Education of the Handicapped Act, now IDEA, which sets the upper age limit at 21. Therefore, the suit continued.]

Justice BRENNAN delivered the opinion of the Court.

As a condition of federal financial assistance, the Education of the Handicapped Act requires States to ensure a "free appropriate public education" for all disabled children within their jurisdictions. In aid of this goal, the Act establishes a comprehensive system of procedural safeguards designed to ensure parental participation in decisions concerning the education of their disabled children and to provide administrative and judicial review of any decisions with which those parents disagree. Among these safeguards is the so-called "stay-put" provision, which directs that a disabled child "shall remain in [his or her] then current educational placement" pending completion of any review proceedings, unless the parents and state or local educational agencies otherwise agree. 20 U.S.C. § 1415(e)(3). Today

we must decide whether, in the face of this statutory proscription, state or local school authorities may nevertheless unilaterally exclude disabled children from the classroom for dangerous or disruptive conduct growing out of their disabilities.

****

Respondent Jack Smith was identified as an emotionally disturbed child by the time he entered the second grade in 1976. School records prepared that year indicted that he was unable "to control verbal or physical outburst[s]" and exhibited a "[s]evere disturbance in relationships with peers and adults." *Id.*, at 123. Further evaluations subsequently revealed that he had been physically and emotionally abused as an infant and young child and that, despite above average intelligence, he experienced academic and social difficulties as a result of extreme hyperactivity and low self-esteem. *Id.*, at 136, 139, 155, 176. Of particular concern was Smith's propensity for verbal hostility; one evaluator noted that the child reacted to stress by "attempt[ing] to cover his feelings of low self worth through aggressive behavior[,] . . . primarily verbal provocations." *Id.*, at 136.

****

At the beginning of the next school year [1980], Smith was assigned to a full-day program; almost immediately thereafter he began misbehaving. School officials met twice with his grandparents in October 1980 to discuss returning him to a half-day program; although the grandparents agreed to the reduction, they apparently were never apprised of their right to challenge the decision through EHA procedures. The school officials also warned them that if the child continued his disruptive behavior—which included stealing, extorting money from fellow students, and making sexual comments to female classmates—they would seek to expel him. On November 14, they made good on this threat, suspending Smith for five days after he made further lewd comments. His principal referred the matter to the SPC [Student Placement Committee], which recommended exclusion from SFUSD [San Francisco Unified School District]. . . . [T]he Committee scheduled a hearing and extended the suspension indefinitely pending a final disposition in the matter. . . .

****

III.

The language of § 1415(e)(3) is unequivocal. It states plainly that during the pendency of any proceedings initiated under the Act, unless the state or local educational agency and the parents or guardian of a disabled child otherwise agree, "the child shall remain in the then current educational placement" § 1415(e)(3). Faced with this clear directive, petitioner asks us to read a "dangerousness" exception into the stay-put provision. . . .

Petitioner's arguments proceed, he suggests, from a simple, common sense proposition: Congress could not have intended the stay-put provision to be read literally, for such a construction leads to the clearly unintended, and untenable, result that school districts must return violent or dangerous students to school while the often lengthy EHA proceedings run their course. We think it clear, however, that Congress very much meant to strip schools of the unilateral authority they had traditionally employed to exclude disabled students, particularly emotionally disturbed students, from school. In so doing, Congress did not leave school administrators powerless to deal with dangerous students; it did, however, deny school officials their former right to "self-

help," and directed that in the future the removal of disabled students could be accomplished only with the permission of the parents or, as a last resort, the courts.

As noted above, Congress passed the EHA after finding that school systems across the country had excluded one out of every eight disabled children from classes. In drafting the law, Congress was largely guided by the recent decisions in *Mills v. Board of Education of District of Columbia*, 348 F. Supp. 866 (1972), and *PARC*, 343 F. Supp. 279 (1972), both of which involved the exclusion of hard-to-handle disabled students. . . .

Congress attacked such exclusionary practices in a variety of ways. It required participating States to educate all disabled children, regardless of the severity of their disabilities, 20 U.S.C. § 1412(2)(C), and included within the definition of "handicapped" those children with serious emotional disturbances. § 1401(1). It further provided for meaningful parental participation in all aspects of a child's educational placement, and barred schools, through the stay-put provision, from changing that placement over the parent's objection until all review proceedings were completed. Recognizing that those proceedings might prove long and tedious, the Act's drafters did not intend § 1415(e)(3) to operate inflexibly, *see* 121 Cong. Rec. 37412 (1975) (remarks of Sen. Stafford), and they therefore allowed for interim placements where parents and school officials are able to agree on one. Conspicuously absent from § 1415(e)(3), however, is any emergency exception for dangerous students. . . .

Our conclusion that § 1415(e)(3) means what it says does not leave educations hamstrung. The Department of Education has observed that, "[w]hile the [child's] placement may not be changed [during any complaint proceeding], this does not preclude the agency from using its normal procedures for dealing with children who are endangering themselves or others." Comment following 34 CFR § 300.513 (1987). Such procedures may include the use of study carrels, timeouts, detention, or the restriction of privileges. More drastically, where a student poses an immediate threat to the safety of others, officials may temporarily suspend him or her for up to 10 schooldays. This authority, which respondent in no way disputes, not only ensures that school administrators can protect the safety of others by promptly removing the most dangerous of students, it also provides a "cooling down" period during which officials can initiate IEP review and seek to persuade the child's parents to agree to an interim placement. And in those cases in which the parents of a truly dangerous child adamantly refuse to permit any change in placement, the 10-day respite gives school officials an opportunity to invoke the aid of the courts under § 1415(e)(2), which empowers courts to grant any appropriate relief.

****

[W]e believe that school officials are entitled to seek injunctive relief under § 1415(e)(2) in appropriate cases. In any such action, § 1415(e)(3) effectively creates a presumption in favor of the child's current educational placement which school officials can overcome only by showing that maintaining the child in his or her current placement is substantially likely to result in injury to either himself or herself, or to others. . . ..

IV.

We believe the courts below properly construed and applied § 1415(e)(3), except insofar as the Court of Appeals held that a suspension in excess of 10 schooldays does not constitute a "change in placement." We therefore affirm the Court of Appeals' judgment on this issue as modified herein. Because we are equally divided on the question whether a court may order a State to provide services directly to a disabled child where the local agency has failed to do so, we affirm the Court of Appeals' judgment on this issue as well.

****

(Footnotes omitted.)

ADDITIONAL COMMENTARY

1. In *Doe v. Rockingham County School Board*, 658 F. Supp. 403 (W.D. Va. 1987), the court applied IDEA protection to a student who had not been found to be disabled before the "expulsion" because the school district should have been aware of the likely disability. *See also Alvord Unified School District*, 17 E.H.L.R. 1021 (SEA CA. 1991).

2. In *Metropolitan School District v. Davila*, 969 F.2d 485 (7th Cir. 1992), the court upheld the interpretive ruling of the Office for Special Education and Rehabilitative Services (OSERS) that requires the continuation of educational services for students with disabilities who have been suspended or expelled.

3. In *Chester County*, the OCR found that the district's in-school suspension program that provided students with the educational services that were regularly provided in the classroom was not a change in placement, even if administered for a period of greater than 10 days. *Chester County School District*, 17 E.H.L.R. 301 (OCR 1990).

4. Two emotionally disturbed students were confined in a janitorial closet for periods of four to seven days as a disciplinary measure. An OCR review found that this was a violation of Section 504, since nondisabled students were not disciplined in this manner. *McCracken County School District*, 18 I.D.E.L.R. 482 (OCR 1991).

5. A 16-year-old student with cerebral palsy and developmental delays was suspended on four occasions, for a total of 18 days, due to violent outbursts. The school's failure to hold an IEP before that last 10-day suspension was found to be a Section 504 violation. *York (SC) School District #3*, 17 E.H.L.R. 475 (OCR 1991).

6. The courts have been willing, on occasion, to enjoin disruptive students from school by using one of the avenues outlined by the court in *Honig*. For example, a school received an injunction to prevent a dangerous/disruptive high school student who had attacked and threatened students and teachers from returning to school. The student had violently struck students and had threatened to kill students, teachers, and staff, stating that he had the means to do so. The school offered homebound instruction or an alternate public high school placement during the pendency of administrative proceedings. The district court enjoined the student from attending his high school until the conclusion of a pending special education due process hearing, and ordered the Board to provide

him 10 hours per week of homebound instruction in the interim. *Township High School District Board of Education v. Kurtz-Imig*, 16 E.H.L.R. 17 (N.D.Ill. 1989).

7. The 10-day suspension "clock" begins again after the students' IEP is reviewed. However, a student's repeated inappropriate behavior may be an indication of an inappropriate placement. *Rhys*, 18 I.D.E.L.R. 217 (OSEP 1991).

8. The district expelled a student with learning disabilities for shooting at a school bus with a bow and arrow. The hearing officer noted that the student's learning disability was not severe and that the student's misbehavior manifested itself, generally, only outside the classroom. Although the student's IEP addressed certain socialization skills, the hearing officer determined that the student's misconduct exceeded the emotional and social concerns listed in the IEP and were, to a great extent, a result of the student's family dynamic. *Elk Grove Unified School District*, 16 E.H.L.R. 622 (SEA CA 1990).

9. In the area of drug and alcohol addiction, the scope of coverage and restrictions of IDEA and Section 504 are not identical. Inconsistencies between the laws are primarily the result of their differing definitions of disabled individuals.

Drug or alcohol addiction does not ordinarily fit into any of the disability categories listed under IDEA. Therefore, chemically dependent children are not considered disabled under IDEA, and IDEA's special disciplinary procedures do not apply to them. Districts should look beyond a child's drug or alcohol addiction, however, to ensure that the chemical dependency has not resulted in disabling conditions as defined under the act, and to ensure that the addiction does not coexist with unrelated disabling conditions.

The Section 504 definition of *handicapped person* does not list specific categories of disabilities. Students with drug or alcohol addiction fall within Section 504's broader definition of "handicapped persons." Students who only occasionally use or abuse drugs or alcohol, however, are *not* viewed as handicapped under Section 504. Therefore, at least in certain cases, a school dis-

trict is required under Section 504 to evaluate a student addicted to drugs or alcohol before making any significant change in educational placement, such as expulsion.

In an official memorandum, OCR has ruled that school districts should not conduct blanket drug and alcohol screening of students. *Marietta City School District,* 353 E.H.L.R. 369 (OCR 1989). Districts should evaluate a student before expulsion, however, when a student is *known* to be addicted or when *strong evidence* exists of addiction. *Garner,* 305 E.H.L.R. 53 (OCR 1989). When evidence reveals only occasional use or abuse of drugs or alcohol by a student, a district is not required to evaluate prior to expulsion. Districts need to make these determinations on a case-by-case basis, looking for substantial, clear evidence that a pupil's condition represents genuine addiction.

OCR has stated in an official memorandum that it is not a violation of Section 504 to suspend or expel an addicted student for violating school rules concerning drugs or alcohol, *provided that* any student would have been similarly suspended or expelled for such violation. *Long-Term Suspension or Expulsion of Handicapped Students,* 15 E.H.L.R. 52 (OCR 1983). OCR based its decision on the policy that schools need not tolerate consumption or possession of drugs or alcohol on school premises or at school-sponsored activities. Thus, when an addicted student commits a drug- or alcohol-related offense, a prior evaluation need not be conducted before suspension or expulsion.

The Americans with Disabilities Act (ADA) amended Section 504 to exclude persons "currently engaging in the illegal use of drugs" from protection. Section 512(a) of the ADA also adds a subsection that states:

> [L]ocal educational agencies may take disciplinary action pertaining to the use or possession of illegal drugs or alcohol against any handicapped student who currently is engaging in the illegal use of drugs or in he use of alcohol to the same extent that such disciplinary action is taken against non-handicapped students.

ENDNOTES

1. U.S. Const. amend. XIV.

2. *E.g.*, San Antonio v. Rodriguez, 411 U.S. 1 (1973).

3. Goss v. Lopez, 419 U.S. 565 (1975).

4. *See* Petrey v. Flaugher, 505 F. Supp. 1087 (E.D. Ky. 1981); Slocum v. Holton Board of Education, 429 N.W.2d 607 (Mich. App. 1988).

5. 429 N.W.2d 607 (Mich. App. 1988); *see also* Mitchell v. Bd. of Trustees of Oxford School District, 625 F.2d 660 (5th Cir. 1980).

6. *E.g.*, Metzger v. Osbeck, 841 F.2d 518 (3rd Cir. 1988); Garcia v. Miera, 817 F.2d 650 (10th Cir. 1987), Hall v. Tawney, 621 F.2d 607 (4th Cir. 1980).

7. *See* Goss v. Lopez, 419 U.S. 565 (1975).

8. For the common law derivation of this concept, *see* O'Rourke v. Walker, 102 Conn. 130, 128 A.25 (1925).

9. 582 F. Supp. 159 (E.D. Ark. 1984).

10. *E.g.*, Claiborne v. Beebe School Dist., 687 F. Supp. 1358 (E.D. Ark. 1988).

11. *Black's Law Dictionary, 6th Ed.*

12. *See* Ingraham v. Wright, 430 U.S. 651 (1977), in which the Court found that corporal punishment did not violate the Eighth Amendment prohibition on cruel and unusual punishment.

13. Ingraham v. Wright, 430 U.S. 651 (1977).

14. Hall v. Tawney, 621 F.2d 607 (4th Cir. 1980); Garcia v. Miera, 817 F.2d 650 (10th Cir. 1987); Metzger v. Osbeck, 841 F.2d 518 (3rd Cir. 1988); Wise v. Pea Ridge School Dist., 855 F.2d 560 (8th Cir. 1988); *Contra.* Fee v. Herndon, 900 F.2d 804 (5th Cir. 1990).

15. *E.g.*, Commonwealth v. Douglass, 403 Pa Super. 105, 588 A.2d 53 (Pa. 1991); Haley v. McManus, 593 So. 2d 1339 (La. Ct. App. 1991).

16. *E.g.*, Rose v. Nashua Bd. of Educ., 679 F.2d 279 (1st Cir. 1982).

17. *E.g.*, Spring Branch I.S.D. v. Stamos, 695 S.W.2d 556 (Tex. 1985); Stone v. Kansas State High School Activities Association, 761 P.2d 1255 (Kan. App. 1988); Hardy v. Univ. Interscholastic Athletic League, 759 F.2d 1233 (5th Cir. 1985); Simkins v. South Dakota High School Activities Association, 434 N.W.2d 367 (S.D. 1989).

18. *E.g.*, Bernstein v. Menard, 557 F. Supp. 90 (E.D. Va. 1982); Poling v. Murphy, 872 F.2d 757 (6th Cir. 1989).

19. *Compare* Hayes v. Unified School Dist., 669 F. Supp. 1519 (D. Kan. 1987) and Cole v. Newton Special Municipal Separate School Dist., 676 F. Supp. 749 (S.D. Miss. 1987).

20. Dickens v. Johnson Cty. Bd. of Educ., 661 F. Supp. 155, 157 (E.D. Tenn. 1987).

21. 419 U.S. 565 (1975).

22. *E.g.*, Strickland v. Inlow, 519 F.2d 744 (8th Cir. 1975); Pervis v. La Marque Indep. School Dist., 466 F.2d 1054 (5th Cir. 1972); Dunn v. Tyler Indep. School Dist., 460 F.2d 137 (5th Cir. 1972).

23. *See* Craig v. Selma City School Bd, 801 F.Supp. 585 (S.D.Ala 1992); Grannis v. Ordean, 234 U.S. 385 (1914).

24. This would violate Section 504's prohibition on discrimination on the basis of handicap which states that "No qualified handicapped person shall, on the basis of handicap, be excluded from . . . or otherwise be subject to discrimination under any program or activity which receives or benefits from Federal financial assistance." 34 C.F.R. 104.4(a). The Office for Civil Rights in response to an inquiry in the area has stated: "This question assumes a direct relationship between the student's handicap and the conduct for which suspension is proposed. If a student were suspended under these circumstances, even though the conduct is characterized as extreme, certain regulatory provisions would be implicated. 34 C.F.R. 104.4(a) prohibits exclusion from participation on the basis of handicap." *Van Vleck*, 305 E.H.L.R. 28, 29 (OCR 1986).

25. S-1 v. Turlington, 635 F.2d 342 (5th Cir. 1981), *cert. denied*, 454 U.S. 1030 (1981); Doe v. Maher, 793 F.2d 1470 (9th Cir. 1986), *aff'd in part and mod. in part*; Honig v. Doe, 108 S. Ct. 592 (1988); School Bd. v. Malone, 762 F.2d 1210 (4th Cir. 1985); Kaelin v. Grubbs, 682 F.2d 595 (6th Cir. 1982).

26. *Malone*, 762 F.2d at 1217.

27. *See Turlington*, 635 F.2d 342; Doe v. Maher, 793 F.2d 1470 (9th Cir. 1986); Thomas v. Davidson Academy, 846 F. Supp. 611 (M.D. Tenn. 1994).

28. *Turlington*, 635 F.2d at 346.

29. *Maher*, 793, F.2d at 1480 n.8.

30. *Turlington*, 635 F.2d at 347. *See also* Kaelin v. Grubbs, 682 F.2d 595 (6th Cir. 1982); Doe v. Koger, 480 F. Supp. 225 (N.D. Ind. 1979).

31. Suspension of handicapped students, 16

E.H.L.R. 491 (OCR 1989). *See also* Bellamy, 213 E.H.L.R. 181 (OSEP 1988).

32. The provisions of IDEA consistently stress the need for parental input in decisions related to the student's educational program. See 20 U.S.C. 1400(c), 1401(19), 1412(7), 1415(b)(1)(A), (C), (D), (E), and 1415(b)(2). To ensure this, IDEA affords various procedural safeguards that guarantee parental input and the right to review of disputed decisions. These safeguards include the right to examine all relevant records pertaining to the identification evaluation, and educational placement of their child; prior written notice whenever the responsible educational agency proposes (or refuses) to change the child's placement or program; and opportunity to present complaints concerning any public education; and an opportunity for 'an impartial due process hearing' with respect to any such complaints. 20 U.S.C. 1415(b)(1), (2).

33. *See* Kristian M., Case No. 273, 507 E.H.L.R. 458 (S.E.A. Pa. 1986). If, however, it is determined that the question of nexus can be determined without parental input, the notice provisions would only come into play when a decision had been made that the behavior was disability related and a consequence for that behavior was being determined through the IEP process or if the proposed discipline constituted a change in place under IDEA.

34. *See* Dysart Unified School Dist., 311 E.H.L.R. 32 (EHA Compliance Review 1983).

35. *See* Tulsa County Area Voc. and Tech. School, 352 E.H.L.R. 387 (OCR Complaint 1987).

36. *Van Vleck,* 305 E.H.L.R. 28, 29 (OCR 1986).

37. Cole v. Greenfield-Central Community Schools, 657 F. Supp. 56 (S.D. ind. 1986).

38. Nash County School Dist., 352 E.H.L.R. 37 (OCR Complaint 1985); Battle Creek Public Schools, 16 E.H.L.R. 665 (OCR 1990).

39. *Accord*, Kaelin v. Grubbs, 682 F.2d 595 (6th Cir. 1982); S-1 v. Turlington, 635 F.2d 342 (5th Cir. 1981), *cert. denied*, 454 U.S. 1030 (1981); Doe v. Koger, 480 F. Supp. 225 (N.D. Ind. 1979); Stuart v. Nappi, 443 F. Supp. 1235 (D. Conn. 1978); OSEP Policy Letter, 211 E.H.L.R. 437 (1987).

40. 108 S. Ct. at 605 n.8.

41. Smith, 18 I.D.E.L.R. 685 (OSERS, 1992); Symkowick, 17 E.H.L.R. 469 (OSERS 1991).

42. 108 S. Ct. 592 (1988).

43. O.S.E.P. Memorandum, 13 E.H.L.R. 372 (1987).

44. OCR Memorandum, 14 E.H.L.R. 306 (1988).

45. *Id.*

46. 765 F.2d 535 (5th Cir. 1985).

47. *Id.* at 538.

48. *See* Victoria L. by Carol A. v. District School Bd., 741 F.2d 369 (11th Cir. 1984); *contra* Kaelin v. Grubbs, 682 F.2d 595 (6th Cir. 1982).

49. 20 U.S.C. 1425(e)(3).

50. 108 S. Ct. at 604 (citation omitted).

51. *Id.* at 605.

52. *Id.*

53. *Id.*

54. *Id.* at 606; Township High School v. Kurtz-Imig, 16 E.H.L.R. 17 (N.D. Ill. 1989).

55. *Id.*

56. H.R. 6 103rd Congress, Second Session, Act 16, 1994. Technically, this provision was passed as an amendment to the reauthorization of the Elementary and Secondary Education Act. As such, its application is limited to one year. However, it is anticipated that Congress will make this a permanent provision of IDEA when IDEA is considered for reauthorization during the next congressional term.

CHAPTER 6

OTHER JUVENILE ISSUES

ABUSED AND NEGLECTED CHILDREN

Introduction

Reports of child abuse and neglect, particularly sexual abuse, have increased significantly over the past few years. In 1990, there were more than 2.5 million reports of child abuse—an increase of more than 30 percent since 1985 and 100 percent since 1980.[1] The rise may be due, in part, to national media attention, school programs that raise students' awareness about their "right to be safe," and the clarification and expansion of child abuse and neglect reporting requirements. No one yet knows how many additional cases remain unreported. Abuse and neglect have serious long-term consequences for its victims. Abused children are more likely than other children to be developmentally delayed and emotionally disturbed. As adults they have a higher probability of becoming abusive parents, psychiatric patients, and criminals.[2] Early detection and reporting of child abuse and neglect by educators can help eliminate its long-term consequences and help prevent the continuing cycle of abuse.

Alfred Alschuler, a clinical psychologist and professor of education at the University of Massachusetts, works with adult victims of abuse and neglect. He stated, "[H]elping to stop child abuse and neglect simultaneously contains the long term human costs, like spotting and stopping a contagious disease before it becomes an epidemic."[3]

In 1974, the federal Child Abuse Prevention and Treatment Act was enacted.[4] This statute provides a model legislative response for the reporting of child abuse and neglect. Since then, all 50 states have enacted similar child abuse protection statutes. These statutes generally contain provisions mandating the reporting of suspected child abuse by those who work with children, encouraging reporting by others, providing good-faith immunity to both groups of reporters, and providing penalties for the failure of mandatory reporters to report.

Definitions

Every state statute sets out the definition for abuse and neglect; however, there is a good deal of consistency in definitions.[5] *Abuse* is generally seen as an affirmative act—an injury that is inflicted intentionally. Abuse can include bodily violation (e.g., beating, burning, cutting, exposure), sexual molestation, and mental injury (e.g., sleep deprivation, berating, and sensory overload or deprivation). *Neglect,* on the other hand, is an omission, such as a caregiver's failure to provide for a child when he or she is otherwise able to do so. It is important to remember that neglect is also intentional. It is intentionally depriving a child of some necessary item. Thus, failure to provide sufficient food and shelter due to poverty is not neglect; but failure to provide sufficient food and shelter when there are adequate funds for them is neglect. It includes the failure to: (1) meet nutritional needs; (2) meet needs of physical shelter from the elements and physical harm from the environment within the control of the parent; (3) protect the child from dangers in the environment within the control of the parent; (4) meet health needs, including specific medical care; (5) meet emotional needs; (6) meet intellectual needs; or (7) meet needs of moral guidance and supervision. One important distinction between abuse and neglect is that neglect occurs at the hands of the child's caregiver, whereas abuse can be inflicted by anyone.

Detection

The written definition of child abuse and neglect is simple. However, making a determination of possible abuse in actuality is very difficult. Table 6.1 provides a list of possible indicators of abuse and neglect. Many resources are available to assist school districts in educating school personnel to recognize signs of physical abuse, physical neglect, emotional maltreatment, and sexual abuse. Literature is available from many organizations, such as the National Committee for Prevention of Child Abuse in Chicago, Illinois; the National School Board Association in Alexandria, Virginia; and the National Education Association in Washington, DC.

Lists containing indicators of abuse in children and families can be obtained from both national and local organizations. Generally, see American Prosecutors Research Institute National Center for Prosecution of Child Abuse, Investigation and Prosecution of Child Abuse (1987); Diane D. Broadhurst, U.S. Dept. of Health, Education, and Welfare, Pub. No. 79-30172; and the Educator's Role in the Prevention and Treatment of Child Abuse and Neglect (1979) (government manual for educators on identification, treatment, and prevention of child abuse and neglect.)

One must remember that often one indicator alone will not create a suspicion; but this is not always true. There are some injuries that may, by themselves, give rise to a suspicion of abuse due to their pattern, intensity, or location. One must also remember that the symptoms of abuse

and neglect manifest themselves differently for children of different ages.

Mandatory Reporting

An integral part of all of the child protection statutes is the mandated reporting by certain professionals of suspected child abuse or neglect. Mandatory reporters are basically those people who have access to children during the course of their professional duties. All states require teachers and other school officials who deal directly with children to report suspected child abuse. Although educators do not have the medical expertise to make an actual diagnosis of abuse or neglect, they can generally surmise the cause of unexplained or unusual injuries. They see children on a day-to-day basis and are more likely to recognize incongruencies in a child's appearance or behavior.

In addition to mandatory reporters, most state protection statutes encourage the reporting of child abuse by anyone who knows or has reasonable cause to suspect that a child is being abused or neglected. Nearly half of all child abuse reports come from this group of permissive reporters. See Figure 6.1.

Source of Report

The states are relatively consistent in the degree of certainty an educator, or other mandatory reporter, must have before he or she is required to report. The statutory message is virtually the same—mandatory reporters are required to report a situation when they believe or have a reasonable suspicion that a child has been abused or neglected. A teacher may wish to confer with other professionals before reporting suspected child abuse to the appropriate authorities. A second opinion may provide the potential reporter with additional information supporting a reasonable suspicion that abuse or neglect is occurring. However, it is the initial

TABLE 6.1 Physical and Behavioral Indicators of Child Abuse and Neglect[1]

TYPE OF CHILD ABUSE/NEGLECT	PHYSICAL INDICATORS	BEHAVIORAL INDICATORS
Physical Abuse	Unexplained bruises and welts: —on face, lips, mouth —on torso, back, buttocks, thighs —in various stages of healing —clustered, forming regular patterns —reflecting shape of article used to inflict (electric cord, belt buckle) —on several different surface areas —regularly appear after absence, weekend, or vacation	Wary of adult contacts Apprehensive when other children cry Behavioral extremes: —aggressiveness, or —withdrawal Frightened of adults Afraid to go home
	Unexplained burns: —cigar, cigarette burns, especially on soles, palms, back, or buttocks —immersion burns (sock-like, glove-like, doughnut shaped on buttocks or genitalia) —patterned like electric burner, iron, etc. —rope burns on arms, legs, neck, or torso	Reports injury by adults
	Unexplained fractures: —to skull, nose, facial structure —in various stages of healing —multiple or spiral fractures	
	Unexplained lacerations or abrasions: —to mouth, lips, gums, eyes —to external genitalia	
Physical Neglect	Consistent hunger, poor hygiene, inappropriate dress Consistent lack of supervision, especially in dangerous activities or long periods Unattended physical problems or medical needs Abandonment	Begging, stealing food Extended stays at school (early arrival and late departure) Constant fatigue, listlessness, or falling asleep in class Alcohol or drug abuse Delinquency (e.g., thefts, truancy) States there is no caretaker

(continued)

TABLE 6.1 continued

TYPE OF CHILD ABUSE/NEGLECT	PHYSICAL INDICATORS	BEHAVIORAL INDICATORS
Sexual Abuse	Difficulty in walking or sitting	Unwilling to change for gym or participate in physical education class
	Torn, stained, or bloody underclothing	
	Pain or itching in genital area	Withdrawal, fantasy, or infantile behavior
	Bruises or bleeding in external genitalia, vaginal, or anal areas	Bizarre, sophisticated, or unusual sexual behavior or knowledge
	Venereal disease, especially in preteens	
	Pregnancy	Poor peer relationships
		Delinquent or run-away
		Reports sexual assault by adult
Emotional Maltreatment	Speech disorders	Habit disorders (sucking, biting, rocking, etc.)
	Lags in physical development	Conduct disorders (antisocial, destructive, etc.)
	Failure to thrive	Neurotic traits (sleep disorders, inhibition of play)
		Psychoneurotic reactions (hysteria, obsession, compulsion, phobias, hypochondria)
		Behavior extremes: —compliant, passive —aggressive, demanding
		Overly adaptive behavior: —inappropriately adult —inappropriately infant
		Developmental lags (mental, emotional)
		Attempted suicide

Source: Adapted from Diane D. Broadhurst, *The Educator's Role in the Prevention and Treatment of Child Abuse and Neglect*, National Center on Child Abuse and Neglect, U.S. Department of Health, Education and Welfare, Publ. No. 79-30172 (1979).

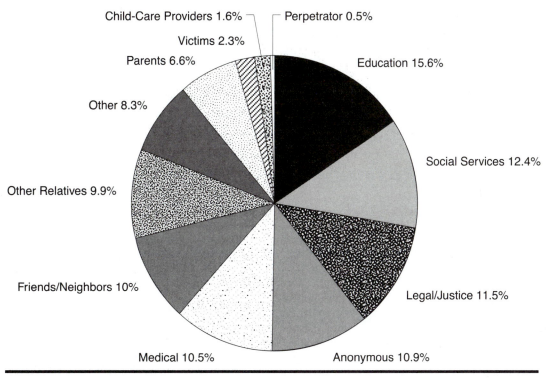

Child-Care Providers 1.6%
Perpetrator 0.5%
Victims 2.3%
Education 15.6%
Parents 6.6%
Other 8.3%
Social Services 12.4%
Other Relatives 9.9%
Friends/Neighbors 10%
Legal/Justice 11.5%
Medical 10.5%
Anonymous 10.9%

FIGURE 6.1 Source of Report

Source: Data taken from the National Center on Child Abuse and Neglect. *National Child Abuse and Neglect Data System: Working Paper 2—1991 Summary Data Component.* Washington, DC: U.S. Government Printing Office, 1993.

reporter who must follow through, and ensure a report is made. He or she is the responsible party.

Educators want to feel confident that a report is legitimate. The laws that mandate reporting generally require a report when there is "suspicion" or "reason to believe." However, there is no law that requires the reporter to have *proof* that child abuse has occurred. Waiting for proof may involve grave risk to the child because proof may be long in coming. A report of suspected child abuse and neglect states that a child *may* be an abused child. Proof is to be left to the proper authorities who are specially trained in handling these sensitive situations.

One of the common features of all of the state child protection statutes is the immunity from

civil or criminal liability granted to those reporters who report in good faith.[6] This provision is intended to combat the fear of liability by protecting reporters from possible legal repercussions for reporting. The statutes grant immunity from all acts required or permitted in the reporting process, including evidence gathering such as taking photographs or interviewing the child. In *Landstrom v. Illinois Department of Children and Family Services*,[7] the school's principal, a social worker, a nurse, and a teacher interviewed two children suspected of being abused without contacting the parents. In fact, they interviewed one of the children a second time even after the parents made their objections known. The parents filed a Section 1983 action and accused the school personnel of violating the student's right to be free from unreasonable questioning. The court decided that in this case, the school and its employees were protected from the Section 1983 claim through qualified immunity. Furthermore, a school district was not held liable for defamation based solely upon a school official's report of suspected child abuse.[8]

Penalties for Failure to Report

To compel compliance with the reporting statutes, most statutes carry penalties for failure to report. Although some states provide for both civil and criminal penalties, most provide for only criminal sanctions, and a minority provide for only civil penalties. Most states have criminal sanctions available for an educator's failure to report suspected child abuse.[9] For example, 7 state statutes provide for the imposition of fines for failure to report, 18 states provide for fines or imprisonment, and 22 states provide for the standard prescribed penalties for misdemeanors (typically up to a $1,000 fine and up to one year in jail). In addition, a school district may pursue the matter through disciplinary proceedings of its own. A district can discipline an employee for failure to follow its own policies regarding the reporting of suspected abuse and neglect, just as it can discipline for failure to follow any district regulation.[10]

A civil suit may be filed on behalf of the child for damages caused by the failure to report. A type of civil liability can be imposed on a mandatory reporter who failed to report suspected child abuse or neglect through a simple negligence action.[11] There, it is claimed that the mandatory reporter's failure to report was a cause of the child's subsequent injuries.

District Liability

Finally, a district could be subject to liability in a civil rights action for abuse that occurred at the hands of a school employee when the district should have known of the abuse and failed to act. Section 1983 creates a type of tort liability for those acting on behalf of the state.[12] Under Section 1983, liability may be applied to school districts and public school officials, individually, when they violate constitutional or federal statutory rights of students.[13] Liability may be imposed if a district's supervisory officials "knew or should have known" that (1) abuse was taking place within a school, yet they failed to take remedial action, or (2) training or supervision was grossly inadequate and represented deliberate indifference or tacit authorization of the offensive acts.[14]

In *DeShaney v. Winnebago County Department of Social Service,*[15] the Supreme Court held that the Department of Social Services could not be held liable in a civil rights action for failing to protect a child from parental abuse. The reason was that the department had not caused the child to be in the home of the parent; it had only failed to remove the child from the abusive home.[16] However, a school has a special obligation to protect its students, particularly from its own employees.[17] Thus, courts have found Section 1983 liability for a school district for failure to protect students from abuse.

In 1988, the U.S. Department of Education reported that one million school children were hit by teachers, coaches, or principals each year.[18] Litigation has centered on situations where teachers or administrators have applied unreasonable or excessive use of force, as well as situations when corporal punishment was used in states or districts where it is prohibited.[19] Injuries due to excessive corporal punishment are not confined to injured buttocks. Excessive corporal punishment has also resulted in "a cerebral concussion and sprained neck, impaired hearing, a perforated eardrum, a sprained arm and facial abrasions, chipped teeth, and fractures of various bones throughout the body."[20] Paddles, straps, straight pins, and lye rinses have been used to reestablish discipline.[21]

Mistreatment of children in schools may take forms in addition to excessive corporal punishment. There is increasing evidence that sexual abuse is occurring in the schools.[22] Child abuse in schools also extends into the emotional and mental realms.[23] It is critical that educators are alert for abusive situations in their own schools and are prepared to report them.

IN THE INTEREST OF B.B.
440 N.W. 2d 594 (Iowa 1989)

LAVORATO, Justice.

At issue here is whether a mildly mentally retarded child should be adjudged a child in need of assistance [CHINA] within the meaning of Iowa Code chapter 232 because of his parents' refusal to send him to school. The juvenile court referee dismissed a CHINA petition, holding that the child was not in need of assistance and that the compulsory education statutes provided the State's only remedy. . . . We reverse and remand with directions.

Barry, the child, is an eleven-year-old . . . who lives with his family. . . .

In 1983 Barry was enrolled in kindergarten in the Tama school district. During the school year, he attended classes 154 days and was absent twenty-six days. School officials recommended that he be placed in special education classes the following year because his progress was unsatisfactory in all categories. Barry's parents objected, and he did not attend school during the 1984–85 school year.

****

Barry reached the age of compulsory school attendance the following year. He was scheduled to return to school for special education tutoring. He, however, attended classes only fifty-one days and was absent 129 days.

During the 1986–87 school year, Barry attended classes nine and one-half days and was absent 170 days. A CHINA petition was filed in January 1988. During the first half of the 1987–88 school year, before the petition was filed, Barry had only attended school eighteen and one-half days and was absent sixty-four and one-half days.

Through these long periods of absenteeism, Anna [Barry's mother] gave Barry's illnesses as the reason for keeping him home. . . . The record, however, is barren of any medical evidence that Barry's health would support his virtual absence from school for nearly three years, . . . Moreover, the parents have not sought a health exemption from compulsory school attendance. . . .

****

Medical and educational professionals who have evaluated Barry agree that he is mildly to moderately mentally retarded but educable. The school psychologist who observed the in-home education during 1984–85 testified that while Anna was a conscientious teacher, Barry had made no educational progress. The psychologist opined that Barry was not receiving enough lesson time and that he was suffering educational, social, and emotional harm by being withheld from school. Simply put, the psychologist believed that Barry needs the skills he would gain by being with other children. The psychologist also believed that Barry was reaching the age when it would be crucial for him to attend school.

****

Anna was convicted in 1987 of violating Iowa's Compulsory Education Act for her refusal to send Barry to school. . . . She received a suspended sentence and was placed on probation on the condition that she give assurances that Barry would attend school regularly.

In January 1988, at about the same time the CHINA petition was filed, the State prosecuted both parents for similar violations. They were found guilty, fined, and given jail time. Part of their jail time was suspended on the condition that Barry would be enrolled in and attend an accredited school. . . .

In alleging that Barry is a child in need of assistance, the State relied on three alternative definitions of a child in need of assistance. Those definitions are found in Iowa Code section 232.2(6) and include children who are (1) physically abused or neglected, (2) likely to suffer harmful effects from the parents' failure to exercise reasonable care in supervising them, and (3) in need of treatment for mental or emotional conditions and whose parents do not or cannot provide the needed treatment. . . .

****

In *In re Devone*, 86 N.C. App. 57, 356 S.E.2d 389 (1987), the facts of which are strikingly similar to the facts here, the court was reviewing a juvenile court determination that a moderately mentally retarded child was neglected and dependent within the meaning of the North Carolina juvenile code. The basis of the juvenile court's determination was the parent's insistence on attempting to teach the child at home, thus denying the child's right to attend special education classes that were critical to his development and welfare.

The North Carolina juvenile code defines "neglected juvenile" as one who does not receive proper care, supervision, or discipline from his parents. N.C.G.S. § 7A-517(21). It defines a "dependent juvenile" as one who is in need of assistance and whose parent is unable to provide for his care or supervision. N.C.G.S. § 7A-517(13).

****

"Neglect" under the North Carolina juvenile code, like "dependent," does include lack of supervision—the very ground the State relies on here in seeking to establish that Barry is a child in need of assistance. Thus, the rationale put forth by the *Devone* court to support its finding of neglect and dependence has pertinent application to our determination here of lack of supervision. Affirming their

trial court's finding that the juvenile was neglected and dependent, the *Devone* court said:

> It is fundamental that a child who receives proper care and supervision in modern times is provided a basic education. A child does not receive "proper care" and lives in an "environment injurious to his welfare" when he is deliberately refused this education, and he is "neglected" within the meaning of [the North Carolina juvenile code].

****

Devone, *86 N.C. App. at 60, 356 S.E.2d at 390-91 (citation omitted).*

Likewise, Barry, although of limited intelligence, is entitled to educational opportunities. . . .

Anna's blind devotion to the child has clouded her thinking. She is simply irrational when it comes to Barry's being in school. She has tried to teach him at home, but to date he has made little progress. In fact, the experts agree that Barry's poor school attendance has adversely affected his educational, social, and emotional development.

It is now time for Anna to give school a chance. There, Barry has at least a chance to acquire the social and self-help skills he so desperately needs just to survive.

For all of these reasons, we think the State has by clear and convincing evidence established that Barry is a child in need of assistance because of his parents' failure to exercise a reasonable degree of care in supervising him. The juvenile court referee and the district court erred in concluding otherwise.

****

REVERSED AND REMANDED WITH DIRECTIONS.

(Footnotes omitted.)

— — — —

STONEKING v. BRADFORD AREA SCHOOL DISTRICT
882 F.2d 720 (Third Circuit 1989)

SLOVITER, Circuit Judge.

I.

This case is before us on remand from the United States Supreme Court which vacated our judgment and remanded for further consideration in light of *DeShaney v. Winnebago County Department of Social Services*, [489] U.S. [189], 109 S. Ct. 998, 103 L. Ed. 2d 249 (1989). . . .

Kathleen Stoneking filed suit under 42 U.S.C. § 1983 against the Bradford Area School District, Frederick Smith, the principal of the Bradford Area High School, Richard Miller, the assistant principal, and Frederick Shuey, the superintendent of the School District. Each of the individual defendants was sued in both his individual and official capacity. . . .

Stoneking's complaint alleged that Edward Wright . . . who was the Band Director at Bradford High, used physical force, threats of reprisal, intimidation and coercion to sexually abuse and harass her and to force her to engage in various sexual acts beginning October 1980, when she was a high school student, and continuing through Stoneking's sophomore, junior and senior years until her graduation in 1983 and thereafter until 1985. Defendants concede that some of these acts occurred in the band room at the high school and on trips for band functions, as well as in Wright's car and in his house while Stoneking babysat or after he gave her a music lesson. Wright was ultimately prosecuted for various sex-related crimes and pled guilty.

Stoneking averred that in 1979, before Wright's actions toward her, another female member of the band informed Smith that Wright had attempted to rape or sexually assault her; that Smith, in his capacity as principal, maintained a personal file on Wright which contained reports of complaints of sexual misconduct by female students in the band program; that Smith announced to Wright a "policy" with respect to his contact with female students under which he was to have no further "one on one" contacts with female band members; that Smith, Miller and Shuey "failed to take any action to protect the health, safety and welfare of the female student body" Stoneking, App. at 10; and that Miller and Shuey were also on notice of the complaints of sexual misconduct by Wright and of the policy adopted by Smith under which Wright was to have no one-on-one contact with female band members, or, if Shuey was not aware, it was because of "the defective and deficient policies and customs" of the School District, App. at 11; and that Wright threatened his victims that if they reported his actions they would incur "loss of parental support, the esteem of friends and the dissolution of the school band which had become . . . a significant institution to the School District and the community in general,". . .

****

In *DeShaney*, the [Supreme] Court held that a minor could not maintain an action against Winnebago County, its Department of Social Services, and various individual employees of the Department for injuries he received at the hands of his father, even though the county caseworker returned DeShaney to the father's custody and allegedly knew or should have known of the risk of violence to him at his father's hands. The Court's analysis was straightforward: it held that "a State's failure to protect an individual against private violence simply does not constitute a violation of the Due Process Clause." 109 S. Ct. at 1004. . . .

The Court held that because there was no constitutional duty on the state to provide its citizens with particular protective services, "the State cannot be held liable under the [Due Process] Clause for injuries that could have been averted had it chosen to provide them." 109 S. Ct. 1004 (footnote omitted). It distinguished DeShaney's situation from those "limited circumstances [in which] the Constitution imposes upon the State affirmative duties of care and protection with respect to particular individuals." 109 S. Ct. at 1004-05. . . .

****

II.

The principal distinction between DeShaney's situation and that of Stoneking is that DeShaney's injuries resulted at the hands of a private actor, whereas Stoneking's resulted from the actions of a state employee. The significance of the status of the perpetrator as a private actor rather than as a state official is referred to on numerous occasions in the *DeShaney* opinion. Not only is the Court's statement of the holding in terms of the identity of the actor ("a State's failure to protect an individual against private violence simply does not constitute a violation of the Due Process Clause," 109 S.Ct. at 1004), but the analytic steps taken by the Court to reach that holding continuously take note of the status of the person responsible for the injuries. See, e.g., "nothing in the language of the Due Process Clause itself requires the state to protect the life, liberty and property of its citizens against invasion by private actors;" the Due Process Clause "forbids the State itself to deprive individuals of life, liberty or property without 'due process of law,' but its language cannot fairly be extended to impose an affirmative obligation on the State to insure that those interests do not come to harm through other means;" the purpose of the Due Process Clause "was to protect the people from the

State, not to insure that the State protected them from each other." 109 S. Ct. at 1003.

Unlike DeShaney's father, who was referred to throughout the *DeShaney* opinion as a private third party, Wright was a school district employee subject to defendants' immediate control. In fact, many of Wright's interactions with Stoneking occurred in the course of his performance of his official responsibilities, such as during school-sponsored events and trips, and sometimes on school property.

****

[S]he argues defendants are liable because of their own actions in adopting and maintaining a practice, custom or policy of reckless indifference to instances of known or suspected sexual abuse of students by teachers, in concealing complaints of abuse, and in discouraging students' complaints about such conduct. She argues that these practices, customs or polices created a climate which, at a minimum, facilitated sexual abuse of students by teachers in general, and that there was a causal relationship between these practices, customs or policies and the repeated sexual assaults against her by Wright. Thus, this is not respondeat superior in another guise, but an assertion of liability against the individual defendants based on theories recognized in a line of Supreme Court cases.

****

A teacher's sexual molestation of a student is an intrusion of the schoolchild's bodily integrity not substantively different for constitutional purposes from corporal punishment by teachers. Reasonable officials would have understood the "contours" of a student's right to bodily integrity, under the Due Process Clause, to encompass a student's right to be free from sexual assaults by his or her teachers. . . .

****

We turn then from the issue of the clearly established constitutional right of Stoneking to be free from sexual abuse by school staff to an inquiry into the objective reasonableness of defendants' conduct from late 1980 through at least 1983 when Stoneking was molested by Wright while still a student. . . .

According to the deposition testimony of Theresa Rodgers, her social studies teacher Richard DeMarte sexually accosted her in late 1977 or early 1978. . . . She immediately reported the incident to Miller and Smith. They responded by warning her that it would be her word against the teacher's and that she should not tell her parents. . . .

According to the deposition testimony of Judith Grove Sowers, she was sexually assaulted by Wright in 1979 and reported the incident to Miller and Smith. She claims that Smith told her "it was my [Sowers'] fault. That's why he wanted to clear up the rumors because he wanted the band to get back on their feet again. . . . He had told me that if the rumors were true . . . I could find myself in front of a jury, in front of a judge, telling exactly what happened, that being that I had been drinking [and that I was] at his house voluntarily . . . I wouldn't look very good is what he said.". . . .

Both Sowers and her father testified that she was presented with the option of recanting her story in front of the band or withdrawing from all band activities. Sowers stated that the band was assembled and she was called before it for this purpose, but fled from the room in tears.

****

Smith's handwritten notes refer to three other incidents in 1981–1982 with respect to sexual harassment by DeMarte, the social studies teacher. . . .

Two months later, two female students reported to Miller that another student, Lorie Lamberson, was crying in the restroom and when she emerged she told Smith and Miller that she had gone to DeMarte's room with a friend to get a make-up assignment, that he sent her friend away, blindfolded her to demonstrate the sense of touch, and after doing so was down on his hands and knees looking up her dress. . . .

. . . . Again, the only action taken was to arrange that the student be scheduled for a different class . . . and no reprimand or other note was placed in DeMarte's file.

The next year, another parent called to complain about DeMarte's relationship with a student because DeMarte had asked the student to sit on his lap at a Halloween party on a social occasion, . . . and again no written warning was placed in DeMarte's file. . . .

In sum, there is evidence in the record that between 1978 and 1982 Smith and Miller received at least five complaints about sexual assaults of female students by teachers and staff members; that Shuey was told about some of these complaints; that Smith recorded these and other allegations in a secret file at home rather than in the teachers' personnel files, which a jury could view as active concealment; that the defendants gave such teachers excellent performance evaluations, which a jury could view as communication by the defendants to the teachers that the conduct of which they were accused would not be considered to reflect negatively on them; and that Smith and Miller discouraged and/or intimidated students and parents from pursuing complaints, on one occasion by forcing a student to publicly recant her allegation.

****

In sum, although the mere failure of supervisory officials to act or investigate cannot be the basis of liability, . . . by at least 1981 . . . it was clearly established law that such officials may not with impunity maintain a custom, practice or usage that communicated condonation or authorization of assaultive behavior.

If the testimony of the various complainants is believed, Smith and Miller discouraged and minimized reports of sexual misconduct by teachers. A jury could construe such actions, as plaintiff's expert did, as "encourag[ing] a climate to flourish where innocent girls were victimized.". . .

****

For the foregoing reasons, we conclude that the district court did not err in denying the motion for summary judgment of defendants Smith and Miller on grounds of qualified immunity, but we conclude that Shuey's motion should have been granted.

****

(Footnotes omitted.)

— — — —

D.R. v. MIDDLE BUCKS AREA VOCATIONAL TECHNICAL SCHOOL
972 F.2d 1364 (Third Circuit 1992)

SEITZ, Circuit Judge.

Plaintiffs . . . appeal the decision and order of the district court dismissing the amended complaints against Middle Bucks Area Vocational Technical School ("Middle Bucks"), Penn Ridge School District ("Penn Ridge"), Bucks County Intermediate Unit No. 22 ("Unit No. 22"), and individually named teachers and officials ("school defendants"). Claims were also asserted against seven male students. Only two students, James Gallagher and Marc Ratcliffe, appeared, but because all seven were allegedly involved in the wrongful conduct we shall include all of them in referring to "student defendants.". . .

Plaintiffs were two female students in a graphic arts class at Middle Bucks. They allege that while attending the arts class during the 1989–90 school year, several male students in the same class physically, verbally and sexually molested them. This conduct took place primarily in the unisex bathroom and a darkroom, both of which were part of the graphic arts classroom.

Plaintiff, D.R., avers that the student defendants grabbed her and either forced or carried her into the bathroom or darkroom on a regular basis and physically abused her. She asserts that such conduct took place on an average of two to four times per week from January to May of 1990. Plaintiff, L.H., claims

that some of the student defendants molested her two to three times per week from December 1989 to May of 1990. Plaintiffs allege that the sexual molestation consisted of offensive touching of their breasts and genitalia, sodomization and forced acts of fellatio. The student defendants also allegedly forced plaintiffs to watch similar acts performed on other students.

****

Plaintiff, L.H., avers that in December of 1988, she told defendant Bazzel, Assistant Director of Middle Bucks, that one student defendant was trying to force her into the bathroom for the purpose of engaging in sexual conduct. She alleges that Bazzel did not take action to correct the situation. Plaintiffs also allege that other individual school defendants had knowledge of the severe non-sexual misconduct occurring in the classroom.

Based on the foregoing allegation, the amended complaints assert violations of plaintiffs' civil rights by the school and student defendants under 42 U.S.C. §§ 1983 and 1985(3) as well as Pennsylvania law.

****

III. DISCUSSION

Plaintiffs' amended complaints allege that the school defendants had knowledge of the physical, verbal and sexual abuse committed by the student defendants and maintained a policy of laxity toward such conduct. . . .

The school defendants respond that the district court's dismissal can be affirmed by this court without reaching the issue of the sufficiency of the factual allegations as to their knowledge of the conduct of the student defendants. They assert that . . . no special relationship of constitutional proportions existed between plaintiffs and the school defendants. Thus, they say that this § 1983 action is not maintainable. We turn to that important and complex issue in this most wrenching factual setting.

****

Generally, the first issue in a § 1983 case is whether a plaintiff sufficiently alleges a deprivation of any right secured by the constitution. . . .

Plaintiffs state that they have a liberty interest in their personal bodily integrity protected by the Fourteenth Amendment as recognized in *Ingraham v. Wright*, 430 U.S. 651, 673-74, 97 S. Ct. 1401, 1413-14, 51 L. Ed. 2d 711 (1977), and *Youngberg v. Romeo*, 457 U.S. 307, 315, 102 S. Ct. 2452, 2457, 73 L. Ed. 2d 28 (1982). Defendants do not argue otherwise. In order to demonstrate a violation of their constitutional rights plaintiffs' amended complaints essentially assert four theories of liability. The first is based upon the finding of the existence of a special relationship between plaintiffs and the school defendants during the school day. Such relationship, they assert, gave rise to an affirmative constitutional duty on the part of state officials to protect students such as these plaintiffs from serious harm. Second, plaintiffs contend that the school defendants are liable for creating a danger that resulted in a violation of plaintiffs' constitutional rights under the Fourteenth Amendment. Third, they assert that the school defendants are responsible for the existence of a policy, custom or practice that permitted injuries to the plaintiffs in violation of their constitutional rights. Fourth, plaintiffs assert that defendants conspired to deprive them of certain constitutional rights. We will deal with each theory in turn.

A. Special Relationship Custody

We commence our analysis by reiterating the well-established principle that the Due Process Clause does not impose an affirmative duty upon the state to protect its citizens. Rather, it serves as a limitation on the state's power to act. *DeShaney v. Winnebago County Dept. of Social Services*, 489 U.S. 189, 195, 109 S. Ct. 998, 1002, 103 L. Ed. 2d 249 (1989); . . . However, when the state enters into a special relationship with a particular citizen, it may be held liable for failing to protect him or her from the private actions of third parties. . . . This liability attaches under § 1983 when the state fails, under sufficiently culpable circumstances, to protect the health and safety of the citizen to whom it owes an affirmative duty. . . .

We must decide at the outset whether the school defendants had such a special relationship with the plaintiffs during school hours that they owed plaintiffs a constitutional duty to protect them from the misconduct of the student defendants. Plaintiffs argue that one way the state can enter into a duty-producing relationship under this theory is by restraining a citizen's freedom to act on his or her own behalf. . . .

In *DeShaney v. Winnebago County Dept. of Social Services*, 489 U.S. 189, 109 S. Ct. 998, 103 L. Ed. 2d 249 (1989), the Court declined to impose a constitutional duty upon a state to protect the life, liberty or property of a citizen from deprivations by private actors absent the existence of a special relationship. . . .

. . . . The Court noted that it first recognized such an exception in *Estelle v. Gamble*, 429 U.S. 97, 97 S. Ct. 285, 50 L. Ed. 2d 251 (1976). The Court in *Estelle* held that the state had an affirmative duty to provide adequate medical care for prisoners since incarceration prevents an inmate from caring for himself. . . .

The Court extended the *Estelle* exception from the Eighth Amendment context to a Fourteenth Amendment substantive due process claim in *Youngberg v. Romeo*, 457 U.S. 307, 102 S. Ct. 2452, 73 L. Ed. 2d 28 (1982). According to the *DeShaney* court, it there held that the Constitution imposed a duty upon the state to provide involuntarily committed mental patients "such services as are necessary to ensure their 'reasonable safety' from themselves and others." *DeShaney*, 489 U.S. at 199, 109 S. Ct. at 1005. . . .

****

. . . . Focusing primarily on physical restraint, the Court concluded that the *Estelle-Youngberg* exception was inapplicable to Joshua DeShaney's case since the conduct did not occur while the child was in the state's custody.

Although the Court decided that Joshua's situation did not amount to state custody, it left open the possibility that the duty owed by a state to prisoners and the institutionalized might also be owed to other categories of persons in custody by means of "similar restraints of personal liberty." *Id.* at 200, 109 S. Ct. at 1006. . . .

Plaintiffs assert that Pennsylvania's scheme of compulsory attendance and the school defendants' exercise of in loco parentis authority over their pupils so restrain school children's liberty that plaintiffs can be considered to have been in state "custody" during school hours for Fourteenth Amendment purposes. We consider this to be an open question in this circuit. . . .

Pennsylvania law mandates that every child of "compulsory school age" attend a day school. Pa. Stat. Ann. tit. 24 § 13-1327. Both children and their parents may be penalized for the child's truancy. . . .

****

[T]he question presented to us is whether compulsory attendance paired with the in loco parentis authority of the school defendants resulted in such an affirmative restraint of D.R.'s liberty by the state that she was left without reasonable means of self-protection and, indeed, whether the focus should be confined to the school day.

****

Here it is the parents who decide whether that education will take place in the home, in public or private schools or, as here, in a vocational-technical school. For some, the options may be limited for financial reasons. However, even when enrolled in public school parents retain the discretion to remove the child from classes as they see fit, . . .

Our view that parents remain the primary caretakers, despite their presence in school, is not affected by section 13-1317 which grants Pennsylvania teachers and principals in loco parentis status. Section 13-1317 operates in conjunction with section 5-510. Together they permit school boards to set reasonable regulations to govern students' conduct. Pa. Stat. Ann. tit. 24 § 5-510 (1962 & Supp. 1991). However, section 13-1317 invests in school officials "only such control as is reasonably necessary to prevent infractions of discipline and interference with the educational process." *Axtell v. Lapenna*, 323 F.

Supp. 1077 (W.D. Pa. 1971). As the Commonwealth court concluded, section 13-1317 "invests authority in public school teachers; it does not impose a duty upon them." *Pennsylvania State Education Association v. Department of Public Welfare*, 68 Pa. Comm. 279, 449 A.2d 89, 92 (1982) . . . .

By requiring D.R. to attend assigned classes at Middle Bucks as part of her high school educational program, and authorizing officials to engage in disciplinary control over the students, the school defendants did not restrict D.R.'s freedom to the extent that she was prevented from meeting her basic needs. . . . Thus, the school defendants' authority of D.R. during the school day cannot be said to create the type of physical custody necessary to bring it within the special relationship noted in *DeShaney*, particularly when their channels for outside communication were not totally closed.

The analogy between school children and prisoners or the involuntarily committed is weakened further by the fact that school children remain resident in their homes. Thus, they may turn to persons unrelated to the state for help on a daily basis. D.R.'s complaint alleges an ongoing series of assaults and abuse over a period of months. Although these acts allegedly took place during the school day, D.R. could, and did, leave the school building every day. The state did nothing to restrict her liberty after school hours and thus did not deny her meaningful access to sources of help.

****

B. State Created Danger

We come to plaintiffs' second basis for their constitutional claim, viz., that the school defendants created the danger that eventuated in a violation of plaintiffs' constitutional rights. Plaintiffs' counsel asserts that this claim exists apart from the claim based on the compulsory attendance law and applies to both plaintiffs. We now address that claim.

We understand plaintiffs' amended complaints, their briefs and the oral assertions of their counsel to advance a claim that the school defendants imperiled plaintiffs, or increased their risks of harm, by : (1) failing to report to the parents or other authorities the misconduct resulting in abuse to plaintiffs; (2) placing the class under the control of an inadequately trained and supervised student teacher; (3) failing to demand proper conduct of the student defendants;

and (4) failing to investigate and put a stop to the physical and sexual misconduct. Plaintiffs say that these acts or omissions "created a climate which facilitated sexual and physical abuse of students." L.H.'s Amended Complaint, App. at 58. Thus, they assert that having placed plaintiffs in the situation alleged, the school defendants were obligated to protect them from violations of their personal bodily integrity by other students who were also under such defendants' control.

The state-created danger theory, utilized to find a constitutional tort duty under § 1983 outside of a strictly custodial context, has been recognized by several courts of appeals. . . .

****

Plaintiffs also argue that school defendants increased their risks of harm by failing to report the abuse to plaintiffs' parents or other authorities. This argument stems in part from their assertion that defendants are under a state imposed duty to report abuse pursuant to 23 P.C.S.A. §§ 6311 and 6312 (1991). It is clear, however, that a violation of a state law duty, by itself, is insufficient to state a § 1983 claim. . . . Section 1983 liability arises only from a violation of federal statutory or constitutional rights under color of state law.

We readily acknowledge the apparent indefensible passivity of at least some school defendants under the circumstances. Accepting the allegations as true, viz., that one school defendant was advised of the misconduct and apparently did not investigate, they show nonfeasance but they do not rise to the level of a constitutional violation. As in *DeShaney*, "[t]he most that can be said of the state functionaries in this case is that they stood by and did nothing when suspicious circumstances dictated a more active role for them." *DeShaney*, 489 U.S. at 203, 109 S. Ct. at 1007; . . .

C. State Established Policy, Custom or Practice

We read plaintiffs' amended complaints to assert a third theory of constitutional liability that is viable even in the absence of a special relationship duty. . . . In *Stoneking II* [882 F.2d 720 (3rd Cir. 1989)], this court recognized that state defendants may be held liable for deliberately and recklessly establishing and maintaining a custom, practice or policy which caused harm to a student when a teacher sexually molested a student. . . . We emphasized that *DeShaney* was distinguishable because the abuse there "resulted at the hands of a private actor." *Id.* at 724.

We agree with the district court that this case lacks the linchpin of *Stoneking II*, namely, a violation by state actors. Sexual molestation committed by an agent of the state is readily distinguishable from the situation present here since the Due Process Clause itself imposes limitations on the state's conduct. Thus, § 1983 liability may not be predicated upon a *Stoneking II* type theory because private actors committed the underlying violative acts.

****

In view of our affirmance of the district court's dismissal of the constitutional claims, we will also affirm the dismissal of the pendent state law claims.

The order of the district court will be affirmed.

SLOVITER, Chief Judge, dissenting, with whom MANSMANN, SCIRICA and NYGAARD, Circuit Judges, join.

The majority opinion is based on the premise that the types of relationships which can give rise to a constitutional duty of a state to protect its school children from harm from third parties is mandated by the Supreme Court's opinion in *DeShaney v. Winnebago County Dept. of Social Servs.*, 489 U.S. 189, 109 S. Ct. 998, 103 L. Ed. 2d 249 (1989). . . .

DeShaney contains no language to support the majority's holding that the duty to protect can be triggered only by involuntary, round-the-clock, legal custody. Nothing in the opinion suggests that compulsory school attendance cannot qualify as the type of state restraint of personal liberty which gives rise to a duty to protect. As this court has previously recognized, "*DeShaney* requires that the state have imposed some kind of limitation on a victim's ability to act in his own interests." *Horton v. Flenory*, 889 F.2d 454, 458 (3d Cir. 1989). However, we continued, "[w]hile specifically referring to imprisonment and institutionalization . . . the [*DeShaney*] court acknowledges that other similar state-imposed restraints of personal liberty will trigger a state duty to prevent harm." *Id.* In fact, the *DeShaney* Court left open the possibility that the state might have a special relationship with a child it places in foster care, 489 U.S. at 201 n. 9, 109 S.Ct. at 1006 n. 9, even though it would no longer be the state that had the direct daily contact with the child.

****

I find inexplicable the majority's conclusion on the record before us that "the school defendants did not restrict D.R.'s freedom to the extent that she was prevented from meeting her basic needs.". . .

It is the majority's thesis that students, unlike prisoners, have meaningful access to sources of help. *See* Maj. op. at 1372. Yet the reluctance of children to disclose sexual abuse is generally acknowledged. *See Myers v. Morris*, 810 F.2d 1437, 1459-60 (8th Cir.) (noting "unique reluctance" of children to disclose sexual abuse), *cert. denied*, 484 U.S. 828, 108 S. Ct. 97, 98 L. Ed. 2d 58 (1987); *Doe v. New York City Dept. of Social Servs.*, 709 F.2d 782, 785 (2d Cir.) (doctor testified that great majority of abused children deny abuse), *cert. denied*, 464 U.S. 864, 104 S. Ct. 195, 78 L. Ed. 2d 171 (1983). Elementary school age children are unlikely to be sufficiently independent of the school authorities to complain promptly to their parents about constitutional deprivations occurring at school, and even older students may be in comparable situations. . . .

****

Thus, in this case I would find that the plaintiffs have sufficiently pled facts alleging a breach of the duty to protect triggered by the special relationship that arises between vulnerable school children and their public schools. Therefore, I need not decide the contours of the duty in all situations except to note that the extent of such a duty would necessarily be commensurate with the lesser custody exercised by schools over school children than prisons over inmates. Of course, there may be situations where the schools can show that the premises underlying the duty to protect were inapplicable to particular students who, because of their maturity or other circumstances, could have effectively secured help. Unless that is shown, then we owe immature school children attending public school who are seriously injured as a result of a policy of deliberate indifference to their danger no less a remedy than we are willing to provide to incarcerated criminals.

(Footnotes omitted.)

ADDITIONAL COMMENTARY

1. The following are the state statutes that parallel the federal Child Abuse Prevention and Treatment Act. Ala. Code §§ 26-14-1 to -13 (1986 & Supp. 1990); Alaska Stat. §§ 47.17.010-.070 (1990); Ariz. Rev. Stat. Ann. §§ 8-531 to -546.10 (West 1989 & Supp. 1991); Ark. Code Ann. §§ 12-12-501 to -517 (Michie 1987 & Supp. 1991); Cal. Penal Code §§ 11165-11174 (West 1982 & Supp. 1991); Colo. Rev. Stat. Ann. §§ 19-3-301 to -313 (West 1990 & Supp. 1991); Conn. Gen. Stat. Ann. §§ 17-38(a)-(g) (West 1986 & Supp. 1991) (transferred to Conn. Gen. Stat. Ann. §§ 17a-101 to -107); Del. Code Ann. tit. 16, §§ 901-909 (1983 & Supp. 1990); D.C. Code Ann. §§ 2-1257 to -1351, 6-2101 to -2127 (1988 & Supp. 1991); Fla. Stat. Ann. §§ 415.501-,514 (West 1986 & Supp. 1991); Ga. Code Ann. §§ 19-7-4 to -5 (1991); Haw. Rev. Stat. §§ 350-1 to -5 (1985 & Supp. 1990); Idaho Code §§ 16-1601 to -1631 (1979 & Supp. 1991); Ill. Ann. Stat. ch. 23, paras. 2051-2061.7 (Smith-Hurd 1988 & Sup. 1991); Ind. Code Ann. §§ 31-6-11-1 to -22 (Burns 1987 & Supp. 1991); Iowa Code Ann. §§ 232.67-77 (West 1985 & Supp. 1991); Kan. Stat. Ann. §§ 38-1501 (1986 & Supp. 1990); Ky. Rev. Stat. Ann. §§ 620-030 (Baldwin 1989); La. Rev. Stat. Ann. §§ 14:403 (West 1986 & Supp. 1991); Me. Rev. Stat. Ann. tit. 22, §§ 4001-4017 (West Supp. 1990); Md. Code Ann. Fam. Law §§ 5-701 to -715 (Supp. 1991); Mass. Gen. Laws Ann. ch. 119, §§ 51A-51G (West Supp. 1991); Mich. Comp. Laws Ann. §§ 722.621-.636 (West Supp. 1991); Minn. Stat. Ann. § 626.556 (West Supp. 1991); Miss. Code Ann. §§ 43-21-353, 43-23-9 1972 & Supp. 1991); Mo. Ann. Stat. §§ 210.110-.165 (Vernon 1983 & Supp. 1991); Mont. Code Ann. §§ 41-3-101 to 407 (1991); Neb. Rev. Stat. §§ 28-710 to -727 (1988 & Supp. 1990); Nev. Rev. Stat. Ann. §§ 432B.010-.255 (Michie 1986 & Supp. 1989); N.H. Rev. Stat. Ann. §§ 169-C:29-:40 (1990 & Supp. 1991); N.J. Stat. Ann. §§ 9:6-8.10-.20 (West 1976 & Supp. 1991); N.M. Stat. Ann. §§ 32-1-15 to 16 (Michie 1989 & Supp. 1991); N.Y. Soc. Serv. Law §§ 411-428 (McKinney

1984 & Supp. 1990); N.C. Gen. Stat. §§ 7A-516 to -517 (1990); N.D. Cent. Code §§ 50-25.2-02 to -14 (1989 & Supp. 1991); Ohio Rev. Code Ann. §§ 2151.01 to -.031, 2151.421 (Anderson 1990 & Supp. 1990); Okla. Stat. Ann. tit. 21, §§ 843 -848 (West 1983 & Supp. 1992); Or. Rev. Stat. §§ 418- 740 to 755 (1989); 23 Pa. Cons. Stat. Ann. §§ 6311-6333 (Supp. 1991); R.I. Gen. Laws §§ 40-11-1 to -16 (1990); S.C. Code Ann. §§ 20- 7-480 to -690 (Law. Co-op. 1985 & Supp. 1990); S.D. Codified Laws Ann. §§ 26-8A-1 to -29 (Supp. 1991); Tenn. Code Ann. §§ 37-1-401 to - 413 (1991); Tex. Fam. Code Ann. §§ 34.01-.54 (West 1986 & Supp. 1991); Utah Code Ann. §§ 62A-4-401 to -605 (1991); Vt. Stat. Ann. tit. 33, §§ 4911-19 (Supp. 1990); Va. Code Ann. §§ 63.1-248.1 to -.17 (Michie 1991); Wash. Rev. Code Ann. §§ 26.55.010-.900 (West & Supp. 1991); W. Va. Code §§ 49-6A-1 to -10 (1986 & Supp. 1991); Wis. Stat. Ann. §§ 48.981 to -.982 (West 1990); Wyo. Stat. §§ 14-3-104 to -215 (1986 & Supp. 1991).

2. The mandatory duty to report suspected child abuse has been upheld, even against a claim that it violates the confidentiality between a psychologist and patient and the child's right to privacy, *Pesce v. J. Sterling Morton High School District 201,* 830 F.2d 789 (7th Cir. 1987).

3. Policies that require abuse and neglect reports be made to an administrator are sometimes troublesome. In reporting, statutes generally require that a report be made to the social service agency or the police. Thus, a report made only to a school administrator that never is further reported outside of the school would not fulfill the obligation. The report made to the administrator by a teacher may create an obligation to report on the administrator's side, but would not fulfill the teacher's obligation, unless the report was made to the proper authorities. *See People v. Bernstein,* 243 Cal. Rptr. 363, 197 Cal. App. 3d Supp. 34 (Cal. Super. 1987).

4. Despite mandatory reporting, studies show educators report a low percentage of the child abuse and neglect that they observe. R. J. Shoop and L.

M. Firestone, Mandatory Reporting of Suspected Child Abuse: Do Teachers Obey the Law? *Education Law Reporter, 46* (1988), p. 1115; N. Abrahams, K. Casey, and D. Daro, *Teachers Confront Child Abuse: A National Survey of Teacher's Knowledge, Attitudes, and Beliefs* (Prepared by the National Center on Child Abuse Prevention Research, a program of the National Committee to Prevent Child Abuse, Working Paper No. 846, 1989).

5. Research indicates that children with special needs tend to be more vulnerable to abuse. J. B. Mullins, The Relationship between Child Abuse and Handicapping Conditions, *Journal of School Health, 56* (1986), pp. 134–136. *See also* the number of cases in which a disabled child was the victim of abuse at home or at school, e.g., *Jane Doe v. Special School District of St. Louis County,* 901 F.2d 642 (8th Cir. 1990); *Spann for Spann v. Tyler Independent School District,* 876 F.2d 437 (5th Cir. 1989).

6. Going to court on behalf of an abused or neglected child is an experience that may or may not happen to the average teacher. It is best, however, to be prepared for the possibility. The following are some suggestions to help during a court appearance. When you learn from the social worker that you may go to court:

   a. Record for yourself the dates and types of injuries you have observed.

   b. Record any contacts you have had with the parent(s) and the content of the conversations. (You may or may not be asked about the content of your conversations. Usually, a court would consider such information hearsay, but a juvenile court will on some occasions allow such testimony.)

   c. Try to remember and jot down pertinent conversations you have had with the child concerning the abuse/neglect.

   d. Review your notes but do not memorize them. You might want to take a few notes to refresh your memory but do not expect to read your testimony.

JUVENILE JUSTICE

Introduction

American society places children in special regard. The law, as a mirror of that society, does likewise. Children have a special status within the U.S. legal system; the law simultaneously confines and protects them. Restrictions on their freedoms include compulsory attendance and bans of drinking and smoking. On the other hand, children are protected from others and often their own poor judgment by being exempted from civil duties, excused when they sign a contract, and treated specially when they commit crimes.

The juvenile justice system—that complex web of courts, social service agencies, and residential facilities that handle only juveniles—is really a set of special subparts of a number of larger social and judicial systems. One component is a law enforcement system for juvenile offenders that interacts on a daily basis with the police and other law enforcement agencies. One component is a subset of the social service agencies that deliver social work, counseling, medical help, or psychiatric treatment services for juveniles, particularly abused and neglected children. Finally, one component is the enforcement agency for the educational system dealing with truancy. Each part of this juvenile justice "system" works independently and yet in coordination with other parts of the juvenile system, the larger social agencies that a subpart belongs to, and other agencies that deal with children, e.g., the schools.

The systems developed by each state are more or less unique. Consistency results from common adoption of suggested standards and rules, e.g., Council of Judges, National Council in Crime and Delinquency, Model Rules for Juvenile Courts, and Juvenile Justice Act. However, there is an underlying philosophy that runs across all the states. Juveniles are *treated* by the law and the systems are different from that of adults. The juvenile justice system is set up to assist and protect juveniles; it is not set up as a punitive system. Even the law enforcement section is undergirded by a philosophy of rehabilitation and growth, not crime and punishment. As stated by Justice Black in his concurring opinion in the landmark juvenile case, *In Re Gault*:

> *The juvenile court laws . . . are the result of plans promoted by humane and forward-looking people to provide a system of courts, procedures, and sanctions deemed to be less harmful and more lenient to children than to adults.*[24]

This philosophy is derived from the reform movement in the late 1800s. In 1899, the first juvenile code was enacted in the state of Illinois. It embodied the following principles, which are still at the heart of the juvenile system today:

— A special court was created for neglected, dependent, or delinquent children under the age of 16.
— The purpose of that court was to rehabilitate rather than punish.
— Theoretically, no stigma would be attached from a juvenile court appearance.
— All records and proceedings were to be confidential.
— Juveniles were to be detained separate from adults.
— Juvenile court proceedings were to be informal.

The juvenile system has two unique parts and, although disposition may be the same, the rights afforded the juvenile differ markedly. Juveniles are treated differently, depending on whether they are being adjudicated due to commission of a crime or a status offense that places them in the judicial system only because they are a juvenile. Juveniles in the first circumstance are afforded more procedural protections, much more like adult court. Unlike the late 1970s, this distinction was drawn between these as "criminal" and "civil" actions, and the protections of adult court were extended to the "criminal" actions. These extensions may have been granted due to a judge's perception that the goals of the juvenile system were not being met. As stated by Chief Justice Burger,

> Although the juvenile court system had its genesis in the desire to provide a distinctive procedure and setting to deal with the problems of youth, including those manifested by antisocial conduct, our decisions in recent years have recognized that there is a gap between the originally benign conception of the system and its realities. . . . [T]he Court's response to that perception has been to make applicable in juvenile proceedings constitutional guarantees. . . .[25]

In the 1980s, juvenile justice became much more punitive—incarceration rates escalated and juveniles were treated much more like adults.[26]

Criminal Conduct

The language of the juvenile court remains different from that in the adult criminal court. Children are not found guilty of crimes and sentenced; rather, they are adjudicated a delinquent and in their disposition placed in confinement. As the Supreme Court noted in *In Re Gault*,[27] a rose by any other name smells as sweet. "The fact of the matter is that, however euphemistic the title, a 'receiving home' or an 'industrial school' for juveniles is an institution of confinement in which the child is incarcerated for a greater or lesser time."[28] Children are held accountable for their actions; they are adjudicated delinquents. A child may be adjudicated a delinquent if he or she violates a state or local criminal law, and they can be adjudicated a delinquent for engaging in acts that would be punishable by incarceration if they were adults.

The Supreme Court, in *In Re Gault*, held that juveniles should be afforded, at a minimum, the same rights adults had in a criminal process. In addition, because of their age and maturity, children have some additional protections in the process. Juveniles have the same rights as adults in regard to police search, arrest, and interrogation. Additionally, during the intake process, they are afforded the right to have their parent or guardian present, but they may be detained before the hearing.[29] During the delinquency proceeding, juveniles have (1) the right to be notified of the charges, (2) the right to counsel (appointed counsel if indigent), (3) the right to confront and cross-examine witnesses, (4) the protection against self-incrimination, (5) the right to be considered innocent until proven guilty beyond a reasonable doubt, and (6) the protection against double jeopardy.[30] As a constitutional matter, however, they do not have the right to trial by jury.[31] Some states afford this right by statute.

Every state provides that juveniles accused of committing a crime may be prosecuted in juvenile court. However, every state also has provisions for prosecuting juveniles—in some circumstances, in adult court. In most states, there is a minimum age below which a juvenile cannot be prosecuted in adult court. However, in some states, juveniles charged with serious offenses may be prosecuted in adult court regardless of age; and in a minority of states, juveniles charged with specific serious offenses must be tried in adult court. The general pattern is that waiver into adult court is at the discretion of the juvenile judge after a hearing has been held on the issue. In *Kent v. the United States*,[32] the Supreme Court stated that this waiver hearing was a critically important stage in the juvenile process, thus many procedural protections are afforded the child at this time. A waiver hearing is a full hearing.

In *Kent*, the Court set out factors that should be considered in the decision. These factors are not constitutionally required but have provided courts and legislatures guidelines in this area; 37 states have by statute or court decision adopted similar criteria.[33] The Court's suggested criteria were:

1. The seriousness of the alleged offense
2. Whether the alleged offense was committed in an aggressive, violent, premeditated, or willful manner
3. Whether the alleged offense was against a person
4. The merit of the complaint
5. If there are others involved in the alleged offense being tried in adult court
6. The juvenile's maturity
7. The juvenile's record and previous history
8. The prospects for protection of the community and for the juvenile's rehabilitation[34]

If the court determines at the close of the hearing to waive the child into adult court, all of the adult protections apply. Additionally, if found guilty, a child may be subjected to any of the criminal sanctions available for the crime charged. This is even true of the death penalty.[35]

Status Offenses

The authority of the juvenile court extends past those minors who engage in criminal conduct. Juvenile misbehavior of a noncriminal nature may also result in the adjudication of delinquency. Some acts bring a juvenile into the system because they exhibit behaviors that society does not accept from a child. These behaviors are referred to as *status offenses*—those acts that are "criminal" because of the child's age. Most often found in the court's jurisdiction is running away from home, violating curfew, being truant from school, or being unmanageable by one's parents. Increasingly, these children are fixed with a newer statutory label: *children in need of supervision.*

The procedural requirements for adjudicating a child in need of supervision or a delinquent due to a status offense is often different from adjudicating a delinquent due to a criminal offense. The procedures are usually looser and

the standards of proof are more lax. It is easier to be adjudicated a delinquent due to a status offense. The standard of proof is typically a preponderance of the evidence rather than beyond a reasonable doubt, and in some states alleged status offenders have no right to counsel. This explains why a child often will be adjudicated a delinquent as a status offender rather than for violating a statute. Nonetheless, in nearly every state, the resulting disposition of the juvenile can be the same.

Arrest and Questioning

The statutory standards for arresting a child—usually termed *taking a child into custody*—generally parallel adult arrest procedures. An officer of the court, a police officer, a social services officer, or a juvenile officer can take a child into custody. The police officer does not always have to have an arrest warrant. A child can be taken into custody by a police officer if there is reasonable or probable cause to believe that the child has committed a delinquent act or a status offense.

When a child is in custody, that child has a right to be told he or she may have a lawyer before any questioning can begin.[36] A child's waiver of these rights must be treated cautiously, since it is questionable when a child, under stress, can make a voluntary and knowing waiver of his or her constitutional rights. This is particularly true when factors such as inexperience, low intelligence, or intoxication enter into the picture.[37] In fact, research has indicated that most juveniles do not understand their rights, even after officials have explained them.[38] When dealing with juveniles, officials must be very selective in the ways questioning is conducted. Juveniles may be more susceptible to self-incrimination than an adult suspect simply by virtue of the circumstance of an official interrogation.[39] For example, the police should have known that placing burglar tools in front of an unaccompanied 13-year-old would illicit an incriminating response. Therefore, the court in *In Re Ronald C.* found that the police should have informed the juvenile of his rights to an attorney and to remain silent.[40]

In virtually all states, statutes require that parents or guardians are notified when a child is taken into custody. The presence of parents is often one of the factors taken into consideration in determining whether a juvenile's waiver of his or her rights has been made knowingly and voluntarily.[41] The Supreme Court recognized that

> *a lawyer or an adult relative or friend could have given the petitioner the protection which his own immaturity could not. Adult advice would have put him on a less unequal footing with his interrogators. Without some adult protection against this inequality, a 14-year-old boy would not be able to know, let alone assert, such constitutional rights as he had.*[42]

Some states require parental presence during police interrogation of a juvenile. Violation of this requirement could make any subsequent statement ruled inadmissible in court.[43]

Miranda warnings are required only for *custodial interrogations*. Thus, if the person is not in "custody," he or she has no rights to an attorney present before questioning and no right to be informed of other procedural rights. The Supreme Court found that a probation interview was not "custodial" for the purposes of *Miranda*. Whether an interrogation in a school official's office would be "custodial" is still in question.[44] However, juvenile defense attorneys consistently claim that *Miranda* rights apply in school settings. "[L]ogic . . . calls for the application of *Miranda* protections to questioning in the school setting, at least when such questioning occurs in the intimidating environment of a principal's or assistant principal's office."[45]

Once a child is detained and questioned, he or she is often released without further proceedings. Statutes and police regulations generally grant broad discretion in juvenile arrests. A warning may be issued and charges dropped.

Some authorities estimate that over 50 percent of juvenile situations end at police questioning.[46] The factors that go into this decision include the seriousness of the offense; the age of the child; the child's prior record; the race, gender, and socioeconomic status of the child (studies indicate that poor African-American males are the least likely candidates for release[47]); the child's demeanor; the parent's demeanor; and the nature of the individual officer involved. Typically, the police maintain some sort of informal record of juvenile contacts so that in future circumstances it can be determined if a child has had prior incidents with the police.

Intake and Diversion

After a minor has been detained but before formal proceedings have begun, some member of the juvenile staff must decide whether to file a petition that will lead to adjudication or that will divert the minor from the formal system. At this step, typically called *intake,* the staff will meet with the juvenile, parents, witnesses, victims, and possibly the police officer involved. Intake is one of the most critical steps in juvenile proceedings, because the entire process may be avoided at this stage. A central premise of diverting juveniles from the system is that certain forms of nonjudicial solutions should be encouraged as more effective at rehabilitation than judicial disposition.[48]

This informal treatment is not without drawbacks. First, there are no formal protections for juveniles in an informal system. The minors may actually serve informal probation longer than they would have been ordered to serve through the formal process. More notable is the problem of deciding which juveniles should have to continue through the juvenile system. Juvenile intake officers generally consider a variety of factors in making this decision, including the following:

— The juvenile's attitude toward the offense
— Parental control over the juvenile

- Employment and school status
- The juvenile's history
- Cooperation of parents
- Age of the juvenile
- Nature of the offense

In essence, the intake process is a screening during which the staff obtains all available information and makes a decision as to the action to be taken. The child may be released, placed on informal probation, sent through the juvenile court, or waived into adult court through a hearing process.[49]

Disposition

One of the effects of the Supreme Court opinion in *In Re Gault*[50] was the separation of the disposition of the juvenile from the determination of delinquency. This bifurcated process requires that the child be adjudicated and then that a determination of what disposition is in his or her best interests be made.

Because of the critical nature of this hearing, the juvenile is again cloaked in a number of procedural guarantees at the disposition hearing, e.g., the right to counsel, the exclusionary rule (however, hearsay is admissible). An important and unique component of a juvenile disposition is the *social study*. This is an individualized report, usually prepared by the probation department, that gives a thorough background of the juvenile and recommendations to the juvenile judge.

The range of dispositional alternatives and the judge's discretion in choosing among them is very broad. State statutes may limit a judge's discretion in disposition in some circumstances. The possibilities, in increasing severity, include the following:

1. Dismissal without retaining any jurisdiction over the juvenile.
2. Probation without verdict. Jurisdiction is retained, but if the juvenile remains arrest free, the case is dismissed after a specified period of time.
3. Restitution may be used alone or in conjunction with some other disposition.
4. Suspended judgment. Jurisdiction is retained, but if the juvenile complies with the court's orders, the case is dismissed after a specified period of time.
5. Probation. This is the most common disposition. The typical probation lasts one to two years but may last until the juvenile becomes an adult. It is common for probation orders to contain conditions, such as meeting with a probation officer, remaining crime free, obeying a curfew, and attending school regularly. Violation of these conditions becomes an offense itself.
6. Prison without walls. As with adults, this is court-ordered confinement, usually to one's own home for a period of time (usually over weekends), monitored by electronic devices.
7. Placement in a group home.
8. Placement in a private residential facility.
9. Placement in a minimum security juvenile facility.
10. Placement in a maximum security juvenile facility.
11. Placement in an adult facility. In some states, juvenile courts can commit a juvenile directly to an adult facility, or a juvenile may be transferred to an adult facility if his or her sentence lasts past the time the juvenile becomes an adult.

In most states, a juvenile placement is not set for a period of time; rather, it is indeterminate. In theory, the placement can last until the child becomes an adult. In some states, even a determinate sentence, set for a specified period of time, can be extended after a court review. For all juveniles who are incarcerated due to a status offense, jurisdiction lasts until they become adults. As a practical matter, once the court makes a disposition, supervision is turned over to the facility in which the child has been

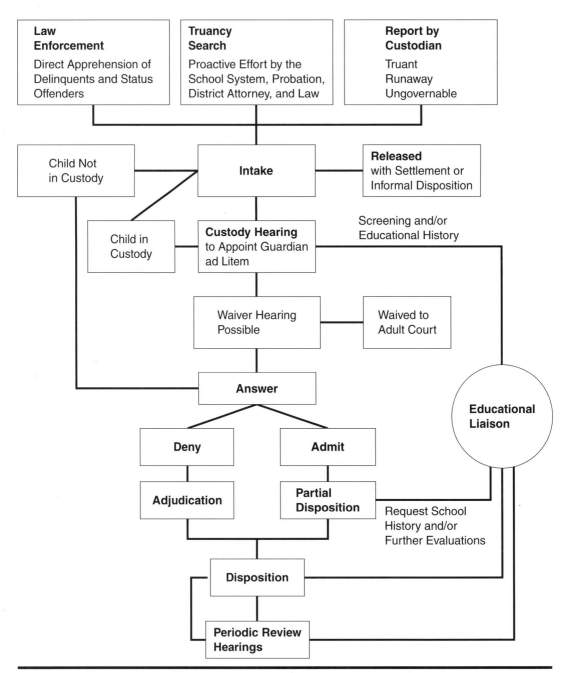

FIGURE 6.2   Path through a Typical State Juvenile System

placed. That agency then determines the child's release date through a series of periodic reviews. Almost all juveniles are released after a period of 12 to 18 months.

Figure 6.2 depicts the path of a juvenile through a typical state's juvenile system.

IN RE GAULT
387 U.S. 1, 87 S. Ct. 1428, 18 L. Ed. 2d 527 (1967)

Mr. Justice FORTAS delivered the opinion of the Court.

This is an appeal under 28 U.S.C. § 1257 (2) from the judgment of the Supreme Court of Arizona affirming the dismissal of a petition for a writ of habeas corpus. . . . The petition sought the release of Gerald Francis Gault, appellants' 15-year-old son, who had been committed as a juvenile delinquent to the State Industrial School by the Juvenile Court of Gila County, Arizona. The Supreme Court of Arizona affirmed dismissal of the writ against various arguments which included an attack upon the constitutionality of the Arizona Juvenile code because of its alleged denial of procedural due process rights to juveniles charged with being "delinquents.". . .

We do not agree, and we reverse.

I.

On Monday, June 8, 1964, at about 10 A.M., Gerald Francis Gault and a friend, Ronald Lewis, were taken into custody by the Sheriff of Gila County. Gerald was then still subject to a six months' probation order which had been entered on February 25, 1964, as a result of his having been in the company of another boy who had stolen a wallet from a lady's purse. The police action on June 8 was taken as the result of a verbal complaint by a neighbor of the boys, Mrs. Cook, about a telephone call made to her in which the caller or callers made lewd or indecent remarks. It will suffice for purposes of this opinion to say that the remarks or questions put to her were of the irritatingly offensive, adolescent, sex variety.

At the time Gerald was picked up, his mother and father were both at work. No notice that Gerald was being taken into custody was left at the home. No other steps were taken to advise them that their son had, in effect, been arrested. Gerald was taken to the Children's Detention Home. When his mother arrived home at about 6 o'clock, Gerald was not there.

Gerald's older brother was sent to look for him at the trailer home of the Lewis family. He apparently learned then that Gerald was in custody. He so informed his mother. The two of them went to the Detention Home. The deputy probation officer, Flagg, who was also superintendent of the Detention Home, told Mrs. Gault "why Jerry was there" and said that a hearing would be held in Juvenile Court at 3 o'clock the following day, June 9.

Officer Flagg filed a petition with the court on the hearing day, June 9, 1964. It was not served on the Gaults. Indeed, none of them saw this petition until the habeas corpus hearing on August 17, 1964. The petition was entirely formal. It made no reference to any factual basis for the judicial action which it initiated. It recited only that "said minor is under the age of eighteen years, and is in need of the protection of this Honorable Court; (and that) said minor is a delinquent minor." It prayed for a hearing and an order regarding "the care and custody of said minor." Officer Flagg executed a formal affidavit in support of the petition.

On June 9, Gerald, his mother, his older brother, and Probation Officers Flagg and Henderson appeared before the Juvenile Judge in chambers. . . . Mrs. Cook, the complainant, was not there. No one was sworn at this hearing. No transcript or recording was made. No memorandum or record of the substance of the proceedings was prepared. . . . [I]t appears that at the June 9 hearing Gerald was questioned by the judge about the telephone call. . . . At the conclusion of the hearing, the judge said he would "think about it." Gerald was taken back to the Detention Home. He was not sent to his own home with his parents. On June 11 or 12, after having been detained since June 8, Gerald was released and driven home. There is no explanation the record as to why he was kept in the Detention Home or why he was released. At 5 P.M. on the day of Gerald's release, Mrs. Gault received a note signed by Officer

Flagg. It was on . . . plain paper, not letterhead. Its entire text was as follows:

> *Mrs. Gault:*
>
> *Judge McGHEE has set Monday June 15, 1964 at 11:00 A.M. as the date and time for further Hearings on Gerald's delinquency*
>
> */s/ Flagg*

At the appointed time on Monday, June 15, Gerald, his father and mother, Ronald Lewis and his father, and Officers Flagg and Henderson were present before Judge McGhee. . . . Again, the complainant, Mrs. Cook, was not present. . . .

At this June 15 hearing a "referral report" made by the probation officers was filed with the court, although not disclosed to Gerald or his parents. This listed the charge as "Lewd Phone Calls." At the conclusion of the hearing, the judge committed Gerald as a juvenile delinquent to the State Industrial School "for the period of his minority (that is, until 21), unless sooner discharged by due process of law.". . .

No appeal is permitted by Arizona law in juvenile cases. On August 3, 1964, a petition for a writ of habeas corpus was filed with the Supreme Court of Arizona and referred by it to the Superior Court for hearing.

At the habeas corpus hearing on August 17, Judge McGhee was vigorously cross-examined as to the basis for his actions. He testified that he had taken into account the fact that Gerald was on probation. He was asked "under what section of . . . the code you found the boy delinquent?"

His answer is set forth in the margin [footnote 5].[51]

. . . . The law which Gerald was found to have violated is ARS § 13--377. This section of the Arizona Criminal Code provides that a person who "in the presence or hearing of any woman or child . . . uses vulgar, abusive or obscene language, is guilty of a misdemeanor. . . ." The penalty specified in the Criminal Code, which would apply to an adult, is $5 to $50, or imprisonment for not more than two months. The judge also testified that he acted under ARS § 8--201, subsec. 6(d) which includes in the definition of a "delinquent child" one who, as the judge phrased it, is "habitually involved in immoral matters."

Asked about the basis for his conclusion that Gerald was "habitually involved in immoral matters," the judge testified, somewhat vaguely, that two years earlier, on July 2, 1962, a "referral" was made concerning Gerald, "where the boy had stolen a baseball glove from another boy and lied to the Police Department about it." The judge said there was "no hearing," and "no accusation" relating to this incident, "because of lack of material foundation." But it seems to have remained in his mind as a relevant factor. The judge also testified that Gerald had admitted making other nuisance phone calls in the past which, as the judge recalled the boy's testimony, were "silly calls, or funny calls, or something like that."

****

II.

The Supreme Court of Arizona held that due process of law is requisite to the constitutional validity of proceedings in which a court reaches the conclusion that a juvenile has been at fault, has engaged in conduct prohibited by law, or has otherwise misbehaved with the consequence that he is committed to an institution in which his freedom is curtailed. This conclusion is in accord with the decisions of a number of courts under both federal and state constitutions.

This Court has not heretofore decided the precise question. . . . Accordingly, while these cases relate only to restricted aspects of the subject, they unmistakably indicate that, whatever may be their precise impact, neither the Fourteenth Amendment nor the Bill of Rights is for adults alone.

****

We do not in this opinion consider the impact of these constitutional provisions upon the totality of the relationship of the juvenile and the state. We do not even consider the entire process relating to juvenile "delinquents.". . . We consider only the problems presented to us by this case. These relate to the proceedings by which a determination is made as to whether a juvenile is a "delinquent" as a result of alleged misconduct on his part, with the consequence that he may be committed to a state institution. As to these proceedings, there appears to be little current dissent form the proposition that the Due Process Clause has a role to play. The problem is to ascertain the precise impact of the due process requirement upon such proceedings.

From the inception of the juvenile court system, wide differences have been tolerated—indeed insisted upon—between the procedural rights accorded to adults and those of juveniles. In practically all jurisdictions, there are rights granted to adults which are withheld from juveniles. In addition to the specific problems involved in the present case, for example, it has been held that the juvenile is not entitled to bail, to indictment by grand jury, to a public trial or to trial by jury. it is frequent practice that rules governing the arrest and interrogation of adults by the police are not observed in the case of juveniles.

****

It is claimed that juveniles obtain benefits from the special procedures applicable to them which more than offset the disadvantages of denial of the substance of normal due process. As we shall discuss, the observance of due process standards, intelligently and not ruthlessly administered, will not compel the States to abandon or displace any of the substantive benefits of the juvenile process. But it is important, we think, that the claimed benefits of the juvenile process should be candidly appraised. Neither sentiment nor folklore should cause us to shut our eyes, for example, to such startling findings as that reported in an exceptionally reliable study of repeaters or recidivism conducted by the Stanford Research Institute for the President's Commission on Crime in the District of Columbia. This Commission's Report states:

> In fiscal 1966 approximately 66 percent of the 16- and 17-year-old juveniles referred to the court by the Youth Aid Division had been before the court previously. In 1965, 56 percent of those in the Receiving Home were repeaters. The SRI study revealed that 61 percent of the sample Juvenile Court referrals in 1965 had been previously referred at least once and that 42 percent had been referred at least twice before. Id., at 773.

Certainly, these figures and the high crime rates among juveniles to which we have referred . . . , could not lead us to conclude that the absence of constitutional protections reduces crime, or that the juvenile system, functioning free of constitutional inhibitions as it has largely done, is effective to reduce crime or rehabilitate offenders. We do not mean

by this to denigrate the juvenile court process or to suggest that there are not aspects of the juvenile system relating to offenders which are valuable. But the features of the juvenile system which its proponents have asserted are of unique benefit will not be impaired by constitutional domestication. For example, the commendable principles relating to the processing and treatment of juveniles separately from adults are in no way involved or affected by the procedural issues under discussion. Further, we are told that one of the important benefits of the special juvenile court procedures is that they avoid classifying the juvenile as a "criminal." The juvenile offender is now classed as a "delinquent." There is, of course, no reason why this should not continue. It is disconcerting, however, that this term has come to involve only slightly less stigma than the term "criminal" applied to adults. It is also emphasized that in practically all jurisdictions, statutes provide that an adjudication of the child as a delinquent shall not operate as a civil disability or disqualify him for civil service appointment. There is no reason why the application of due process requirements should interfere with such provisions.

Further, it is urged that the juvenile benefits from informal proceedings in the court. The early conception of the Juvenile Court proceeding was one in which a fatherly judge touched the heart and conscience of the erring youth by talking over his problems, by paternal advice and admonition, and in which, in extreme situations, benevolent and wise institutions of the State provided guidance and help "to save him from downward career." Then as now, goodwill and compassion were admirably prevalent. But recent studies have, with surprising unanimity, entered sharp dissent as to the validity of this gentle conception. They suggest that the appearance as well as the actuality of fairness, impartiality and orderliness—in short, the essentials of due process—may be more impressive and more therapeutic attitude so far as the juvenile is concerned. . . .

****

Ultimately, however, we confront the reality of that portion of the Juvenile Court process with which we deal in this case. A boy is charged with misconduct. The boy is committed to an institution where he may be restrained of liberty for years. It is of no constitutional consequence—and of limited practical meaning—that the institution to which he is committed is called an Industrial School. The fact of the matter is that, however euphemistic the title, a "receiving home" or an "industrial school" for juveniles is an institution of confinement in which the child is incarcerated for a greater or lesser time. His world becomes "a building with whitewashed walls, regimented routine and institutional hours . . . ." Instead of mother and father and sisters and brothers and friends and classmates, his world is peopled by guards, custodians, state employees, and "delinquents" confined with him for anything from waywardness to rape and homicide.

In view of this, it would be extraordinary if our Constitution did not require the procedural regularity and the exercise of care implied in the phrase "due process." Under our Constitution, the condition of being a boy does not justify a kangaroo court. The traditional ideas of Juvenile Court procedure, indeed, contemplated that time would be available and care would be used to establish precisely what the juvenile did and why he did it—was it a prank of adolescence or a brutal act threatening serious consequences to himself or society unless corrected? Under traditional notions, one would assume that in a case like that of Gerald Gault, where the juvenile appears to have a home, a working mother and father, and an older brother, the Juvenile Judge would have made a careful inquiry and judgment as to the possibility that the boy could be disciplined and dealt with at home, . . . The essential difference between Gerald's case and a normal criminal case is that safeguards available to adults were discarded in Gerald's case. The summary procedure as well as the long commitment was possible because Gerald was 15 years of age instead of over 18.

If Gerald had been over 18, he would not have been subject to Juvenile Court proceedings. For the particular offense immediately involved, the maximum punishment would have been a fine of $5 to $50, or imprisonment in jail for not more than two months. Instead, he was committed to custody for a maximum of six years. . . .

****

We now turn to the specific issues which are presented to us in the present case.

****

. . . . We cannot agree with the court's conclusion that adequate notice was given in this case. Notice, to comply with due process requirements, must be given sufficiently in advance of scheduled court proceedings so that reasonable opportunity to prepare will be afforded, and it must "set forth the alleged misconduct with particularity." It is obvious, as we have discussed above, that no purpose of shielding the child from the public stigma of knowledge of his having been taken into custody and scheduled for hearing is served by the procedure approved by the court below. The "initial hearing" in the present case was a hearing on the merits. Notice at that time is not timely; and even if there were a conceivable purpose served by the deferral proposed by the court below, it would have to yield to the requirements that the child and his parents or guardian be notified, in writing, of the specific charge or factual allegations to be considered at the hearing, and that such written notice be given at the earliest practicable time, and in any event sufficiently in advance of the hearing to permit preparation. Due process of law requires notice of the sort we have described—that is, notice which would be deemed constitutionally adequate in a civil or criminal proceeding. It does not allow a hearing to be held in which a youth's freedom and his parents' right to his custody are at stake without giving them timely notice, in advance of the hearing, of the specific issues that they must meet. . . .

IV. RIGHT TO COUNSEL

Appellants charge that the Juvenile Court proceedings were fatally defective because the court did not advise Gerald or his parents of their right to counsel, and proceeded with the hearing, the adjudication of delinquency and the order of commitment in the absence of counsel for the child and his parents or an express waiver of the right thereto. The Supreme Court of Arizona . . . referred to a provision of the Juvenile Code which it characterized as requiring "that the probation officer shall look after the interests of neglected, delinquent and dependent children," including representing their interests in court. The court argued that "[t]he parent and the probation officer may be relied upon to protect the infant's interests." Accordingly it rejected the proposition that "due process requires that an infant have a right to counsel." It said that juvenile courts have the discretion, but not the duty, to allow such representation; it referred specifically to the situation in which the Juvenile Court discerns conflict between the child and his parents as an instance in which this discretion might be exercised. We do not agree. Probation officers, in the Arizona scheme, are also arresting officers. They initiate proceedings and file petitions which they verify, as here, alleging the delinquency of the child; and they testify, as here, against the child. And here the probation officer was also superintendent of the Detention Home. The probation officer cannot act as counsel for the child. His role in the adjudicatory hearing, by statute and in fact, is as arresting officer and witness against the child. Nor can the judge represent the child. There is no material difference in this respect between adult and juvenile proceedings of the sort here involved. In adult proceedings, this contention has been foreclosed by decisions of this Court. A proceeding where the issue is whether the child will be found to be "delinquent" and subjected to the loss of his liberty for years is comparable in seriousness to a felony prosecution. The juvenile needs the assistance of counsel to cope with problems of law, to make skilled inquiry into the facts, to insist upon regularity of the proceedings, and to ascertain whether he has a defense and to prepare and submit it. The child "requires the guiding hand of counsel at every step in the proceedings against him.". . .

V. CONFRONTATION, SELF-INCRIMINATION, CROSS-EXAMINATION

Appellants urge that the writ of habeas corpus should have been granted because of the denial of the rights of confrontation and cross-examination in the Juvenile Court hearings, and because the privilege against self-incrimination was not observed. The Juvenile Court Judge testified at the habeas corpus hearing that he had proceeded on the basis of Gerald's admissions at the two hearings. Appellants attack this on the ground that the admissions were obtained in disregard of the privilege against self-incrimination. . . .

****

We shall assume that Gerald made admission of the sort described by the Juvenile Court Judge, as quoted above. Neither Gerald nor his parents were advised that he did not have to testify or make a statement, or that an incriminating statement might result in his commitment as a "delinquent."

The Arizona Supreme Court rejected appellants' contention that Gerald had a right to be advised that

he need not incriminate himself. It said: "We think the necessary flexibility for individualized treatment will be enhanced by a rule which does not require the judge to advise the infant of a privilege against self-incrimination."

In reviewing this conclusion of Arizona's Supreme Court, we emphasize again that we are here concerned only with a proceeding to determine whether a minor is a "delinquent" and which may result in commitment to a state institution. Specifically, the question is whether, in such a proceeding, an admission by the juvenile may be used against him the absence of clear and unequivocal evidence that the admission was made with knowledge that he was not obliged to speak and would not be penalized for remaining silent. In light of *Miranda v. State of Arizona*, 384 U.S. 436, 86 S. Ct. 1602, 16 L. Ed. 2d 694 (1966), we must also consider whether, if the privilege against self-incrimination is available, it can effectively be waived unless counsel is present or the right to counsel has been waived.

****

The privilege against self-incrimination is, of course, related to the question of the safeguards necessary to assure that admissions or confessions are reasonably trustworthy, that they are not the mere fruits of fear or coercion, but are reliable expressions of the truth. . . . One of its purposes is to prevent the state, whether by force or by psychological domination, from overcoming the mind and will of the person under investigation and depriving him of the freedom to decide whether to assist the state in securing his conviction.

Against the application to juveniles of the right to silence, it is argued that juvenile proceedings are "civil" and not "criminal," and therefore the privilege should not apply. It is true that the statement of the privilege in the Fifth Amendment, which is applicable to the States by reason of the Fourteenth Amendment, is that no person "shall be compelled in any criminal case to be a witness against himself." However, it is also clear that the availability of the privilege does not turn upon the type of proceeding in which its protection is invoked, but upon the nature of the statement or admission and the exposure which it invites. . . .

It would be entirely unrealistic to carve out of the Fifth Amendment all statements by juveniles on the ground that these cannot lead to "criminal" involvement. In the first place, juvenile proceedings to determine "delinquency," which may lead to commitment to a state institution, must be regarded as "criminal" for purposes of the privilege against self-incrimination. To hold otherwise would be to disregard substance because of the feeble enticement of the "civil" label-of-convenience which has been attached to juvenile proceedings. . . . For this purpose, at least, commitment is a deprivation of liberty. It is incarceration against one's will, whether it is called "criminal" or "civil." And our Constitution guarantees that no person shall be "compelled" to be a witness against himself when he is threatened with deprivation of his liberty—a command which this Court has broadly applied and generously implemented in accordance with the teaching of the history of the privilege and its great office in mankind's battle for freedom.

For the reasons stated, the judgment of the Supreme Court of Arizona is reversed and the cause remanded for further proceedings not inconsistent with this opinion. It is so ordered.

Judgment reversed and cause remanded with directions.

****

(Footnotes omitted.)

ADDITIONAL COMMENTARY

1. The courts have found that the use of corporal punishment—including paddling, severe behavior modification, and drug treatments—in a juvenile detention facility violates the Eighth Amendment prohibition on cruel and unusual punishment. *E.g., Nelson v. Heyne*, 491 F.2d 352 (7th Cir. 1974) *cert. denied* 417 U.S. 976; *Milonas v. Williams*, 691 F.2d 931 (10th Cir. 1982).

2. A number of courts have found that juveniles, when involuntarily incarcerated, have a right to rehabilitative treatment. The reasoning is twofold. First, relying on the Supreme Court's decision in *Jackson v. Indiana*, 406 U.S. 715 (1972), "The nature and duration of commitment must bear some reasonable relation to the purpose for which the individual is committed." Since a juvenile incarceration is supposedly for the child's benefit and rehabilitation, then that rehabilitation must be forthcoming. Second, courts have found a right to treatment arising from a quid pro quo exchange for diminished procedural rights within the juvenile justice structure. *E.g., Morgan v. Sproat*, 432 F. Supp. 1130 (S.D. Miss. 1977).

3. All 50 states have procedures for not disclosing documents produced in the course of juvenile proceedings. This is in keeping with the basic premises of the juvenile system.

> *Confidentiality by statute of juvenile offenses . . . are promises with a purpose, i.e., to provide incentive that if a youngster . . . will straighten out and clean up his life, the state will give the security that his past offenses will be behind him and not used as a cloud over him or his family forever.*
> Montesano v. Donrey, *99 Nev. 644, 668 P.2d 1081, 1089 (Nev. 1983) (Zenoff, J., dissenting).*

However, two Supreme Court cases have ruled that once the information, including a juvenile's name, becomes public, publication cannot be prohibited. *Smith v. Daily Mail Publishing Co.*, 443 U.S. 97 (1979); *Oklahoma Publishing Co. v. District Court*, 430 U.S. 308 (1977).

4. For purposes of fulfilling the obligation to report child abuse, police liaison officers in schools are often considered police officers. *E.g., People v. Bernstein*, 243 Cal. Rptr. 363, 197 C.A.3d Supp. 34 (1987), for statutes relating to resisting arrest. *E.g., Comm. v. Mitchell*, 554 A.2d 542 (Pa. Super, 1989). *But see* searches, *supra*.

5. Unlike IDEA, when a court is making a placement decision, factors such as appropriateness or least restrictive environment do not have to be considered, unless set forth by the state juvenile code. *In re Michael G.*, 243 Cal. Rptr. 224, 747 P.2d 1152 (Cal. 1988).

6. A juvenile court may not exercise its authority over a child to place him or her in a special education program and circumvent the IDEA. *In Interest of J.D.*, 510 So. 2d 623 (Fla. App. 1987); *Morgan v. Chris L.,*—F. Supp.—(E.D. Tenn. 1994). But a court may order, during juvenile proceedings, that a child be evaluated and suitably placed if found to be in need of special education. *Matter of Jackson*, 84 N.C. App. 167, 352 S.E.2d 449 (1987).

ENDNOTES

1. National Committee for Prevention of Child Abuse, 1991.

2. J. S. Wodarskik, P. Kurtz, J. Gaudin, and P. Howing, Maltreatment and the School-Age Child: Major Academic, Socioemotional, and Adaptive Outcomes, *Social Work, 35* (1990), pp. 506–513; A. Cohn, D. Finkelhor, and C. Holmes, Preventing Adults from Becoming Child Sexual Molesters (Prepared by the National Center on Child Abuse Prevention Research, a program of the National Committee to Prevent Child Abuse, Working Paper No. 825, 1985); D. Goleman, Sad Legacy of Abuse: The Search for Remedies, *New York Times,* Jan. 24, 1989, at C1 (studies show that as many as one-third of abused children become abusive adults).

3. Alfred Alschuler, Foreword to Tower, C. C. (1987). *How Schools Can Help Combat Child Abuse and Neglect* (2d ed.) Washington, DC: National Education Association.

4. 42 U.S.C. 5101-5107.

5. The Model Act includes the following definition: Child abuse and neglect means the physical or mental injury, sexual abuse, negligent treatment or maltreatment of a child [under the age of eighteen] by a person who is responsible for the child's welfare under circumstances which indicate that the child's health or welfare is harmed or threatened thereby. 42 U.S.C. 5106g.

6. *E.g.,* McDonald v. State, 71 Or. App. 751, 694 P.2d 569 (Or. App. 1985).

7. 892 F.2d 670 (7th Cir. 1990).

8. *E.g.,* Davis v. Durham City Sch., 91 N.C.App. 520, 372 S.E.2d 318 (1988).

9. This criminal liability has been upheld even against claims of vagueness and overbreadth. *E.g.,* State v. Grover, 437 N.W.2d 60 (Minn. 1989).

10. *E.g.,* Bellevue Public School v. Benson, 41 Wash. App. 730, 707 P.2d 137 (1985); Pesce v. J. Sterling Morton School Dist. 201, 830 F.2d 789 (7th Cir. 1987).

11. *E.g.,* Landeros v. Flood, 17 Cal. 3d 399, 551 P.2d 389 (Cal. 1976). See Note, J. Aaron, Civil Liability for Teachers' Negligent Failure to Report Suspected Child Abuse, *Wayne Law Review, 28* (1981), pp. 183–213.

12. 42 U.S.C. § 1983 (1988) states in part: "[E]very person who, under color of any statute, ordinance, regulation, custom, or usage, of any State or Territory or the District of Columbia, subjects, or causes to be subjected, any citizen of the United States or other person within the jurisdiction thereof to the deprivation of any rights, privileges, or immunities secured by the Constitution and laws, shall be liable to the party injured in an action at law, suit in equity, or other proper proceeding for redress."

13. *See* Carey v. Piphus, 435 U.S. 247 (1978); Ingraham v. Wright, 430 U.S. 651 (1977). Qualified or good faith immunity affords limited protection to certain individuals from civil rights liability. However, the Supreme Court has stated that qualified immunity is limited because if it were not, boards would not be deterred from promulgating unconstitutional policies. *See* Kentucky v. Graham, 473 U.S. 159 (1985), *on remand sub nom.* Graham v. Wilson, 791 F.2d 932 (6th Cir. 1986).

14. Stoneking v. Bradford Area Sch. Dist., 856 F.2d 594 (3rd Cir. 1988), *vacated sub nom.* Smith v. Stoneking, 489 U.S. 1062 (1989), *on remand sub nom.* Stoneking v. Bradford Area Sch. Dist., 882 F.2d 720 (3rd Cir. 1989), *cert. denied sub nom.* Smith v. Stoneking, 493 U.S. 1044 (1990).

15. 489 U.S. 189 (1989).

16. The Court stated: "The affirmative duty to protect arises not from the State's knowledge of the individual's predicament or from its expressions of intent to help him, but from the limitation which it has imposed on his freedom to act on his own behalf." *Id.* at 200. However, in *DeShaney,* the Court found that no duty to protect existed because the Department of Social Services had not placed the child in the position of peril. *Id.* at 200-01.

17. In *Stoneking,* the court stated: "There is thus an adequate basis from the Pennsylvania child abuse reporting and *in loco parentis* statutes, coupled with the broad common law duty owed by school officials to students, to conclude there was a desire on the part of the state to provide affirmative protection to students." Stoneking, 856 F.2d at 603. *Also* Pagano v. Massapequa Public Sch., 714 F. Supp. 641 (E.D. N.Y. 1989); Doe v. Taylor Independent School Dist., 975 F.2d 137 (5th Cir. 1992). But *see,* J.O. v. Alton Community Unit School Dist. 11, 909 F.2d 267 (7th Cir. 1990); D.T. v. Independent School Dist. No. 16, 894 F.2d 1176 (10th Cir. 1990).

18. C. S. Moelis, Banning Corporal Punishment: A Crucial Step Toward Preventing Child Abuse,

Children's Legal Rights Journal, 9 (3) (1988), pp. 2–5 (citing Department of Education, Office for Civil Rights national projected data).

19. D. J. Messina, Corporal Punishment v. Classroom Discipline: A Case of Mistaken Identity, *Loyola Law Review, 34* (1988), pp. 35–110, at 57–69.

20. *Id.* at 59.

21. *Id.*

22. The Pennsylvania Superior Court gave a male elementary school gym teacher a 5- to 10-year aggregate sentence for sexually abusing two girls who were 5 and 8 years old. Commonwealth v. Willis, 553 A.2d 959 (Pa. 1989). In another case, a principal sexually molested a male student for 4 years. Fisher v. Independent Sch. Dist., 357 N.W.2d 152 (Minn. Ct. App. 1984). In one case, a male music teacher was found guilty of engaging in a 1-year affair with a 13-year-old girl. Osterback v. State, 789 P.2d 1037 (Alaska Ct. App. 1990).

23. Psychological maltreatment can be associated with "rejecting, degrading, terrorizing, isolating, corrupting, exploiting, and denying emotional responsiveness." *See generally* Broadhurst, *supra* note 9.

24. *In Re Gault,* 387 U.S. 1, 59 (1967) (Black, J., concurring).

25. Breed v. Jones, 421 U.S. 519, 528 (1975).

26. For a discussion *see* I. Schwarts, M. Steketee, and J. Butts, Business as Usual: Juvenile Justice During the 1980s, *Notre Dame Journal of Law Ethics and Public Policy, 5* (1991), pp. 377–396.

27. 387 U.S. 1 (1967).

28. 387 U.S. at 27.

29. Schall v. Martin, 467 U.S. 253 (1984).

30. *In Re Winship,* 397 U.S. 358 (1970); Breed v. Jones, 421 U.S. 519 (1975); Illinois v. Vitale, 447 U.S. 410 (1980).

31. McKeiver v. Pennsylvania, 403 U.S. 528 (1971).

32. 383, U.S. 541 (1966).

33. R. O. Dawson, An Empirical Study of Kent Style Juvenile Transfers to Criminal Court, *St. Mary's Law Journal, 23* (1992), pp. 975–1054, at p. 980.

34. Kent, 383 U.S. at 566-567.

35. Stanford v. Kentucky, 492 U.S. 937 (1989); *but see* Thompson v. Oklahoma, 487 U.S. 815 (1988); Woods v. Florida, 479 U.S. 954 (Marshall dissenting to denial of certiorari) (1986).

36. Miranda v. Arizona, 384 U.S., 436 (1966).

37. *See* Fare v. Michael C., 442 U.S., 707 (1979); Woods v. Clusen, 794 F.2d 293 (7th Cir. 1986); *In Re Thompson,* 241 N.W.2d 2 (Iowa 1976); Beecher v. Alabama, 389 U.S. 35 (1967).

38. Grisso, *Evaluating Competencies: Forensic Assessments and Instruments* (1986), pp. 113–155; State v. Benoit, 126 N.H. 6, 490 A.2d 295, 300 (1985).

39. Rhode Island v. Innis, 446 U.S. 291 (1980).

40. 107 A.D.2d 1053, 486 N.Y.S.2d 575 (N.Y. App. 1985).

41. *E.g.,* McIntyre v. State, 309 Md. 2d 607, 526 A.2d 30 (1987).

42. Gallegos v. Colorado, 370 U.S. 49, 54 (1962).

43. *E.g.,* Colo. Rev. Stat. 19-2-102 (1981); Iowa Code 232.11; NC. Gen. Stat. 7A-595; Okla. Title 10 Stat. 1109.

44. In *People in Re P.E.A.,* 754 P.2d 382 (Colo. 1988) the court found that a statute that required the statements made by juvenile be suppressed unless a parent or guardian had been present during questioning was *not* applicable to questioning by a school principal and security officer. *Also* Cason v. Cook, 810 F.2d 188 (8th Cir. 1987), *cert. denied* 107 S. Ct. 3217.

45. American Law Institute, 1 Trial Manual for Defense Attorneys in Juvenile Court, 650 (1991). R. Hertz, M. Guggenheim, & A. G. Amsterdam, Philadelphia: American Law Institute—American Bar Association Committee on Continuing Professional Education.

46. American Law Institute, 1 Trial Manual for Defense Attorneys in Juvenile Court, 20 (1991). R. Hertz, M. Guggenheim, & A. G. Amsterdam, Philadelphia: American Law Institute—American Bar Association Committee on Continuing Professional Education.

47. *Id.,* R. O. Dawson, An Empirical Study of Kent Style Juvenile Transfers to Criminal Court, *St. Mary's Law Journal, 23* (1992), pp. 975–1054, at p. 993.

48. *E.g., In re Walker,* 282 N.C. 28, 191 S.E.2d 702 (N.C. 1972); *In Re K.,* 26 Or. App. 451, 554 P.2d 180 (1976).

49. Kent v. U.S., 383 U.S. 541 (1966).

50. 387 U.S. 1 (1967).

51. *Q. All right. Now, Judge, would you tell me under*

what section of the law or tell me under what section of—of the code you found the boy delinquent?

A. Well, there is a—I think it amounts to disturbing the peace. I can't give you the section, but I can tell you the law, that when one person uses lewd language in the presence of another person, that it can amount to—and I con-sider that when a person makes it over the phone, that it is considered in the presence, I might be wrong, that is one section. The other section upon which I consider the boy delinquent is Section 8—201, Subsection (d), habitually involved in immoral matters.

CHAPTER 7

NEGLIGENCE

INTRODUCTION

A *tort* is a civil wrong, as when an individual commits a wrong against another individual. Defamation, assault, and trespass are examples of intentional torts. Negligence differs from these in that it is an unintentional tort. It occurs when one person unintentionally causes an injury to another through a breach of duty. *Negligence* is the failure to exercise due care when subjecting another to a risk or danger that causes harm. The court redresses this wrong by awarding the injured party monetary damages to compensate for the injuries incurred.

Schools and their employees are not automatically responsible for every injury that may occur within the school. In order to be held liable for negligence, the following four questions must be answered in the affirmative:

1. Did the defendant owe a duty to the plaintiff?
2. Did the defendant breach that duty?
3. Was the plaintiff injured?
4. Was the breach the proximate cause of the injuries?

Further, there can be no defenses to the action. Generally speaking, to recover damages, it must be shown that the defendant owes a duty to the injured person, that the behavior fell short of that required, that this caused a real injury to the person, and that the injured person was not responsible for causing the injury.

DUTY

There is a duty of due care that the law recognizes one person owes to another. This duty may arise from a contract, a statute, common sense, or a special relationship the parties have to one another. Basically, a duty exists between two people when the relationship between them is such that one is obligated to exercise at least ordinary care that the other person not be injured. Regarding students, the courts have found that schools and their employees have the duty to supervise students, provide adequate and appropriate instruction prior to commencing an activity that may pose a risk of harm, and provide a safe environment. Usually, that duty extends to students while they are in the custody or control of the school. However, duties can be extended if a person assumes additional responsibilities, such as assuming the duty to supervise students before and after school.

In this connection, it is important to note that in education, no one is automatically responsible for the acts of another. School administrators are not automatically held liable for the negligent acts of teachers and other employees. The doctrine of *respondeat superior*, which requires an employer to be responsible for acts of their employees, does not operate the same way in schools as in business and industry. School administrators are not normally employers of the staff they supervise. The doctrine only works to impose liability on the *school district*, not the administrators. Additionally, the doctrine is often not found applicable to instructional staff because of the history of autonomous actions in the classroom. Thus, in school situations, a plaintiff must find a separate duty on the part of each defendant that is brought into the action.

BREACH OF DUTY

A breach of duty amounts to a failure of one person to conform to the standard of care required toward another. One has a legal duty to act as an ordinary, prudent, reasonable person considering all of the circumstances involved. The court determines if a reasonable person would have acted similarly under the circumstances. This "reasonable person" has been described as one who has: (1) the physical attributes of the defendant himself or herself, (2) normal intelligence, (3) normal perception and memory with a minimum level of information and experience common to the community, and (4) the same skills and knowledge as the defendent has or holds himself or herself out to the public as having.

The reasonable person standard varies to take into consideration a person's position or training. Defendants who are professional will be held to a standard based on the skills and training they should have acquired in order to hold themselves out as professionals. This standard will be higher than that which would apply to an ordinary person. In essence, the court will be looking at whether this defendant acted as a reasonable teacher (or administrator) would have under the circumstances.

In assessing negligence, students are not held to the same standard of care as an adult; rather, their actions must be reasonable for a child of similar age, maturity, intelligence, and experience. Some courts have further classified minors according to a presumption of capability for negligence: (1) children under the age of 7 are considered incapable of negligence; (2) children over the age of 14 are presumed capable of negligence; and (3) children between 7 and 14 years of age are considered incapable of negligence, but the presumption can be rebutted. The noted exception is that children are held to the standard of an adult when they are engaged in adult activities, e.g., driving a car, handling a weapon, and so on.

The standard of care requires not only consideration of the defendant but also the circumstances involved. Each situation gives rise to a unique set of circumstances, and each situation should be assessed independently. Some factors that should be examined include the age and maturity of the plaintiff, the nature of the risk to which he or she was exposed, and the precautions that were taken by the defendant to avoid injury. The degree of care for supervision most often would be determined by factors such as the age, maturity, and disposition of the students, the environment, the type of instructional activity, and previous practice and experience.

The circumstance of having responsibility for a child who is disabled may increase the amount of supervision necessary to be deemed reasonable. For example, the court in *Payne v. North Carolina Department of Human Resources*[1] found that increased precautions had to be considered in supervising a deaf student in a shop class. The standard for reasonableness regarding safe facilities also varies depending on the age, maturity, and physical abilities of the students, the environment, the use of such facilities, the extent and likelihood of harm to the student, and sometimes the cost of alternative equipment. For example, in *Bertetto v. Sparta Community District,*[2] the student sued the school after being thrown from a wheelchair while being transported. The question hinged on the reasonableness of the equipment for the student.

CAUSATION

Just because a school or an employee has not been reasonable in carrying out the duty owed to students does not mean that a student will recover monetary damages. To recover for an injury, a student must also show that the negligence (failure to be reasonable in carrying out the duty) was the cause of the injury in question. In other words, if the accident would have occurred, even if there had been no negligence, there can be no recovery. In addition, when a series of events leads up to the injury, such as the actions of another person, the type of injury actually incurred must be a foreseeable result of the negligence. Foreseeability suggests that the defendant could or should have seen the potentially dangerous consequences of the action when it was taken. This does not mean that the defendant subjectively or personally foresaw the actual danger, but rather that a reasonable person would have foreseen the possibility of the type of injury.

Increasingly, schools are becoming more aware of the potential for liability when a student is injured by a third party. These cases arise often when one student has injured another. In addition, there has been an increase in the number of cases that involve injuries caused by others who are not a part of the school community. Often, these are situations in which the outsider has intentionally harmed the student—not just the injury caused by throwing snowballs or roughhousing on the playground, but intentional assault. In these situations, the court looks to whether the intentional act of the outsider was a foreseeable result of the defendant's negligence. Thus, if the school is negligent for not providing proper security in a school, and a student is assaulted by an intruder, the school will be liable for those damages.

INJURY

To recover, the plaintiff must show an actual loss or real damages. Nominal damages sought to indicate a technical right or the threat of future harm is not sufficient grounds for a negligence action. Compensation may include direct monetary damages, such as medical expenses, replacement of property, as well as compensation for pain and suffering.

DEFENSES

Once these elements have been established, the court may look to the possibility of defenses before a damage award is granted. These defenses range from governmental immunity to the more usual affirmative defenses or assumption of the risk, and comparative or contributory negligence. This area differs widely between states.

As recent as 30 years ago, tort liability in public schools was virtually nonexistent because such actions were precluded by the doctrine (statutory or common law) of *sovereign immunity.* In states that have sovereign immunity, an individual may not bring an action against the state. Immunity is motivated by the public policy interest in not allowing individuals to receive money to compensate them from the public treasury. The thinking is that this money should be protected and used only for the intended public purpose—in this instance, education.

Sovereign immunity has greatly eroded in recent years, generally allowing an individual to recover for injuries, but not allowing an action that would undermine or question its decision-making power as a governmental actor, or actions taken to carry out official functions. This distinction is usually noted between proprietary and governmental function. Thus, a student may sue a school for failing to provide adequate playground supervision but not for setting the start of the schoolday at 8:00 A.M. In many states, the courts have abolished sovereign immunity, or the legislature has abolished it or passed some limiting statute.

Assumption of the risk is an affirmative defense that, if successful, is a complete bar to a plaintiff's recovery. It is based on the idea that the plaintiff knew that his or her actions would lead to injury. This is a difficult defense to use in the school setting because of the age and maturity level of students. It must be shown that the plaintiff understood the specific action or activity was dangerous and nonetheless voluntarily went forward with the action. Assumption of the risk is often used successfully in sports injuries. For instance, students who are playing tennis know there is always a risk of falling or twisting their elbows or ankles. When such an injury occurs during the normal course of a match, the school is not responsible.

Many people mistakenly believe that parents assume all risks when they sign permission slips for their children to participate in activities. Although parents may assume the normal risks associated with the activity, they do not assume all risks. They cannot assume risks of which they have no knowledge. A permission slip will not be interpreted to assume unreasonable risks of harm because parents would not have known of those risks.

The defenses of contributory and comparative negligence offer a complete bar or a reduction in the damage award due to the plaintiff being partially responsible for his or her injuries. Making this determination is similar to making the determination of the defendant's negligence, i.e., the court will inquire into the plaintiff's duty and whether the plaintiff failed to act reasonably under the circumstances.

Contributory negligence is a total bar from recovery regardless of the degree of fault. In other words, if the plaintiff is responsible for the injuries sustained in any way, no matter how slight, he or she cannot be awarded any damages. Since children are held to the standard of care of similarly aged children, it is difficult to find contributory negligence on the part of a very young child.

Comparative negligence, however, apportions the damage award among the negligent parties depending on their level of fault or contribution to the injuries. Comparative negligence is distinguished between pure and modified forms. Pure comparative negligence allows the plaintiff to recover any amount of damages for which the defendant was negligent. Even if the plaintiff is 90 percent negligent, he or she can recover 10 percent of his or her damages from a negligent defendant. In states that have adopted modified comparative negligence, damages are awarded to a negligent plaintiff only if the defendant's negligence is greater than his or her own. Over the last 15 years, states have rapidly moved to replace their system of contributory negligence with some form of comparative negligence. Today, a majority of states operate with some type of comparative negligence.

BODANESS v. STATEN ISLAND AID, INC.
144 Misc. 2d 245, 544 N.Y.S. 2d 115 (1989)

CUSICK, Justice.

****

Staten Island Aid, Inc., a non-profit corporation, provides vocational training and employment for self-sufficient mentally retarded adults. The program is run pursuant to the Mental Hygiene Law of the State of New York.

Staten Island Aid, Inc., located at 219 Bay Street operates daily weekday sessions from approximately 8:00 A.M. to 3:00 P.M. and does not assume responsibility for its participants' travelling arrangements. Upon dismissal for the day, approximately one-third of the 160 participants leave the facility and walk one block to the public bus stop on the north side of Victory Boulevard, at the corner of Bay Street. While at the bus stop, on the afternoon of November 12, 1984, Gregory Yurek, a program participant, began to chase Susan McWalters, another program participant. After catching up with McWalters, Yurek pushed her into plaintiff Evelyn Bodaness. Bodaness was thrown to the ground, causing her to sustain serious injuries. Affidavits submitted by the plaintiff aver that the program participants often engaged in such horseplay. . . .

At issue is whether S.I. Aid, Inc., is liable, as a matter of law, to the plaintiff for the activities of its program participants committed subsequent to their dismissal for the day. Negligence consists, inter alia, of a duty of care owed to another and a breach of such duty. . . .

Plaintiff has been unable to cite to any cases reported in New York which squarely define a school's liability for injuries caused by students to third parties off school premises and after dismissal. However, authority in this area has established that a school's duty to protect students terminates once they are outside of its custody and control. . . . *Fornaro v. Kerry*, 139 A.D.2d 561, 527 N.Y.S.2d 61. In *Fornaro*, the infant plaintiff was injured after being struck with a rock thrown by another student. This incident occurred while the students were waiting for the school bus at the designated pick-up location. (*Id.*, at 561, 527 N.Y.S.2d 61). . . . The court reasoned that a school district's duty was premised on its physical control of the students. . . . By logical extension of this reasoning, it is proper to conclude that once S.I. Aid., Inc., discharged its program participants at 3:00 P.M., it no longer had physical control upon which to base a duty owed to Evelyn Bodaness. To hold S.I. Aid., Inc., liable for program participants' activities which occur outside of its custody or physical control after dismissal constitutes an unrealistic burden, lacking any guidelines or boundaries. Its duty must end at some time or place, and to consider the duty terminated upon discharge at 3 P.M. each day is not unreasonable.

****

The plaintiff argues that a question of fact is presented regarding whether Staten Island Aid, Inc., was negligent for failing to reasonably foresee that an accident would occur and to provide appropriate supervision. This approach to the problem at hand is akin to leading the cart before the horse.

. . . As aptly stated by the Court of Appeals in *Pulka v. Edelman,* 40 N.Y. 2d 781, at p. 785, 390 N.Y.S.2d 393, 358 N.E. 2d 1019:

****

Foreseeability should not be confused with duty. The principle expressed in Palsgraf v. Long Island Railroad Co., *248 N.Y. 339, . . . is applicable to determine the scope of duty—only after it has been determined that there is a duty. Since there is no duty here, that principle is inapplicable.*

In holding that there is no duty here, it must be stressed that not all relationships give rise to a duty. One should not be held legally responsible for the conduct of others merely because they are within our sight or environs. . . .

****

The plaintiff also argues that S.I. Aid, Inc., was statutorily negligent in failing to maintain updated records and statistics on the program participants, as required by the Rules and Regulations of the NYS Department of Mental Hygiene, Part 85 (14 NYCRR). The declared purpose of these rules and regulations is to provide the mentally retarded with programs most conducive to their personal growth. Mental Hygiene Law § 13.01. Thus, Bodaness is not within the class of persons which the statute seeks to protect. (*See*, Prosser, Law of Torts, § 35 (4th Ed.)). She therefore cannot be said to have any cause of action accruing from the violation of these regulations, nor can the failure to comply create a duty where none otherwise exists.

****

(Footnotes omitted.)

— — — —

BERTETTO v. SPARTA COMMUNITY UNIT DISTRICT NO. 140
188 Ill. App. 3d 954, 544 N.E.2d 1140
(Appellate Court of Illinois 1989)

HARRISON, Justice.

****

The pleadings at issue here alleged that plaintiff suffers from a medical condition diagnosed as spinal muscle atrophy with scoliosis and that she is confined to a wheelchair. She was a student at the Sparta-Lincoln Attendance Center . . . . On the other side of North St. Louis Street from the center was a playground which the School District also controlled and maintained.

The pleadings further alleged that on September 8, 1986, the School District transported plaintiff from the center to the playground in her wheelchair. That wheelchair had been entrusted to the District by plaintiff's parents. Although plaintiff's parents had advised the School District that plaintiff had to be secured in the wheelchair by her seat belt whenever she was moved, plaintiff's seat belt was not fastened on this occasion. One of plaintiff's classmates was allowed to push plaintiff along in the wheelchair, and as this was being done, the wheels of the wheelchair hit a "crevice," "thereby throwing the plaintiff with force and violence upon the pavement." As a result of this accident, plaintiff suffered numerous injuries, including a fractured right femur, bruises, contusions of the body and internal injuries.

****

Count I of plaintiff's amended complaint in this case alleged negligence . . . when plaintiff was being transported from the center to the playground, . . . the School District, "through its agents and servants acting in its behalf, owed the duty of exercising due care and caution in providing, operating and utilizing adequate equipment, namely the entrusted wheelchair and attached seat belt."

Count I further alleged that the District breached this duty when it "[c]arelessly and negligently failed to provide, operate and utilize adequate equipment, namely, the entrusted wheelchair and seat belt, which would have prevented Lara Bertetto from being thrown from the wheelchair. . . .

The School District attempts to . . . argu[e] that because the equipment alleged to be inadequate here,

the wheelchair and seat belt, was supplied to the School District by plaintiff's parents, the District cannot be held liable. This argument must fail. The affirmative duty to furnish adequate equipment . . . belongs to the School District, not the parents. Accordingly, if the equipment supplied by parents is not adequate for a particular activity, we believe that the District must provide alternate equipment which is adequate. Unless the activity is one which is required to be provided pursuant to some other provision of the law, the District may, of course, also choose not to allow the student to participate in the activity. But in any case, the School District may not evade its duty by attempting to shift responsibility for providing adequate equipment to the parents of the children in its charge. . . .

****

For the foregoing reasons, the judgment of the circuit court of Randolph County dismissing . . . [the] complaint . . . is reversed, and this cause is remanded to the circuit court for further proceedings not inconsistent with the views expressed in this opinion.

REVERSED AND REMANDED.
(Footnotes omitted.)

— — — —

GREIDER v. SHAWNEE MISSION UNIFIED SCHOOL DISTRICT NO. 512
710 F. Supp. 296 (U.S. District Court, District of Kansas 1989)

SAFFELS, District Judge.

****

The uncontroverted facts for purposes of these motions are as follows.

In the fall of 1985, plaintiff Alexander Greider was an eighth grader at Trail Ridge Junior High. He was enrolled in an industrial arts class taught by defendant, Mark Isenberg and was injured in that class while using a table saw. Greider has been classified by the defendant school district as a behaviorally disturbed child and therefore "handicapped" under the Education for All Handicapped Children Act of 1975 ("EHA"), 20 U.S.C. § 1401 *et seq.* . . .

One of the special education teachers at Trail Ridge Junior High determined that Greider should be enrolled in Isenberg's woodworking class. The special education instructor claims she notified Isenberg that Greider was a special education student, and further advised him of Greider's particular problems and needs. However, Isenberg does not recall receiving any such notice.

While in Isenberg's woodworking class, Greider severely injured his hand on a table saw. He now brings suit . . . contending the school district and Isenberg were negligent in several regards. He contends that defendants failed to take reasonable steps to protect his safety. According to Greider, those failures included placing him in the class despite his behavioral disturbance, failing to properly notify Isenberg of his enrollment in the class and of his particular problems and needs, failing to properly instruct plaintiff on safety procedures while taking into consideration his behavioral disturbance, and failing to provide proper guards and warnings on the table saw. Further, Greider contends defendants were negligent in failing to properly supervise Greider's activities in the woodworking class.

****

The court finds that the defendants here were under a legal duty to properly supervise Greider in the woodworking class and to take reasonable steps to protect his safety. Reasonable steps would at least include properly instructing him on safety procedures and providing proper guards and warning signs on the table saw on which he was injured. Such matters were not "discretionary" and the defendants are not entitled to immunity.

Defendants do contend that they are entitled to immunity concerning their decision to place Greider in the woodworking class and to notify defendant Isenberg of his presence there and his special needs and problems. 34 C.F.R. § 300, App. C(17)(c) requires that a child's "regular" teachers should be informed of the child's IEP. Since the district was under a legal duty to notify Isenberg, the district would not be entitled to immunity if it failed in this duty. Finally, the court finds that in assigning Greider to the woodworking class, the school district had a duty to take into consideration Greider's safety. This of course would include determining whether Greider could safely operate the power tools in the class, despite his behavioral disorder. This is a minimal duty it would owe to any student, whether handicapped or not. Thus, the discretionary function exception does not apply in this instance, and defendants are not entitled to immunity under the KTCA [Kansas Tort Claims Act]. Accordingly, defendants' motion for summary judgment will be denied and plaintiff's motion for summary judgment on the issue of the applicability of the KTCA will be granted.

****

IT IS BY THE COURT THEREFORE ORDERED that defendants' motion for summary judgment is denied. . . .

(Footnotes omitted.)

— — — —

JACKSON v. CHICAGO BOARD OF EDUCATION
192 Ill. App. 3d 1093, 549 N.E. 2d 829
(Appellate Court of Illinois 1989)

BUCKLEY, Justice.

Betty Jackson (plaintiff) brought an action in the circuit court of Cook County against defendants Chicago Board of Education (the Board), Ruby L. Rhodes, Bertha Easterling, and Keith Washington for personal injury she sustained in an educably mentally handicapped (EMH) classroom in February 1982, when she was struck by a chalkboard clip thrown by defendant Washington. . . .

. . . . Rhodes testified that on February 24, 1982, she taught 14 children, ages ranging from 12 to 15 years, in an EMH class at Bryn Mawr Elementary School in Chicago, Illinois. On her 20-minute scheduled break that day, she left the classroom at 1:12 P.M. to be attended by Easterling, a teacher's aide who simultaneously supervised a "regular" second grade class during this recess period. Rhodes returned to the classroom by 1:32 P.M.

Easterling testified that during the recess period, as part of her regular duties, she went back and forth between the EMH classroom and the regular second grade classroom, leaving each class unattended for a minute at a time. While she monitored the "regular" second grade classroom, she heard yelling in the EMH classroom. She then returned to the EMH classroom.

Plaintiff testified that Easterling did not enter the room during the recess break. The children in the classroom were acting "wild," sitting on the desks, standing at the back of the room, and play-fighting. While she was in the back of the room, someone called her name. When she turned around, she was hit in the eye by a chalkboard clip.

Washington testified that Rhodes was gone a short time when he began tossing a "paper clip" in the air and catching it. He mistakenly threw the clip backwards over his shoulder. He was not aware that it hit plaintiff until he heard her holler. He further testified that 20 minutes elapsed from the time of the accident until Rhodes returned, and no adult was present during the recess period.

****

Plaintiff introduced an affidavit of Dr. Patricia Shafer, a psychologist, wherein Shafer stated her opinion that a mentally handicapped 15-year-old child, functioning educationally at a seven-year-old child's level, without the presence of an authority figure is "more likely to act on his immediate impulses resulting in unintended consequences." She further stated her belief that "a class of mentally handicapped children, functioning at the mental age of 7 or 8, should not be left unattended for any period of time."

In granting summary judgment in favor of defendants, the circuit court applied the willful and wanton standard as set forth in *Kobylanski v. Chicago Board of Education* (1976), 63 Ill. 2d 165, 347 N.E.2d 705. In *Kobylanski*, our supreme court interpreted the Illinois School Code . . . as conferring upon teachers and other certificated educational employees in disciplinary and nondisciplinary supervisional matters the status of in loco parentis, thereby extending to them the parental immunity from ordinary negligent conduct and requiring proof of willful and wanton misconduct as a prerequisite to imposition of liability.

****

We turn now to plaintiff's . . . contention that the circuit court erred in granting summary judgment to defendants under the willful and wanton misconduct standard. To establish that a person's conduct has been willful and wanton, a plaintiff must show that the act was "committed under circumstances exhibiting a reckless disregard for the safety of others, such as a failure, after knowledge of impending danger, to exercise ordinary care to prevent it or a failure to discover the danger through recklessness or carelessness when it could have been discovered by ordinary care." *Lynch v. Board of Education, Collinsville Community Unit School District 10* (1980), . . . 412 N.E.2d 447, 457;. . . Defendants argue that even ac-

cepting the disputed fact that the EMH students were left without any supervision during the 20- or 30-minute recess period, Illinois case law demonstrates that plaintiff did not present sufficient evidence to create a factual question as to whether defendants had the requisite knowledge to meet the above standard.

Illinois courts have consistently held that a teacher's mere act of leaving children unsupervised will not be sufficient to establish willful and wanton misconduct. . . . Rather, a plaintiff must show that a teacher or school was aware or should have known that the absence of supervision posed a high probability of serious harm or an unreasonable risk of harm. . . . A plaintiff's general allegation that a teacher or school should have known the harm would occur without adult supervision is insufficient to satisfy this standard. . . .

The specific allegations necessary to raise a jury question as to whether a teacher or school's lack of supervision is willful and wanton is best illustrated by the following cases. In *Gammon v. Edwardsville School District* (1980), 82 Ill. App. 3d 586, 38 Ill. Dec. 28, 403 N.E.2d 43, where a student was injured when a classmate struck him in the eye, a jury question was raised by the fact that the guidance counselor was previously warned of the student's threats to plaintiff's safety but failed to supervise the students. In *Hadley v. Witt Unit School Dist. 66* (1984), 123 Ill. App. 3d 19, 78 Ill. Dec. 758, 462 N.E.2d 877, summary judgment was improperly granted where the plaintiff had alleged that the teacher left students unattended without directing them to wear goggles during a dangerous experiment involving the hammering of metal.

The record here discloses no evidence of any knowledge by the school or its employees as to prior behavioral problems with Keith Washington. To the contrary, Rhodes testified that Washington was well-mannered and had never given her problems before. The school psychologist stated that Washington's school records gave no indication of behavioral disorders or problems with aggressive behavior. Finally, plaintiff testified that Washington was not a troublemaker.

The evidence is also insufficient to create a factual question as to whether defendants should have known of a high probability of impending danger because the children were EMH students. No evidence was presented that this particular EMH class contained children with behavioral problems or that EMH students by their nature have behavioral disorders. The school psychologist testified that children are placed in the EMH program for academic deficiencies, not behavioral problems. . . .

Accordingly, we affirm the circuit court's order entering summary judgment in favor of defendants Rhodes, the Board and Easterling.

AFFIRMED.

(Footnotes omitted.)

— — — —

WAGENBLAST v. ODESSA SCHOOL DISTRICT
758 P.2d 968 (Washington 1988)

ANDERSEN, Justice.

FACTS OF CASE

****

The plaintiffs in these cases are public school children and their parents.

Odessa School District students Alexander and Charles Wagenblast and Ethan and Katie Hendrick all desired to participate in some form of interscholastic athletics. As a condition to such participation, the Odessa School District requires its students and their parents or guardians to sign a standardized form which releases the school district from "liability resulting from any ordinary negligence that may arise in connection with the school district's interscholastic activities programs." The releases are required by a group of small Eastern Washington school districts, including Odessa, which "pooled" together to purchase liability insurance.

****

ISSUE

Can school districts require public school students and their parents to sign written releases which release the districts from the consequences of all future school district negligence, before the students will be allowed to engage in certain recognized school related activities, here interscholastic athletics?

DECISION

Conclusion

We hold that the exculpatory releases from any future school district negligence are invalid became they violate public policy.

The courts have generally recognized that, subject to certain exceptions, parties may contract that one shall not be liable for his or her own negligence to another. As Prosser and Keeton explain:

It is quite possible for the parties expressly to agree in advance that the defendant is under no obligation of care for the benefit of the plaintiff, and shall be liable for the consequences of conduct which would otherwise be negligent. There is in the ordinary case no public policy which prevents the parties from contracting as they see fit, as to whether the plaintiff will undertake the responsibility of looking out for himself.

In accordance with the foregoing general rule, appellate decisions in this state have upheld exculpatory agreements where the subject was a toboggan slide, a scuba diving class, mountain climbing instruction, an automobile demolition derby, and ski jumping.

As Prosser and Keeton further observe, however, there are instances where public policy reasons for preserving an obligation of care owed by one person to another outweigh our traditional regard for the freedom to contract. Courts in this century are generally agreed on several such categories of cases.

Courts, for example, are usually reluctant to allow those charged with a public duty, which includes the obligation to use reasonable care, to rid themselves of that obligation by contract. Thus, where the defendant is a common carrier, an innkeeper, a professional bailee, a public utility, or the like, an agreement discharging the defendant's performance will not ordinarily be given effect. Implicit in such decisions is the notion that the service performed is one of importance to the public, and that a certain standard of performance is therefore required.

****

This court has also gone beyond these usually accepted categories to hold future releases invalid in other circumstances as well. It has struck down a lease provision exculpating a public housing authority from liability for injuries caused by the authority's negligence and has also struck down a landlord's exculpatory clause relating to common areas in a multi-family dwelling complex.

In reaching these decisions, this court has focused at times on disparity of bargaining power, at times the importance of the service provided, and at other times on other factors. In reviewing these decisions, it is apparent that the court has not always been particularly clear on what rationale it used to decide what type of release was and was not violative of "public policy." Undoubtedly, it has been much easier for courts to simply declare releases violative of public policy in a given situation than to state a principled basis for so holding.

Probably the best exposition of the test to be applied in determining whether exculpatory agreements violate public policy is that stated by the California Supreme Court. In writing for a unanimous court, the late Justice Tobriner outlined the factors in *Tunkl v. Regents of Univ. of Cal.*, 60 Cal. 2d 92, 383 P.2d 441, 32 Cal. Rptr. 33, 6 A.L.R.3d 693 (1963):. . .

****

1. The agreement concerns an endeavor of a type generally thought suitable for public regulation.
   ****

2. The party seeking exculpation is engaged in performing a service of great importance to the public, which is often a matter of practical necessity for some members of the public.
   ****

3. Such party holds itself out as willing to perform this service for any member of the public who seeks it, or at least for any member coming within certain established standards.
   ****

4. Because of the essential nature of the service, in the economic setting of the transaction, the party invoking exculpation possesses a decisive advantage of bargaining strength against any member of the public who seeks the services.
   ****

5. In exercising a superior bargaining power, the party confronts the public with a standardized

adhesion contract of exculpation, and makes no provision whereby a purchaser may pay additional reasonable fees and obtain protection against negligence.
   ****

6. The person or property of members of the public seeking such services must be placed under the control of the furnisher of the service, subject to the risk of carelessness on the part of the furnisher, its employees or agents.

A school district owes a duty to its students to employ ordinary care and to anticipate reasonably foreseeable dangers so as to take precautions for protecting the children in its custody from such dangers. This duty extends to students engaged in interscholastic sports. As a natural incident to the relationship of a student athlete and his or her coach, the student athlete is usually placed under the coach's considerable degree of control. The student is thus subject to the risk that the school district or its agent will breach this duty of care.

In sum, the attempted releases in the cases before us exhibit all six of the characteristics denominated in *Tunkl v. Regents of Univ. of Cal.*, 60 Cal. 2d 92, 98-101, 383 P.2d 441, . . . (1963). Because of this, and for the aforesaid reasons, we hold that the releases in these consolidated cases are invalid as against public policy.

Having decided the case on this basis, only two remaining aspects of the cases require discussion.

The first of these aspects is the relationship of this decision to the doctrine of assumption of risk. Another name for a release of the sort presented here is an express assumption of risk. . . . [T]o the extent that the release portions of these forms represent a consent to relieve the school districts of their duty of care, they are invalid whether they are termed releases or express assumptions of risk.

Nonetheless, risks other than that of a school district's negligence may be present in any sporting event. For instance, an opponent may play recklessly, or the sport may be so inherently dangerous that no amount of reasonable supervision or training can eliminate all the vestiges of danger. If a student knowingly encounters one of these risks, but chooses to play on, it could be argued that the student has voluntarily encountered the risk. By our opinion today we do not rule on this question; the law of assumption of risk has developed and will continue to develop . . . .

****

[I]n order to prove an express assumption of risk, the evidence must show that the plaintiff (1) had full subjective understanding, (2) of the presence and nature of the specific risk, and (3) voluntarily chose to encounter that risk. By their very nature, the existence of these characteristics can only be determined with reference to the facts of an actual lawsuit.

****

The decision of the trial court in the Odessa School District case is affirmed. . . .
(Footnotes omitted.)

ADDITIONAL COMMENTARY

1. The absence of statutorily required curb cuts on school premises could render applicable the "dangerous condition of sidewalks" exception under a state governmental immunity statute. Therefore, the trial court erred when it granted summary judgment in the school district's favor on the claim of negligence where a woman with arthritis fell while stepping from a curb at a district high school. *Gilson v. Doe*, 600 A.2d 267 (Pa. Commw. Ct. 1991).

2. The district's decision to transport a child with developmental disabilities to school by taxi was a matter of discretionary policy making. Thus, the district was immune from liability in a suit alleging that the child had been sexually assaulted by the taxi driver, and the trial court's entering of a partial directed verdict for the district had not been in error. *Tinkham v. Groveport Madison Local School District*, 18 IDELR 291 (Ohio Ct. App. 1991). However, another court has reached the opposite result. In affirming nearly all of a $1.8 million judgment in favor of a 6-year-old girl with Down syndrome who sued a school bus driver, the transportation service, and the school district for her sexual molestation by the driver, the state supreme court ruled that the school district was not immune from liability under the "discretionary function" provision of the state's Tort Claims Act. Moreover, the court ruled that the jury had been properly kept from comparing the intentional misconduct of the driver to the negligence of the transportation service and the school district for the purposes of reducing the assigned percentages of fault. *Kansas State Bank & Trust Company v. Specialized Transportation Services, Inc.* 819 P.2d 587 (Kan. 1991).

3. School counselors have a duty to use reasonable means to prevent a suicide when they are on notice of a student's suicidal intent. Therefore, on the basis of the facts developed to date, a trier of fact could conclude that the duty to prevent a suicide included warning the parent about the danger to his teenage daughter after she made suicidal statements to other students and these statements were relayed to two school counselors before the girl's suicide. *Eisel v. Montgomery County Board of Education*, 597 A.2d 447 (Md. 1991).

4. After a 14-year-old female student with learning and emotional disabilities was allegedly taken from the schoolgrounds and raped by several male students, her parents sued the school board for negligent breach of its statutory and common law duty to provide adequate supervision of its students. Because a genuine issue of material fact existed as to whether the school board breached that duty, the trial court erred in granting summary judgment to the school board, and the case was remanded for jury determination of the questions of fact. *Doe v. Escambia County School Board*, 599 So. 2d 226 (Fla. Dist. Ct. App. 1992).

5. A genuine issue of fact existed regarding whether the school district acted in a grossly negligent manner in deciding to place a 15-year-old student, identified as educably mentally disabled, under the supervision of a janitor. Moreover, the school district's decision regarding the student's supervision was not an exercise of a discretionary function, and even if it were, there was sufficient evidence to indicate that the janitor had acted in a grossly negligent manner in carrying out his duty to supervise. Thus, the trial court's grant of sum-

mary judgment to the school district was reversed, and the case was remanded for further proceedings on the school district's liability for the student's injuries. *Grooms v. Marlboro County School District*, 414 S.E.2d 802 (S.C. Ct. App. 1992).

6. A school bus driver who was attacked on her bus by a student with a mental disturbance was limited to recovering worker's compensation benefits. However, the student was permitted to proceed with a negligence action against the school board and several school employees who may have precipitated the attack when they forcibly placed the student on the bus. *Rankins v. Aytch*, 591 So. 2d 387 (La. Ct. App. 1991).

7. A school district's policy of placing disruptive or potentially violent students in regular education settings is not unconstitutional, in and of itself. Moreover, in the absence of prior knowledge on the part of the school district that a special education student who assaulted a regular education student in a high school hallway had previously exhibited aggressive tendencies, the school district's failure to prevent the attack did not rise to a level of a constitutional violation for which the school district could be held liable. *Cohen v. Philadelphia School District*, 18 IDELR 911 (E.D. Pa. 1992).

8. A taxi company may be held liable as a common carrier for the alleged sexual assault by one of its drivers on a child with developmental disabilities who was being transported to school, regardless of whether the driver was considered an employee or an independent contractor. Therefore, because sufficient evidence was presented at trial that the alleged abuse had occurred, the lower court erred in entering a directed verdict for the company. *Tinkham v. Groveport Madison Local School District*, 18 IDELR 291 (Ohio Ct. App. 1991).

9. Courts have not accepted the Civil Rights Act as a proper vehicle to litigate simple negligence claims. For example, in *Arroyo v. Pla*, 748 F. Supp. 56 (D.P.R. 1990) the court found no civil rights liability for the school's failure to prevent a student from shooting and killing a fellow student. Likewise, in *Maldonado v. Josey*, 975 F.2d 727 (10th Cir. 1992) the court found no civil rights liability involved when a student was accidently strangulated by being caught on his bandana in the cloakroom.

MALPRACTICE

A phrase that quickly strikes fear in the hearts of school personnel is *educational malpractice*. As in medical malpractice, the term refers to negligence on the part of a professional. Educational malpractice cases can be divided into two categories: those arising from a student's failure to achieve, called *instructional malpractice,* and those arising from the classification or placement of children with disabilities, called *diagnostic malpractice*. So far, there has not yet been an award of damages for either type of educational malpractice upheld by an appellate court.

The seminal case in instructional malpractice is *Peter W. v. San Francisco Unified School District*.[3] Peter W. was illiterate. Contrary to a statute requiring graduates to be able to read at over the eighth-grade level, he received a high school diploma from the San Francisco schools. He sued the district for not teaching him these skills and allowing him to graduate without them. His case was dismissed. The court found no legal duty on which to base the action. Second, the court concluded that there was no workable standard of care for teaching against which the defendants' actions could be judged. In addition, the court noted that the degree of certainty that the plaintiff had suffered any injury, the extent of the injury, and the establishment of a causal link between defendants' conduct and the plaintiff's injuries were all highly problematic. Apparently, the primary motive for the court's reluctance in wrestling with these problems was the public policy involved. The court found a public policy argument against allowing such suits because of the burdensome litigation that would be generated.

Few of our institutions, if any, have aroused the controversies, or incurred the public dissatisfaction, which have attended the operation of the public schools during the last few decades. Rightly or wrongly, but widely, they are charged with outright failure in the achievement of their educational objectives; according to some critics, they bear responsibility for many of the social and moral problems of our society at large. Their public plight in these respects is attested in the daily media, in bitter governing board elections, in wholesale rejections of school bond proposals, and in survey upon survey. To hold them to an actionable "duty of care," in the discharge of their academic functions, would expose them to the tort claims—real or imagined—of disaffected students and parents in countless numbers. They are already beset by social and financial problems which have gone to major litigation, but for which no permanent solution has yet appeared. The ultimate consequences, in terms of public time and money, would burden them—and society—beyond calculation.[4]

Other courts have struck similar actions.[5] These decisions are equally based on public policy concerns. The concern is expressed that recognition of this cause of action would require the courts to make judgments on the validity of broad educational policies and may eventually require their hand in the review of day-to-day implementation of these policies. This would contravene the judicial policy of not becoming involved in educational questions. Additionally, courts have noted that the public has other avenues of relief when dissatisfied with schools in general: through school board elections, individual student achievement in the school, and IDEA reviews. The following are most common reasons for not recognizing the cause of actions:

1. There is a lack of an appropriate standard of care against which to measure conduct.
2. Recognition of the cause of action will likely cause a flood of litigation that would overburden the courts.
3. The award of monetary damages would be uncertain and inappropriate.
4. Litigation of such claims would lead to judicial interference in educational policymaking.

Unfortunately, the summary rejection of these claims has been carried over to cases involving diagnostic malpractice without an examination by the courts of the significant differences between the claims and facts involved. The best known diagnostic malpractice is *Hoffman v. Board of Education of New York*.[6] The action was based on a psychologist's failure to evaluate a student pursuant to a psychologist's order. The action was dismissed, relying on its earlier decision in *Donohue* that educational malpractice as a cause of action did not exist in the state of New York. Other courts have summarily rejected claims for failing to evaluate.[7]

It appears that the general arguments against instructional malpractice are not as strong as those against diagnostic malpractice. The standard of care of the underlying profession, e.g., psychologist, can be applied in these situations. There would not be an open flood of litigation since, in these situations, a new cause of action is really not being recognized. For many years, professional malpractice has been recognized by the courts. Recognition of diagnostic malpractice would merely disallow professionals use of the fact that they are employed by a school as a defense. The argument concerning the appropriateness of monetary damages is probably the same in both types of cases; however, there may be damages other than lack of education that a child or parent has incurred as the result of malpractice. Those issues should be addressed. Finally, the policy argument of not interfering in educational policymaking is not as strong in diagnostic malpractice. Here, there have been clear issues (e.g., Was the evaluation performed and interpreted properly?) that do not involve the broader public matters in educational policymaking.

Although the judicial landscape may change, it does not appear that either cause of action will soon be recognized by the courts. It is more likely that if change occurs, it will be to recognize diagnostic malpractice rather than instructional malpractice. Nonetheless, it is likely that students and parents will seek other avenues and theories for relief.

HOFFMAN v. BOARD OF EDUCATION OF THE CITY OF NEW YORK
49 N.Y.2d 121, 400 N.E. 2d 317, 424 N.Y.S. 2d 376
(Court of Appeals of New York, 1979)

JASEN, Judge.

The significant issue presented on this appeal is whether considerations of public policy preclude recovery for an alleged failure to properly evaluate the intellectual capacity of a student.

The facts in this case may be briefly stated. Plaintiff Daniel Hoffman entered kindergarten in the New York City school system in September, 1956. Shortly thereafter, plaintiff was examined by Monroe Gottsegen, a certified clinical psychologist in the school system, who determined that plaintiff had an intelligence quotient (IQ) of 74 and recommended that he be placed in a class for Children with Retarded Mental Development (CRMD). Dr. Gottsegen was, however, not certain of his findings. The apparent reason for this uncertainty was that plaintiff suffered from a severe speech defect which had manifested itself long before plaintiff entered the school system. Plaintiff's inability to communicate verbally made it difficult to assess his mental ability by means of the primarily verbal Stanford-Binet Intelligence Test administered by Dr. Gottsegen. As a result, Dr. Gottsegen recommended that plaintiff's intelligence "be re-evaluated within a two-year period so that a more accurate estimation of his abilities can be made."

Pursuant to Dr. Gottsegen's recommendations, plaintiff was placed in a CRMD program. While enrolled in the program, plaintiff's academic progress was constantly monitored through the observation of his teachers and by the use of academic "achievement tests" given twice a year. Although in 1959 and 1960 plaintiff received a "90 percentile" rating as to "reading readiness," indicating that his potential for learning to read was higher than average, the results of his achievement tests consistently indicated that he possessed extremely limited reading and mathematical skills. As a result of plaintiff's poor performance on the standardized achievement tests and, presumably, because his teacher's daily observations confirmed his lack of progress, plaintiff's intelligence was not retested on an examination designed specifically for that purpose.

In 1968, plaintiff was transferred to the Queens Occupational Training Center (OTC), a manual and shop training center for retarded youths. The following year plaintiff's mother requested, for the first time, that Plaintiff's intelligence be retested. Plaintiff was administered the Wechsler Intelligence Scale for Adults (WAIS). The results of the test indicated that plaintiff has a "verbal" IQ of 85 and a "performance" IQ of 107 for a "full scale" IQ of 94. In other words, plaintiff's combined score on the WAIS test indicated that he was not retarded. Inasmuch as his course of study at the OTC was designed specifically for retarded youths, plaintiff was no longer qualified to be enrolled. As a result, plaintiff was allowed to complete the spring semester of 1969, but was not allowed to return in the fall.

Thereafter, plaintiff commenced this action against the Board of Education of the City of New York, alleging that the board was negligent in its original assessment of his intellectual ability and that the board negligently failed to retest him pursuant to Dr. Gottsegen's earlier recommendation. Plaintiff claimed that these negligent acts and omissions caused him to be misclassified and improperly enrolled in the CRMD program which allegedly resulted in severe injury to plaintiff's intellectual and emotional well-being and reduced his ability to obtain employment. At trial, the jury awarded plaintiff damages in the amount of $750,000. The Appellate Division affirmed this judgment, two Justices dissenting, as to liability, but would have reversed this judgment and required plaintiff to retry the issue of damages had he not consented to a reduction in the amount of the verdict from $750,000 to $500,000. . . .

At the outset, it should be stated that although plaintiff's complaint does not expressly so state, his cause of action sounds in "educational malpractice." Plaintiff's recitation of specific acts of negligence is, in essence, an attack upon the professional judgment of the board of education grounded upon the board's alleged failure to properly interpret and act upon Dr. Gottsegen's recommendations and its alleged failure to properly assess plaintiff's intellectual status thereafter. As we have recently stated in *Donohue v. Copiague Union Free School Dist.*, 47 N.Y.2d 440, 418 N.Y.S.2d 375, 391 N.E.2d 1352, such a cause of action, although quite possibly cognizable under traditional notions of tort law, should not, as a matter of public policy, be entertained by the courts of this State. (47 N.Y.2d at p. 444, 418 N.Y.S.2d at p. 378, 391 N.E.2d at p. 1354.)

In *Donohue*, this court noted that "(c)ontrol and management of educational affairs is vested in the Board of Regents and the Commissioner of Education (N.Y. Const., art. V, § 4; art. XI, § 2; Education Law, §§ 207, 305;) . . . In that case, the court was invited to undertake a review not only of broad educational policy, but of the day-to-day implementation of that policy as well. We declined, however, to accept that invitation and we see no reason to depart from that holding today. We had thought it well settled that the courts of this State may not substitute their judgment, or the judgment of a jury, for the professional judgment of educators and government officials actually engaged in the complex and often delicate process of educating the many thousands of children in our schools. (*Donohue v. Copiague Union Free School Dist.*, 47 N.Y.2d 440, 444, 418 . . . .) Indeed, we have previously stated that the courts will intervene in the administration of the public school system only in the most exceptional circumstances involving "gross violations of defined public policy." (*Donohue v. Copiague Union Free School Dist.*, 47 N.Y.2d 440, 445 . . . .) Clearly, no

such circumstances are present here. Therefore, in our opinion, this court's decision in *Donohue* is dispositive of this appeal.

****

Our decision in *Donohue* was grounded upon the principle that courts ought not interfere with the professional judgment of those charged by the Constitution and by statute with the responsibility for the administration of the schools of this state. In the present case, the decision of the school officials and educators who classified plaintiff as retarded and continued his enrollment in CRMD classes was based upon the results of a recognized intelligence test administered by a qualified psychologist and the daily observation of plaintiff's teachers. In order to affirm a finding of liability in these circumstances, this court would be required to allow the finder of fact to substitute its judgment for the professional judgment of the board of education as to the type of psychometric devices to be used and the frequency with which such tests are to be given. Such a decision would also allow a court or a jury to second-guess the determinations of each of plaintiff's teachers. To do so would open the door to an examination of the propriety of each of the procedures used in the education of every student in our school system. Clearly, each and every time a student fails to progress academically, it can be argued that he or she would have done better and received a greater benefit if another educational approach or diagnostic tool had been utilized. Similarly, whenever there was a failure to implement a recommendation made by any person in the school system with respect to the evaluation of a pupil or his or her educational program, it could be said, as here, that liability could be predicated on misfeasance. However, the court system is not the proper forum to test the validity of the educational decision to place a particular student in one of the many educational programs offered by the schools of this State. In our view, any dispute concerning the proper placement of a child in a particular educational program can best be resolved by seeking review of such professional educational judgment through the administrative processes provided by statute. (*See* Education Law, § 310, subd. 7.)

Accordingly, the order of the Appellate Division should be reversed and the complaint dismissed. (Footnotes omitted.)

— — — —

SQUIRES v. SIERRA NEVADA EDUCATIONAL FOUNDATION
823 P. 2d 256 (Nevada 1991)

ROSE, Justice:

Brandon Squires (Brandon) attended Cambridge School from pre-kindergarten through second grade. Brandon's parents, Bonnie and Burke Squires (the Squires), chose to send him to Cambridge because they suspected that he might experience difficulties learning to read, based upon his difficulties in articulating words and the difficulties his father had experienced in learning to read. In her affidavit, Bonnie Squires states that she expressed this concern to the principal of Cambridge, Linda Fisher, when she was choosing a school for Brandon. Ms. Fisher specifically advised her that Cambridge had the capabilities and the facilities to diagnose and remediate any reading difficulties which might develop. In addition, Bonnie states that Ms. Fisher told her that Cambridge could provide an education superior to that provided by public schools because of smaller classes, individualized instruction, and a highly qualified staff.

The Squires contend that, in reliance upon Ms. Fisher's statements, they elected to send Brandon to Cambridge, foregoing a public school education. . . .

****

After Brandon's second grade year at Cambridge, the Squires transferred him to a public school where, as a result of his reading deficiencies, he was required to repeat the second grade. As of last February, Brandon was twelve years old and in the fourth grade, and he had been identified as a special education student. Brandon alleges injuries consisting of permanent injury to his mental and emotional development and the pain, frustration, and shame associated with being held back. Furthermore, according to Verlinda Thompson's affidavit, Brandon is likely to suffer future harm because, as a very bright older child with markedly discrepant reading skills, he possesses traits which would characterize him as being at a high risk of dropping out of school. Brandon's parents also allege monetary damages in the form of wasted tuition expenses, the cost of remediation services at the University of Nevada at Reno's Reading Clinic, and three years of private tutoring.

Appellants brought several claims for relief before the district court, alleging primarily (1) educational malpractice, (2) misrepresentation, and (3) breach of contract. . . .

This case presents issue of first impression to this court. A cause of action in contract for educational claims was recognized in dicta in *Paladino v. Adelphi University,* 89 A.D.2d 85, 454 N.Y.s.2d 868, 873 (1982), which held that a cause of action in contract can exist against a private educational institution when that institution provides no service or does not provide certain specified services, such as an agreed upon number of hours of instruction. . . .

The claims presented by appellants in the instant case are similar to those presented in *Paladino.* The Squires allege that a contract existed, whereby they promised to pay tuition in exchange for Cambridge's promise to provide Brandon with a quality elementary education. Unlike the contract alleged in *Paladino,* the quality education for which the Squires contracted was to include certain specified services, such as appropriate individualized reading instruction and adequate diagnostic and remediation services should reading problems develop. Thus, in the instant case, the contract is alleged to contain sufficiently particularized services to support a claim for breach of contract.

The allegations of misrepresentation in the instant case are also similar to those in *Paladino.* The Squires allege that Ms. Fisher made specific representations as to the quality of Cambridge's educational offerings in response to the Squires' specific questions concerning Brandon's potential reading problems. As in *Paladino,* the Squires allege that Brandon's teachers sent progress reports which negligently or knowingly misrepresented that he was not having academic difficulties. . . . [A]ppellants' claim of misrepresentation is also valid.

Because we conclude that appellants have successfully articulated claims of breach of contract and misrepresentation upon which relief may be granted, we decline to address the justiciability of the claim for educational malpractice at this time. Accordingly, we reverse and remand for trial.

(Footnotes omitted.)

SAVINO v. THE BOARD OF EDUCATION OF SCHOOL DISTRICT #1, WESTBURY, N.Y.

123 A.D.2d 314, 506 N.Y.S. 2d 210 (1986)

Before BROWN, J.P., and NIEHOFF, RUBIN and KUNSEMAN, J.J.

****

The complainant alleges that the defendant, by its agents, conducted certain psychological evaluations of the infant plaintiff while he was enrolled at a school, or schools, operated by the defendant. It is further alleged that these evaluations revealed that the infant plaintiff was suffering from severe psychological problems, but that the defendant, while knowing that these problems would worsen if left untreated, nonetheless refused or failed to notify the plaintiff's mother of his condition. It is alleged that as a result of this failure, the psychological problems of the infant plaintiff worsened to the extent that he now displays "chronic antisocial behavior."

The defendant moved to dismiss the complaint on the ground that . . . it is based on educational malpractice, and hence is barred as a matter of public policy under the rule of *Donohue v. Copiague Union Free School Dist.*, 47 N.Y.2d 440, 418 N.Y.S.2d 375, 391 N.E.2d 1352, and *Hoffman v. Board of Educ.*, 49 N.Y.2d 121, 424 N.Y.S.2d 376, 400 N.E.2d 317. . . .

On appeal, the sole issue before us is whether the complaint in this action is one based on educational malpractice. . . . A claim of educational malpractice is based on allegations that a public or private school failed to properly educate a student. . . . This includes cases where the failure to properly educate results from an incorrect assessment of a student's intellectual capacity (*see, e.g., Hoffman v. Board of Educ., supra; Torres v. Little Flower Children's Servs.*, 64 N.Y.2d 119, 485 N.Y.S.2d 15, 474 N.E.2d 223, *cert. denied* --- U.S. ----, 106 S. Ct. 181, 88 L. Ed. 2d 150). However, the complaint under review does not allege that the infant plaintiff was improperly educated, and hence, the complaint is not one based on educational malpractice. Therefore, the complaint should not be dismissed on this basis. . . .

ADDITIONAL COMMENTARY

1. Seeking damages for allegedly negligent evaluation of a student who is disabled is not a suit for professional malpractice; rather, it is an action for educational malpractice that must be dismissed. *Doe v. Board of Education of Montgomery County Maryland*, 453 A.2d 814 (Ct. App. Md. 1982).

2. There is no cause of action in the state of Florida for educational malpractice. *Tubell v. Dade County Public Schools*, 419 So. 2d 388 (Fl. Ct. App. 1982).

3. To the extent that a claim attempts to state a common law cause of action for educational malpractice, it must be dismissed as contrary to public policy. *Silano v. Tirozzi*, 651 F. Supp. 1021 (D. Conn. 1987).

4. In light of the Montana state constitution, statutes, and policies concerning educational goals, compulsory attendance, and special education programs, and since the child clearly falls within the class of students for whom special education programs are provided, school authorities owed the child a duty of reasonable care in testing and placing her in appropriate special education program. *Burger v. Montana*, 649 P.2d 425 (Mont. 1982).

5. A cause of action seeking damages for acts of negligence in the educational process is precluded by considerations of public policy, among them being the absence of a workable rule of care against which the defendants' conduct may be measured, the inherent uncertainty in determining the cause and nature of any damages, and the extreme burden that would be imposed on the already strained resources of the public school system and the judiciary. *Hunter v. Board of Education of Montgomery County*, 439 A.2d 582 (Md. Ct. App. 1982).

6. Under Pennsylvania Public School Code, a school district has a statutory duty to identify exceptional children and provide them with a proper education, but there is no statutory provision whatsoever for a monetary remedy arising out of a breach of these statutory duties. Accordingly, a student with learning disabilities who alleged that she was incorrectly diagnosed as educable mentally retarded cannot establish a claim for relief. *Agostine v. Philadelphia School District,* 527 A.2d 193 (1987).

7. The court in *Torres v. Little Flower Children's Services,* 474 N.E. 2d 223 (N.Y. Ct. App. 1984) refused to allow a suit to go forward against a public social services department and the private agency it authorized. The department had custody of a minor child and had authorized a private agency as responsible for his care. The suit alleged negligence in the provision of educational services. The court ruled that the case was barred by public policy concerns regarding educational malpractice and because of the nature of the determinations the court would be required to make in ruling on the claim.

8. Although a tort of educational malpractice is not recognized in New York, where a deaf child was incorrectly identified as mentally retarded, a teacher or the board of education may be held liable in common law negligence based not on duty to teach, but on duty to observe that a hearing loss rather than retardation caused the child's educational problems. Such duty does not fall within pedagogical methodology and is therefore actionable. *DeRosa v. New York City,* 517 N.Y.S.2d 754 (1987). *See also Cantone v. Rosenblum,* 587 N.Y.S.2d 743 (A.D. 2 1992).

9. As justification for its refusal to recognize a cause of action in educational malpractice, the court concurred with school officials that a cause of action would lack a satisfactory standard of care for measuring the conduct of educators, would produce inherent uncertainty in determining the cause and nature of any damages, would result in an ensuing flood of litigation against schools, and would force courts to blatantly interfere with the internal operations and daily workings of educational institutions. *Rich v. Kentucky Country Day, Inc.,* 793 S.W.2d 832 (Ky. Ct. App. 1990).

ENDNOTES

1. 382 S.E.2d 449 (N.C. App. 1989).
2. 544 N.E.2d 1140 (Ill. App. 1989).
3. 131 Cal. Rptr. 854 (1976).
4. *Peter W.,* 131 Cal. Rptr. at 861.
5. *E.g.,* Donohue v. Copiague Union Free School Dist., 418 N.Y.S.2d 375, 391 N.E.2d 1352 (1979); Rich v. Kentucky Country Day, Inc., 793 S.W.2d 832 (Ky. App. 1990) which involved a private school.
6. 400 N.E.2d 317 (N.Y. App. 1979).
7. Johnson v. Clark, 418 N.W.2d 466 (Mich. App. 1987); Keech v. Berkeley Unified School Dist., 162 Cal. App. 3d 464 (Cal. App. 1984); errors in diagnosis—D.S.W. v. Fairbanks North Star Borough School Dist., 628 P.2d 554 (Alaska 1981); De Rosa v. City of New York, 517 N.Y.S.2d 754 (1987); and placement in the wrong program—Smith v. Alameda County Social Services Agency, 153 Cal. Rptr. 712 (Cal. App. 1979); Hunter v. Bd. of Educ. of Montgomery County, 439 A.2d 582 (Md. App. 1982).

CHAPTER 8

STUDENT CONFIDENTIALITY

INTRODUCTION

In order to properly educate and monitor a child's educational achievement, schools maintain considerable information about each student they encounter. Records of current and past performance, behavioral incidents, health concerns, intelligence tests, psychological examinations, and special education evaluations may all be collected by various school personnel. Understandably, students and their parents have concerns that this personal information be used properly and that confidentiality be respected. These concerns are manifested in two aspects of student confidentiality. First, concerns for student privacy spring to mind—that is, that what students tell school personnel, especially counselors, remains private. Second, school records themselves must be protected, their accuracy assured, and their access restricted to those with a legitimate reason for their use.

PRIVACY

Under the Family Educational Rights and Privacy Act of 1974 (FERPA),[1] the school is bound to restrict access to student information. Often, school personnel, particularly when serving as counselors, assume that this act gives them the right of confidential communications with students. However, this is usually not true. The term *confidentiality* has specific meaning in legal terms, i.e., no one can compel disclosure of information which has been exchanged within a confidential relationship. Within legal terms, this confidentiality generally arises in terms of privileged communications. A privilege protects individuals from information being disclosed, even in courtroom proceedings, i.e., the relationship is so confidential that not even a judge can compel disclosure. This privilege is only recognized from special relationships between two parties—attorney/client, clergy/penitent, physician/patient, or husband/wife. Courts have been reluctant to extend this privilege past these common-law privileges without specific statutory authority.

Some states have granted this privilege to teachers, psychologists, and counselors. Regarding state statutes, Fisher and Sorenson reported the following:

Michigan provide[s] the most complete protection. . . . Similarly, the state of Nevada extends the privilege to both teachers and counselors in civil and criminal proceedings, except for proceedings in criminal offenses where the punishment might be life imprisonment or death. South Dakota provides immunity from testifying to counselors only, not to teachers, which Montana exempts anyone who teaches psychology or is "engaged in the observation of child mentality." The latter provision is sufficiently vague and broad to include counselors and teachers. Delaware, Idaho, Indiana, Maine, Maryland, North Carolina, Oklahoma, Oregon, Pennsylvania, South Carolina, South Dakota, and Washington are the only other states that grant the privilege directly to counselors or teachers, but some favorable arguments can be made by analogy in states where psychologists have received the privilege by statute. . . . 47 states and the District of Columbia have privileged communication stat-utes for psychologists, and 28 states have privi-leged communication statutes for social workers.[2]

This privilege is relevant for court proceed-ings. When a counselor is asked to testify in court—generally in cases involving divorce, abuse, or custody—if the privilege exists, the counselor will not have to disclose the privi-leged information. The adult child or the parent of a minor child may choose to waive the privi-lege, in which case the counselor could be com-pelled to testify.

The more typical situation is when school personnel are asked information from parties other than the court. In these situations, the school is bound by the rules set forth in FERPA and may not disclose information regarding a student without permission. The other typical situation is the question of whether school per-sonnel may withhold information from a parent. Within the bounds of FERPA, school personnel have discretion to withhold information from parents. States may enact statutes specifically giving this authority. For example, in Wiscon-sin, a school psychologist, counselor, social worker, nurse, teacher, or administrator who is working in drug and alcohol abuse programs must keep confidential information received from a student that he or she or others are using or experiencing problems because of use of drugs or alcohol.[3] School districts may also en-act policies regarding the disclosure or with-holding of specific information from parents. Certainly, the overriding concern must be for the student, and good judgment must prevail.

There are situations when, even if the infor-mation is privileged under statute or common law, for the best interests of the student or oth-ers, information must be divulged. The best ex-ample of this is when one in a confidential relationship knows that the student intends to do harm to himself or herself or another specific person. In these situations, one must weigh the possibility of harm against the harm that disclo-sure will cause. If there is a significant possibil-ity that the student will follow through with the threats of harm, disclosure is warranted. States may also, by statute or case law, impose a duty upon counselors to warn known victims, or to actively protect a known victim, or to detain the client to prevent harm.[4] These duties may apply to a greater extent to teachers, school counse-lors, and school psychologists because their claim to true confidentiality is weaker than that of psychiatrists, attorneys, and doctors.

TARASOFF v. THE REGENTS OF THE UNIVERSITY OF CALIFORNIA
17 Cal. 3d 425, 131 Cal. Rptr. 14, 551 P.2d 334
(California 1976)

TOBRINER, Justice.

On October 27, 1969, Prosenjit Poddar killed Tatiana Tarasoff. Plaintiffs, Tatiana's parents, allege that two months earlier Poddar confided his intention to kill Tatiana to Dr. Lawrence Moore, a psycholo-gist employed by the Cowell Memorial Hospital at the University of California at Berkeley. They allege that on Moore's request, the campus police briefly detained Poddar, but released him when he appeared rational. They further claim that Dr. Harvey Powelson, Moore's supervisor, then directed that no further action be taken to detain Poddar. No one warned plaintiffs of Tatiana's peril.

****

Plaintiffs' complaints predicate liability on two grounds: defendants' failure to warn plaintiffs of the impending danger and their failure to bring about Poddar's confinement. . . .

We shall explain that defendant therapists cannot escape liability merely because Tatiana herself was not their patient. When a therapist determines, or pursuant to the standards of his profession should determine, that his patient presents a serious danger of violence to another, he incurs an obligation to use reasonable care to protect the intended victim against such danger. The discharge of this duty may require the therapist to take one or more of various steps, depending upon the nature of the case. Thus it may call for him to warn the intended victim or others likely to apprise the victim of the danger, to notify the police, or to take whatever other steps are reasonably necessary under the circumstances.

****

In the landmark case of *Rowland v. Christian* (1968), . . . , 443 P.2d 561, Justice Peters recognized that liability should be imposed "for an injury occasioned to another by his want of ordinary care of skill" as expressed in section 1714 of the Civil Code. Thus, Justice Peters, quoting from *Heaven v. Pender* (1883) 11 Q.B.D. 503, 509 stated: "whenever one person is by circumstances placed in such a position with regard to another . . . that if he did not use ordinary care and skill in his own conduct . . . he would cause danger of injury to the person or property of the other, a duty arises to use ordinary care and skill to avoid such danger."

We depart from "this fundamental principle" only upon the "balancing of a number of considerations"; major ones "are the foreseeability of harm to the plaintiff, the degree of certainty that the plaintiff suffered injury, the closeness of the connection between the defendant's conduct and the injury suffered, the moral blame attached to the defendant's conduct, the policy of preventing future harm, the extent of the burden to the defendant and consequences to the community of imposing a duty to exercise care with resulting liability for breach, and the availability, cost and prevalence of insurance for the risk involved."

****

Although, . . . under the common law, one person owed no duty to control the conduct of another, . . . nor to warn those endangered by such conduct, . . . the courts have carved out an exception to this rule in cases in which the defendant stands in some special relationship to either the person whose conduct needs to be controlled or in a relationship to the foreseeable victim of that conduct . . . . Applying

this exception to the present case, we note that a relationship of defendant therapists to either Tatiana or Poddar will suffice to establish a duty of care; as explained in section 315 of the Restatement Second of Torts, a duty of care may arise from either "(a) a special relation . . . between the actor and the third person which imposes a duty upon the actor to control the third person's conduct, or (b) a special relation . . . between the actor and the other which gives to the other a right of protection."

****

Defendants contend, however, that imposition of a duty to exercise reasonable care to protect third persons is unworkable because therapists cannot accurately predict whether or not a patient will resort to violence. In support of this argument amicus representing the American Psychiatric Association and other professional societies cites numerous articles which indicate that therapists, in the present state of the art, are unable reliably to predict violent acts; their forecasts, amicus claims, tend consistently to overpredict violence, and indeed are more often wrong than right. Since predictions of violence are often erroneous, amicus concludes, the courts should not render rulings that predicate the liability of therapists upon the validity of such predictions.

****

We recognize the difficulty that a therapist encounters in attempting to forecast whether a patient presents a serious danger of violence. Obviously we do not require that the therapist, in making that determination, render a perfect performance; the therapist need only exercise "that reasonable degree of skill, knowledge, and care ordinarily possessed and exercised by members of (that professional specialty) under similar circumstances.". . . Within the broad range of reasonable practice and treatment in which professional opinion and judgment may differ, the therapist is free to exercise his or her own best judgment without liability; proof, aided by hindsight, that he or she judged wrongly is insufficient to establish negligence.

****

Amicus contends, however, that even when a therapist does in fact predict that a patient poses a serious danger of violence to others, the therapist should be absolved of any responsibility for failing to act to protect the potential victim. In our view, however, once a therapist does in fact determine, or under applicable professional standards reasonably should have determined, that a patient poses a serious danger of violence to others, he bears a duty to exercise reasonable care to protect the foreseeable victim of that danger. . . .

****

For the reasons stated, we conclude that plaintiffs can amend their complaints to state a cause of action against defendant therapists by asserting that the therapists in fact determined that Poddar presented a serious danger of violence to Tatiana, or pursuant to the standards of their profession should have so determined, but nevertheless failed to exercise reasonable care to protect her from that danger. . . .

. . . . The judgment of the superior court in favor of Defendants Gold, Moore, Powelson, Yandell, and the Regents of the University of California is reversed, and the cause remanded for further proceedings consistent with the views expressed herein. (Footnotes omitted.)

— — — —

EISEL v. BOARD OF EDUCATION OF MONTGOMERY COUNTY
324 Md. 376, 597 A. 2d 447 (Court of Appeals of Maryland 1991)

RODOWSKY, Judge.

The legal theory advanced by the plaintiff in this wrongful death and survival action is that school counselors have a duty to intervene to attempt to prevent a student's threatened suicide. . . .

The decedent, Nicole Eisel (Nicole), was a thirteen year old student at Sligo Middle School in Montgomery County. She and another thirteen year old girl consummated an apparent murder-suicide pact on November 8, 1988. Nicole's father, Stephen Eisel (Eisel), brought the instant action. His amended complaint alleges negligence on the part of two counselors at Nicole's school, among others. . . .

****

II.

The amended complaint avers that Nicole became involved in satanism, causing her to have an "obsessive interest in death and self-destruction." During the week prior to the suicide, Nicole told several friends and fellow students that she intended to kill herself. Some of these friends reported Nicole's intentions to their school counselor, Morgan, who relayed the information to Nicole's school counselor, Jones. Morgan and Jones then questioned Nicole about the statements, but Nicole denied making them. Neither Morgan nor Jones notified Nicole's parents or the school administration about Nicole's alleged statements of intent. Information in the record suggests that the other party to the suicide pact shot Nicole before shooting herself. The murder-suicide took place on a school holiday in a public park at some distance from Sligo Middle School. The other party to the pact attended another school.

****

On the issue of duty Eisel argued that, by the School Board's own policy, counselors were required to contact the parents of any child who had expressed suicidal thoughts. Eisel pointed to deposition testimony on that subject by the principal, who said: "If the student is in danger, of course, you take care of that first. Then the next thing you do would be to notify a parent. If the student is in no apparent danger, you will notify the parent." There appear to be two broad categories of cases in which a person may be held liable for the suicide of another. The first type occurs when the defendant's conduct actually causes the suicide. . . .

The second type of case holds that a special relationship between a defendant and the suicidal person creates a duty to prevent a foreseeable suicide. . . .

****

Recent attempts to extend the duty to prevent suicide beyond custodial or therapist-patent relationships have failed. . . .

Given the peculiar mix of factors presented, it is an open question whether there is a duty to attempt to prevent an adolescent's suicide, by reasonable means, including, in this case, by warning the parent. Therefore, we must analyze whether we should recognize a duty in this case.

****

IV.

A. Foreseeability and Certainty of Harm

Foreseeability is the most important variable in the duty calculus, *Ashburn*, 306 Md. at 628, 510 A.2d at 1083, and without it there can be no duty to prevent suicide. Comment, Civil Liability for Suicide, 12 Loy. L.A.L. Rev. at 991. Here Nicole's suicide was foreseeable because the defendants allegedly had direct evidence of Nicole's intent to commit suicide. That notice to the defendants distinguishes this case from *Bogust v. Iverson*, 10 Wis.2d 129, 102 N.W.2d 228, where the counselor had no notice of contemplated suicide.

Nor would reasonable persons necessarily conclude that the harm ceased to be foreseeable because Nicole denied any intent to commit suicide when the counselors undertook to draw out her feelings, particularly in light of the alleged declarations of intent to commit suicide made by Nicole to her classmates. "An adolescent who is thinking of suicide is more likely to share these feelings with a friend than with a teacher or parent or school guidance counselor. But, we all—parents, teachers, administrators, service providers and friends—can learn what the warning signs are and what to do." 3 Maryland Office for Children Youth, Monthly Memo, at 3 (Apr. 1986). Jurors, as triers of fact, may well conclude that the quoted point of view is consistent with their own experiences with adolescents. On the other hand, when the facts of this case are fully developed, the court may conclude that the duty did not arise, or jurors may conclude that it had not been negligently breached.

****

C. Closeness of Connection Between Conduct and Injury

This factor is the proximate cause element of a negligence action considered on the macroscale of policy. Consideration is given to whether, across the universe of cases of the type presented, there would ordinarily be so little connection between breach of the duty contended for, and the allegedly resulting harm, that a court would simply foreclose liability by holding that there is no duty. . . .

The defendants say that the law considers suicide to be a "deliberate, intentional and intervening act which precludes a finding that a given defendant is responsible for the harm." Brief of Appellees at 6. . . . Here, however, we deal with the relationship between an adolescent and school counselors who allegedly were informed that the adolescent was suicidal. Legally to categorize all suicides by adolescents as knowing and voluntary acts which insulate

the death, as a matter of law, from all other acts or omissions which might operate, in fact, as causes of the death is contrary to the policy manifested by the Act. The Act does not view these troubled children as standing independently, to live or die on their own. In a failure to prevent suicide case, Maryland tort law should not treat an adolescent's committing suicide as a superseding cause when the entire premise of the Act is that others, including the schools have the potential to intervene effectively.

****

E. Burden on the Defendant

****

The harm that may result from a school counselor's failure to intervene appropriately when a child threatens suicide is total and irreversible for the child, and severe for the child's family. It may be that the risk of any particular suicide is remote if statistically quantified in relation to all of the reports of suicidal talk that are received by school counselors. We do not know. But the consequence of the risk is so great that even a relatively remote possibility of a suicide may be enough to establish duty. . . .

Moreover, when the risk of death to a child is balanced against the burden sought to be imposed on the counselors, the scales tip overwhelmingly in favor of duty. . . .

The counselors argue that there are elements of confidentiality and discretion in their relationships with students that would be destroyed by the imposition of a duty to notify parents of all reports of suicidal statements. Confidentiality does not bar the duty, given that the school policy explicitly disavows confidentiality when suicide is the concern.

The defendants further point out that ocunselors are required to exercise discretion when dealing with students. Their discretion, however, cannot be boundless when determining whether to treat a student as a potential suicide. Discretion is relevant to whether the standrd of conduct has been breached under the circumstances of a given case. Discretion does not create an absolute immunity, which would be the effect of denying any duty.

****

Considering the growth of this tragic social problem in the light of the factors discussed above, we hold that school counselors have a duty to use reasonable means to attempt to prevent a suicide when they are on notice of a child or adolescent student's suicidal intent. On the facts of this case as developed to date, a trier of fact could conclude that that duty included warning Eisel of the danger.

JUDGMENT OF THE CIRCUIT COURT FOR MONTGOMERY COUNTY REVERSED AND CASE REMANDED TO THAT COURT FOR FURTHER PROCEEDINGS. . . .

****

(Footnotes omitted.)

— — — —

ARNOLD v. BOARD OF EDUCATION OF ESCAMBIA COUNTY
880 F.2d 305 (Eleventh Circuit 1989)

FAY, Circuit Judge:

****

The complaint alleges the following facts. On March 10, 1986, Jane Doe and John Doe discovered that Jane was pregnant. On March 27, 1986, Kay Rose [high school guidance counselor] summoned Jane to her office for counseling. After speaking with Jane, Rose summoned John Doe to her office where he admitted paternity. At the expense of the school board, Rose procured a pregnancy test for Jane which proved positive. Rose informed Powell [high school vice principal] of Jane's pregnancy on April 2, 1986.

The counselors then allegedly coerced the children to agree to abort the child. Because the children were financially unable to afford the medical services attendant to an abortion, the school officials paid Jane and John to perform menial tasks for them. On May 8, 1986, Powell allegedly gave $20.00 to the individual who drove the children to the medical facility in Mobile, Alabama where Jane obtained the abortion.

The complaint alleges that Rose and Powell "coerced" the children "in diverse respects and so fundamentally imposed their wills upon the children that the children were unable to exercise any freedom of choice with regard to the decision whether or not to agree to the termination of the pregnancy." Further, the plaintiffs allege that the school officials "coerced these children to refrain from notifying their parents regarding the matter" and "to maintain the secrecy of their plan" to obtain an abortion for Jane.

****

The plaintiffs argue that the above allegations state eight causes of action. They assert several claims under 42 U.S.C. § 1983 that the various defendants violated the plaintiffs' constitutional rights of due process, free exercise of religion, privacy and equal protection under the first and fourteenth amendments and freedom from involuntary servitude under the thirteenth amendment. The plaintiffs also allege a claim for civil conspiracy under 42 U.S.C. § 1985 (3) (1982). After the plaintiffs filed several amended complaints and the parties conducted discovery, the defendants filed a 12(b)(6) motion to dismiss the complaint for failure to state a claim for relief. The district court granted the motion and dismissed the complaint. The plaintiffs now appeal the complaint's dismissal.

III. SECTION 1983 CLAIMS

Section 1983 creates a private right of action for damages and injunctive relief against individuals and governmental bodies whose conduct under the color of state or local law deprives a plaintiff of rights, privileges or immunities "secured by the Constitution or laws." 42 U.S.C.1983 (1982). To state a prima facie § 1983 claim grounded on a constitutional violation, a plaintiff must allege that 1) the defendant's conduct caused the constitutional violation, and 2) the challenged conduct was "under color of state law." 42 U.S.C. § 1983 (1982). . . .

A. Constitutional Rights

1. The Right to Privacy

Both Jane Doe and her father claim that the school officials coerced Jane into having an abortion. We find that coercing a minor to abort a child violates the minor's constitutionally protected freedom to choose whether to abort or bear her child. Further, the allegations in the complaint are sufficient to state a cause of action on behalf of Jane Doe. Any cause of action alleged by Charles Davis as the father of Jane Doe can only be stated in terms of an impermissible interference with family relations which we will discuss later in this opinion. . . .

****

2. Familial Relations

The second cause of action alleges that the defendants wrongfully coerced the minors to refrain from consulting with their parents prior to determining whether to proceed with the abortion and that this unconstitutionally interfered with the right of privacy existing between the plaintiffs and their children. We find that a parent's constitutional right to direct the upbringing of a minor is violated when the minor is coerced to refrain from discussing with the parent an intimate decision such as whether to obtain an abortion; a decision which touches fundamental values and religious beliefs parents wish to instill in their children. Hence, the complaint sufficiently states a cause of action for invasion in the familial right to privacy on behalf of Charles Davis, the father of Jane Doe and Helen Arnold, the mother of John Doe.

****

These cases demonstrate a willingness to protect from unjustified state interference the parental right to structure the education and religious beliefs of one's children. Likewise, in this case we encounter a state intrusion on this parental right. Coercing a minor to obtain an abortion or to assist in procuring an abortion and to refrain from discussing the matter which the parents unduly interferes with parental authority in the household and with the parental responsibility to direct the rearing of their child. This deprives the parents of the opportunity to counter influences on the child the parents find inimical to their religious beliefs or the values they wish instilled in their children.

****

Further, we are not, as appellees argue, constitutionally mandating that counselors notify the parents of a minor who receives counseling regarding pregnancy. We hold merely that the counselors must not coerce minors to refrain from communicating with their parents. The decision whether to seek parental guidance, absent law to the contrary, should rest within the discretion of the minor. As a matter of common sense, not constitutional duty, school counselors should encourage communication with parents regarding difficult decisions such as the one involved here. . . .

****

B. State Action and Official Policy and Custom Requirement

As previously discussed, under § 1983, in addition to alleging a constitutional right violation, a plaintiff must also allege that the challenged conduct was "under color of state law." Moreover, to impose liability on the school board as a unit of local government, the plaintiff must allege that the challenged conduct executed an official policy or custom of the school board. As school employees, Rose and Powell apparently operated with the authority of the state. Thus, their conduct in their capacity as school officials constitutes action under the color of state law. We find that the complaint sufficiently states a § 1983 claim against the school officials individually.

****

While we find the complaint sufficiently sets forth several claims, we emphasize that none of our findings indicate an opinion as to whether the appellants will or will not be able to present sufficient evidence in support of these claims to withstand a motion for summary judgment or prevail at trial. . . .

****

(Footnotes omitted.)

ADDITIONAL COMMENTARY

1. Confidentiality rights generally apply to educational records of students, not to classroom visits. Access to classrooms is controlled by state law and district policy. *Blades*, 213 E.H.L.R. 169 (OSERS 1988).

2. A school violates a parent's right to privacy when the school conditions a student's receipt of counseling services on the parent receiving counseling. *Teresa Diane P. v. Alief Independent School District*, 744 F.2d 484 (5th Cir. 1984).

3. The parents of a student who had been asked to repeat a grade sought a private evaluation for learning disabilities and then brought an action for reimbursement. The local newspaper printed an article about the request and then the parents sued the paper. The court found that because the parents sought reimbursement of public funds, thereby making the issue a public concern, neither the newspaper nor the reporter could be sued for an invasion of privacy. *Culver v. Port Allegany Reporter*, 598 A.2d 54 (Pa. Super. Ct. 1991).

4. Giving advice regarding contraception and birth control is increasingly becoming a trouble spot for school counselors. Counselors may give this information to minors, unless there is a specific state statute or school district policy forbidding it. As in any area, incompetent advice given that causes injury could result in liability. In *Arnold v. Board of Education of Escambia County*, 754 F. Supp. 853 (S.D. Ala. 1990), the parents of a child who procured an abortion after seeking counseling sought damages against the counselor but lost. In *Hodgson v. Minnesota*, 110 S. Ct. 2926 (1990), the Supreme Court found unconstitutional a statute that prohibited abortions on minors until at least 48 hours after *both* parents had been notified. *See also Bellotti v. Baird*, 428 U.S. 132 (1976); *Bellotti v. Baird (Bellotti II)*, 443 U.S. 622 (1979); *H.L. v. Matheson*, 450 U.S. 398 (1981)); and *City of Akron v. Akron Center for Reproductive Health*, 462 U.S. 416 (1983), in which the Court upheld the requirements of notice and consent of the parents of minor or a judicial determination that the minor is sufficiently mature to make the decision herself.

RECORDS

In 1974, Congress passed the Family Educational Rights and Privacy Act, also known as FERPA, or the Buckley Amendment.[5] The act was passed in response to many concerns that outsiders had more access to children's records than parents, that information was being abused, and that records often contained speculations and erroneous information with no systematic method to correct them.[6] The act addresses these concerns by setting forth restrictions to access to student records, rights to parental access, and a procedure for challenging information. FERPA is applicable to "any public or private elementary, secondary or postsecondary educational agency or institution that receives federal funds,"[7] giving these rights to all students and their parents. Further, parents and students must be notified of their rights under the act on an annual basis.

The act applies to all "education records." This is defined as any personally identifiable record collected, maintained, or used[8] by a school that the student has attended. There are several exceptions outlined:

1. *Personal logs*—records of instructional, supervisory, administrative, and associated educational personnel that are in the sole possession of the maker of the record and not accessible or revealed to any person other than a person substituting for the maker.

2. *Treatment records*—records of a physician, psychiatrist, psychologist, or other recognized professional acting in his or her professional capacity and used only in connection with the treatment of the student.

3. *Directory information*—records that include the student's name, address, telephone listing, date and place of birth, major field of study, participation in officially recognized activities or sports, weight and height of members of athletic teams, dates of attendance, degrees and awards received, and name of school most recently attended. Directory information may be disclosed if the school has given public notice of the categories of information and allowed the parents and students an opportunity to prohibit the disclosure. Directory information about former students need not include an opportunity to prohibit the disclosure.[9]

With these exceptions, all other personally identifiable records are subject to the nondisclosure and access rights contained in FERPA. Under the act, parents and adult students have the right (1) to be informed about the kinds and location of education records maintained by the school and the officials responsible for them and (2) to receive an explanation or interpretation of the records if requested. Officials must comply with a parental request to inspect records within a reasonable time, but in no case more than 45 days after the request, or for special education students, at least 5 days before any pertinent meeting or hearing. Either parent, including a noncustodial parent, has the right to inspect the records, unless prohibited by court order. Although a school may not deny parental access to student records, it may charge the parent a reasonable fee to copy records the parent wishes to keep.

If the parents of minor students or adult students believe the record contains information that is inaccurate, misleading, or otherwise in violation of their privacy or other rights, they must be given an opportunity to challenge the information. If the school disagrees, or refuses to alter the record, they must be provided an opportunity for a hearing on the issue. The hearing must provide an opportunity to correct or delete such information and for the parent or student to insert a written explanation regarding the content of the record.[10]

Regarding the nondisclosure provision, these records generally may not be released without the prior consent of a minor student's parent or an adult student.[11] For special education students, this consent must be in writing. In seeking consent, the school should inform the parents of the purpose of the disclosure, which records are to be disclosed, and to whom and when the disclosure will be made. Exceptions are provided for the following disclosures:

1. To school officials, including teachers, who the school determines have legitimate educational interests in the records

2. To comply with a judicial order or a lawfully issued subpoena, if a reasonable effort is made to notify the parent of a minor student or an adult student of the order or subpoena in advance of compliance

3. To authorized federal, state, and local officials in connection with the audit and evaluation of a federally or state supported education program (the information must be (a) protected in a manner that will not permit identification of students and parents by others and (b) destroyed when it is no longer needed for those purposes)

4. In connection with an emergency, if necessary to protect the health or safety of the student or other persons

5. To the parents of an adult pupil who is a dependent of the parent for federal income tax purposes

6. To officials of other schools in which the student seeks to enroll, provided that an opportunity is provided for a hearing to challenge the content of the records

7. In connection with a student's application for financial aid

8. To organizations conducting certain education-related studies, if conducted in such a manner that identification of the student and his or her parents is not permitted and the information is destroyed when no longer needed[12]

Each school must keep with the educational records of students a record of each person who has requested or obtained access to a student's records. The record must include the legitimate interest that each such person has in obtaining the information.[13]

The Individuals with Disabilities Education Act (IDEA) provides some additional regulations regarding the handling of records, including the following: Under FERPA, a student over the age of 18 assumes the rights granted by FERPA. However, under IDEA, each state is to develop policies regarding access to student records by students themselves. Those policies must be consistent with FERPA but could grant access earlier than age 18. The regulations also indicate that the severity of a student's disability may be a factor in the development of state policy.[14]

Student rights differ under FERPA and IDEA in the area of destruction of records. Under FERPA, schools may destroy some or all of a student's educational records at any time, unless there is an outstanding request to inspect them. However, under IDEA, schools must notify parents before the destruction of any records, and must destroy records at the request of a parent (although a record of directory information may be maintained).[15] The General Educational Provisions Act requires federal grantees to retain records at least five years after the completion of the activity for which the records were used.[16] This may then create a conflict between the obligation to save and a request to destroy.[17] In practice, destroying a file before a child is past the age of graduation would create all sorts of problems for the district and student alike.

PAGE v. ROTTERDAM-MOHONASEN CENTRAL SCHOOL DISTRICT
109 Misc. 2d 1049, 441 N.Y.S.2d 323 (1981)

MINER, Justice:

****

Petitioner is the natural father of Eric Page, a fifth grade student at the Herman L. Bradt Elementary school. The child was born on December 6, 1969 and resides with his natural mother, Michiko Page, in the Town of Rotterdam, Schenectady County. It appears that the child's parents are living separate and apart under the terms of a separation agreement executed in June of 1979. Although a copy of the agreement has not been furnished to the court, it is uncontroverted that the agreement provides for custody in the mother with rights of visitation to the father. The parents are not divorced and there is no court order affecting custody, visitation or support.

Various requests by petitioner to review his son's school records and to meet with school authorities respecting his son's academic progress have been refused. These requests were made both orally and in writing, ...

The Family Educational Rights and Privacy Act of 1974 (20 U.S.C.A., § 1232g) does not support the position taken by respondents. It is specifically provided therein that funds shall not be available to educational agencies which deny to parents the right to inspect and review the education records of their children. The regulations implementing the act (34 CFR 99.11) allow inspection by either parent, without regard to custody, unless such access is barred by state law, court order or legally binding instrument. There is no such bar to petitioner's access here.

Finally, the provisions of the State Education Law, relied on by respondents to thwart the relief sought by petitioner, have no applicability to the case at bar. . . . Section 3212 defines the duties of persons "in parental relation" to assure the attendance and proper condition of children for instruction. It is significant that both parents are charged with responsibility under the terms of this statutory provision. . . .

Petitioner does not seek to alter custodial rights, . . . indeed, petitioner seeks no relief which will inequitably affect the rights, duties and obligations of the child's mother. Accordingly, it was not necessary to join Michiko Page as a party in this proceeding. . . . Educators and school districts, including respondents, are charged with the duty to act in the best educational interests of the children committed to their care. Although it may cause some inconvenience, those interests dictate that educational information be made available to both parents of every school child fortunate enough to have two parents interested in his welfare.

WEBSTER GROVES SCHOOL DISTRICT v.
PULITZER PUBLISHING COMPANY
898 F.2d 1371 (Eighth Circuit 1990)

BOWMAN, Circuit Judge.

In November 1988, T.B., a fourteen-year-old public school student who had been classified as a handicapped child under the Education of the Handicapped Act (EHA) [now IDEA], 20 U.S.C. § 1401(1) (1988), brought a loaded handgun to school, in violation of school policy, and threatened classmates with it. He was first suspended and then expelled from school. Before expulsion, T.B.'s individualized education program (IEP) committee met to determine whether the behavior that resulted in the discipline was a result of the child's handicapping condition. T.B.'s grandmother and legal guardian, a member of the IEP committee, disagreed with the committee's findings of no relation between the gun incidents and the handicap, thus entitling her to seek administrative review on T.B.'s behalf. . . . The school District then sought in Missouri circuit court to enjoin T.B. from attending school pending exhaustion of his administrative remedies, ...

On February 3, 1989 (the day following the hearing), Pulitzer filed motions to intervene and to open the courtroom. In an amended motion, Pulitzer also requested that the District Court unseal the court file. . . .

****

Pulitzer urges us to find a constitutional right of access to civil proceedings and to apply First Amendment standards to this case. The District Court's order denying Pulitzer's motions appears to take that approach. Although the Supreme Court has held "that the right to attend criminal trials is implicit in the guarantees of the First Amendment," *Richmond Newspapers,* 448 U.S. at 580, . . . it never has held that there is a constitutional right of access to civil trials. . . .

We find it unnecessary to our decision in this case to decide whether there is a First Amendment right of access applicable to civil proceedings. Any First Amendment right of access that might apply would be qualified, not absolute. Given the nature and the circumstances of this case, our decision must be the same whether the case is governed by a First Amendment qualified right of access or a common law right of access. We take this view because this case involves a handicapped child proceeding under the EHA, records and testimony regarding his disability, and his educational records. Under any qualified right of access of which we can conceive, the District Court properly granted the motion of T.B.'s guardian to shelter the proceedings from public view.

The privacy of juveniles is protected by the legislatures and the courts of this country in a variety of ways. . . . Juvenile court records are neither to be inspected nor disclosed, except to those who have a legitimate interest in them. Certain juvenile records may be destroyed or sealed when the child reaches seventeen years old. . . . These measures all reflect a strong public policy favoring the special protection of minors and their privacy where sensitive and possibly stigmatizing matters are concerned. This strong public policy applies forcefully to students classified as handicapped because of a learning disability or some other disability that affects their educational progress.

Under the Family Educational Rights and Privacy Act (FERPA) and the regulations thereunder, a school's release of a student's records or personally identifiable information to unauthorized persons will result in the withholding of federal funds. 20 U.S.C. § 1232g(b) (1988); 34 C.F.R. § 99.30 (1988). FERPA applies to T.B., and Congress, through the EHA, has further restricted the release of information when a handicapped student is involved. 20 U.S.C. § 1417(c) (1988). Identifying information about such students is not to be released absent parental consent and its confidentiality is to be protected. 34 C.F.R. §§ 300.571, .572 (1988). Much of the information is to be destroyed at the parent's request when no longer needed by the school. Id. § 300.573. In judicial proceedings brought pursuant to the EHA, a great deal of this statutorily protected information inevitably will be placed before the court. "In addition to reviewing the administrative record, courts are empowered to take additional evidence at the request of either party. . . ." *Honig*, 484 U.S. at 312, 108 S. Ct. at 598. In order to safeguard the confidentiality of such information in judicial proceedings, it therefore is appropriate to restrict access to the courtroom and the court file. . . .

ADDITIONAL COMMENTARY

1. Schools do not have to release test items or protocols; however, they must make test results and evaluations available for parental inspection and provide an interpretation of them for parents. *E.g., Tri County Special Education Cooperative*, 257 E.H.L.R. 529 (OCR 1984).

2. *In re Handicapped Child*, 460 N.Y.S.2d 256 (Supp. 1983), the school was not allowed to subpoena the records of an independent psychological evaluation for use in a hearing with the parents regarding the child's eligibility under IDEA. In *Zaal v. Maryland*, 602 A.2d 1247 (Md. 1992), the defendant in a criminal action was allowed access to a student's educational records since it was probable that evidence that was both relevant and admissible would be found.

3. Noncustodial divorced parents are entitled to the same rights as custodial parents. Thus, if requested, a school must provide access to a student's records to a noncustodial parent unless they have been given a court order indicating that this right has been terminated. See *Doe v. Anrig*, 651 F. Supp. 424 (D.Mass. 1987).

4. Section 504 does not explicitly address student records. However, its regulations require that elementary and secondary institutions that receive federal funds must implement procedural safeguards for students with disabilities. These safeguards include an opportunity for parents to examine relevant records. Compliance with IDEA is one manner of meeting this requirement. 34 CFR 104.36 (1991).

5. Courts generally have held that FERPA does not create a private right of action for damages. *E.g., Tarka v. Franklin*, 891 F.2d 102 (5th Cir. 1989); *Fay v. South Colonie School District*, 802 F.2d 21 (2nd Cir. 1986). But parents may sue for compensatory damages for wrongful failure to disclose records under Section 1983. *E.g., Fay v. South Colonie Cent. School District*, 802 F.2d 21 (2nd Cir. 1986). *But see Francois v. University of District of Columbia*, 788 F. Supp. 31 (D.D.C. 1992).

6. Third parties who receive information under FERPA may do so only on the condition that they will abide by FERPA disclosure regulations. 34 CFR 99.33-.36 (1991).

ENDNOTES

1. 20 USC 1232g.

2. L. Fischer and G. P. Sorenson (1991). *School Law for Counselors, Psychologists, and Social Workers* (2d ed.). New York: Longman, pp. 15–16.

3. Wis. Stat. 118.126. Exceptions are provided if the pupil using the substances or experiencing the problems consents to the disclosure, in writing; if there is reason to believe that there is serious and imminent danger to the health, safety, or life of another person and the disclosure will alleviate the danger; or if the information is required to be reported under the child abuse and neglect laws.

4. *See* Lipari v. Sears, Roebuck & Co., 497 F. Supp. 185 (D. Neb. 1980); Leedy v. Hartnett, 510 F. Supp. 1125 (M.D. Pa. 1981); Mavroudis v. Superior Ct. for Cty of San Mateo, 162 Cal. Rptr. 724 (Ca. Ct. App. 1980).

5. 20 USCA 1232g; implementing regulations 34 C.F.R. 99.

6. For a discussion of abuses and concerns, *see* D. Divoky, Cumulative Records: Assault on Privacy, *Learning Magazine*, 2 (1) (Sept. 1973); pp. 18–23; M. Stone, Off the Record: The Emerging Right to Control One's School Files, *New York University*

Review of Law and Social Change, 5 (1975), pp. 39–64, at p. 42.

7. 20 USCA 1232g(a)(3)(A).

8. IDEA increases the Buckley definition to include personally identifiable records that are used by the educational institution.

9. 20 USC 1232g(a)(5); 34 CFR 99.3.

10. 20 USC 1232g (a)(2).

11. 20 USCS 1232g(b)(1); 34 CFR 99.3.

12. 20 USCA 1232g(b)(1),(2),(3),(5); 34 CFR 99.31(a)(9)(i).

13. 20 USC 1232g(b)(4)(A).

14. 34 CFR 300.574.

15. CFR 300.573.

16. 20 USC 1232(f) (1988); 34 CFR 75.734 (1991).

17. Breecher, 17 E.H.L.R. 56(OSEP 1990).

CHAPTER 9

STUDENT HEALTH CONCERNS

INTRODUCTION

Schools have always been concerned about the health of students and school staff. It is only when diseases are dangerous, or perceived as dangerous, that questions arise about special care for some students. In the early 1920s, the federal government established a public health service that is today responsible for public safety. Most cases involving schools, such as measles outbreaks, are handled in a routine manner by schools and the Public Health Department. When an individual within a school has a communicable disease, questions often arise concerning the conflict between the right of the infected individual and the safety (or perceived danger) of all of those within the facility.

EXCLUSION

In addition to the public relations and political problems caused by the existence of communicable diseases in the school community, schools must consider the legal implications of their decisions and actions. The presence of people with communicable diseases raises concerns about others' welfare and the spread of infection. However, these people still retain rights to employment and an education. The legal question usually arises when the school has attempted to exclude a person due to a communicable disease. The most common legal authorities used against exclusion in these situations are the equal protection clause of the Fourteenth Amendment, Section 504, and the Individuals with Disabilities Education Act (IDEA) (when discussing students).

The equal protection arguments are straightforward discrimination issues: Does the school have sufficient justification to treat the person with the contagious disease differently than any other person? The courts have not determined that this category of people should be afforded the protections of a suspect classification; thus, the analysis used would be the rational basis test, or minimal scrutiny.[1] It is relatively easy for the school to justify exclusion under this argument since its rationale need only be to show that it had some logical basis for its actions. It may be rational to exclude people due to the risk of infection, even when that risk is relatively low.

Section 504 defines a handicapped person as "any person who (i) has a physical or mental impairment which substantially limits one or more of such person's major life activities, (ii) has a record of such an impairment, or (iii) is regarded as having such an impairment."[2] In *School Board of Nassau County v. Arline,*[3] the Supreme Court determined that a person with a communicable disease may be handicapped under Section 504 if the disease is such that it creates an impairment or if that person is regarded as being impaired due to the disease.

If a person qualifies as disabled under Section 504, any exclusion would have to be based on a lack of qualifications for the program or position. If the person is disabled, then one must determine if that individual is nonetheless qualified, or if he or she can be made to be qualified using reasonable accommodations. The Supreme Court identified four factors to use to determine if a person with a contagious disease was such a substantial risk to others to render him or her unqualified.

1. The nature of the risk, i.e., how the disease is transmitted
2. The duration of the risk, i.e., how long the carrier is infectious
3. The severity of the risk, i.e., what the potential harm to others is
4. The probability that the disease will be transmitted and will cause varying degrees of harm

A lower court applied this analysis in *Chalk v. U.S. District Court*.[4] A teacher diagnosed with acquired immune deficiency syndrome (AIDS) was removed from his classroom duties and given a noninstructional job. The court specifically held that AIDS is a "handicap" within the meaning of Section 504. Further, although the teacher was "disabled," he was otherwise qualified to perform his job within the meaning of the act. The court, finding that the casual contact incident to the performance of Chalk's teaching duties presented no significant risk of harm to others, ordered Chalk's reinstatement. This analysis was also used in *Jeffrey S. v. State Board of Education*,[5] where the court found that nondiscrimination mandates in Section 504 were strong enough to prohibit total exclusion of a student with Hepatitis B.

When enacting the Civil Rights Restoration Act, Congress qualified the definition of the term *handicapped individual* in the employment context. The amendment states:

> *For the purpose of Sections [503] and [504], as such sections related to employment, [handicapped] does not include an individual who has a currently contagious disease or infection and who, by reason of such disease or infection, would constitute a direct threat to the health or safety of other individuals or who, by reason of the currently contagious disease or infection, is unable to perform the duties of the job.[6]*

This merely restates the current standard. To be protected, a person must be "otherwise qualified" for the employment at issue. Pursuant to this amendment, an individual with a contagious disease who constitutes a threat to others or who is unable to perform the duties of the job is not "otherwise qualified." This codified previous case law.

The issues under IDEA are a bit different. First, in order to be covered by IDEA, the person must be between the ages of 3 and 21; second, the student must fit under one of the statute's handicapping conditions (presumably, this would be other health impairments); and, finally, the student's condition must be such that he or she is in need of special education. Once these eligibility criteria have been met, the issues for students with a communicable disease are the same as for any other handicapped student, i.e., What is an appropriate program in the least restrictive environment? The twist on the placement is the issue of least restrictive environment and mainstreaming. The individualized education program (IEP) team must determine (1) What is the least restrictive placement for the student? and (2) If the child should be in a mainstreamed placement, are there any compelling reasons to remove him or her.[7]

DISCLOSURE

Students and employees have rights to privacy within the school setting. These rights may have to be balanced with the safety concerns for others in questions of disclosing the identities of people with contagious diseases. Officials will likely need compelling reasons to justify disclosure of this information beyond those few people who need to know a person's condition to deliver necessary services.

Students have additional rights to privacy granted by the Family Educational Rights and Privacy Act (FERPA). There is an exception in FERPA that allows disclosure of personally identifiable student information without parental consent in the event of a medical emergency. Such emergencies would rarely exist if there was no risk of transmission of the disease through casual contact. The Office for Civil Rights (OCR) has stated in a memorandum that children with communicable diseases may not be treated differently than others with regard to confidentiality.[8] The best rule of thumb to follow appears to be not to disclose the actual identity of a person with a contagious disease except to those who need to know in order to deliver services.

SCHOOL BOARD OF NASSAU COUNTY, FLORIDA v. ARLINE
480 U.S. 273, 107 S. Ct. 1123, 94 L. Ed. 2d 307 (1987)

Justice BRENNAN delivered the opinion of the Court.

Section 504 of the Rehabilitation Act of 1973, 87 Stat. 394, as amended, 29 U.S.C. § 794 (Act), prohibits a federally funded state program from discriminating against a handicapped individual solely by reason of his or her handicap. This case presents the questions whether a person afflicted with tuberculosis, a contagious disease, may be considered a "handicapped individual" within the meaning of § 504 of the Act, and, if so, whether such an individual is "otherwise qualified" to teach elementary school.

I.

From 1966 until 1979, respondent Gene Arline taught elementary school in Nassau County, Florida. She was discharged in 1979 after suffering a third relapse of tuberculosis within two years. . . .

The superintendent of schools for Nassau County, testified as to the school board's response to Arline's medical reports. After both her second relapse, in the spring of 1978, and her third relapse in November 1978, the school board suspended Arline with pay for the remainder of the school year. At the end of the 1978–1979 school year, the school board held a hearing, after which it discharged Arline, "not because she had done anything wrong," but because of the "continued reoccurrence [sic] of tuberculosis." *Id.*, at 49-52.

****

Section 504 of the Rehabilitation Act reads in pertinent part:

No otherwise qualified handicapped individual in the United States, as defined in section 706(7) of this title, *shall, solely by reason of his handicap, be excluded from participation in, be denied the benefits of, or be subjected to discrimination under any program or activity receiving Federal financial assistance. . . . 29 U.S.C. § 794.*

In 1974 Congress expanded the definition of "handicapped individual" for use in § 504 to read as follows:

[A]ny person who (i) has a physical or mental impairment which substantially limits one or more of such person's major life activities, (ii) has a record of such an impairment, or (iii) is regarded as having such an impairment. 29 U.S.C. § 706(7)(B).

The amended definition reflected Congress' concern with protecting the handicapped against discrimination stemming not only from simple prejudice, but also from "archaic attitudes and laws" and from "the fact that the American people are simply unfamiliar with and insensitive to the difficulties confront[ing] individuals with handicaps.". . . U.S. Code Cong. & Admin. News 1974, p. 6400. To combat the effects of erroneous but nevertheless prevalent perceptions about the handicapped, Congress expanded the definition of "handicapped individual" so as to preclude discrimination against "[a] person who has a record of, or is regarded as having, an impairment [but who] may at present have no actual incapacity at all." *Southeastern Community College v. Davis*, 442 U.S. 397, 405-406, n.

****

Within this statutory and regulatory framework, then, we must consider whether Arline can be considered a handicapped individual. According to the testimony of Dr. McEuen, Arline suffered tuberculosis "in an acute form in such a degree that it affected her respiratory system," and was hospitalized for this condition. App. 11. Arline thus had a physical impairment as that term is defined by the regulations, since she had a "physiological disorder or condition . . . affecting [her] . . . respiratory [system]." 45 CFR § 84.3(j)(2)(i) (1985). [Also,] Arline's hospitalization for tuberculosis in 1957 suffices to establish that she has a "record of . . . impairment" within the meaning of 29 U.S.C. s. 706(7)(B)(ii), and is therefore a handicapped individual.

Petitioners concede that a contagious disease may constitute a handicapping condition to the extent that it leaves a person with "diminished physical or mental capabilities," Brief for Petitioners 15, and concede that Arline's hospitalization for tuberculosis in 1957 demonstrates that she has a record of a physical impairment, see Tr. of Oral Arg. 52-53. Petitioners maintain, however, that Arline's record of impairment is irrelevant in this case, since the school board dismissed Arline not because of her diminished physical capabilities, but because of the threat that her relapses of tuberculosis posed to the health of others.

****

Allowing discrimination based on the contagious effects of a physical impairment would be inconsistent with the basic purpose of § 504. . . . By amending the definition of "handicapped individual" to include not only those who are actually physically impaired, but also those who are regarded as impaired. . . . Congress acknowledged that society's accumulated myths and fears about disability and disease are as handicapping as are the physical limitations that flow from actual impairment. Few aspects of a handicap give rise to the same level of public fear and misapprehension as contagiousness. Even those who suffer or have recovered from such noninfectious diseases as epilepsy or cancer have faced discrimination based on the irrational fear that they might be contagious. The Act is carefully structured to replace such reflexive reactions to actual or perceived handicaps with actions based on reasoned and medically sound judgments: the definition of "handicapped individual" is broad, but only those individuals who are both handicapped and otherwise qualified are eligible for relief. The fact that some persons who have contagious diseases may pose a serious health threat to others under certain circumstances does not justify excluding from the coverage of the Act all persons with actual or perceived contagious diseases. Such exclusion would mean that those accused of being contagious would never have

the opportunity to have their condition evaluated in light of medical evidence and a determination made as to whether they were "otherwise qualified." Rather, they would be vulnerable to discrimination on the basis of mythology—precisely the type of injury Congress sought to prevent. We conclude that the fact that a person with a record of a physical impairment is also contagious does not suffice to remove that person from coverage under § 504.

IV.

The remaining question is whether Arline is otherwise qualified for the job of elementary schoolteacher. To answer this question in most cases, the district court will need to conduct an individualized inquiry and make appropriate findings of fact. The basic factors to be considered in conducting this inquiry are well established [footnote 17].[9] In the context of the employment of a person handicapped with a contagious disease, we agree with amicus American Medical Association that this inquiry should include:

> [Findings of] facts, based on reasonable medical judgments given the state of medical knowledge, about (a) the nature of the risk (how the disease is transmitted), (b) the duration of the risk (how long is the carrier infectious), (c) the severity of the risk (what is the potential harm to third parties) and (d) the probabilities the disease will be transmitted and will cause varying degrees of harm. Brief for American Medical Association as Amicus Curiae 19.

In making these findings, courts normally should defer to the reasonable medical judgments of public health officials. The next step in the "otherwise-qualified" inquiry is for the court to evaluate, in light of these medical findings, whether the employer could reasonably accommodate the employee under the established standards for that inquiry. . . .

V.

We hold that a person suffering from the contagious disease of tuberculosis can be a handicapped person with the meaning of § 504 of the Rehabilitation Act of 1973, and that respondent Arline is such a person. We remand the case to the District Court to determine whether Arline is otherwise qualified for her position.

The judgment of the Court of Appeals is Affirmed.

(Footnotes omitted.)

—   —   —   —

KOHL v. WOODHAVEN LEARNING CENTER
865 F. 2d 930 (Eighth Circuit 1989)

WOLLMAN, Circuit Judge.

The Woodhaven Learning Center and Woodhaven School, Inc. (WLC and WS, or collectively Woodhaven) . . . are not-for-profit corporations. . . . Both receive federal funding through various programs. WLC provides residential placement for handicapped individuals and is also a "life-skills facility" that seeks to enable its clients to function more independently. WS is a habilitation facility that provides educational, pre-vocational, and vocational day programs for handicapped individuals. . . .

Kohl is thirty-two years old, mentally retarded, bilaterally blind, and an active carrier of hepatitis B. As a result of his physical and mental impairments, he frequently exhibits maladaptive behavior, including scratching, biting, open masturbation, and self-abuse.

****

On September 10, 1984, WLC informed Kohl's DMH [Department of Mental Health] case manager by letter that Kohl was "determined to be appropriate" for WLC's program, but that he was being refused admission because WLC would not accept a hepatitis B carrier until all its clients and staff were inoculated and screened. Similarly, although a certified vocational evaluator from WS rated Kohl as a "good candidate" for its programs, Kohl was denied admission to WS. . . .

****

Hepatitis is an infection that primarily affects the liver and is often caused by specific viruses, one of which is the hepatitis "B" virus. . . .

Although the transmission of hepatitis B is not fully comprehended, most medical experts agree that it is transmitted through body fluids, chiefly blood but also through saliva, tears, and seminal fluid, and not by casual contact. Infection occurs when contaminated body fluid comes into contact with breaks in the skin, even breaks too small to be visible to the human eye, or mucosal surfaces such as the mouth or eyes of an uninfected person. Not every contact with contaminated body fluids will result in infection, but a single exposure involves a 10–15 percent chance

that the exposed person will become infected. More prolonged exposure increases the risk, and in the high risk groups—clients of mental institutions, promiscuous homosexual men, and intravenous drug users—the risk is nearly 100 percent.

****

A. KOHL IS HANDICAPPED WITHIN THE MEANING OF THE ACT

The statute [Section 504] defines an individual with handicaps as "any person who (i) has a physical or mental impairment which substantially limits one or more of such person's major life activities, (ii) has a record of such an impairment, or (iii) is regarded as having such an impairment." 29 U.S.C. § 706(8)(B) (1988).

The district court found that hepatitis B is a physical impairment affecting one or more of Kohl's major life functions and that Kohl has a record of physical impairment. Although Woodhaven strenuously argues, and not without substantial support in the record, that Kohl does not have a physical impairment, we will accept the district court's finding as not clearly erroneous for the purposes of this appeal. Accordingly, we need not address the district court's additional finding that Kohl is handicapped as a result of his carrier status regardless of whether being a carrier causes him physical impairment. . . .

B. WOODHAVEN REJECTED KOHL SOLELY BECAUSE OF HIS CARRIER STATUS

The district court found that Woodhaven had discriminated against Kohl "solely by reason of" his carrier status. Woodhaven contends that Kohl was excluded for other reasons as well.

On September 10, 1984, James Michael, the assistant executive director of WLC, wrote Kohl's case manager at the DMH that Kohl had been found "appropriate" for the Woodhaven programs, but that WLC could not take him because WS had refused him and WLC would therefore be unable to provide for him during the day. WS rejected Kohl, according to Michael's letter, because its staff had not been inoculated and screened. Other communications from WLC made it clear that Kohl's contagiousness, and not the lack of a day program, was the reason for his exclusion. In May and in July of 1985, WLC informed Kohl's parents that Kohl could return when the immunization of WLC's clients and staff was completed. Charles Brewer, the executive director of WLC, wrote Kohl's parents that it was WLC's "policy" to refuse hepatitis carriers until the staff was inoculated. Kohl's maladaptive behavior was never mentioned in these communications.

****

Woodhaven now offers four reasons for rejecting Kohl other than his carrier status: (1) because his maladaptive behavior increased the risk of contagion, (2) the maladaptive behavior itself, (3) the fact that the staff was not immunized, and (4) WLC could not accept Kohl unless WS did. All of these rationales, with the exception of Kohl's maladaptive behavior itself, boil down to Kohl's being a carrier. Kohl's behavior and the non-inoculation of the staff are irrelevant except as they pertain to the risk of infection. . . .

C. OTHERWISE QUALIFIED–REASONABLE ACCOMMODATION

The district court found that Kohl was otherwise qualified for the Woodhaven programs and that Woodhaven could reasonably accommodate him. The two concepts are related: if a handicapped individual cannot be reasonably accommodated, then he cannot be otherwise qualified. . . .

Arline sets out a two-part test for determining whether a contagious individual is otherwise qualified. First, the district court must analyze the following four factors to assess the threat to others: " '(a) the nature of the risk (how the disease is transmitted), (b) the duration of the risk (how long the carrier is infectious), (c) the severity of the risk (what is the potential harm to third parties), and (d) the probabilities the disease will be transmitted and will cause varying degrees of harm.' " Arline, 107 S. Ct. at 1131 (citation omitted). In evaluating these factors, "courts normally should defer to the reasonable medical judgments of public health officials." Id.

If the individual is found to pose a significant risk to others, the second part of the test is whether the accommodation necessary to eliminate that risk is

reasonable. Id. "Accommodation is not reasonable if it either imposes 'undue financial and administrative burdens' on a grantee, or 'requires a fundamental alteration in the nature of [the defendant's] program.' " Id. 107 S. Ct. at 1131 n. 17. . . . It is "for the court to evaluate, in light of these medical findings," whether the recipient of federal funds can reasonably accommodate the individual with handicaps. Id. 107 S. Ct. at 1131.

****

The nature of the risk in the present case is the possibility of infection with hepatitis B through the transfer of body fluids. . . .

The probability that the disease will be transmitted and cause varying degrees of harm must be considered high. Because of Kohl's maladaptive behavior, there is a substantial likelihood that others could come into contact with his body fluids. Kohl averages several acts of aggression against the staff and several acts of self abuse per day. On at least one occasion during Kohl's evaluation at Woodhaven, staff members came into contact with Kohl's blood after he inflicted an injury upon himself.

The district court did not reach a conclusion as to whether Kohl posed a significant risk to others, focusing instead on considerations of how the risk could be minimized. The district court found that a combination of the vaccine that generally confers immunity to roughly 90 percent of those inoculated, the screening test to determine who has been successfully immunized, and the post-exposure prophylaxis hepatitis B immune globulin would "provide a means for eliminating virtually any potential harm to third parties imposed by [Kohl]."

Discussing the probability that clients or staff will be infected, the fourth factor of the Arline test, the district court noted that by the time of the trial all the clients at WLC had been or were being inoculated, as had all but three clients of WS. The district court recommended that those three clients be inoculated and that all the clients be screened.

To protect the staff from the threat of infection, the district court's plan called for creating "a barrier of protection" around Kohl by inoculating and screening those staff members who would routinely deal with Kohl and by also immunizing a small number of supervisors or other staff who would function as "backup in an emergency situation.". . . The district court concluded that such a plan would "eliminate any significant risk of [Kohl's] transmitting hepatitis B."

Concluding its reasonable accommodation analysis, the district court found that the cost of its plan would be reasonable. The district court foresaw an initial cost to WLC of $6,500 and an annual cost of $4,400 a year thereafter. The district court found that this cost was not an "undue financial burden" on WLC in light of its $4 million annual budget. . . .

Before discussing the merits of the district court's plan, it should first be pointed out that the plan's costs are deceptively low. The district court considered only the cost of the medical supplies and lab tests necessary to inoculate and screen the direct contact and backup staff. Many obvious costs were not considered, including the cost of inoculating and screening additional staff to replace the ten percent who do not develop immunity, the cost of screening the clients, the cost of administering the shots and tests, and the cost of the regular booster shots. . . .

****

After reviewing the record, we are left with a firm conviction that the limited inoculation plan would expose the Woodhaven staff to an unreasonable risk. Both Woodhaven facilities are open and allow clients full access to all areas of their facilities. At WLC there are many large group activities including choir, dances, bible study, religious services, and recreation. The clients have free access to the nursing station, gymnasium, and swimming pool, as well as the administrative offices. WLC also gathers all clients and staff together twice a week for meetings. At WS the clients freely intermingle during breaks from classes. In this setting, it is impossible to isolate Kohl or to insure that unimmunized staff will not be required to give assistance in emergencies involving Kohl. . . . Even attempting to isolate Kohl would be a fundamental alteration in Woodhaven's open program and would deny Kohl one of the most important therapeutic benefits of the Woodhaven program, that of social interaction with others. In addition to the fact that instructing unimmunized staff not to assist in emergencies involving Kohl is conceivably dangerous, a Woodhaven official testified that a staff member's refusal to give reasonable care to a client in a situation amounting to neglect of that client could result in a review of Woodhaven's license. . . .

Given the open environment at Woodhaven and Kohl's unpredictable and violent nature, it is inevitable that unimmunized staff would eventually be exposed to a significant risk of infection.

We cannot consider a 10–15 percent chance of infection so small as to be insignificant. This is particularly true since the immune globulin post-exposure treatment is only 75 percent effective under the best circumstances. Protecting 3 out of 4 unimmunized staff members is not equivalent to "eliminat[ing] any significant risk," as the district court found. This risk is unacceptable. *See Arline*, 107 S. Ct. at 1131 n. 16 ("[a] person who poses a significant risk of communicating an infectious disease will not be otherwise qualified for his or her job if reasonable accommodations will not eliminate the medical testimony indicates that inoculating the staff who could reasonably come into contact with Kohl or who would be required to assist him should an emergency arise would eliminate that risk; *Davis*, 442 U.S. at 409,. . . On the other hand, the medical testimony indicates that inoculating the staff who could reasonably come into contact with Kohl or who would be required to assist him should an emergency arise would eliminate any significant risk of infection. *See Chalk*, 840 F.2d at 708 (plaintiff permitted to reassume teaching position when the "overwhelming consensus of medical opinion" was that he posed no significant risk to others).

In the light of the contradiction between Dr. Donnell's proposal and the DMH's procedures, the hypothetical nature of Dr. Donnell's proposed plan, and the unanimity of opinion among all the medical experts, including Dr. Donnell, that it was preferable to inoculate all the staff that could reasonably come into contact with Kohl, we conclude that the district court erred in finding that limited inoculation would eliminate all significant risk. Therefore, regardless of the cost of the plan, which was seriously understated, a program of limited inoculation cannot reasonably accommodate Kohl. The evidence and testimony established that to eliminate all significant risk of infection, all staff who reasonably would come into contact with Kohl should be inoculated.

The district court's order granting injunctive and declaratory relief is reversed. . . .
(Footnotes omitted.)

— — — —

MARTINEZ v. SCHOOL DISTRICT OF HILLSBOROUGH COUNTY, FLORIDA
861 F.2d 1502 (Eleventh Circuit 1988)

VANCE, Circuit Judge:

This case involves the appropriate educational placement of a mentally retarded child infected with the human immunodeficiency virus, the virus that causes Acquired Immunodeficiency Syndrome (AIDS). Appellant, Eliana Martinez, is seven years old and has an I.Q. of 41. This classifies her as a trainably mentally handicapped child. Eliana was born prematurely and received thirty-nine blood transfusions in the first four months of life. In April 1985 Eliana was diagnosed as suffering from AIDS Related Complex. She now is in the late stages of AIDS but her condition has been stabilized for several months. The court below found that Eliana is not toilet trained and suffers from thrush, a disease that can produce blood in the saliva. Eliana sucks her thumb and forefinger frequently, resulting in saliva on her fingers. In the past Eliana has suffered from skin lesions. When these occurred, Mrs. Rosa Martinez, her adoptive mother, has kept her at home.

In the summer of 1986, Mrs. Martinez attempted to enroll Eliana in the special classroom for trainably mentally handicapped ("TMH") children in the public school system of Hillsborough County, Florida. Based on the recommendation of an interdisciplinary review team, the Hillsborough County School Board decided that the appropriate educational placement for Eliana was homebound instruction. . . .

****

Two overlapping federal statutes establish the framework for determining appropriate educational placement for handicapped children—the Education of the Handicapped Act (the "EHA") [now IDEA], and section 504 of the Rehabilitation Act of 1973 ("section 504"). . . .

****

When a child with an infectious disease seeks relief under both the EHA and section 504 of the Rehabilitation Act, the relationship between these two statutory frameworks is particularly intricate. The trial judge must first determine the most appropriate educational placement for the handicapped child under EHA procedures. Next, the court must determine whether the child is otherwise qualified within the meaning of section 504 to be educated in this setting, despite the communicable disease. *See Arline*, 107 S. Ct. at 1131 n. 16. If not, the court must consider whether reasonable accommodations could reduce the risk of transmission so as to make the child otherwise qualified to be educated in that setting. In considering accommodations that would make the child "otherwise qualified," the court must bear in mind the requirement that to the maximum extent appropriate, the child is to be educated in the least restrictive environment.

****

As the parties agreed, the appropriate educational placement for Eliana under the EHA would be the regular TMH classroom if she did not suffer from AIDS. This presented the question whether the exclusion of Eliana from that setting is unlawful under section 504. In conducting this inquiry, the trial court had to determine whether Eliana was otherwise qualified to be educated in the regular TMH classroom. The trial court found a "remote theoretical possibility" of transmission with respect to tears, saliva and urine. This does not rise to the "significant" risk level that is required for Eliana to be excluded from the regular TMH classroom. . . . The court below made no findings with respect to the overall risk of transmission from all bodily substances, including blood in the saliva, to which other children might be exposed in the TMH classroom. Accordingly, we remand with directions that the trial court make findings as to the overall risk of transmission so that it can determine whether Eliana is otherwise qualified to attend classes in the TMH classroom.

If the risk of transmission supports a finding that Eliana is not "otherwise qualified" to attend classes with the other children in the TMH classroom, the court must consider whether reasonable accommodations would make her so. In evaluating possible accommodations, a trial court must consider the effect of each proposed accommodation on the handicapped child and the institution. . . . The court must be guided by the requirement that, to the maximum extent appropriate, these accommodations place the child in the least restrictive environment that would make the child otherwise qualified. Additionally, the court must consider the financial burden the accommodation would impose on the institution. . . .

****

We vacate the judgment of the district court and remand the case so that the district court may make the further required findings. The district court should receive such additional evidence as it deems necessary in light of such requirements. It should thereafter enter such judgment as is appropriate. (Footnotes omitted.)

ADDITIONAL COMMENTARY

1. The Center for Disease Control recommends that most school-aged children infected with AIDS be allowed to attend school or day-care programs. This is based on the belief that AIDS is not transmitted by casual contact; therefore, the benefits of school attendance outweigh the risks of infection. But, as is true of any situation, these decisions must be made on an individual basis.

    Additionally, the Center for Disease Control makes the following recommendations:

    - Those caring for AIDS children should wash hands thoroughly after exposure to body fluids.
    - All schools and day-care centers should adopt routine procedures for handling body fluids, including using disposable towels and tissues and disinfecting soiled surfaces.
    - Blood tests to screen for AIDS should not be routinely required.
    - Those dealing with AIDS children—doctors, school officials and others—should respect the children's right to privacy.

    OCR has issued the following:

    The following policies will be applied to children handicapped solely by reason of AIDS:

    - *The regulatory definition of a handicapped person will be applied to children with AIDS, who are virtually always "regarded as handicapped" within the meaning of this definition.*
    - *Children handicapped solely by reason of AIDS are "qualified" if they meet the age-related regulatory definition.*
    - *Unless currently presenting a risk of contagion due to the stage of the disease, a child with AIDS will remain in the regular classroom.*
    - *A full evaluation is not required when neither recipients nor parents believe that a child is in need of special education or related services.*
    - *In all other respects, school districts should apply to children with AIDS the process and procedures required by the Section 504 regulation. Placement decisions must be made drawing on all relevant sources mentioned in the regulation, including the latest medical information on AIDS. The group of persons making the placement decision must include persons knowledgeable about the meaning of that information.*
    - *All procedural safeguards required in Subpart D of the regulation apply to children handicapped solely by reason of AIDS.*
    - *Children with AIDS may not be subjected to different treatment with respect to confidentiality.*

    OCR Memorandum, 16 EHLR 712 (1990).

2. The final chapter for teacher Gene Arline was that the Supreme Court remanded her case back to the trial court. The trial court found she was otherwise qualified for her position when she was wrongfully terminated and she was due back pay and reinstatement. *Arline v. School Board of Nassau County*, 692 F. Supp. 1286 (M.D. Fla. 1988).

3. Members of a religious group brought suit challenging regulations promulgated by the Commissioner of Education requiring all primary and secondary school students to receive instruction about AIDS as violative of their First Amendment right to freely exercise their religious beliefs. The Supreme Court granted summary judgment in favor of defendants, and plaintiffs appealed. The Court of Appeals held that genuine issues of material fact regarding burden imposed upon plaintiffs' religious exercise by exposure to AIDS

curriculum, and whether compelling interest in educating youth against AIDS would be adversely affected by granting exemption to plaintiffs, precluded summary judgment. *Ware v. Valley Stream High School District*, 75 N.Y.2d 114, 551 N.Y.S.2d 167, 550 N.E.2d 420 (1989).

4. For a thorough and practical discussion of students with AIDS *see* M. M. Murphy, Special Education Children with HIV Infection: Standards and Strategies for Admission to the Classroom, *Journal of Law and Education, 19* (1990), pp. 345–370.

5. A Nebraska human services agency that provided services to people who are mentally disabled adopted a communicable diseases policy. Personnel having frequent contact with clients were required to take blood tests for AIDS and Hepatitis B. The policy also required all employees to notify personnel officers when they knew or suspected that they had one of the diseases. The Eighth Circuit Court of Appeals found that mandatory blood testing was a search under the Fourth Amendment, and the agency had to comply with its reasonableness mandates. This required balancing the employees' privacy rights with the public and client interests and safety. Using the district court's finding that the risk of transmission was minuscule, the Court of Appeals held that the policy was unreasonable. *Glover v. Eastern Nebraska Community Office of Retardation*, 867 F.2d 461 (8th Cir. 1989).

ENDNOTES

1. District 27 Community School Bd. v. Bd. of Educ., 502 N.Y.S.2d 325 (S.Ct. 1986).

2. 29 USC 706(8)(B).

3. 107 S. Ct. 1123 (1987).

4. 832 F.2d 1158 (9th Cir. 1987).

5. 441 E.H.L.R. 576 (S.D. Ga. 1989).

6. 29 U.S. Ca. 706 (8)(D)(1990).

7. OCR Memorandum, 16 E.H.L.R. 712 (1990).

8. OCR Memorandum, 16 E.H.L.R. 712 (1990).

9. "An otherwise qualified person is one who is able to meet all of a program's requirements in spite of his handicap." *Southeastern Community College v. Davis*, 442 U.S. 397, 406, (1979). In the employment context, an otherwise qualified person is one who can perform "the essential functions" of the job in question. 45 CFR § 84.3(k) (1985). When a handicapped person is not able to perform the essential functions of the job, the court must also consider whether any "reasonable accommodation" by the employer would enable the handicapped person to perform those functions. *Ibid.* Accommodation is not reasonable if it either imposes "undue financial and administrative burdens" on a grantee, *Southeastern Community College v. Davis*, 442 U.S., at 412, or requires "a fundamental alteration in the nature of [that] program," id., at 410. . . . ("[W]here reasonable accommodation does not overcome the effects of a person's handicap, or where reasonable accommodation causes undue hardship to the employer, failure to hire or promote the handicapped person will not be considered discrimination"); *Davis, supra*, at 410-413. . . .

CHAPTER 10

PRESCHOOL AND EARLY CHILDHOOD

INTRODUCTION

Part B of the Individuals with Disabilities Education Act (IDEA) grants children from ages 3 through 21 a right to a free appropriate education. Amendments in 1986, P.L. 99-457, provide for incentive grants in two ways. First, additional grant funds are provided to states for programming for children with disabilities from ages 3 through 5. Second, financial assistance is provided to states that establish early intervention programs for infants and toddlers with disabilities.[1] The statute sets forth the policy for the latter broadly:

It is therefore the policy of the United States to provide financial assistance to States

1. *to develop and implement a statewide, comprehensive, coordinated, multidisciplinary, interagency program of early intervention services for infants and toddlers with disabilities and their families,*
2. *to facilitate the coordination of payment for early intervention services from Federal, State, local, and private sources (including public and private insurance coverage), and*
3. *to enhance its capacity to provide quality early intervention services and expand and improve existing early intervention services being provided to infants and toddlers with disabilities and their families.*[2]

EARLY CHILDHOOD EDUCATION

The first part of P.L. 99-457 provides that states should develop a statewide system of coordinated multidisciplinary interagency programs delivering appropriate early intervention services for infants and toddlers with disabilities. Infants and toddlers with disabilities within the meaning of the act are those children, from birth through age 2, who require services because they are experiencing developmental delays or have a diagnosed physical or mental condition that has a high probability of resulting in developmental delay.[3] States are not mandated to provided free appropriate services to this population, but may instead set out a system of payment, including a schedule of sliding fees. However, the standards for payment may not be used to deny services to an eligible child because of the family's inability to pay.[4]

Early intervention services under P.L. 99-457 are developmental services provided under public supervision designed to meet the child's developmental needs in terms of physical, cognitive, language, speech, psychosocial, and self-help skills.[5] These services may include:

— Family training, counseling and home visits
— Special instruction
— Speech pathology and audiology
— Occupational therapy
— Physical therapy
— Psychological services
— Case management services
— Medical services only for diagnostic or evaluation purposes
— Early identification, screening, and assessment services
— Health services necessary to enable the infant or toddler to benefit from the other early intervention services

— Social work services

— Vision services

— Assistive technology devises and assistive technology services

— Transportation and related costs that are necessary to enable an infant or toddler and the infant's or toddler's family to receive early intervention services[6]

Case management is a service that must be provided to infants and toddlers that does not have to be provided to school-age children and preschoolers under IDEA. Under Part H of 99-457, each eligible child and family must be provided with a case manager who is responsible for coordinating services and serving as the contact to help parents obtain the services and assistance they may need.[7] Case management services, which are all carried out in conjunction with the family, include:

— Coordinating the performance of evaluations and assessments

— Facilitating and participating in the development, review, and evaluation of individualized family service plans

— Assisting families in identifying available service providers

— Coordinating and monitoring the delivery of available services

— Informing families of the availability of advocacy services

— Coordinating with medical and health providers

— Facilitating the development of a transition plan to preschool services[8]

The focus is on the family, particularly in providing services to and through the family unit. The implementing document is called an individualized family service plan (IFSP). Further, it is not intended that services be provided in a central facility, such as a school, but in the natural environment of infants and toddlers—the home. The statute provides that services be provided "to the maximum extent appropriate . . . in natural environments, including the home, and community settings in which children without disabilities participate."[9]

An IFSP is to be developed after a multi-disciplinary assessment of the child and resources and concerns of the family.[10] The IFSP must include the following:

— A statement of the child's present levels of development

— A statement of the family's resources, priorities, and concerns

— A statement of the major outcomes expected to be achieved for the child and family

— A statement of specific early intervention services needed to meet the unique needs of the child and family

— A statement of the natural environments in which early intervention services are to be provided

— Projected dates for initiation, and the anticipated duration of services

— The name of the case manager

— The steps to be taken to support transition to services available to 3 year olds and above[11]

Like IDEA, procedural safeguards are set forth; they are basically identical to IDEA. They include the requirements of parental notification and consent. Either party, i.e., the public agency and the family, can initiate a due process hearing to resolve a dispute. There must be an administrative resolution before the public agency can change, identify, evaluate or place a child for services. States may choose to use the due process mechanisms already established for IDEA or may develop similar systems. There are three notable differences. First, a due process decision must be made no later than 30 days (rather than 45) after the receipt of a parent's complaint. Second, there must be a single level of appeal, i.e., there cannot be a two-tier administrative appeal system like many states use under IDEA. Finally, parents do not have a right to obtain an independent evaluation, as under IDEA.

A child with a disability that impacts education is entitled to receive a free appropriate public education as of his or her third birthday. In order to avoid disruption of services on that day, 99-457 requires states to ensure a transition into services. To facilitate that transition, a meeting between the service providers and the family should be held at least 90 days before the child's third birthday. At this meeting, a transition plan should be written. To assist in the transition, 99-457 authorizes states to allow the family and the district to agree to permit implementation of the IFSP beyond the third birthday and to place the child into school-based services at a logical time within the general school calendar.

Because this statute went into effect in July 1992 and is not a mandatory program on the states, there is little administrative or judicial guidance. However, noting the impact that early intervention can have on a child's life, the statute is of great significance.

ENDNOTES

1. 20 USC 1419 (1990).
2. 20 USC 1471.
3. 20 USC 1472(1).
4. OSEP Policy Memorandum, 16 E.H.L.R. 709 (1990).
5. 20 USC 1472(1), 1472(2)(C).
6. 20 USC 1472(E).
7. 34 CFR 303.6 (a)(2).
8. 34 CFR 303.6(b).
9. 20 USC 1472 (2)(G).
10. 20 USC 1477(a).
11. 20 USC 1477(d).

GLOSSARY OF LEGAL TERMS

Action a lawsuit brought by one or more individuals to seek redress for a legal wrong or for protection of a right or prevention of a wrong. A *right of action* is the legal right to sue; a *cause of action* is the facts that give rise to a right to sue. If the complaint fails to state a proper cause of action, it will be dismissed.

Affidavit a written statement made or taken under oath before a person duly authorized to administer an oath. Generally used as evidence, much as live testimony would be.

Affirm the approval of an appellate court that the judgment of the court below is correct and should stand.

Allegation an assertion of fact; the statement of the issue that the party is prepared to prove.

Amicus Curiae a Latin term meaning "friend of the court." The court grants permission for a person or organization with an interest in the suit to appear in the case, file briefs, and present oral arguments even though such person or organization is not a party to the action.

Answer The first pleading by the defendant in a lawsuit; a response to the plaintiff's allegations.

Appeal the review taken by a higher court of a lower court's actions. In an appeal, new evidence is not taken; the reviewing court only corrects errors, e.g., a misinterpretation of the law, an incorrect application of the law to the facts, or conclusions that are not substantiated by the evidence.

Appellant the party who appeals a decision.

Appellate court a court having jurisdiction to review the law as determined by a lower court.

Appellee the party prevailing in the court below, who argues against the setting aside of the judgment.

Certiorari a request made by a party asking a higher court to review a lower court's decision. The granting of the writ of certiorari is discretionary with the reviewing court, i.e., the court can refuse to review the case.

Civil that branch of law that pertains to suits outside of criminal prosecution.

Class action a lawsuit brought by one or more representative members of a large group on behalf of all the members of a group. The trial court must certify the action, i.e., rule that the special criteria applicable to such suits have been met.

Code a systematic compilation of laws, e.g., the education code refers to the laws relating to education.

Common law the body of law based on judicial decision (precedents) generally derived from principles based on justice, reason, and common sense, rather than legislative enactments.

Compensatory damages a monetary remedy awarded to a party that is based on the actual loss suffered, e.g., medical expenses. See **Damages**.

Complainant the party who initiates the complaint in an action (generally synonymous with *plaintiff* or *petitioner*).

Complaint the first main legal document filed in a civil lawsuit in which the plaintiff informs the court and the defendant(s) of the action, asserts the reasons for the suit, and makes a request for the court's help (relief or remedy wanted). Generally, the first papers filed to initiate a lawsuit.

Consent written permission from the parents or guardians to test the child, to place the child in a special education program, or to change the child from one special education program to another.

Consent decree a consent decree is an agreement of the parties made under the sanction of the court, and is not appealable.

Damages monetary compensation that a court may award to one who has been injured by the action of another; recompense for a legal wrong. For example, *actual damages* consist of compensation for those monetary losses that can readily be proven to have been incurred and for which compensation is a matter of right. *Punitive damages* are an amount in excess of actual monetary loss; this is awarded as a form of punishment to the wrongdoer in those rare instances where malicious and willful misconduct by the defendant is shown.

Declaratory judgment establishes the rights of

the parties or expresses the opinion of the court on a question of law without ordering anything to be done.

De facto   in fact; in reality; actually. De facto segregation, for example, exists regardless of the law as a result of social and psychological conditions. Latin for "in fact, actual."

Defendant   one who is sued. In civil proceedings, the party responding to the complaint.

Defense   a denial, answer, or plea opposing the truth or validity of the plaintiff's case.

De jure   by right; lawful; legitimate. For example, de jure segregation is segregation directly intended and sanctioned by law or otherwise issuing from an official racial classification. Latin for "by law."

De minimis   insignificant; an act that is not sufficiently important to be dealt with judicially.

De novo   new; In a de novo hearing, for example, the reviewing court determines the case as though it originated in the reviewing court and gives no attention to the findings and judgment of the trial court except as they may be helpful in the reasoning.

Dicta, Dictum   an observation in a judicial opinion not necessary for the decision of the case. It differs from the holding in that it is not binding on the courts in subsequent cases.

Dismiss   to terminate a case without a complete trial.

Due process   the steps and rules established to ensure fairness in providing educational opportunities to all children, disabled or otherwise.

En banc   by the full court. Appellate courts are usually divided into panels of three or more judges to hear cases. In cases of special significance, sometimes all members of the court sit to hear and decide the matter. Those cases then carry the notation *en banc*.

Evaluation   includes all testing and diagnostic work for determining the level of performance with regard to a child's skills or behaviors.

Evidence   the means (testimony of witnesses, introduction of records, documents, exhibits, objects, or any other admissible matter) offered for the purpose of establishing or disproving the truth of alleged facts.

Expert witness   a person called to testify who has special knowledge, skill, or experience in the sub-

ject matter under consideration by a court.

Ex rel   a Latin term meaning "on behalf of"; used in the title of a case when one party is bringing an action on behalf of another person.

Fact finder   trier of fact; in a judicial or administrative proceeding, the person or group that has the responsibility of determining the facts relevant to deciding a dispute.

Hearing   a proceeding where evidence is taken for the purpose of determining an issue of fact and reaching a decision on the basis of that evidence.

Holding   any ruling of the court in a case; the portion of a court opinion that applies the rule of law to the particular facts of a case.

Injunction   a judicial remedy involving a court order that requires a defendant to perform or refrain from doing a particular act or activity. Types of injunctive relief include temporary restraining orders, preliminary injunctions, and permanent injunctions. Compare this to a **mandamus,** which requires someone to take an action.

In re   a Latin term used in the name of a case meaning "in the matter of." This is often used to describe cases involving children, where the action involves a child, but is not a civil or criminal action.

Irreparable injury (harm)   any damage or wrong resulting from a violation of a legal right for which money damages would be inadequate compensation, and that may require some form of equitable intervention, such as an injunction.

Judgment   the determination of the rights of the parties in a judicial controversy. A judgment of the merits is determined by adjudication of the factual issues posed, rather than by a technical or procedural defect that allows one party to prevail.

Jurisdiction   a court's power to hear and decide a case. The term also refers to particular legal systems or geographical areas where a given court has authority.

Litigation   dispute resolution in a court; a judicial contest through which legal rights are sought to be determined and enforced.

Local educational agency (LEA)   a public board of education or other public authority legally constituted within a state for either administrative control or direction of, or to perform a service function for public elementary or secondary schools.

Mandamus a court order requiring someone to take an action. Compare this to an **injunction,** which requires someone to refrain from or stop an action.

Mitigation reduction. Used often to describe actions that reduce someone's injury, or a court order reducing a damage award.

Monitoring the activities conducted to ensure that particular requirements or procedures are being carried out.

Motion a request to a judge to take certain action or make a ruling in favor of the applicant.

Notice actual communication of a fact to another. In special education, parents and students must be notified of their rights and of intended evaluation, programming, and placement.

Opinion a judge's statement of the reason for a court's judgment finding, or conclusion, as opposed to the judgment itself. There are often different types of opinions written in a case. The *majority opinion* is one that is agreed to by a majority of the court. It is the binding precedent of the case. However, a judge who disagrees may write a *dissenting opinion.* A judge who agrees in outcome, but differs in reasoning, may write a *concurring opinion.* When there is no majority opinion, the opinion that represents the greatest number of judges, but is short of a majority, is a *plurality opinion.* Nearly the opposite is also possible: A decision to which all judges agree, but is issued, unsigned, i.e., without a specific attribution to the writing judge, is called a *per curiam opinion.*

Parent a parent, a guardian, a person acting as a parent of a child, or a surrogate parent who has been properly appointed.

Pleadings statements, in logical and legal form, of each side of a case. Legal procedure includes submission of such successive statements until the real matter in controversy has been fully disclosed to the court.

Precedent a decision in a prior case that is recognized as authority for deciding future cases involving similar questions of law and similar facts.

Preponderance of the evidence a general standard of proof in civil cases. Evidence is considered to "preponderate" where it is more convincing to the trier of fact than the opposing evidence.

Proceeding the cumulative events comprising the process by which administrative or judicial action is initiated and resolved.

Related services developmental, corrective, and other supportive services as are necessary to assist a child with disabilities to benefit from special education. Such services may include but are not limited to speech pathology, audiology, psychological services, physical and occupational therapy, recreation, transportation, counseling services, and medical services for diagnostic or evaluation purposes.

Relief (remedy) the redress or assistance awarded to a plaintiff or complainant by a court. Examples include monetary damages, specific performance of a contractual obligation, temporary restraining orders, preliminary injunctions, etc.

Remand to send back for further deliberation to the tribunal from which a judgment was appealed or moved.

Restraining order an order granted, pending a hearing, to preserve the status quo until a hearing can be held to determine whether a preliminary or permanent injunction should be issued.

Reverse the decision of an appellate court that the judgment of a lower court or other body should be set aside, vacated, or changed.

Section 504 a federal statute prohibiting the discrimination of individuals with disabilities in institutions receiving or benefitting from federal funds.

Special education specially designed instruction to meet the unique needs of a child who has a disability. It includes classroom instruction, instruction in physical education, home instruction, and instruction in hospitals and institutions.

Standing the legal right of a person or group to invoke administrative or judicial proceedings, especially with respect to governmental action.

Stare decisis to stand by that which was decided; under this doctrine, previously decided cases serve as a precedent for the disposition of future cases.

State Educational Agency (SEA) the state board of education or other agency or officer primarily responsible for the state supervisor of public elementary and secondary schools.

Summary judgment a decision made by trial court on the basis of written documentation submitted before any trial occurs. Summary judgment can only be granted when there are no genuine issues of material fact.

Testimony   a statement made under oath by a witness.

Case Index

Note: Edited cases are indicated by boldface page numbers.